T0230207

Lecture Notes in Computer Science 1153

Edited by G. Goos, J. Hartmanis and J. van Leeuwen

Advisory Board: W. Brauer D. Gries J. Stoer

Springer
Berlin
Heidelberg
New York
Barcelona
Budapest
Hong Kong
London
Milan
Paris
Santa Clara
Singapore
Tokyo

Edmund Burke   Peter Ross   (Eds.)

Practice and Theory of Automated Timetabling

First International Conference
Edinburgh, U.K.
August 29 - September 1, 1995
Selected Papers

 Springer

Series Editors

Gerhard Goos, Karlsruhe University, Germany

Juris Hartmanis, Cornell University, NY, USA

Jan van Leeuwen, Utrecht University, The Netherlands

Volume Editors

Edmund Burke
Department of Computer Science, University of Nottingham
University Park, Nottingham NG7 2RD, UK
E-mail: ekb@cs.nott.ac.uk

Peter Ross
Department of Artificial Intelligence, University of Edinburgh
5 Forrest Hill, Edinburgh EH1 2QL, UK
E-mail: peter@dai.ed.ac.uk

Cataloging-in-Publication data applied for

Die Deutsche Bibliothek - CIP-Einheitsaufnahme

Practice and theory of automated timetabling : ... international
conference ; selected papers. - Berlin ; Heidelberg ; New York
; Barcelona ; Budapest ; Hong Kong ; London ; Milan ; Paris ;
Santa Clara ; Singapore ; Tokyo : Springer
1. Edinburgh, U.K., August 29 - September 1, 1995. - 1996
  (Lecture notes in computer science ; 1153)
  ISBN 3-540-61794-9 (Berlin ...)
NE: GT

CR Subject Classification (1991): I.2.2, I.2.8, H.4.1-2, J.1, K.3

ISSN 0302-9743
ISBN 3-540-61794-9 Springer-Verlag Berlin Heidelberg New York

This work is subject to copyright. All rights are reserved, whether the whole or part of the material is
concerned, specifically the rights of translation, reprinting, re-use of illustrations, recitation, broadcasting,
reproduction on microfilms or in any other way, and storage in data banks. Duplication of this publication
or parts thereof is permitted only under the provisions of the German Copyright Law of September 9, 1965,
in its current version, and permission for use must always be obtained from Springer-Verlag. Violations are
liable for prosecution under the German Copyright Law.

© Springer-Verlag Berlin Heidelberg 1996
Printed in Germany

Typesetting: Camera-ready by author
SPIN 10525549   06/3142 - 5 4 3 2 1 0   Printed on acid-free paper

Preface

The range of practical timetabling problems is enormous. Teachers and lecturers have to arrange classes or exams; transport planners have to devise bus and train schedules; conference organisers have to contrive parallel streams of events; hospitals have to plan appointments; airlines have to devise staff rotas; distribution managers have to fix delivery routes and schedules; and so on. The common thread of all such activities is the solving, as far as is reasonably possible, of an elaborate constraint satisfaction task. Such problems are sometimes still tackled by hand, especially in the world of education, and everyone has a story to tell about a bad timetable.

Computers ought to be the ideal tool for timetabling, but it is still surprisingly hard to find the right algorithm or to buy suitable software that fits your particular flavour of problem. Academic papers that describe particular ways of approaching a class of problems are dispersed throughout the computing, mathematical, and business management literature and the choice of commercial packages is still fairly limited. Nevertheless, given the diversity of requirements, is there much to be said that is generally useful?

The answer is yes. There has been a vast amount of applicable research over the past decade, and the first international conference on the Practice and Theory of Automated Timetabling attempted to bring much of it together. The conference was held at Napier University in Edinburgh on 30th August - 1st September 1995 and brought together people from all over the world. People with interesting problems were able to meet others with ingenious possible answers, and theoreticians were able to swap ideas with implementors. This book contains a selection of the papers presented at that conference. Hopefully, it goes some way towards meeting the clear need for a single wide-ranging survey of the state of the art.

Timetabling is still a mix of practical art and science. It may be tempting to look at the whole area in terms of the kind of functional taxonomy suggested by the first paragraph of this introduction, but it is more useful to categorise it in terms of constraint types and requirements. For example, exam timetablers are faced with large numbers of binary constraints (two exams cannot coincide if a student is to take them both), capacity constraints (several exams may happen in the same room at the same time if it is big enough) and global constraints (each student wants his exams to be reasonably spread out rather than in close sequence). Lecture timetablers often have to worry more about capacity constraints, since lecture halls are typically more at a premium than exam halls and you certainly cannot have two lectures in the same hall at once. Transport and distribution managers must worry more about such matters as time windows and the legal constraints on drivers' hours. More generally, there are binary and non-binary constraints; global constraints on the solution as a whole and local constraints on small fragments; soft constraints that should be obeyed if at all feasible and hard constraints that cannot be broken under any circumstances; and so on. The solutions can usually be judged in terms of some kind of resource utilisation, but the criteria vary. In some cases, any answer is better than none ('sorry, you're stuck with an evening lecture') and in others you need to aim for the best lest your competitors steal your market ('their buses run more frequently and more regularly').

The range of techniques is impressive. Graph-colouring, in itself a fascinating branch of mathematics, can be an excellent method for handling binary constraints. Hyper-graph colouring can handle some varieties of non-binary constraint. Expert systems can be used when there is a lot of useful knowledge available about where to look for solutions. Theorem-proving and constraint-directed search methods can be useful if all or most of the constraints are hard ones. Various optimisation techniques can be used to handle soft constraints; for example, simulated annealing and tabu search can be used to conduct a very wide-ranging tour of the possibilities and genetic algorithms can be used to evolve an excellent solution, especially if there is some compositional aspect to such solutions, even though such an aspect may not be humanly discernible within the statement of the problem.

You will find all of these represented within this book. We hope you will get pleasure and intellectual stimulation out of exploring this broad, difficult, but deeply practical area; and if the work reported in this book helps to improve the quality and reduce the labour of timetabling then it will have served its purpose.

The Conference Series

The conference in Edinburgh was the first in a series of international conferences on the Practice And Theory of Automated Timetabling (PATAT). The second conference in the series will be held in Toronto, Canada on 20th- 22nd August 1997. For further information, contact the steering committee (see below).

Acknowledgements

The first conference was a considerable success thanks to the efforts of many people. The organising committee (members are listed below) worked very hard to make it the enjoyable and interesting event that it was, and we would like to extend our thanks to them. Particular thanks go to Ben Paechter, Guiti Saberi, and Amanda Coulter for the many hours of extra work that they cheerfully undertook. We would also like to thank Napier University. The institution was tremendously helpful, being prepared to give the idea its full support, even when it was just a speculative notion in the minds of a few people.

The papers were fully refereed for the conference itself and had to undergo a second round of careful refereeing for this volume. A lot of work has gone into the process of selecting those papers which now appear in this book. We are very grateful to the members of the programme committee (listed below) who helped to referee the papers during these two rounds. We would also like to thank Jacques Ferland and John Beasley for helping with the first round of refereeing. Thanks must also go to the staff of Springer-Verlag for their support and encouragement. As editor of the Lecture Notes in Computer Science Series, Jan van Leeuwen was particularly helpful throughout the duration of this project. His comments and advice were invaluable in bringing the book to publication. We are also particularly grateful to Farida Alibhai for all the secretarial support she has given us during the preparation of this volume.

The book could not have arisen without the delegates at the conference and the authors of submitted papers. Their enthusiasm and participation were a fundamental factor in the success of the event. Finally, we would like to thank the steering committee (listed below) for their continuing work in bringing us this and future timetabling conferences. We apologise for any omissions that have been inadvertently made. So many people have helped with the conference and with the series of conferences that it is difficult to remember them all.

March 1996   Edmund Burke
                                                                 Peter Ross

The 1st International Conference on the Practice and Theory of Automated Timetabling Programme Committee

Edmund Burke (co-chair)   University of Nottingham, UK
Peter Ross (co-chair)   University of Edinburgh, UK
Victor Bardadym   International Renaissance Foundation, Ukraine
Patrice Boizumault   Ecole des Mines de Nantes, France
Mike Carter   University of Toronto, Canada
Dave Corne   University of Reading, UK
Andrew Cumming   Napier University, UK
Marco Dorigo   Universite Libre de Bruxelles. Belgium
Wilhelm Erben   Fachhochschule Konstanz, Germany
Alain Hertz   EPFL, Switzerland
Hideto Ikeda   Ritsumeikan University, Japan
Jeff Kingston   University of Sydney, Australia
Fumio Kitagawa   Okayama University of Science, Japan
Gilbert Laporte   Ecole des Hautes Etudes Commerciales, Montreal, Canada
Henri Luchian   AL. I. Cuza University of Iasi, Romania
Ben Paechter   Napier University, UK
Jan Schreuder   University of Twente, The Netherlands
Dennis Spuck   University of Houston Clear Lake, USA
Jonathan Thompson   University of Wales Swansea, UK
Rupert Weare   Hoskyns Group plc, UK
Dominique de Werra   EPFL, Switzerland
George White   University of Ottawa, Canada
Anthony Wren   University of Leeds, UK

The 1st International Conference on the Practice and Theory of Automated Timetabling Organising Committee

Ben Paechter (Chair)	Napier University, UK
Edmund Burke	University of Nottingham, UK
Dave Corne	University of Reading, UK
Amanda Coulter	Napier University, UK
Andrew Cumming	Napier University, UK
Denis Edgar-Nevill	Napier University, UK
Kirk Jackson	University of Nottingham, UK
Peter Ross	University of Edinburgh, UK
Guiti Saberi	Napier University, UK
Rupert Weare	Hoskyns Group plc, UK

The international series of conferences on the Practice And Theory of Automated Timetabling (PATAT) Steering Committee

Edmund Burke (Chair)	University of Nottingham, UK
Ben Paechter (Treasurer)	Napier University, UK
Victor Bardadym	International Renaissance Foundation, Ukraine
Michael Carter	University of Toronto, Canada
Dave Corne	University of Reading, UK
Jeff Kingston	University of Sydney, Australia
Gilbert Laporte	Ecole des Hautes Etudes Commerciales, Montreal, Canada
Peter Ross	University of Edinburgh, UK
Rupert Weare	Hoskyns Group plc, UK
Dominique de Werra	EPFL, Switzerland
Anthony Wren	University of Leeds, UK

Contents

Surveys

Recent Developments in Practical Examination Timetabling 3
M.W.Carter and G.Laporte

Computer-Aided School and University Timetabling: The New Wave 22
V.A.Bardadym

Scheduling, Timetabling and Rostering - A Special Relationship? 46
A.Wren

Examination Timetabling in British Universities - A Survey 76
E.K.Burke, D.G.Elliman, P.H.Ford and R.F.Weare

Reasoning About Constraints

Employee Timetabling, Constraint Networks and Knowledge-Based Rules:
A Mixed Approach 93
A.Meisels, E.Gudes and G.Solotorevsky

Automated Time Table Generation Using Multiple Context Reasoning with
Truth Maintenance 106
V.Ram and C.Scogings

Investigations of a Constraint Logic Programming Approach to
University Timetabling 112
C.Cheng, L.Kang, N.Leung and G.M.White

Building University Timetables Using Constraint Logic Programming 130
C.Guéret, N.Jussien, P.Boizumault and C.Prins

Complete University Modular Timetabling Using Constraint Logic
Programming 146
G.Lajos

Using Oz for College Timetabling 162
M.Henz and J.Würtz

Genetic Algorithms

A Smart Genetic Algorithm for University Timetabling 181
D.C.Rich

A Genetic Algorithm Solving a Weekly Course-Timetabling Problem 198
W.Erben and J.Keppler

GA-Based Examination Scheduling Experience at Middle East Technical
University 212
A.Ergül

Peckish Initialisation Strategies for Evolutionary Timetabling 227
D.Corne and P.Ross

A Memetic Algorithm for University Exam Timetabling 241
E.K.Burke, J.P.Newall and R.F.Weare

Extensions to a Memetic Timetabling System 251
B.Paechter, A.Cumming, M.G.Norman and H.Luchian

Automatic Timetabling in Practice 266
R.C.Rankin

Complexity Issues

The Complexity of Timetable Construction Problems 283
T.B.Cooper and J.H.Kingston

Some Combinatorial Models for Course Scheduling 296
D.de Werra

The Phase-Transition Niche for Evolutionary Algorithms in Timetabling . 309
P.Ross, D.Corne and H.Terashima-Marín

Tabu Search and Simulated Annealing

Three Methods Used to Solve an Examination Timetable Problem 327
J.P.Boufflet and S.Nègre

General Cooling Schedules for a Simulated Annealing Based
Timetabling System 345
J.Thompson and K.A.Dowsland

How to Decompose Constrained Course Scheduling Problems into
Easier Assignment Type Subproblems 364
V.Robert and A.Hertz

Other Timetabling Papers

A list of other papers presented at the conference 377

Author Index 381

Surveys

Recent Developments in Practical Examination Timetabling

Michael W. Carter
Dept. of Industrial Engineering
University of Toronto
4 Taddlecreek Road
Toronto, Canada M5S 1A4

E-mail: carter@ie.UToronto.ca

Gilbert Laporte
GERAD
École des Hautes Études
 Commerciales de Montréal
5255 avenue Decelles
Montreal, Canada H3T 1V6
E-mail: gilbert@crt.UMontreal.ca

Abstract

In 1986, Carter published a survey of papers on practical examination timetabling, in the intervening years, there have been a number of new applications, and several innovative techniques have been attempted. In this paper, we will classify the algorithms, discuss their reported results and try to draw some conclusions on the state of the art. We have not attempted to perform any experimental comparisons on the different methods.

1 Introduction

Examination timetabling is a difficult combinatorial problem that must normally be faced by educational institutions up to four times each year. There have been hundreds of research papers on the subject and probably thousands of computer programs written (mostly by amateurs at each of these schools) to "solve" their own particular variation on the theme. With all of this effort being expended on the timetabling, it is somewhat surprising that there have been relatively few published papers describing actual successful implementations. The purpose of this paper is to present an overview of such applications. While we have made every possible effort to produce an exhaustive review, we are conscious that some references may have been left out. We would therefore appreciate hearing from anyone who has been overlooked.

Initially, we had intended to include only those papers that had been implemented in a practical application and published; but that would have been a very short survey. We decided to extend our review to include some working papers (which are available from the authors) and papers describing algorithms that had been tested on real timetabling data. In the latter case, it is difficult to determine whether or not the algorithm has subsequently been implemented, but it is somewhat reassuring to see realistic results.

In 1986, Carter, published a fairly comprehensive survey of the literature on practical applications of examination timetabling. Our intention here is to update that often-cited survey with some of the more recent developments in the area. Therefore, we have not repeated the discussion of papers included in the previous review. A few older papers have been included here that were omitted from the original survey.

2 The Examination Timetabling Problem

The basic problem is to assign examinations to a limited number of available time periods in such a way that there are no *conflicts* or *clashes*. i.e., no student is required to write two examinations at the same time. In some cases, this constraint is relaxed, and the objective is to *minimize* the number of student conflicts. The following represents some of the more common side constraints that are observed in practice:

1) Certain groups of exams may be required to take place at the same time (e.g., some common examination questions);

2) Precedence constraints between exams restrict the ordering;

3) Certain exams are required to be in consecutive periods;

4) Certain exams are required to be on the same day;

5) Rules of the form "No student can write x examinations in any y consecutive periods";

6) Certain periods are excluded for an examination (e.g., an exam may be restricted to "evening periods only");

7) Certain (groups of) students are restricted to a subset of the available periods (note that this is a simple extension of excluding exams from certain periods);

8) There is a limit on the total number of students who can write examinations at the same time (total seats);

9) There is a limit on the number of examinations that can occur at the same time (e.g., number of rooms or invigilators).

There may also be a variety of constraints with respect to resources and examiners associated with each examination:

1) Limited number/size of rooms available;
   - Multiple exams in one location
   - Exams may be split over several geographically similar locations
   - Exams may have specific room/building preferences
   - Exams may be preassigned or excluded from certain rooms

2) Special resource requirements (large desks, TV, computers, etc.);

3) Schedule examiners (no examiner should have two exams on the same day; or examiners with two exams should have them in nearby locations);

4) Assign invigilators to exam rooms (minimize number of invigilators depending on the actual number of students in the room);

5) For special students, need to specify exam spacing, length, location, and special resources.

As described above, the primary objective is to find a conflict free timetable (or minimize the number of conflicts). However, there are a variety of secondary objectives:

1) Minimize the number of occurrences of x examinations in any y consecutive periods for all students;

2) Spread examinations out as evenly as possible (for each student);

3) Try to schedule all examinations as early as possible. Note that criterion 3) is directly contrary to objectives 1) and 2);

4) Retain the optimized timetable from the previous year as much as possible. This last criterion is not very appropriate unless there is very little change in student demand patterns from one year to the next. (Some schools want the opposite: do not put the same exam late every year);

5) Maximize flexibility: maximize the number of exams that can be moved to another time period without disrupting the rest of the schedule.

3 Algorithmic Approaches

In Tables 1 and 2, we have summarized a number of papers published in the past ten years. Not surprisingly, there are no exact algorithms being used. The papers can be divided roughly into four types of approaches which we have labelled Cluster, Sequential, Generalized Search and Constraint Based. We also briefly discuss the possibility of a global optimisation solution.

3.1 Cluster Methods

In these methods, the set of examinations are first combined into blocks corresponding to a set of compatible examinations, e.g., this group can feasibly be assigned to some period with no (or only few) conflicts. In a second phase, the clusters are sequenced into specific periods to minimize some objective or satisfy some constraints. The first published application paper describing an application of this approach was by White & Chan [1979] (discussed in Carter [1986]).

Table 1: Problem Descriptions

Reference	Institution (Exams, Students, Periods)	Problem Description
FOXLEY & LOCKYER(1968)	Nottingham University 1967: (651,15000,23)	Conflict-free; fixed spread between exams; user priorities.
FISHER & SHIER (1983)	Clemson University (—,10875,18)	Minimize occurrence of consecutive exams (2 in 2)
LEONG & YEONG (1987,1990)	National University of Singapore (800,16000,44)	Conflict-free, and minimize occurrence of (2 in 2)
JOHNSON (1990)	University of the South Pacific (200,2350,20)	Conflict-free; minimize occurrence of (2 in 2) with capacity constraints
LOTFI & CERVENY (1991)	SUNY at Buffalo (858,11331,15)	Minimize conflicts, 2 in 2, and 2 per day
HERTZ (1991)	Swiss Federal Institute of Technology in Zürich (1851,4529,—)	Minimize 2 in 2, 2 in 4
BALAKRISHNAN, LUCENA & WONG (1992)	Purdue University (3569,—,30)	Minimize conflicts plus capacity constraints
CORNE, FANG & MELISH (1993)	University of Edinburgh, Dept. of Artificial Intelligence 1991: (38,60,28), 1992: (44,93,28)	Minimize conflicts and second and third order conflicts (2 in 2 and 2 in 3)
NUIJTEN, KUNNEN, AARTS, DIGNUM (1994)	Eindoven University of Technology (275,7000,33)	Conflict-free; mandatory spread between exams within each program
BOIZUMAULT, DELON & PERIDY (1994)	l'Université Catholique de l'Ouest, Angers, France (308, 4000,33)	Conflict-free, time windows, consecutives, fixed spacing (some exams), precedence.
THOMPSON & DOWSLAND (1994,1995)	Swansea University 1992: (600,3000,24)	Conflict-free; consecutives; minimize no. of students with consecutive exams.
CARTER, LAPORTE & CHINNECK (1994)	University of Toronto Faculty of Engineering (200,2400,20), and Carleton University (682,16925,34)	No x in y (any x ≤ 3), or, Minimize x in y (any x ≤ 3) plus capacity, and preference constraints
CARTER, LAPORTE & LEE (1995)	Eleven institutions (81 to 2419, 611 to 30032, 20 to 51)	No x in y (any x ≤ 3), or, Minimize x in y (any x ≤ 3) plus capacity, and preference constraints
LEONG (1995)	National University of Singapore (1000,16000,44)	Conflict-free.
Ergül (1995)	Middle East Technical University (1438,16000,39)	Minimize conflicts, 2 in 2, 2 in 3, 2 in 4; evenly spread required (must) course exams.

Table 2: Results on Practical Problems

Reference	Algorithm	Results
FOXLEY & LOCKYER (1968)	Sequential Approach	Implemented and used since 1967
FISHER & SHIER (1983)	Cluster Approach with TSP	Tested on real data but not shown to be implemented
LEONG & YEONG (1987,1990)	Cluster Approach with QAP	Tested on real data; probably not implemented (see Leong (1995))
JOHNSON (1990)	Cluster Approach with Simulated Annealing	Implemented 'very successful'
LOTFI & CERVENY (1991)	Cluster Approach with QAP & TSP	Implemented
HERTZ (1991)	Tabu Search	Tested on real data but not shown to be implemented
BALAKRISHNAN, LUCENA & WONG (1992)	Cluster Approach with TSP	Tested on real data but not implemented
CORNE, FANG & MELISH (1993)	Genetic Algorithm	Implemented
NUUTEN, KUNNEN, AARTS, DIGNUM (1994)	Constraint Satisfaction	Tested on real data
BOIZUMAULT, DELON & PERIDY (1994)	Constraint Logic Programming	Tested on real data
THOMPSON & DOWSLAND (1994,1995)	Simulated Annealing	Implemented since 1993
CARTER, LAPORTE & CHINNECK (1994)	Sequential with Backtracking	Implemented
CARTER, LAPORTE & LEE (1995)	Sequential with Backtracking	Implemented in three, tested in eight Institutions
LEONG (1995)	Constraint Satisfaction ILOG	Implemented for 1994/95 year
Ergül (1995)	Genetic Algorithm	Implemented for Spring '95

There are a variety of approaches used to address the cluster phase. White & Chan create conflict free groups by selecting exams, one at a time, beginning with the largest ones first. Leong & Yeong [1990], do the same except that they select each exam in descending order of number of conflicts. This exam is added to a group with which it has no conflicts and has the largest number of conflicting exams in common. i.e., they try to minimize the number of new group conflicts that will be created.

A similar approach is used by Lotfi & Cerveny [1991]. They sort the exams by the degree times the number of student conflicts with all other exams. Exams are assigned to the first available conflict free block (with no instructor conflict and sufficient remaining capacity). If there are no conflict free blocks, the exam is assigned to the block with the minimum number of conflicts (subject to instructor and capacity constraints). (They do not explain what they do if this fails.) They then apply simple interchange rules to improve the assignment (from Arani & Lotfi [1989]).

Johnson [1990] uses a linear combination of two criteria: the size of the exam (enrolment) and the number of conflicts with other courses. By varying the relative weights, a wide variety of different schedules will be produced. Johnson's algorithm constructs a sequence of solutions, discards the infeasible ones, and saves several of the best ones for the user to choose from. He also assigns rooms and verifies capacity constraints on each period as he constructs the groups.

In the algorithm of Fisher & Shier [1983] conflict free groups are constructed by using the original *course* timetable. i.e., two exams belong to the same group if their corresponding lectures occurred on overlapping time periods. At Clemson University, course lecture patterns appear to be very regular; they describe a pattern consisting of all courses offered at 9:00 on any day. Apparently, these patterns do not overlap with any courses offered at 10:00. In many schools, this grouping would not work. Since lectures are 1, 2 or 3 hours long, combining courses that overlap would often produce a single group!

Once the examinations have been divided into compatible groups, there are several different methods used to sequence the groups. The simplest approach uses the objective of trying to minimize the number of students who have two exams in a row where the last examination on day t is considered *adjacent* to the first exam on day $t+1$. This problem can be modelled as a "Travelling Salesman Problem" (TSP) where each cluster is a city, and the "cost" to travel from cluster i to cluster j is equal to the number of students who must write an examination in *both* group i and in group j. Finding a *tour* that visits each city at minimum cost is equivalent to finding a *sequence* for the groups that minimizes the number of students with consecutive exams (see White & Chan [1979]). (A dummy city (group) with no students must be added to the tour so that our final sequence, when we remove the dummy city, is a linear ordering as opposed to a closed tour.)

Initially, Fisher & Shier sort the groups based on the number of students in each group, σ_i. They arrange the periods in the order: $\sigma_n \ \sigma_1 \ \sigma_{n-2} \ \sigma_3 \ \cdots \ \sigma_4 \ \sigma_{n-3} \ \sigma_2 \ \sigma_{n-1}$. If the students were uniformly randomly distributed, this sequence would minimize total 2 in 2 conflicts. They then use a simple pairwise interchange heuristic to solve the TSP.

A variation of this problem is studied by Balakrishnan, Lucena & Wong [1992]. Here, the last exam on day t is *not* considered adjacent to the first exam on day $t+1$. They model the problem as a "time dependent" TSP in the sense that adjacent groups over a day boundary have no cost. They use a network model with a Lagrangian penalty function and report very good results on large realistic problems; they produce upper and lower bounds that are always under 6%. They assume that the exams have already been divided into groups.

As pointed out by Arani, Karwan & Lotfi [1988], when there are exactly two periods per day, and no cost over a day boundary, then the problem can be solved as a minimum weighted matching problem, dividing the groups up into compatible pairs. In Johnson's application, there are two periods per day, over 10 days, and the objective at this stage was to minimize the number of same day conflicts. However, he chose to solve the problem using simulated annealing. He then solves the final step of the problem of sequencing these "days" based on the criterion that the day with the most "large" exams should be scheduled first; and all days are ordered using this rule.

The group sequencing problem can also be modelled as a Quadratic Assignment Problem (QAP) where the objective is to minimize the number of students who have two examinations in any y consecutive periods. The most common choice for y is 2 or 3. Leong & Yeong [1990] consider the objective:

$$minimize \ \Sigma_i \ \Sigma_j \ q_{ij} \ c_{p(i)p(j)}$$

where

q_{ij}	is the degree of interaction between lists i and j
c_{rs}	is the cost of time spacing between sessions (periods) r and s, and
$p(i)$	is the session (period) that examination i has been assigned to.

For example, q_{ij} represents the number of students who have an exam in group i and in group j, and c_{rs} represents the "cost" associated with a student having exams in period r and period s. Leong & Yeong argue that, since the QAP approach uses costs associated with specific periods, it is possible to take advantage of natural breaks like weekends and holidays (where "consecutive exams" have no cost), while this is not easily done in the TSP. They used costs of 1000 for 2 in 2, 100 for 2 in 3, and 10 for 2 in 4. They construct an initial ordering randomly, and search for improving pairwise exchanges.

Lotfi & Cerveny [1991] include an additional stage in this type of approach; they first cluster the exams into "low conflict" groups. They then organize these groups into *days* using a simple QAP heuristic where they have three exam periods per day. In a third stage, they take the period each day with the least conflicts to the other two and put it in the middle, and then use a simple TSP heuristic to sequence the *days* based on the number of conflicts between the first and last period of each pair of days.

In general, the cluster approaches represent a form of decomposition of the problem. By combining exams into low conflict groups first, the size of sequencing problem is reduced which, theoretically, allows the use of more sophisticated optimization techniques on the period sequencing problem. This must necessarily detract from the potential quality of the final solution since the search space is drastically reduced. Moreover, in practical applications, people seem to be using fairly simple heuristics to solve the decomposed problem. It is not clear to us that the approach is beneficial. A further disadvantage of these methods is that it becomes virtually impossible to implement rules such as "No student should have three exams in any four periods". Any reference back to individual exams or students has been lost. At the same time, Johnson [1990] reports success on a fairly small problem; and Lotfi & Cerveny [1991] report that their algorithm has been successfully implemented on a fairly large instance.

3.2 Sequential Methods

In sequential methods, examinations are assigned to a specific period one at a time, chosen using some *sequencing strategy*. There exist a wide variety of approaches distinguished by the order for selecting the next exam, and the way the period is chosen. The period may be chosen as the earliest feasible period (in an attempt to minimize the total number of periods required), or it may be the best feasible period (where "best" is a measure of the objectives). These algorithms typically employ a two phase approach: a construction phase produces an initial timetable, and an improvement phase makes modifications and improvements. (Note that some of the papers described earlier used sequential methods to create an initial set of conflict-free blocks.)

Several earlier papers describe sequential methods, (cf. Barham & Westwood [1978], Broder [1964, 1966, 1968], Cole [1964], Desroches, Laporte & Rousseau [1978], Laporte & Desroches[1984], Mehta [1981,1982]) which are discussed in Carter [1986].

The following list illustrates some of the sequencing strategies that have been employed for the construction phase:

1) *Largest degree*: largest number of conflicting examinations. i.e., exams which conflict with many other exams should be scheduled early.

2) *Saturation degree*: number of *periods* in conflict. i.e., the exam with the least number of available periods should be selected next. This is a dynamic selection rule. Ties are broken using largest degree.

3) *Largest weighted degree*: total number of students in conflict with other exams.

4) *Largest enrollment*: select the exam with the largest number of students.

5) *Largest number of papers*: some exams may require multiple papers to be written in different, possibly consecutive, exam periods.

6) *User defined priority groups*: select high priority examinations first (e.g., exams for final year students may have high priority).

7) *Random ordering*: select examinations in random order (or select them in the order they appear in the input stream).

For almost 30 years, Nottingham University has been using an algorithm developed by Foxley & Lockyer [1968] based on Cole's [1964] method. The approach is a simple construction algorithm that fills the periods, one at a time from the beginning. There is no automatic improvement phase (although there is allowance for manual adjustments after the schedule has been generated). The structure of the procedure allows the authors to easily accommodate conflicts, consecutive exams, required minimum exam spacing and user defined exam priorities. They employ a flexible exam ordering and priority routine to allow the user to construct several different schedules and then choose the best.

Carter, Laporte & Chinneck [1994] include sequence strategies 1-4 and 7 as user selected options. Some strategies work better on some problems. In general, the "saturation degree" strategy proved the most robust, but occasionally, other strategies worked better. For a comparison of the strategies, refer to Carter, Laporte & Lee [1995]. They also include "random tie breaking" so that the algorithm can be run several times to generate a selection of timetables for the scheduler to choose from. A "limited backtracking" approach is used to try to ensure that the initial solution is feasible.

Typically, the improvement phase involves performing "k-opt" interchanges looking for improvements. For example, 1-opt checks if any single exam can move to a better period; 2-opt looks for interchanging or reassigning pairs of exams. Carter, Laporte & Chinneck use 1-opt and 2-opt to improve their final solution.

It is interesting to note that most of the algorithms use a *Conflict Matrix* as the internal method of representing the problem. Element i, j of the matrix represents the *number* of students who must write both exams i and j. This representation allows the implementation of rules like "minimize the number of students who have 2 exams in any y consecutive periods; they do not allow the evaluation of rules like "minimize the number of students who have 3 (or more) exams in y periods". In order to handle these types of measures, we need to retain the examination list for each student. Carter, Laporte & Chinneck do work directly with the list of exams by student, and allow rules of the form "no x in y" or "minimize x in y" for $x = 2, 3$ or 4, and any y.

3.3 Generalized Search Strategies

We use the term *Generalized Search* to describe the class of algorithms that begin with one or more initial solutions, and employs a search strategy that tries to avoid getting stuck in local solution areas, and investigates a more global region of the space. Examples of such approaches include simulated annealing, tabu search and genetic algorithms. These techniques all share the property that, if they are run long enough, they will almost certainly discover the "optimal" solution. They also share the characteristic that, for most problems, it is not practical to really run them "long enough", but they are still interesting as heuristic methods. In some respects, they are similar to sequential methods; they use a (usually simple) sorting criteria to construct one or more initial timetables, and then apply a search procedure to investigate a variety of related solutions. In these algorithms, initial feasibility is not critical; they prefer to get started quickly, so backtracking is not used. The majority of the computation time will be spent in the improvement phase.

Simulated annealing has been applied to a wide range of problems. We already mentioned that Johnson [1990] used simulated annealing to solve one part of his "cluster" approach. The basic concept is that one tries to find a feasible solution fairly quickly, and then randomly, and iteratively, selects a "neighbourhood" solution. For example, one could define a neighbourhood as the set of all solutions with any single exam moved to a new period. If the new solution improves the objective function, it is accepted. If it is not an improvement, it is accepted with some probability. Initially, the probability is high so that most solutions are accepted. As the algorithm proceeds, the probability is slowly lowered (analogous to lowering the temperature in an annealing process) which eventually forces the solution into a local minimum. The temperature can then be increased again, and the procedure repeated until a new local minimum is discovered. The algorithm keeps track of the best solution(s) encountered. When some stopping criteria is met (total time or no improvement for a certain time), the best solution is reported.

Thompson & Dowsland [1995a, 1995b, 1996] used a two phase approach. In the first phase, they only consider the more important, "binding" criteria (conflict-free, limited number of students per period and preassignments). Assuming that they can find a feasible solution, they optimize secondary constraints in the second phase (prefer large exams early, minimize students writing consecutive exams), while the neighbourhood search is restricted to maintaining feasibility of the binding constraints. By restricting the search space in this way, they may disconnect it and thereby lose the "global search" property of simulated annealing. They attempt to counter this behaviour by borrowing some "diversification" ideas from tabu search and constructing several runs investigating a variety of local solutions. They also employ "Kempe chains" which consist of two subsets of exams in time periods i and j where the two sets of assignments can be feasibly interchanged. This increases the size of the neighbourhood. They construct solutions in under an hour on a DEC alpha computer (equivalent to about 18.5 hours on a 486 PC according to the authors) although this can be reduced by using a faster cooling schedule with a corresponding reduction in solution quality. The system has been used successfully at Swansea since 1993.

In simple terms, tabu search is similar to simulated annealing in the sense that neighbourhood moves are used to move out of a local optimum. However, instead of choosing randomly, the method maintains a list of "tabu moves". These represent solutions that have been visited before, and the algorithm is forced to look elsewhere. Subject to this constraint, the algorithm looks for the best improving move it can find without going backwards. The new move is accepted, even if it leads to a worse solution.

Tabu search has been applied to both course and examination timetabling problems by Hertz [1991]. He does not state exactly how he generated an initial solution; but one can assume that he used one of the simple ordering strategies. For exam timetabling, the neighbourhood is defined as the set of schedules obtained by moving a single exam to a new period. Since this set is quite large, he restricts it by considering a random subset; he chooses ½*n* potential moves where *n* is the number of exams. Each selection consists of randomly picking an exam which violates a constraint, and randomly choosing a new period. The algorithm selects the best of these as the new solution. The tabu list "of all previous solutions" is also too large to save directly. Therefore, a list of the last seven moves is saved as pairs {*x*, *i*} where *x* is an exam and *i* represents the previous period; he does not allow any shift that would move course *x* back to period *i*. The number seven is a program parameter. This type of restriction is typical of tabu search algorithms.

Boufflet and Negre [1996] have applied Tabu search to the examination timetabling problem at the University of Technology of Compiègne in France. Their problem involved up to 130 exams in 20 periods.

Genetic algorithms derive their name from the underlying process; they attempt to imitate the genetic function of combining chromosomes to produce new "children". Initially, a large "population" of schedules is constructed (using a simple sequential method). Although there are a variety of coding schemes, the simplest way to represent an examination timetable is in the form of a vector (the chromosome) of length *n* (the number of exams) where the *i*-th entry (gene) of the vector states which period the exam is assigned to. Two different solutions (parents) can be combined to produce two new solutions (children) by randomly selecting a point to split the two vectors into a front and back part. The front of the "father" is merged with the back of the "mother" to produce one child, and vice versa to produce a second child. Both children are new feasible schedules in the sense that every exam is assigned to a unique period. Some algorithms will also include a feature to try to make the children feasible using simple moves. The hope is that perhaps good parts of the father will match with good parts of the mother to produce an improved child. The new solutions are evaluated in a "fitness" function which evaluates how good the schedule is with respect to the criteria. Corne, Fang & Mellish [1993] use a population of size 50. Each one is evaluated, and then 25 pairs are randomly selected (with a bias toward the fittest solutions). These 50 parents produce the next generation of 50 children, and they repeat the procedure for 300 generations. They repeat the whole process ten times and select the best schedule from all runs.

There are many different coding schemes, different strategies for producing children, a process called "mutation" where individual genes are randomly selected to be randomly moved, and "elitism" where the best "parents" are always selected. Corne, Fang and Mellish [1993] used a fairly simple strategy on the exam timetable for the A.I. Dept. at the University of Edinburgh. The evaluation function included conflicting exams (weight 30), more than two exams in a day (weight 10), two consecutive exams (weight 3) and two exams just before and after lunch on the same day (weight 1). They achieved far better solutions compared to those that had been produced manually in 1991/92. One student had consecutive exams (score 3), compared with the manual score of 135 from 33 consecutives, 16 before & after lunch, and two students with three exams on one day. Their approach was implemented in 1992/93. Corne and Ross [1996] looked at alternate initialization strategies using the same data sets.

In 1995, Middle East Technical University (METU) in Ankara, Turkey used a genetic algorithm approach called GUNES developed by Ergül [1996]. The *fitness* (objective) function included costs associated with conflicts and attempting to spread exams out for students. It also gave a higher weight to the spread between "must" (required) course exams. The author used a surrogate for "must" exams as all those exams with a *low* conflict density. Exams with a high conflict density are assumed to be electives. One assumes that elective courses can be taken by a wider variety of students than must courses. The schedule produced by the program was accepted in the Spring '95 exams after 46 exams were moved to new slots. This implies, perhaps, that the results are good, but the fitness function still requires work.

Burke et al [1996] have used a memetic algorithm for examination timetabling and tested it on a number of real problems including the University of Nottingham. A memetic algorithm is similar to a genetic algorithm except that a local improvement heuristic is applied to each child so that every member of the population represents a local optimal solution. This will dramatically reduce the population size; however, it also requires considerable additional time for each iteration. The authors presented evidence of the value of their approach; but they did not compare directly with a genetic approach.

All of these techniques are relatively recent innovations in the area of heuristic search. If one only considers problem size, all of these techniques have been applied successfully on some rather large example problems. This looks like a very promising area for future research. Of course, all of these search algorithms require considerable computer time and/or horse power. It is difficult to draw more accurate conclusions without comparisons with other approaches on identical problems to see if the additional effort produces better quality solutions.

3.4 Constraint Based Approaches

There are a number a papers from the AI (Artificial Intelligence) research community that use general systems for constraint representation. They are described as Constraint Satisfaction Problems or Constraint Logic Programming. Most of the constraint programming literature models a problem as a set of variables with a finite domain, to which values must be assigned so as to satisfy a number of constraints. However, the approaches can also be presented based on the concept that a wide variety of optimization problems can be described as a set of "activities" (exams) which require "resources" (rooms and/or periods) and there are "constraints" which apply to groups (pairs) of activities, and constraints that restrict the use and/or timing on resources. Examples of constraints include two exams that cannot be assigned to the same period;

two exams that must be consecutive, rooms that have seating limits, etc. i.e., most of the exam scheduling rules can be translated into constraints. Typically, these systems employ fairly simple rules for assigning exams to periods. They will not allow infeasible assignments, and when they get stuck, they use backtracking until they find a feasible solution that satisfies all of the constraints. They do not explicitly minimize or maximize an objective function. The beauty of these systems is that they are not designed for exam scheduling. They are general solvers that simply interpret constraints. The user enters a list of constraints to describe their particular application. (In practice, the search strategy or heuristics that are used to guide the search are often specific to the application.)

A general constraint satisfaction technique has been applied to the problem of examination timetabling at the Eindoven University of Technology, Netherlands by Nuijten, Kunnen, Aarts and Dignum [1994]. (They tested their approach on real data, but there is no indication that it has been implemented.) The problem is fairly small with 275 examinations, 7,000 students and 33 exam periods over three weeks. They have constraints on the number of students per period, "time windows" on when the exams can take place, conflict constraints, and mandatory spread constraints (between exams in exam groups corresponding to programs). They had two variations on their algorithm, and both required about 3,000 constraints. The random selection algorithm consists of assigning as many exams as possible to the first period using random selection, and then continuing with the second period. If no feasible solution is found, they try backtracking. If backtracking is not successful after a while, they try a complete restart in the expectation that random selection will provide a different path. They ran several different tests varying the capacity of the exam room to test their approach. On average, the successful runs required between two and twelve minutes of CPU time on a SUN SPARC station ELC.

Constraint logic programming (CLP) uses techniques inherited from Constraint Satisfaction Problems (CSP). In simple terms, the difference is that CSP methods ask the user to specify their constraints, while CLP is an actual programming language, so that the user can do much more customization in the solution design. Presumably, the added flexibility also increases the development time required. Boizumault, Delon & Péridy [1994] describe using Constraint Logic Programming for l'Université Catholique de l'Ouest in Angers, France. In addition to the usual rules (conflicting exams, preassignments, consecutive exams, precedence constraints), they include room assignment where multiple exams may be assigned to each of seven rooms. i.e., a bin packing problem. They tested there model on the 308 examinations which produced a set of 2600 constraints. Of these, the most frequent were 1930 exam conflict constraints. Their search procedure used a "Best Fit Decreasing" (bin packing) strategy. They solved the real problem in under one minute of CPU time (although they did not mention the processor).

Although there are no formal papers presenting the problem or the results, there is an article that appeared in Computerworld (Leong [1995]) describing the use of a commercial package called the ILOG SOLVER and ILOG SCHEDULE. ILOG is a

French company that has become very successful in the development of constraint based object oriented tools. The article gives an overview of an implementation of examination timetabling at the National University of Singapore where one of the systems analysts, Goh Guay Im, in the University Computer Centre, developed and implemented a model in about one month. Unlike the previous two examples, this problem was fairly large with over 1,000 examinations. However, there is an indication in the article that the problem may have been decomposed, and each faculty solved separately. There was no indication of CPU solve times. The article was primarily an interview with Ms. Goh. The system has been used for two exam schedules in 1994-95. The ILOG system allows the user to model one or more objective functions. As the branch and bound search progresses, the program will locate feasible solutions. The system can then add a constraint that only allows solutions with a lower objective function value. In the case of multiple objectives, the user can interact with the system to determine which objectives should be restricted.

All of the papers that we considered for constraint based methods have been used to solve fairly small problems (around 300 examinations). We are not sure what size problem the ILOG solver has tackled, but it is likely around the same size. In constraint methods, the number of constraints grows quite quickly as problem size increases (at least as the square), so it would appear that they may have trouble with large examples in the range of 1,000 exams. Obviously, this limitation will be reduced over time.

3.5 Global Optimization Approaches

Of course, it would be marvellous if someone could develop a globally optimal algorithm for examination timetabling. Although there have been some research papers on this topic, there is only one paper that we are aware of where the author, Tripathy [1980, 1984], has attempted to solve the problem on real data. The approach is described in Carter [1986]. It is probably fair to say that the algorithm is not a feasible way to solve typical practical problems.

4 Room Assignment

Several of the algorithms (Leong & Yeong [1990], Carter, Laporte & Chinneck [1995], Lotfi & Cerveny [1991], Boizumault, Delon & Péridy [1995]) include a routine for assigning examinations to rooms after the exams have been assigned to periods. All of them are similar. Lotfi & Cerveny describe their approach as follows. For each examination period, sort the available rooms in descending order by capacity; sort the examinations in descending order by number of participants. The largest exam is assigned to the smallest room with sufficient capacity to hold the students. If no room is large enough, then the largest room is filled, and remaining students are assigned to a different room.

As mentioned earlier, Johnson assigns rooms as part of the timetable construction. In producing the initial clusters, he first checks if there is an available room for the exam in that cluster, and then assigns the exam to the smallest room which is large enough.

Carter [1995] has recently added a room assignment module to the EXAMINE program that allows a wide variety of additional criteria: some exams cannot be split in multiple rooms, some rooms can handle more than one exam, split exams or exams with the same instructor need to be geographically nearby, some exams require special room facilities, some exams are preassigned to specific (groups of) rooms.

5 Conclusions

One of the most striking observations from preparing this survey is that the algorithms that have been implemented in practice are uniformly relatively simple. For example, there has been a considerable interest in genetic algorithms and a wide variety of approaches. However, the ones that have been implemented are among the simplest of GA strategies. The same is true for the other successful approaches. Part of this simplicity is that most algorithms only address a subset of the constraints and objectives of the general timetabling problem as outlined at the beginning of this paper. Some authors claim that additional criteria could easily be incorporated. For example, an *evaluation* function for a GA can be very flexible. However, complex evaluation functions may severely restrict the speed required to produce large potential populations. There is a trade-off between speed and comprehensiveness.

Carter, Laporte and Chinneck incorporate most of the criteria. Their algorithm is also the only algorithm in the literature that has been implemented at more than one institution. It is currently in use at the University of Toronto (Engineering), Carleton University, London School of Economics, the University of Otago (New Zealand), and the University of Limerick (Ireland).

We should state that this survey is in a sense rather restricted in scope. There has been a lot of practical work on the related, but more complex problem of course timetabling with practical applications. In many cases, course timetabling algorithms can be applied directly to the examination timetabling problem with excellent results. However, a detailed survey of applications in course timetabling will have to wait for another paper. We strongly encourage future researchers make use of the test problems now available at the ftp site: ftp.cs.nott.ac.uk or the web site site http://tawny.cs.nott.ac.uk/ttg/ttp.html. By reporting test results on some of these benchmark problems, it will be possible to gain a better understanding of the relative merits of the various approaches.

References

Arani, T., Karwan, M., and Lotfi, V., "A Lagrangian Relaxation Approach to Solve the Second Phase of the Exam Scheduling Problem", **European Journal of Operations Research 34**, 1988, 372-383.

Arani, T., and Lotfi, V., "A Three Phased Approach to Final Exam Scheduling", **IIE Transactions 21**, 1989, 86-96.

Balakrishnan, N., Lucena, A., and Wong, R.T., "Scheduling Examinations to Reduce Second-order Conflicts", **Computers & Operations Research 19**, 1992, 353-361.

Balakrishnan, N., "Examination Scheduling: A Computerized Application", **Omega 19**, 1991, 37-41.

Barham, A.M. and Westwood, J.B., "A Simple Heuristic to Facilitate Course Timetabling", **Journal of the Operational Research Society 29**, 1978, 1055-1060.

Boizumault, P., Delon, Y., and Péridy, L., "Constraint Logic Programming for Examination Timetabling", **Journal of Logic Programming**, 1995, 1-17.

Boufflet, J.P., and Negre, S., "Three Methods Used to Solve an Examination Timetabling Problem", in The Practice and Theory of Automated Timetabling (E.K. Burke and P. Ross eds.), Springer-Verlag Lecture Notes in Computer Science, 1996.

Broder, S., "Final Examination Scheduling", **Communications of the A.C.M. 7**, 1964, 494-498.

Broder, S., "A Heuristic Algorithm for Timetable Construction", **Journal of Educational Data Processing 5**, 1968, 117-123.

Broder S., On the Problem of Time Table Construction, **Communications of the ACM, 9**, 1966, 257.

Burke, E.K., Newal, J.P., and Weare, R.F., "A Memetic Algorithm for University Exam Timetabling", in The Practice and Theory of Automated Timetabling (E.K. Burke and P. Ross eds.), Springer-Verlag Lecture Notes in Computer Science, 1996.

Carter, M.W., "A Survey of Practical Applications of Examination Timetabling Algorithms", **Operations Research 34**, 1986, 193-202.

Carter, M.W., Laporte, G., and Chinneck, J.W., "A General Examination Scheduling System", **Interfaces 24**, 1994, 109-120.

Carter, M.W., Laporte, G., and Lee, S.Y., "Examination Timetabling: Algorithmic Strategies and Applications", **Journal of the Operational Research Society 47**, No. 3, 1996, 373-383.

Carter, M.W., "Examination Room Assignment for EXAMINE", Working Paper, May 1995.

Cole, A.J., "The Preparation of Examination Timetables Using a Small-Store Computer", **The Computer Journal 7**, 1964, 117-121.

Corne, D., Fang, H.L., and Mellish, C., "Solving the Modular Exam Scheduling Problem with Genetic Algorithms", in **Proc. of the Sixth International Conf. on Industrial and Engineering Applications of Artificial Intelligence and Expert Systems**, P.W.H. Chung, G. Lovegrove & M. Ali (eds), 1993, 370-373.

Corne, D., and Ross, P., "Peckish Initialization Strategies For Evolutionary Timetabling" in The Practice and Theory of Automated Timetabling (E.K. Burke and P. Ross eds.), Springer-Verlag Lecture Notes in Computer Science, 1996.

Desroches, S., Laporte, G. and Rousseau, J., "HOREX: A Computer Program for the Construction of Examination Timetables", **INFOR 16**, 1978, 294-298.

Ergül, A., "GA-Based Examination Scheduling Experience at Middle East Technical University" in The Practice and Theory of Automated Timetabling (E.K. Burke and P. Ross eds.), Springer-Verlag Lecture Notes in Computer Science, 1996.

Fisher, J.G. and Shier, D.R., "A Heuristic Procedure for Large-Scale Examination Scheduling Problems", Tech. Report 417, Dept. of Mathematical Sciences, Clemson University, March, 1983.

Foxley, E., and Lockyer, K., "The Construction of Examination Timetables by Computer", **The Computer Journal 11**, 1968, pp. 264-268.

Hertz, A., "Tabu Search for Large Scale Timetabling Problems", **European Journal of Operations Research 54**, 1991, 39-47.

Johnson, D., "Timetabling University Examinations", **Journal of the Operational Research Society 41**, 1990, 39-47.

Laporte, G. and Desroches, S., "Examination Timetabling by Computer", **Computers and Operations Research 11**, 1984, 351-360.

Leong, T.Y., and Yeong, W.Y., "Examination Scheduling: A Quadratic Assignment Perspective", **Proc. Int'l Conf. on Optimization: Techniques and Applications**, Singapore, April 1987, 550-558.

Leong, T.Y., and Yeong, W.Y., "A Hierarchical Decision Support System for University Examination Scheduling", working paper, National University of Singapore, Sept., 1990.

Leong Y.L., "Right on Schedule: Exam Timetabling at the National University of Singapore Gets an Added Boost with New Tools", **ComputerWorld**, May 12-18 1995, 22-23.

Lotfi, V., and Cerveny, R., "A Final-exam-scheduling Package", **Journal of the Operational Research Society 42**, 1991, 205-216.

Mehta, N.K., "The Application of a Graph Coloring Method to an Examination Scheduling Problem", **Interfaces 11**, 1981, 57-64.

Mehta N.K., Computer-Based Examination Management System, **Journal of Educational Technology Systems, 11**, 1982, 185-198.

Nuijten, W.P.M., Kunnen, G.M., Aarts, E.H.L. and Dignum, F.P.M., "Examination Time Tabling: A Case Study for Constraint Satisfaction", **Proceedings of the ECAI '94 Workshop on Constraint Satisfaction Issues Raised by Practical Applications**, 11-19.

Thompson, J.M., and Dowsland, K.A., "Variants of Simulated Annealing for the Examination Timetabling Problem", working paper, European Business Management School, Swansea University, Swansea, UK 1995a, to appear in **Annals of O.R.**

Thompson, J.M., and Dowsland, K.A., "TISSUE Wipes Away Exam Time Tears: A Computerised System Helps Swansea University Improve Examination Timetabling", **O.R. Insight 8**, No. 4, 1995, 28-32.

Thompson, J.M., and Dowsland, K.A., "General Cooling Schedules for a Simulated Annealing Based Timetabling System" in The Practice and Theory of Automated Timetabling (E.K. Burke and P. Ross eds.), Springer-Verlag Lecture Notes in Computer Science, 1996.

Tripathy, A., "A Lagrangian Relaxation Approach to Course Timetabling", **Journal of the Operational Research Society 31**, 1980, 599-603.

Tripathy, A., "School Timetabling - A Case in Large Binary Integer Programming", **Management Science 30**, 1984, 1473-1489.

White, G.M. and Chan, P.W., "Towards the Construction of Optimal Examination Timetables", **INFOR 17**, 1979, 219-229.

White, G.M., and Haddad, M., "An Heuristic Method for Optimizing Examination Schedules Which Have Day and Night Courses", **Computers and Education 7**, 1983, pp. 235-238.

Wood, D.C., "A System for Computing University Examination Timetables", **Computer Journal 11**, 1968, 41-47.

Computer-Aided School and University Timetabling: The New Wave

Victor A. Bardadym

International Renaissance Foundation
PO Box 358/3
Kiev-30 252030 Ukraine
bardadym@issep.freenet.kiev.ua

Abstract

During the last five years a peak of interest has been observed in the problems related to computer-aided timetabling. The most recent works in this area are based on the application of modern information technologies. Here the main directions of modern research and design are reviewed. A classification is proposed for academic timetabling problems, requirements for the timetables, mathematical models, solution methods, data representation, and interface design. Modern problem solution and software design approaches are represented in connection with the theoretical background and world experience of 35 years. The integration of several algorithmic and interactive tools is discussed. Criticisms of timetabling computer support practicability and related myths are also reviewed. Related topics, like sport scheduling and scheduling sport, are represented. Some unsolved matters are outlined.

1 Introduction

Various scheduling problems in education including construction of lectures' and exams' timetables, and course and classroom scheduling are among the most difficult in educational planning. The difficulties of a typical scheduling problem arise from its large scale, great number of contradictory requirements, constraints and criteria of assignments' quality. The sufficient difficulty for the scheduler is the large amount of routine work, namely finding acceptable alternatives, requirements' fulfilment analysis, looking for mistakes, and filling out several report forms (tables of classes, teachers, and classrooms).

The preparation of a class-teacher timetable for secondary school may need up to two weeks, and the mistakes found during the teaching term may cause sufficient changes in a timetable. Carter [15], Samofalov and Simonenko [64] mentioned that the manual preparation of university timetables may take up to one month.

The interest of school and university administrations in timetabling automatisation has caused numerous challenges to this problem, and problem statements of automated school/university timetable design are well known. But school and university timetabling problems remain a reality for Operations Research and Computer Science in spite of numerous attempts to solve them.

The timetabling problems can be sufficiently varied in different universities depending on their specific requirements and conditions. Due to this, timetabling systems usually are applied only in the institutions where they were designed.

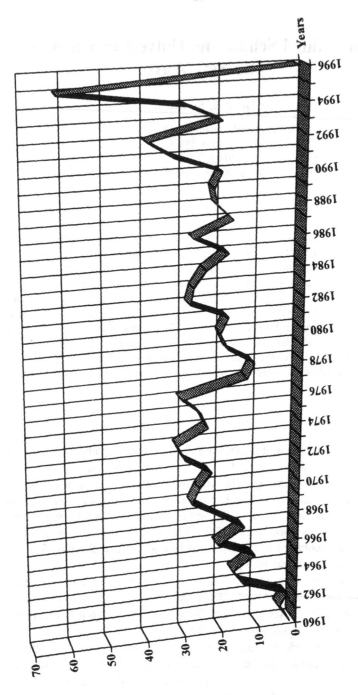

Fig. 1. The distribution of publications related with timetabling by years

Nevertheless, some timetabling systems have been distributed in numerous institutions, mostly in secondary schools [43].

The first attempts at computer-aided timetabling were made in the early 60's when universities obtained computers. Since that time many researchers and programmers have challenged this problem. Author knows more than 700 published writings dealing with these problems, including monographs, results of theoretical analyses and computational experiments, conceptual projects of software tools, articles describing experience in design and usage, surveys and bibliographies, theses for degrees, discussional papers, technical documentation, commercial catalogues, advertising, and private communications. Naturally, all of them cannot be mentioned here, and it is mostly pioneering works, new approaches, or original points of view are quoted in this paper.

Research in school timetabling has brought about many significant results in combinatorics, discrete optimisation and heuristic approaches, as well as technical solutions of its implementation. These results have proved useful in several theoretical and applied fields, and the problem of academic timetabling can be considered a model for the more general problems of decision making, scheduling, etc.

At present, many timetabling researchers world-wide are continuing their studies and software designs at a new level of quality using recent successes in artificial intelligence, decision making, discrete optimisation, and information technologies, as well as the power of modern computers and software. During the last five years a peak in publications related to timetabling and based on new approaches has been observed (See Fig. 1).

The aims of this paper are:
(i) to classify the problem statements, timetable requirements, formalisation approaches, and solution methods;
(ii) to study the logic of 35 years of timetabling software evolution, reasons and consequences of some decisions;
(iii) to find the emerging analogies and impacts between problems and solution approaches having quite different roots;
(iv) to formulate the concept of "new wave" timetabling software tools; and
(v) to outline some problems for future studies.

2 Timetabling Problems Classification

The common educational timetabling problems can be classified as follows:

1) *Faculty Timetabling.* A set of instructors, a set of lessons, and availabilities of instructors to teach several courses are defined. The problem is to distribute courses between the instructors under specified conditions.
2) *Class-Teacher Timetabling.* This problem considers a set of classes, and a set of teachers. Each class is a set of students having a common curriculum and studying together. For several pairs *<class, teacher>* the required lessons and their numbers are defined. Each single lesson must be assigned to the time period

in such a way that no teacher and no class should have two or more simultaneous lessons.

3) *Course Scheduling.* A set of students is given; students are not grouped into classes having fixed curricula. For each student the set of lectures is defined. The lectures must be scheduled to time periods in such a way that no student can have two or more simultaneous lectures.

4) *Examination Timetabling.* The set of students (classes) and the sets of examinations for each student (class) are given. Each examination must be assigned to a time period so that no students (classes) should have two or more exams simultaneously.

5) *Classroom Assignment.* When the class-teacher lessons or student-professor lectures are scheduled, they must be assigned to classrooms according to given availabilities. No classrooms should be used simultaneously by different classes.

Sometimes these problems are considered together or in combination with other educational planning problems, like curricula development or student advising. This leads to the inclusion of corresponding solvers or support tools into integrated computer-aided management systems assuming preliminary scheduling as well as real-time dispatching.

3 Main Timetable Requirements

In addition to above conditions, different general and specific requirements must be satisfied. The main requirements of the ultimate schedule may be classified as follows (See Fig. 2):

(i) *Completeness,* i.e. :

1) complete correspondence of timetable to curriculum. The curriculum is considered here as the set of lessons to be scheduled with specified multiplicities per whole planning period (usually a term, fortnight, or week). There are many ways to define a single curriculum item. The most common items are:

   <class, subject, multiplicity>,
   <class, teacher, multiplicity>,
   <class, subject, teacher, multiplicity>,
   <class, subject, teacher, classroom, multiplicity>,
   <student, subject, multiplicity>,
   <student, subject, professor, multiplicity>;

2) preassignments of some lessons to specified time periods according to the requirements determined for teachers, classes, subjects, or classrooms;

(ii) *Non-contradictoriness,* i.e. absence of any types of conflicts, namely:

1) simultaneous lessons in the same students' group or in the several groups having the same students,

2) simultaneous lessons with the same teacher,

3) simultaneous lessons in the same classroom,
4) lessons for some teachers or classes when they are unavailable, and
5) assignment of lessons to classrooms unacceptable (improperly equipped) for the corresponding subject or having insufficient workspace;

(iii) *Proper Sequencing,* including:

1) continuity of the lessons for all students meaning the absence of gaps. The gap (also spoken of as "window") is a time interval when a class or teacher has no lessons during some period, and has lessons before and after this period on this day. Several special cases (for example, when a lunch break must be scheduled) can be considered as lessons on fictive subjects, but not as gaps. The absence of gaps in teachers' timetables is often desirable also.
2) sequencing requirements reflecting logical structure of courses and defined by the curriculum for lessons on different subjects, or lessons of different types (for example, labs must follow the lectures on this subject),
3) minimisation of students' and teachers' travels between different buildings (usually taking into account whether pairs of buildings are near or far to each other);

(iv) *Uniform Distribution:*

1) the number of lessons per day for each teacher, each student or class, or each pair <*class, teacher*> cannot exceed specified limit,
2) the same lessons in the same classes must be distributed uniformly over the week,
3) the disciplines must be distributed by days of the week and time intervals according to pedagogical, psychological and ergonomic requirements. For example, it might be recommended that the lessons on Mathematics be assigned to Tuesday, Wednesday, or Thursday between the second and fourth lessons; physical training and workshops be assigned to the last lessons in the day; and that easy and hard lessons would be alternated;
4) the time interval between two successive exams cannot exceed the specified minimal interval;

(v) *Others,* for example, reliability meaning maximal opportunities to change a teacher when necessary.

From another point of view, the requirements can be divided into necessary and desirable ones. This subdivision can be varied in different institutions. When the timetabling problem is formulated as one of Mathematical Programming problems, the necessary conditions determine the set of feasible solutions, and desirable conditions determine the optimality criteria.

	By types				By sufficiency
Completeness	Non-contradictoriness	Sequencing	Uniform Distribution	Others	
1) correspondence to curriculum 2) preassignments	1) no student clashes 2) no teacher clashes 3) no classroom clashes 4) availability of teachers 5) availability of students 6) acceptable assignments of classrooms	1) no gaps 2) logical course sequencing 3) minimisation of travels	1) daily limits 2) uniformity within a week 3) pedagogical, psychological and ergonomic requirements	1) reliability ... etc.	1) necessary 2) desirable

Fig. 2. Classification of timetable requirements

4 Data Representation And Mathematical Models

4.1 Sources: Bookkeeping vs Mathematical Models

Due to hardware and system software poor abilities to support interface, early timetabling software tools assumed automatic timetable generation: the responsible person prepared the input information including lists of teachers, classes or students, and classrooms, curriculum, preassignments and availabilities, and special data. The software unit read this information, tried to generate a timetable, and printed out the timetable or the message about generation fault (possibly with some diagnostics concerned with input data incompatibility, or exhaustion of hardware resources or time). The reason for failure often could not be diagnosed.

The orientation to completely automatic solutions caused the development of appropriate data representation and mathematical models. Early software was usually based on one of two main approaches: simulation of timetabling by hand vs reduction of the timetable problem to some mathematical problem. Data representation for handmade timetables usually was straightforward and often was oriented to specific features of universities or schools.

4.2 Mathematical Programming and Combinatorial Approaches

Graph Colouring. The most timetabling software is based on graph representation. The curriculum and other initial information are represented by graphs, multigraphs, hypergraphs, or set of graphs. Teachers, students or classes, and classrooms are usually represented by graph nodes; lessons to be scheduled. Availabilities or possible conflicts are represented by edges, multiedges or hyperedges. The problem is to assign time periods to edges representing lessons to satisfy the requirements. For instance,

(I) class-teacher is directly reduced to colouring single edges of curriculum bipartite multigraph (possibly, with additional constraints to colouring) [27],

(ii) the timetable for a single period must be an assignment in this graph;

(iii) classroom assignment problem is reduced to assignment finding in availability bipartite graph; and

(iv) course scheduling is directly reduced to graph nodes' colouring [22, 53, 70].

Network Flows And Transportation Problems. Graph representation is not enough to take into account more complicated requirements, and graph models can be generalised. To make the lessons' distribution more uniform by subperiods (weeks in a term, or days in a week), network flows optimisation [17, 22, 57] and transportation problems [5] are used. The obtained solutions can define natural decomposition of the problem to subperiods. Schniederjans and Kim [67] consider the faculty timetabling problem to be a multicriteria assignment problem.

Other Combinatorial Structures. The first representation of this kind was proposed by Gotlieb [38]. It assumed hypergraph simultaneously representing curriculum and availabilities by means of 3-dimensional array; the timetabling was in fact reduced to a 3-dimensional assignment problem (the requirements for the subjects were not taken into account). Many later studies used the representation of Gotlieb and its generalisations as background for precise and heuristic solutions. Barraclough [10] also studied the classes' divisions into subgroups and merging into streams. Kitagawa and Ikeda [46] used 11-dimensional tuples of sets and functions to consider similar divisions and merges, classrooms' requirements and different lessons' lengths. Junginger [43] reduced timetabling to 3-dimensional transportation problem.

Some approaches are based on matrix representation, for instance, choice matrices [26, 64], or double stochastic matrices [66], but search of distinct representatives' sets is closely connected with the search of matchings in graphs. The use of Latin squares [41] appears similar to network flow methods reviewed by de Werra [22]. Kostyuk et al. [47] and Lukyanets [54] represented the timetables construction by operations of set theory.

Integer Mathematical Programming. In order to take into account the most difficult requirements, timetabling is often reduced to some general mathematical programming problem. Zarubitskaya and Samoilenko [77] formulated the integer linear programming problem to take into account the division of classes to subgroups and their merging to streams. Classroom assignment problem is also reduced to integer linear programming in [35, 37]. In more complicated cases the quadratic assignment problem can appear [4].

General Scheduling Theory. Network planning [39, 60] and calendar scheduling representations [9, 48, 74] were used when lesson sequencing was sufficient, or when travels between classrooms in different buildings were to be minimised, or when lessons were assumed to have different lengths. These methods are similar to scheduling methods used in computer-aided manufacturing and often referred to assignment or network flow problems as subproblems.

4.3 The Features of New Wave

Mathematical Logic appeared in some early attempts to solve timetabling problems but had no significant success due to restricted abilities of computers and high complexity of general problems. In recent years the successes in expert systems have attracted researchers to use these representations with new approaches to problems' solution [36, 44, 49].

Database Representation. At present general purpose database management systems and computer-aided software engineering tools (like FoxPro) are widely available, and many designers apply standard database structures (usually a set of relational database tables, forms, reports and utilities) with simple 'bookkeeping' heuristics simulating handmade timetable construction. This approach is often used for timetabling modules in general management information systems of universities and schools. Database representation is sometimes also combined with the above mathematical models [6].

Bookkeeping	Graph Theory	Combinatorics	Mathematical Programming	Mathematical Logics	Databases
	1) edges colouring 2) nodes colouring 3) assignments 4) 3-dimensional assignments	1) n-dimensional arrays 2) n-dimensional tuples 3) Latin squares	1) network flows 2) transportation problems 3) 3-dimensional transportation problems 4) integer linear programming 5) quadratic programming 6) scheduling theory		

Fig. 3. Classification of mathematical models

5 Theoretical Problems in Timetabling

Existence Conditions. Timetable existence conditions were usually studied through matrix representation [46, 50, 58, 64]. Simple necessary or sufficient conditions of feasible timetable existence are useful in backtracking algorithms to reject dead end search branches [6].

Analysis of Algorithmic Complexity. Timetabling problems proved to be hard practically as well as theoretically. Although the edges' colouring of a bipartite multigraph can be obtained by $O (E \log E)$ operations, where E is the total number of single multigraph edges [19], the other sufficient requirements lead the extended problems to be *NP*-complete or *NP*-hard. Even et al. [27] proved the *NP*-completeness when some single periods are unavailable for several teachers. De Werra [22] mentioned that this problem is mutually reducible with the problem assuming lessons' preassignments. Also in this paper the course scheduling problem was considered as well known *NP*-complete graph nodes colouring problem. Bardadym [8] studied the problems combining class-teacher and course scheduling. In these problems the classes were considered as divisible into subgroups and able to be combined into lecture streams. The timetabling problems appeared to be *NP*-complete both for the whole planning period and for single periods. Cater and Tovey [13] studied the complexity of several classroom assignment problems; the single-period optimal assignment problem was shown to be polynomially solvable, and the noninterval feasible and interval satisfice problems were shown to be *NP*-complete.

Many of the above-mentioned works also reduce timetabling to problems well known as *NP*-complete or *NP*-hard (integer linear programming, 0-1 integer linear programming, three-dimensional transportation problem, quadratic assignment problem, travelling salesman problem, graph vertices colouring) (Garey and Johnson, 1982).

Estimation of Timetable Quality. The great number of contradictory requirements may necessitate the omission of some constraints, and treatment of conflicts as unavoidable [25, 56]. When the number of conflicts is to be minimised, the problem of comparison of the influence of different requirements appears. Statistical analogies are most often used for this comparison. Estrada [26], Samofalov and Simonenko [64] studied the function estimating the timetable quality via mean square deviation between proposed and desired timetables. Smith [71] defined the timetable quality by the entropy depending on the number of satisfied requirements.

6 Solution Methods

6.1 Precise Methods

The timetabling problem was investigated simultaneously with numerous theoretical and applied problems, and this caused the researchers to use general solution methods for mathematical programming problems, including backtracking, branch-and-bound, Gomory algorithms, dynamic programming, successive variants' analysis, etc. However, precise methods were found to be too inefficient to solve real scheduling problems. Only few-dimensional problems or problems in which certain sufficient requirements are discarded usually can be solved precisely [27].

Due to this reason a great majority of timetabling software units have been based on heuristic problem solvers.

6.2 Heuristics

Simulation of Handmade Ttimetables' Construction. The first heuristic approaches in timetabling simulated the work of a person making handmade timetables, and usually were based on common sense. These algorithms may be classified as follows:

1) greedy algorithms selecting each assignment by some local optimality rule and making no changes in lessons assigned previously. These algorithms cannot return from dead ends when no lessons can be assigned;

2) choosing each assignment with some local optimality rule, and changing earlier assignments when no lessons can be assigned for the period at hand. This approach can be treated as incomplete backtracking with restrictions on local variants' analysis;

3) algorithms finding the possibility of each given assignment simultaneously with the reassignment of conflicting lessons assigned earlier [10]. If the elementary reassignment proves impossible, some algorithms try to find alternating paths to reassign a set of lessons and to assign more lessons. This is called "pushing and pulling" by schools administrators, and in fact this heuristic is a restricted variant of known augmenting paths methods [61]; and

4) decomposition, i.e. reduction of the given problem to similar problems with smaller cardinality, and applying to these subproblems the same decomposition (if possible) or other methods [2]. The most applicable decomposition is natural decomposition by time periods (like weeks or days).

These heuristics, with numerous modifications and combinations, have been applied in many timetabling programs. The variety of heuristics is defined by some decision rules or preference rules choosing the local search directions.

Decision Rules and Preference Rules. The simplest rules to define the local search step choose the first available assignment or a randomly defined assignment. More common are decision rules [3, 11] or rules optimising some preference function [62]. The order can be defined statically, i.e. in the form of pre-processing without possibility of further changes; or dynamically, i.e. taking into account the lessons assigned earlier at the time of each assignment. The recursive rules may be used to prognosticate the influence of a choice on the ability to choose the next assignments properly. Instead of deterministic rules, randomised choice can be applied. It can be based on the Monte Carlo approach, or can use analogies with mixed strategies in games theory [62] where the probability of search direction choice is proportional to some preference function.

Simultaneously with the suggestions for obtaining feasible solutions, decision rules and preference functions can take into account the psychological, pedagogical and ergonomic requirements of the timetable (difficulty, sequencing, and uniformity). These rules and functions should be defined by experts.

A description of the most common decision rules for graph colouring was made by Carter [15]. In order to summarise the discussion of this kind of heuristics, let us note only the classification criteria:

1) largest degree first vs smallest degree last;
2) depth first vs width first;
3) static vs dynamic rules;
4) recursive prognosis vs no prognosis;
5) deterministic vs stochastic choice;
6) feasible solution search vs optimisation.

In addition to the above approaches, the heuristic algorithms for the general mathematical programming problems mentioned above, like the falling vector method for integer linear programming proposed by Ivan Sergienko and implemented in timetabling by Zarubitskaya and Samoilenko [77]; and artificial intelligence heuristic tools were applied. Loskutov [52] described the heuristic approach in terms of simulation.

Restricted versions of special methods were also used. The solution of a problem with the restricted model without guarantee of some conditions' satisfaction can also be considered as heuristic. On the other hand, the above heuristic approaches are also used to make local modifications of more general methods.

6.3 Metaheuristics: a Feature of New Wave

The principal difficulty of combinatorial problems like timetabling is the existence of numerous feasible solutions disjoint from each other and numerous local extrema. The heuristics described above often have no tools to leave local extremum, to jump over the barrier, and to reach better solutions.

In recent years new approaches have been actively studied and applied to timetabling and other problems having great practical use. They tend to find better solutions than already defined local ones, and may be subdivided in:

(i) *Mathematical Programming*

1) tabu search, assuming transfers to the locally best feasible solution with possible local change for worse to jump over barriers, and maintaining tabu list to avoid cycling [40]. Tabu search can be considered as a modification of the above mentioned falling vector method, although they were proposed independently;

2) exchange procedures [30];

3) Lagrangean relaxation [14, 74]. The connections and analogies among the above three approaches were discussed by Ferland and Lavoie [30];

(ii) *Artificial Intelligence Tools*

1) resolution rules implemented most commonly by logical programming based on PROLOG [28, 44];

2) timetabling expert systems and students advising expert systems with timetabling components [36, 49]; and

(iii) *Simulation*

1) simulated annealing, using a thermodynamic analogy to treat a feasible solution as a 'substance' (a set of 'molecules'). When the substance is heated, molecules can jump over potential barriers, and when cooled, they fill positions with minimal potential [1, 25];

2) genetic algorithms, making analogies with an evolution of a 'population' of solutions as sequence of solutions' combinations (crossovers), mutations, and selections of sets of the best solutions [12].

6.4 Interactive Timetabling: a Feature of New Wave

Database Corrections. Numerous heuristics do not guarantee that the schedule will be built even if it exists. Moreover, optimal solution of mathematical programming problem may be unacceptable due to incomplete mathematical models. These considerations and the possible necessity of changing the schedule during a term [45] have led to the development of interactive tools to correcting the input data or the timetable. In early stages these tools appeared in several systems; initially they assumed batch command mode to modify data.

Check of Handmade Timetables. A specific type of timetabling software that appeared in the first stage of the PC epoch consisted of utilities that checked the handmade timetables and formed lists of diagnostics [20, 63]. A person must analyse these diagnostics, correct the timetable with general purpose editing tools, and check the corrected timetable once more. This procedure was repeated until an acceptable timetable appeared.

Use of Universal Spreadsheets and Database Management Systems. The appearance of PC's with powerful interactive general-purpose information tools, like spreadsheets, database management systems, and integrated systems allowed new abilities to be used for interactive timetabling. General purpose text processors and spreadsheets proved useful to input, access and print timetables [16], but these common software tools did almost nothing to check timetables' correctness.

Special Timetabling Editors. When hardware and software allowed interactive work with computers, timetabling systems were completed with facilities allowing interactive choice of alternatives [31], command interface [17, 43] or prompt-response interface [75]. These facilities allowed input and correction of initial data and timetables, and also influence on the automatic problem solution by choice of alternatives, changing of critical assignments, etc.

More developed interactive tools supply the timetabler with the ability to input initial data and timetable using form dialogue boxes and spreadsheets. These tools check the data correctness, prevent the input of incorrect or conflicting data, or warn about emerging mistakes or conflicts. Common methods of database integrity, completeness, and non-contradictoriness are used for this purpose. Several types of menu, like single-choice, multiple-choice, list boxes or combo boxes (editable menu) with location by hot keys or automatic entry expand are also used to make the input easy and correct. The data structures' representation is extremely important for minimising the response time.

These systems can also be used to retrieve information necessary to design a timetable (free time intervals for classes and teachers, free classrooms, unassigned lessons, etc.). Timetabling systems of this type are often integrated and unified with other applications of management information systems and joined to the same databases.

Sometimes there are no automatic problem solvers supplied in systems of this type. As observed by Mathaisel and Comm [55], in many cases users work only with the interactive facilities and reject automatic problem solvers.

Object-Based Interface. The next generation of interactive software is connected with object-oriented programming and event-driven programming. Drag-and-drop data handling was implemented by Mathaisel and Comm [55] to simulate a method of handmade timetable composition using a desktop sheet with cells and a deck of cards representing lessons to be assigned. The cards must be put to the cells of the sheet. In computer implementation these 'cards' (windows with slots filled by lesson attributes) may be picked up, moved and placed by mouse.

When the interface is designed in this manner, the correctness of the timetable is checked after each action; in case of conflict or requirement failure, the system warns the user. Another way to support correct data handling is to lock and to hide impossible lesson assignments. Also certain total values are updated and displayed after each action. Navigation tools for the spreadsheet and decks for scrolling, search and direct access are also assumed.

6.5 Integrating of Interactive and Algorithmic Tools in Decision Support Systems

This section conceptually describes a modern timetabling software system based on the concept of decision support systems. The system integrates:
1) internal data structures and/or access to external databases;
2) object-based user interface with scrolled windows, special spreadsheets, editable two-dimensional menu, forms, drag-and-drop facilities; and
3) problem solvers for automatic generation of timetables based on mathematical programming, artificial intelligence, or simulation metaheuristics.

The person working with the DSS is able to enter and change/edit initial data and parametric settings. The input/editing operations get data from menus or tables when it is possible rather than input alphanumeric data from the keyboard. This manner takes less time and involves fewer misspells. The possibility of simultaneous location of menu items by their string identifiers is assumed.

The timetable is constructed/edited within table interface (spreadsheet) where, for instance, students groups are ranged horizontally, and days/lessons vertically, and each cell is a dialogue box consisting, for example, of a teacher's name, subject, classroom and the quality estimating number (weight function value) of a single assignment. One can construct a handmade timetable from the very beginning, or edit or complete a timetable used previously or generated automatically by picking data up from decks of 'cards' or menus and putting data to table form.

The satisfaction of requirements can be managed for the different timetabling stages as follows. Any requirement and constraint check may be switched to *On/Warning/Off* mode. If switched *On*, the check prohibits and hides choices conflicting with the requirement or contradicting with previously chosen items. In *Warning* mode all cells involved in a conflict receive "hot" status and become visually highlighted. The warnings appear when hot cells exist on the sheet or new hot cells have appeared. The hot cells may be located and operated upon. At any time automatic generation methods are available to propose variants of completing or continuing the construction. The initial data and timetables are stored in external memory, and the system obviously may be used for information retrieval and dispatching (free classroom search for an event, looking for changes when a teacher is ill, etc.).

The problem solver can assume batch and interactive mode with requests to choose alternatives, solution methods, or search directions, or to adjust parameters.

Precise	Heuristics		Metaheuristics	Interactive	
	by algorithm	by local rules		by facilities	by organisation
1) backtracking 2) branch-and-bound 3) Gomory algorithms 4) dynamic programming 5) successive analysis	1) greedy algorithms 2) decision rules 3) preference functions 4) incomplete backtracking 5) incomplete augmenting paths 6) decomposition	1) largest degree first vs smallest degree last 2) depth first vs width first 3) static vs dynamic rules 4) recursive prognosis vs no prognosis 5) deterministic vs stochastic choice 6) feasible solution search vs optimisation	1) mathematical programming • tabu search • exchange procedures • Lagrangean relaxation 2) artificial intelligence • resolution rules 3) simulation • simulated annealing, • genetic algorithms	1) database corrections 2) universal spreadsheets 3) special editors	1) choice of alternatives 2) command interface 3) prompt-response interface 4) popup/pulldown menu, lict boxes and combo boxes 5) object-based interface, drag-and-drop
Combined (expert systems, decision support systems)					

Fig. 4. Classification of solution methods

7 Survey of Surveys

As stated above, timetabling has attracted hundreds of researchers, and it is natural that surveys and bibliographies have followed.

The best-known published representative timetabling bibliography is [66]. The bibliography contains more than 200 references followed by references to most popular review magazines. An annotation classifies problems and solution approaches.

A survey of several timetabling problems' statements, corresponding mathematical models based on graph nodes and edges colouring, and network flows with detailed descriptions and theoretical results has been written by de Werra [22].

Carter [15] considered examination timetabling, including analysis of several practical applications. It also considered wide range of heuristics applicable also to other timetabling problems, and to general graph colouring problems. Some recommendations on approach selecting were stated.

Bardadym [7] reviewed the formalisation and solution approaches, compared and studied impacts of the precise, heuristic and interactive methods, observed relations between different timetabling problems and other applications, and formulated the concept of a modern timetabling decision support system.

Some surveys described the experience of design and use of timetabling software in several countries: Germany and Austria [43], the Netherlands [20], East Europe [65], the USSR [42, 59].

8 Related Topics

8.1 Curricula Development and Planning Components in CAI/CAL

Numerous works are concerned with other problems of automated teaching planning. Works on automated curricula development mostly deal with the sequencing of items to be studied (topics, concepts or problems) according to the relations between them. The subject is represented by an oriented graph or network scheme; loops are diagnosed and/or removed, and then the order of items studying is defined. For example, a concept must be introduced only after introduction the concepts used in its definition. This sequencing is known as topological sorting [76], and it can be found by $O(N+E)$ operations, where N and E denote the numbers of graph nodes and edges correspondingly. More developed models assume optimisation on the set of topological sortings, where optimality criterion takes into account the connections between items, their studying lengths, and forgetting functions depending on time. These models are equivalent or close to the NP-complete travelling salesman problem. These approaches were reviewed in [51, 60]. Similar tools are implemented in computer-aided learning software to control the real-time learning process [72].

The application of simulation and linear programming for curricula development is described by Fedotov [29]. Petri nets were used by Ferraris et al. [33]. In recent years expert systems have been designed to develop individual curricula [24].

8.2 Similar Problems in Other Applications

Many scheduling and planning problems have mathematical models similar to timetabling: vehicle routing, resource sharing, computer-aided manufacturing, multiprocessor systems' scheduling, meetings scheduling [23], terminals scheduling [69], sport scheduling [21, 32, 68].

8.3 Scheduling Sports

Software designers' and users' competitions have been popular in recent years. School timetabling was also involved in this process. In 1993 the Russian Ministry of Education organised an open competition of timetabling software. The authors of programs had to design the class-teacher-classroom timetables with initial data from real secondary schools (usually about 50 classes x 100 teachers x 5-6 days per week x 6 lessons per day). The timetabling process had to be completed within a limited time period. Successfully completed timetables were estimated by experts - vice-principals of Moscow secondary schools responsible for timetable construction in their schools. First prize was awarded to program ASSR 2.5 by Igor Beender and Leonid Chernenko (Odessa, Ukraine).

8.4 Criticisms and Myths

35 years of computer-aided timetabling have provided no ultimate solution. This fact has led to many critical and mythical opinions. Some of them are contrary to each other. The most popular are:

1a) 'The computer is unable to make timetables' vs 1b) 'My students can design a timetabling program within a month'.

2a) 'Computer-aided timetable construction is not economical (for small schools)'; 2b) 'A handmade timetable is always better than one produced by a computer' vs 2c) 'When I have a computer, I'll have no problem with timetabling'.

3a) 'Interactive timetabling is useless without an automatic timetable generator' vs 3b) 'Interactive facilities are useful for timetabling but problem solvers are not'.

4a) 'You have bad timetable due to the computer, not to me', a vice-principal says; 4b) 'If a computer made the timetable I would be dismissed'; 4c) 'If a computer made the timetable I would lose my influence on teachers'.

The specialists need not comment. Nevertheless, let us explain our reaction to opponents' criticism:

1a), 2b), 3a): Even if you make handmade timetables using only interactive editors, you will save a lot of time through avoiding misspellings and routine work on filling paper table cells with repetition of teachers' names, timetable checks, and report making.

1b): Let them try.

2a): As derived from answer to 1a), automated timetabling is not economical only if computer and software are too expensive for the school.

2c): Be ready to have more problems than usual the first time. If you have good software, you will be completely overjoyed once you have:

- overcome the psychological barrier against the computer,
- studied how to handle data correctly,
- completed filling all necessary databases, and finally
- made your own methodology of work with your software.

Moreover, you will consider timetabling as attractive as puzzle like Patience or a Rubik cube 50x50x100.

3b): This point of view is extreme but reasonable, because solvers often leave incomplete timetables in deep search dead ends that are hard to improve manually or automatically.

4a)-4c): A computer is only a tool. It makes only things specified by man. If 'the computer' makes a gap in a teacher's timetable, the reason may be that the vice-principal 'forgot' to prohibit gaps for this teacher.

9 Unresolved Matters

The further development of scheduling DSS's and extension of their application fields will lead to the design of special software tools of specific DSS applications implementation. These tools must be based on research in the following matters of computer science:

1) design of simple language and/or interactive environment to express relationships between different items in the informational structure in order to support specific (auxiliary) requirements and constraints;
2) maintenance and visualisation of hierarchical structures allowing decomposition of interactive problem solutions according to time intervals (for example, terms, weeks, days) and object hierarchies (for example, departments, streams, groups, subgroups); and
3) research on the algebraic properties of interactive operations over informational structures; for example, research on invariants of some operations in order to preserve the data integrity including integrity of partial schedules constructed earlier.

Acknowledgements

I greatly appreciate persons who helped me to find the information about automated timetabling. Their kind help enforced the design of collection involving numerous pearls of human intelligence applied to this really intractable but necessary problem. The most sufficient contributions were made by Michael Carter (Canada), Jacques Ferland (Canada), Alexander Leibovich (Russia), Michael Pleskach (Ukraine), Hana Prochazkova (Czechia), and Valery Simonenko (Ukraine).

I would like to thank Jaime Taber for her help with preparation of this paper.

References

1. Abramson D. (1991) "Constructing School Timetables using Simulated Annealing", *Management Science*, **37**, 98-113.
2. Almond M. (1969) "A University Faculty Timetable", *Computer Journal*, **12**, 215-217.
3. Anisimov B.V. and Vlasov V.P. (1971) "Analysis of Decision Rules Applied to Lessons Timetabling", *Mathematical and Information Problems of Science Prognostication and Management*, Kiev, V.Glushkov Inst. for Cybernetics, 113-122 (Russian).
4. Aubin J. and Ferland J.A. (1989) "A Large Scale Timetabling Problem", *Computers and Operational Research*, **16**, 67-77.
5. Babich V.I. and Raetski V.I. (1991) "Models and Results of Automated Academic Timetabling", *Methods and Systems of Technical Diagnostics*, Saratov State University, 99-102 (Russian).
6. Bardadym V.A. and Vasilyeva-Sklyarova T.V. (1994) "A Decision Support System For Computer-Aided School Timetabling", *Proceedings of East-West International Conference on Computer Technologies in Education*, Crimea, Ukraine, Part 2, 33-35.
7. Bardadym V.A. (1991a) "Computer-Aided Lessons Timetables Construction. A Survey" *USIM (Management Systems and Computers)*, **#8**, 119-126 (Russian).
8. Bardadym V.A. (1991b) "The Complexity Estimate for Two Timetable Construction Problems", in: A.M.Dovgiallo (Ed.), *Computer Assisted Learning Techniques*, Kiev, Glushkov Institute for Cybernetics, 72-78 (Russian).
9. Barkan S.A. and Tanaev V.S. (1970) "About the Construction of Lesson Timetables", *Vesti Akademii Nauk BSSR (Communications of Byelorussian Academy of Sciences), Physical and Mathematical Serie*, **#1**, 76-82 (Russian).
10. Barraclough E.D. (1965) "The Application of a Digital Computer to the Construction of Timetables", *The Computer Journal*, **8**, 136-146.
11. Belova N.B. and Krasner N.Ya. (1984) "Timetabling Models and Methods", *Models and Methods for Rational Planning in the University*, Voronezh State University, 43-55 (Russian).
12. Burke E.K., Elliman D.G. and Weare R.F. (1994) "A Genetic Algorithm Based University Timetabling System", *Proceedings of East-West International Conference on Computer Technologies in Education*, Crimea, Ukraine, part 1, 35-39.
13. Carter M.W. and Tovey C.A. (1992) "When is the Classroom Assignment Problem Hard?", *Operations Research*, **40**, 28-39.
14. Carter M.W. (1989) "A Lagrangian Relaxation Approach to the Classroom Assignment Problem", *INFOR*, **27**, 230-246.
15. Carter M.W. (1986) "A Survey of Practical Applications of Examination Timetabling Algorithms" *Operations Research*, **34**, 193-202.
16. Chan S.K. and Lam C.Y. (1990) "The Electronic Spreadsheet as a Tool for Course Co-ordination in a School of Engineering", *Computers and Education*, **14**, 231-238.

17. Chahal N. and de Werra D. (1989) "An Interactive System for Constructing Timetables on a PC", *European Journal of Operational Research*, **40**, 32-37.
18. Chow K.O., Loo W.S., Kwan C.M., Martinsons M.G. (1991) "An Object-oriented Expert System in Academic Timetabling", *Proc. of National Conference on Information Technology*, Malaysia, 1991, 90-96.
19. Cole R. and Hopcroft J. (1982) "On Edge Coloring Bipartite Graphs", *SIAM Journal on Computing*, **11**, 540-546.
20. De Gans O. (1981), "A Computer Timetabling System for Secondary Schools in the Netherlands", *European Journal of Operational Research*, **7**, 175-182.
21. De Werra D., Jacot-Descombes L. and Masson P. (1990) "A Constrained Sports Scheduling Problem", *Discrete Applied Mathematics*, **26**, 41-49.
22. De Werra D. (1985) "An Introduction to Timetabling", *European Journal of Operational Research*, **19**, 151-162.
23. De Werra D. (1975) "On a Particular Conference Scheduling Problem", *INFOR*, **13**, 308-315.
24. Dovgiallo A.M., Mehtiev H.B. and Petrushin V.A. (1989) "An Expert System for Curricula Development", *Methods and Systems of Technical Diagnostics*, Saratov State University, 98-101 (Russian).
25. Dowsland K.A. (1990) "A Timetabling Problem in which Clashes are inevitable", *Journal of Operations Research*, **41**, 907-918.
26. Estrada Senti V. (1986) "Structures, Algorithms and Software for University Planning in the Republic of Cuba", PhD Thesis, Kiev Polytechnical Institute (Russian).
27. Even S., Itai A. and Shamir A. (1975) "On the Complexity of Timetable and Multicommodity Flow Problems", *SIAM Journal of Computing*, **5**, 691-703.
28. Fahrion R. and Dollanski G. (1992) "Construction of University Faculty Timetables using Logic Programming Techniques", *Discrete Applied Mathematics*, **35**, 221-236.
29. Fedotov A.V. (1985) " Simulation in University Management", Leningrad State University (Russian).
30. Ferland J.A. and Lavoie A. (1992) "Exchange Procedures for Timetable Problems", *Discrete Applied Mathematics*, **35**, 237-253.
31. Ferland J.A. and Fleurent C. (1991a) "SAPHIR: A Decision Support System for Course Scheduling", Publication #764, Universite de Montreal.
32. Ferland J.A. and Fleurent C. (1991b) "Computer Aided Scheduling for a Sport League", *INFOR*, **29**, 14-25.
33. Ferraris M., Midoro V. and Olimpo G. (1984) "Petri Nets as a Modelling Tool in the Development of CAL Software", *Computers and Education*, **8**, 41-49.
34. Garey M. and Johnson D. (1982) "Computers and Intractability", Moscow, Mir Publ (Russian edition).
35. German E.I., Pak L.V. and Chudinov V.N. (1978) "Lecture Room Distribution in the University", *Automated Management Systems in the University*, Novosibirsk State University, 138-142 (Russian).

36. Golumbic M.C., Markovich M., Tsur S. and Schild U.I. (1986) "A Knowledge-based Expert System for Student Advising", *IEEE Transactions on Education*, **E-29**, 120-123.

37. Gosselin K. and Truchon M. (1986) "Allocation of Classrooms by Linear Programming", *Journal of Operations Research*, **37**, 561-569.

38. Gotlieb C.C. (1962) "The Construction of Class-Teacher Time-Tables", in Popplewell C.M. (ed.): *Information Processing 1962. Proc. IFIP Congress 62,* Amsterdam, North-Holland, 73-77.

39. Grigorishin I.A. (1984) "Instrumental Support of Teaching Using Computer Courses", PhD Thesis, Kiev, V.Glushkov Institute for Cybernetics (Russian).

40. Hertz A. (1992), "Finding a Feasible Course Schedule using Tabu Search", *Discrete Applied Mathematics*, **35**, 225-270.

41. Hilton A.J.W. (1981) "School Timetables", *Annals of Discrete Mathematics*, **11**, 177-188.

42. Indushkin V.L., Lysenko V.I. and Tarasov S.B. (1977) "Principles of Automated Management System Design in Higher Education", Moscow, NIIVSh (Res. Inst. for Higher Education) (Russian).

43. Junginger W. (1986) "Timetabling in Germany - a Survey", *Interfaces,* **16**(4), 66-74.

44. Kang L., Von Schoenberg G.H. and White G.M. (1991) "Computer University Timetabling Using Logic", *Computers and Education*, **17**, 145-153.

45. Kirilichev A.M., Kochetkov G.M. and Stepin Yu.P. (1976) "The Principles of Construction of Calendar Planning Subsystem for University Automated Management System", *Design and Implementation of University Automated Management System*, Proceedings of Moscow Institute for Oli and Gas Industry, **128**, 46-51 (Russian).

46. Kitagawa F. and Ikeda H. (1988) "An Existential Problem of a Weight-Controlled Subset and its Application to School Timetable Construction", *Discrete Mathematics*, **72**, 195-211.

47. Kostyuk V.I., Martines J.O. and Zorin V.V. (1976) "The Use of Successive Execution Algorithms in Timetabling", *The Problems of Automated University Management System Implementation*, Moscow, NIIVSh (Res. Inst. for Higher Education), 3-5 (Russian).

48. Knyazeva T.A. and Portugal V.M. (1969) "Computer-aided University Department Timetable Construction", *Computer-Aided Manufacturing*, Kiev, Institute for Cybernetics (Russian).

49. Kowalski K. and Ealy D. (1991) "Schedule Advisement Expert System", *Computers and Education*, **17**, 259-265.

50. Lazak D. (1968) "Die Beziehungen des Kollisionsindexverfahrens zum GOTLIEB-Verfahren, Die Ableitung eines Kriteriums für die Existenz von Losungen bei einer Dienstplanmatrix", *Elektronische Datenverarbeitung*, **10**, 26-37, 58-61.

51. Logvinov I.I. (1980) "Teaching Processes Simulation", Moscow, Pedagogica Publ (Russian).

52. Loskutov S.I. (1983) "About Educational Timetabling", *Mathematical Methods of Management and Information Processing*, Moscow Inst. for Physics and Technology, 151-157 (Russian).

53. Lotfi V. and Sarin S. (1986) "A Graph-Coloring Algorithm for Large-Scale Scheduling Problems", *Computers and Operations Research*, 13, 27-32.

54. Lukyanets N.B. (1980) "School Timetable Construction and Editing with the Aid of the Computer", *The Problems of Computer-Aided Management in Education*, Moscow, Res. Inst. for Pedagogics, 70-82 (Russian).

55. Mathaisel D.F.X. and Comm C.L. (1991) "Course and Classroom Scheduling - an Interactive Computer-Graphics Approach", *Journal of Systems and Software*, 15, 149-157.

56. Mehta N.K. (1981) "The Application of a Graph Coloring Method to an Examination Scheduling Problem", *Interfaces*, #11, 57-64.

57. Mulvey J.M. (1982) "A Classroom/Time Assignment Model", *European Journal of Operational Research*, 9, 64-70.

58. Neufeld G.A. and Tartar J. (1974) "Graph Coloring Conditions for the Existence of Solutions to the Timetable Problem", *Communications of the ACM*, 17, 450-453.

59. Orlov V.N. (1976) "An Analysis of Automated Lessons Timetabling Systems", *Automated Management Systens and Higher Education*, Cheboksary State University, 68-74 (Russian).

60. Ovchinnikov A.A., Puginski A.A. and Petrov G.F. (1972) "The Network Methods for Education Planning and Organisation", Moscow, Vysshaya Shkola (Russian).

61. Papadimitriou C. and Steiglits K. (1985) "Combinatorial Optimisation", Moscow, Mir Publ (Russian edition).

62. Potashnik V.Ya. and Pichko S.P. (1977) "A Randomized Scheme for Timetabling in a University", *The Efficiency of Automated Management Systems in Education*, Kiev, Znanie Publ., 23-27 (Russian).

63. Romero B.P. (1982) "Examination Scheduling in a Large Engineering School: A Computer-assisted Participative Procedure" *Interfaces*, 12, #2, 17-24.

64. Samofalov K.G. and Simonenko V.P. (1972) "Automatisation of University Timetabling", Kiev Polytechnical Institute Publ (Russian).

65. Saveliev A.Ya., Zubarev Yu.B., Kovalenko V.E. and Koloskova T.A. (1984) "Automated Management in University", Moscow, Radio I Svyaz (Russian).

66. Schmidt G. and Strohlein T. (1980) "Timetable Construction - an Annotated Bibliography", *Computer Journal*, 23, 307-316.

67. Schniederjans M.J. and Kim G.C. (1987) "A Goal Programming Model to Optimize Departmental Preference in Course Assignments", *Computers and Operations Research*, 14, 87-96.

68. Schreuder J.A.M. (1992) "Combinatorial Aspects of Construction of Competition Dutch Professional Football Leagues", *Discrete Applied Mathematics*, 35, 301-312.

69. Sebo A. (1991) "A Particular Timetabling Problem - Terminal Scheduling", *Computers and Mathematics with Applications*, 21, 137-156.

70. Selim S.M. (1988) "Split Vertices in Vertex Colouring and Their Application in Developing a Solution to the Faculty Timetable Problem", *Computer Journal*, **31**, 76-82.

71. Smith W.E. (1984) "Efficiency of a University Timetable - an Application of Entropy of Choice", *Bulletin of the Australian Mathematical Society*, **30**, 19-26.

72. Tretiak V.A. (1990) "The Design and Implementation of Problem-Oriented Language Tools to Design CAI/CAL Software", PhD Thesis, Kiev, V.Glushkov Inst. for Cybernetics (Russian).

73. Tripathy A. (1984) "School Timetabling - A Case in Large Binary Integer Linear Programming", *Management Science*, **30**,1473-1489.

74. Vishnevskij L.D. (1976) "About a Problem of Calendar Planning", *Kibernetika*, **#3**, 115-118 (Russian).

75. White G.M. and Wong S.K.S. (1988) "Interactive Timetabling in Universities", *Computers and Education*, **12**, 521-529.

76. Wirth N., (1989) "Algorithms and Data Structures", Moscow, Mir Publ (Russian edition).

77. Zarubitskaya T.F. and Samoilenko A.T. (1976) "On the Automated Timetabling Subsystem", *Experience of Automated Management System Design and Use in Kiev State University*, Moscow, NIIVSh (Research Inst. for Higher Education), 35-40 (Russian).

Scheduling, Timetabling and Rostering - A Special Relationship?

Anthony Wren

Professor of Scheduling and Constraint Management
School of Computer Studies, University of Leeds, Leeds LS2 9JT
wren@scs.leeds.ac.uk

Abstract

Computer solution of timetabling, scheduling and rostering problems has been addressed in the literature since the 1950's. Early mathematical formulations proved impossible to solve given the limited computer power of the era. However, heuristics, often very specialised, were used for certain problems from a very early date, although the term *heuristic* was not generally recognised until later; a few guaranteed optimality, some consistently produced good solutions, but most became unwieldy when adjusted to deal with practical situations. In some cases, weaknesses in the heuristics were overcome by appeal to manual intervention. Mathematical approaches to some problems returned to favour, successfully, around 1980. Some of the subsequent developments of these are very powerful in practical situations, but they are no panacea, and metaheuristics are the flavour of the nineties.

This paper explores the relationships between the problem types, and traces the above developments as applied principally in the areas of Vehicle Routeing and Scheduling, Driver Scheduling, Job Shop Scheduling and Personnel Rostering. Parallels are drawn with Class and Examination Timetabling, but these subjects themselves are not examined, as they are covered extensively elsewhere in this volume.

1.   Introduction

It is tempting in presenting a paper with the present title to start by setting up some definitions so that we may distinguish the three terms of the title. However, a browse through relevant literature reveals very different uses of the terms. We shall therefore start by surveying some of these uses, and then introduce definitions which we shall use within the current paper.

We shall then trace some developments of scheduling, timetabling and rostering as defined below, drawing to a great extent from the author's own principal areas of experience, but introducing parallels from a wider domain.

We start with the most widely used term: scheduling. What is Scheduling?

Authors of works on scheduling have tended to pre-empt the term to their own domain:

The Vehicle Scheduling Problem (VSP), discussed in OR since the 1960's, refers only to the construction of routes for commercial vehicles, as if these were the only vehicles to be scheduled. This is now often called the Vehicle Routeing Problem (VRP);

A particular range of literature [1-5] implicitly refers to buses, trains and their drivers when discussing scheduling;

French's text on Sequencing and Scheduling [6] discusses nothing that moves;

Most OR/AI people mean some form of production scheduling when they use the term "scheduling";

Some literature on class and examination timetabling refers to the process of drawing up the timetable as scheduling.

Scheduling is ...

Definition of a pattern among objects or resources so as to satisfy certain criteria?

Ordering or sequencing objects in order best to satisfy certain objectives within certain restrictions?

Allocation, subject to constraints, of resources to objects being placed in space-time?

We shall consider the objective of scheduling to be:

to solve practical problems relating to the allocation, subject to constraints, of resources to objects being placed in space-time, using or developing whatever tools may be appropriate. The problems will often relate to the satisfaction of certain objectives.

Although some may consider scheduling and timetabling to be separate activities, we shall use the term *scheduling* both as a generic term and to cover specific types of problem, and shall consider timetabling, sequencing and rostering as special cases of the generic scheduling activity.

Scheduling may be seen as the arrangement of objects into a pattern in time or space in such a way that some goals are achieved, or nearly achieved, and that constraints on the way the objects may be arranged are satisfied, or nearly satisfied.

The objects may be people, vehicles, classes, examinations, machines, jobs in a factory, etc. Often the formation of objects may be seen as part of the scheduling process. For example, items of work may be arranged into personnel shifts which have to be grouped into a roster. The formation of shifts may be seen as a specific scheduling process within the larger process.

The pattern may be an ordering of events, a set of legal shifts defined in terms of work to be done during the shifts, a structure of routes, a matrix of allocations, etc.; the overall pattern may have to be created as part of the scheduling process, or may pre-exist as a template which is characteristic of the problem being tackled.

The constraints define physical or legal relationships among the objects or between the objects, other objects and the pattern. They govern the ways in which objects may be fitted together or into the pattern. Constraints may be seen as rules which hinder the achievement of goals. However, they may also be seen as part of the problem specification which may be used to guide the solver towards a solution. Some constraints may exist only in the eye of the problem owner, and it may be part of the solution process to indicate the extent to which a solution might be improved if a constraint or constraints were to be relaxed, so that the owner might decide whether the constraint is necessary or how much it might be worth spending to abolish the constraint.

Sometimes the words schedule, sequence and timetable are loosely used as if they were synonymous. Here we shall make some distinctions, and although we may sometimes have to overstep our definitions in order to conform to accepted practice, we shall try to be consistent as far as possible.

A *timetable* shows when particular events are to take place. It does not necessarily imply an allocation of resources. Thus a published bus or train timetable shows when journeys are to be made on a particular route or routes. It does not tell us which vehicles or drivers are to be assigned to particular journeys. The allocation of vehicles and drivers is part of the scheduling process. Although timetabling is strictly the design of the pattern of journeys, this pattern may be devised as part of a process which bears in mind whether it is likely that an efficient schedule may be fitted to the resulting journey pattern.

In the rail domain, the term timetabling is often used to refer to the construction of a path (with times) for a train through a system. Thus, the Flying Scotsman used to leave Edinburgh (Waverley) at 10 a.m.; the job of timetabling was the process of finding times and paths through the rail system which did not conflict with other traffic (revising such other traffic as necessary) until it reached Kings Cross at 6.30

p.m. (in 1922) or 6.05 p.m. (1948). This form of timetabling has been the subject of some research, but little, if any, practical implementation over any but the simplest systems. Carey [7] has recently reported on timetabling and track allocation in large stations.

A class timetable also shows when particular events are to take place. In certain circumstances there may be no scheduling activity necessary in drawing up such a timetable. In an infants' school where a single teacher is responsible for all the activities of a particular class, and where these activities all take place in the same room, a timetable is nothing more than a statement as to the times at which particular activities will take place (as is the public train timetable above). By contrast, a university examination timetable will normally include room assignments drawn up in the knowledge of group sizes and of special facilities needed. It will have been devised subject to hard or soft constraints, for example on the numbers of examinations to be taken by individual students in consecutive periods. A university class timetable has also to take into account the availability of individual lecturers. The activities of drawing up examination and university class timetables may be considered as scheduling activities.

A *sequence* is simply an order in which activities are carried out. For example, the order in which jobs are processed through the machines of a factory, if jobs pass through each machine in the same order, is a sequence. Sequencing may take into account costs related to one particular job being followed by another (machine conversion costs etc.). The problem of sequencing jobs in these circumstances is known as a flow shop problem.

A *schedule* will normally include all the spacial and temporal information necessary for a process to be carried out. This will include times at which activities are to take place, statements as to which resources will be assigned where, and workplans for individual personnel or machines.

We have already tentatively defined scheduling as allocation, subject to constraints, of resources to objects being placed in space-time. Thus scheduling is the process of forming the schedule, including assignment of resources. We note that French [6] uses the term *timetabling* for this process, and other authors will use other conventions.

2. A Simple Sequencing Example

We shall introduce here a simple example of a sequencing problem, showing some common types of solution heuristic.

A travelling salesman problem (TSP) in which cities have to be visited in the order which minimises the total distance travelled or the total time elapsed is an example of a sequencing problem, as is the more general vehicle scheduling problem (VSP), nowadays more usually and properly called the vehicle routeing problem (VRP), where routes have to be constructed from one or more depots to delivery outlets subject to limits on vehicle capacity and on route distance or duration. The solutions to such problems may be expressed as sequences of points, although depots may each have to appear several times in a sequence. Where further constraints exist on times when certain points are visited, on mixtures of goods which may be carried, or on sizes of trucks which may serve particular points, we may consider ourselves to have a true scheduling problem.

In fact, the TSP and a simple job sequencing problem may be considered as logically equivalent, and we shall shortly introduce a particular example of these. Just as the TSP is a simple example of a range of routeing problems, so the single machine problem is a simple example of a range of job scheduling problems. In both cases we may gain an insight which may be useful in the more complex problems by studying these simple ones.

Consider the processing of nine jobs passing through a machine. The machine may have to be adjusted or cleaned between operations, i.e. between pairs of jobs. There will be costs associated with the adjustment or cleaning. These costs may be combinations of time delays and actual costs of materials used in a conversion process, and we shall want to find the sequence of jobs which minimises the total of these; the cost of job j following job i (c_{ij}) will be the conversion cost of the machine from processing i to processing j. Let us assume that there are costs c_{oj} associated with setting up the machine for job j and costs c_{io} for clearing the machine after job i. In practice such costs are often ignored and can be treated as zero in the table, but we shall assume non-zero costs here. Diagonal elements of the table are infinite, since a job cannot follow itself.

	J0	J1	J2	J3	J4	J5	J6	J7	J8	J9
J0	X	35	33	11	20	17	36	45	25	15
J1	33	X	50	44	22	26	21	43	38	46
J2	36	47	X	40	48	27	34	25	13	21
J3	12	46	39	X	26	28	47	56	34	19
J4	22	25	45	27	X	24	34	52	37	35
J5	16	27	30	25	25	X	19	29	14	21
J6	33	22	38	44	31	22	X	22	24	39
J7	48	42	26	59	51	26	22	X	22	40
J8	22	35	13	33	38	15	23	20	X	18

| J9 | 13 | 45 | 23 | 17 | 33 | 20 | 41 | 41 | 17 | X |

Let us now consider a trial solution in which the jobs are processed in an arbitrary, here numerical, order.   This solution, including setting up and clearing may be written:

$$J0-J1-J2-J3-J4-J5-J6-J7-J8-J9-J0$$
with cost:
$$35+50+40+26+24+19+22+22+18+13 = 269$$

There is no reason to think that this is a good solution, but we shall consider this question later.   We have simply ordered the jobs into an arbitrary sequence and determined the cost of the result.

Now consider a travelling salesman based at city J0 who has to visit nine other cities, J1 - J9, and return to base.   Distances d_{ij} between cities are given as in the table above.   We require to find the route (or sequence of cities visited) which minimises the total distance travelled.   (Since the route returns to base it doesn't really matter which we consider as the starting point, but for comparison with the flow shop problem, we have chosen city J0).   The sequence J0, J1, J2, J3, J4, J5, J6, J7, J8, J9, J0 represents a solution:

$$J0-J1-J2-J3-J4-J5-J6-J7-J8-J9-J0$$
with distance:
$$35+50+40+26+24+19+22+22+18+13 = 269$$

Suppose now we have a class timetabling problem in which a cohort of students attends nine classes in a day.   There may be notional costs associated with moving between classes, as shown in the above table, and with starting the day with any class or finishing with any class. The sequence J1, J2, J3, J4, J5, J6, J7, J8, J9 represents a solution, but we may include coming in the morning and going home at night in the representation:

$$J0-J1-J2-J3-J4-J5-J6-J7-J8-J9-J0$$
with cost:
$$35+50+40+26+24+19+22+22+18+13 = 269$$

The timetabling of this particular cohort of students may be just part of a larger timetabling problem, but given a tentative solution to the overall problem, it may be possible to make piecewise improvements to that solution by revising the above sequence (which may involve reallocating the calls on teachers or rooms).

More briefly, we may represent the given arbitrary solutions to any of these problems as:

```
0   1   2   3   4   5   6   7   8   9, with cost:
35  50  40  26  24  19  22  22  18  13  = 269.
```

Commonly scheduling problems are treated by heuristics, for example we may seek to improve the solution by switching a pair of jobs, cities or classes in the sequence, e.g. 2 and 5, to obtain the new sequence:

```
0   1   5   3   4   2   6   7   8   9, with cost:
35  26  25  26  45  34  22  22  18  13  = 266.
```

If this does not violate any constraints, we have achieved an improvement, although other swaps might have produced a worsening.   The heuristic given above, if continued by trying every pair of swaps iteratively until no improvement can be found, is an example of a very common class of heuristics leading (usually) to a local optimum.   It may be applied to very many timetabling and scheduling problems.   If swaps are processed in the logical sequence 1-2, 1-3 , ... 1-9, 2-3, 2-4 etc., repeating after trying 8-9, one obtains the solution:

```
0   3   4   1   5   6   7   8   2   9, with cost
11  26  25  26  19  22  22  13  21  13  = 198
```

The solution is known as 2-optimal;   no pairwise change will produce an improvement.   The quality of this (possibly) local optimum in a general problem type usually depends on the starting solution, although in one problem type known to the author [8-11] a similar process has in many thousand problem instances always led to solutions believed to be optimal.

There is no way in general of knowing whether the solution is optimal, although in this particular case a better solution is known (obtained from the same first solution by considering moving each object in turn to its best position in the sequence):

```
0   4   1   6   7   5   8   2   9   3, with cost
20  25  21  22  26  14  13  21  17  12  = 191
```

Although this better solution is the best that can be achieved by the particular heuristic, given the starting solution, it is not necessarily optimal.   The reader may wish to check whether it is 2-optimal.

Better solutions may often be reached by considering changing the positions of triples of objects, but this requires much more computer time which may not be justified (there are six ways of arranging triples, all of which may have to be evaluated, but only two ways of arranging pairs).   Some n-optimal processes depend on the links between successive objects rather than on the sequencing of the objects.   Pairs of links may be arranged in three ways (AB, CD; AC, BD; AD, BC), but triples of links may be arranged in fifteen ways;   often many of these ways are infeasible.

3.   Definitions Revisited

We have already defined the goal of scheduling in its broadest sense as:

> to solve practical problems relating to the allocation, subject to constraints, of resources to objects being placed in space-time, using or developing whatever tools may be appropriate.   The problems will often relate to the satisfaction of certain objectives.

The activities known as *timetabling, rostering* and *sequencing* all conform to the above definition.   However, we shall use the following more restrictive definitions in the remainder of this paper:

> *Scheduling* is the allocation, subject to constraints, of resources to objects being placed in space-time, in such a way as to minimise the total cost of some set of the resources used.   Common examples are transport scheduling or delivery vehicle routeing which seek to minimise the numbers of vehicles or drivers and within that minimum to minimise the total cost, and job shop scheduling which may seek to minimise the number of time periods used, or some physical resource.

> *Timetabling* is the allocation, subject to constraints, of given resources to objects being placed in space-time, in such a way as to satisfy as nearly as possible a set of desirable objectives.   Examples are class and examination timetabling and some forms of personnel allocation, for example manning of toll booths subject to a given number of personnel.

> *Sequencing* is the construction, subject to constraints, of an order in which activities are to be carried out or objects are to be placed in some representation of a solution.   Examples are flow-shop scheduling and the travelling salesman problem.

> *Rostering* is the placing, subject to constraints, of resources into slots in a pattern.   One may seek to minimise some objective, or simply to obtain a feasible allocation.   Often the resources will rotate through a roster.

Some problems may fit more than one of the above definitions, and the terms tend to be used rather loosely in the workplace and in the scheduling community.

In some of the above we have referred to satisfying or to minimising.   It should be remarked that many of the problems which we are treating do not have a well-defined objective.   We may sometimes justify the use of ameliorating or non-optimising methods partly because different players will have different views of the objective, but in reality such methods are often used simply because no optimising (or exact) method is practicable.

4.   Scheduling Problems Reviewed

The author first formally met scheduling problems in 1961 when he was assigned to a rail locomotive scheduling exercise for which he subsequently assumed full responsibility and designed simple heuristics. This led in 1963 to the implementation of what was probably the world's first computer-produced rail locomotive schedule. In 1966 he turned to delivery vehicle routeing, and with a student developed heuristics which were used in practical exercises with a number of clients over the next few years.

In 1967 he was approached by the bus industry, for whom he and his group developed a wide range of scheduling programs over the next twenty-eight years. The earlier programs, until the end of the 1970's, were based on heuristics. Although these heuristics were designed independently, they can be classified according to the scheme of Müller-Merbach [15]. Some of these (for bus scheduling) are very robust and still in commercial use. In another problem, however, the heuristics tended to work only in cases very similar to those for which they were designed.

The 1960's also saw the start of research into computer methods for many other scheduling, sequencing, timetabling and rostering problems. Some of these problems will be introduced here, referring mainly to early research. In many fields the first approach of the researchers, most of whom came from mathematics or physical sciences, was to design a mathematical model. However, practical implementations of the models were impossible given the computer power then available. The first serious solution attempts therefore almost always involved specially designed heuristics, although the term *heuristic* was not yet generally known.

In almost all cases this work was followed through the 1970's and 1980's by further heuristic developments, coupled in some cases with integer linear programming. By the 1990's a variety of recently discovered or rediscovered approaches was being enthusiastically applied to most scheduling problems, often, perhaps regrettably, driven more by a desire to use the approach than by a need to solve the problem (see Section 5).

4.1   Job Shop Scheduling

Almost certainly the most frequently discussed form of scheduling in the OR/AI literature, job shop scheduling concerns the processing of jobs through a number of machines, subject to limits on various resources. A number of objectives have been identified, for example, minimising the makespan (the total time to completion of all jobs), the total lateness of jobs, or the number of late jobs. A simple form of job shop scheduling is flow shop scheduling, in which jobs move through each machine in the same order; flow shop scheduling is essentially a sequencing problem.

Most job shop scheduling problems are very specialised and are solved to local optima by special heuristics. No optimising method is known for the general problem of more than two machines. However, even before the 1960's, Johnson [12] had developed an optimal strategy for a two-machine problem. Johnson's work is a rare example of a heuristic which can be proved to produce the optimal result, as are the later heuristics of Moore [13] and Lawler [14] for single machines. Johnson's paper was published in the first volume (1954) of the Naval Research Logistics Quarterly which was for many years a standard source of scheduling papers.

4.2   Travelling Salesman Problem

The TSP has already been introduced. It is widely studied, perhaps more as a theoretical exercise than in order to solve practical problems. However, many problems can be reduced to TSP's (see above), so that solution methods for TSP's can be adapted for them, while vehicle routeing problems may be seen as extensions of TSP's. Müller-Merbach [15] used the TSP to illustrate a wide range of heuristics which he classified as either First Feasible Solution or Iteratively Improving, with sub-classifications. This seminal paper was perhaps the first to try to bring together a theory of heuristics which previously had been introduced as diverse ad hoc, often trial and error, methods.

One of the most successful approaches to the TSP in the early era was due to Lin [16], using an n-optimal method.

4.3   Vehicle Routeing Problem

The delivery vehicle routeing problem attracted much attention in the operational research community during the late 1960's and early 1970's. Commonly (and arrogantly) known within OR as *the* vehicle scheduling problem (VSP), it was originally formulated as the problem of designing routes for delivery vehicles from a single depot subject to constraints of load and distance. Although Dantzig and Ramser [17] postulated a solution based on linear programming, the first practical method was probably the heuristic of Clarke and Wright [18] which built up a first feasible solution and was successfully implemented, first for the Co-operative Wholesale Society based in Manchester. The method formed the basis of several commercial routeing packages, although it was already known to the research community to produce poor solutions; these were nonetheless often much better than existing manual solutions. Gaskell [19] experimented with several variations of the

Clarke and Wright method, introducing six test data sets which have since been widely used.

Christofides and Eilon [20] introduced a 3-optimal method for the VRP, building on Lin's work on the TSP. This applied the approach to several randomly generated starting solutions. They applied their method to the six problems of Clarke and Wright, and to three further ones, showing that it was significantly better than any known variants of Clarke and Wright.

The author, initially with a student [21, 22], designed a multi-depot system which out-performed the above single depot systems on the nine data sets referred to above, and which was used to assist in strategic decision making (e.g., depot siting, creating routes to be operated regularly over a long time period) by Phillips Industries and by Christian Salvesson for deliveries to Marks and Spencer.

The heuristics of Wren and Holliday [22] commenced by building up routes, considering delivery points in order of directional angle (orientation) from the depot. Points were inserted in the cheapest position in an existing route where possible, and otherwise a new route was begun. Where the number of vehicles was limited some points might remain unserved. The search was repeated using a number of different initial orientations, and the cheapest set of resulting routes initiated a set of refining heuristics. (The same approach was later proposed by Gillett and Miller [23], who introduced it as the *sweep algorithm*, without the refinement stages.)

Wren and Holliday used a number of refining heuristics, principally with the goal of reducing costs; some attempted to reduce the number of routes used, and others sought to fit in points that were omitted initially, replacing others of lower priority. The cost reduction routines each performed a different action: moving points from one route to another; exchanging points between two routes; removing crossovers from routes; rebuilding routes according to the initial route construction method applied to a single route or to two adjacently oriented routes which may have become tangled, and keeping the new route structures only if they were better than the old.

These refining heuristics each searched all points or routes until no improvement remained, and were called cyclically in turn until no improvement resulted from a complete cycle, or until a certain time limit was reached (computer time was severely rationed in 1970!). Thus each call of each heuristic found a local optimum. Moving on to another heuristic corresponded to changing the shape of the search space. Overall, the solutions achieved were very good, and generally out-performed Christofides and Eilon on the nine test problems. As in many applications of heuristics, best results were achieved when cost-neutral changes were allowed, although this implied that each heuristic should be continued through several non-improving cycles before being terminated.

Although further mathematical programming formulations of the VRP were produced, these were generally too complicated for solution (but see [24] for an approach using heuristics to reduce the size of a problem which was then solved using integer linear programming). Laporte [25], and others earlier, have surveyed the development of computer methods for the VRP.

Although many more attempts were made to find good algorithms for the VRP, complicating factors such as many depots, different vehicle types, time windows for certain deliveries, etc., inhibited their application to practical problems, and it became evident through the 1970's that fully automatic systems were seldom suitable for solution of tactical problems. For this reason, many commercial systems were developed which used some (often primitive) form of heuristic to build an initial solution, but expected the user to adjust this interactively, using the computer to check out possibilities.

4.4   Timetabling

As timetabling is the theme of this volume, it is unnecessary in this paper to review in detail the large body of research devoted to this subject. Most timetabling research has been undertaken on problems in educational institutions, partly because these were real problems in the researchers' organisations, and partly because of their interesting complexity.

The rail timetabling problem has already been introduced and is the subject of continuing research by Carey (e.g. [7]). Other timetabling problems in the transport areas have been tackled by Kwan [26] and Keudel [27] among others.

Kwan introduced a method for determining suitable timings for regular bus journeys along common stretches of route where any individual service might share different common stretches with different groups of services. The objectives were to produce an acceptable solution to the problems of minimising the number of vehicles and of achieving even intervals between the different services on the common stretches. The method used the computer to present possible solutions to the user, allowing the goals to be changed interactively.

Keudel built on a method of Günther [28] to develop a system which designed timetables for intersecting bus services so as to achieve a good compromise between the number of buses and the waiting times of passengers making interchanges.

One of the earliest educational timetabling systems (for examinations) was developed in the University of Leicester by Cole [29] and published in 1964, while another by Wood [30] four years later took advantage of the greater power of the Atlas computer. Both these authors, and many later ones, used strategies that might now come under the constraint satisfaction banner. Wood used real 1967 data from the

University of Manchester to schedule 5730 students taking 1323 papers into between 24 and 30 periods according to a range of alternative constraints; each schedule took 10 minutes to produce, which seems remarkable for that era. Wood's strategy was basically to schedule the subject that needed the largest room first, but much of his paper is taken up with the technicalities of the binary representation needed to fit the information into what was then the world's largest computer.

If one reads the papers of Cole, Wood and their many successors, one finds that most claim success for their methods, yet none have survived in their institutions for more than a few years, if that. Wood quotes the University of Manchester authorities as saying in 1967 that "the existing system is stretched to its limits", yet most, possibly all, British universities (even the larger ones) struggled on using manual examination and class timetabling into the 1990's until pressures of modularisation forced proper consideration of automatic methods. A major reason for the lack of proper implementation of earlier methods appears to have been the distrust of university administrators of anything emanating from their academic colleagues.

An unusual timetabling problem tackled by Parker, Parker and Proll [31] will be mentioned here as an indication that serious timetabling problems arise elsewhere than universities. This related to the scheduling of interviews during parent-teacher evenings in a high school; a single evening concerned one year's pupils and might be attended by approximately forty teachers and 150 parents. Commitments of both teachers and parents might prevent either from being present during the whole evening. The method commenced with a heuristic which produced a feasible schedule, this being followed by optimisation of each teacher's schedule in turn while the remainder of the schedule was fixed, the goals of the optimisation taking into account parents' as well as teachers' goals. This treatment was possible because gaps in the parents' schedules allowed significant restructuring. The program was used successfully in Leeds schools for several years until with the advent of PC's commercial programs became available which linked some kind of scheduler with a school database.

More recent advances in class and examination timetabling are discussed elsewhere in this volume, and are therefore not considered further here, although timetabling problems are noted in some of the sections below in relation to the techniques outlined.

4.5   Rostering

Rostering problems arise in a large number of situations. Once shifts have been produced showing the daily work of personnel, these shifts are placed into a roster to show which shifts are worked by individuals on particular days. Usually the pattern of shifts for an individual in any week (or over a longer period of time) has to conform to particular rules. Rostering research has covered a wide range of occupations; policemen, nurses, bus and train drivers, etc.

We mention here bus driver rostering, where the daily shifts are grouped into rows of weeks or fortnights according to given hard or soft rules. These rules govern such factors as the positioning of rest days in the roster, grouping of shifts of particular types into certain rows, the observance of minimum times between the end of one day's work and the beginning of the next, and the maintenance of similar starting times on successive days. Drivers then rotate through cycles of rows. The cost depends on the extent to which individual rows exceed a target amount of work, so that an objective is to even out the amount of work in each row while minimising the violation of soft constraints. Bennett and Potts [32] in Adelaide tackled this in 1968 by considering a matrix in which rows represented fortnights of work (early week followed by late week) and the elements identified the shifts to be worked on the appropriate days. A two stage process was developed.

The first stage developed a pattern of rest days such that the correct number of working days could be fitted into each of the fourteen columns. The objective was to maximise first the number of four-day weekends, then three-day, then two-day weekends, then consecutive days off during the week. An initial solution was fitted to this and refined by a heuristic which kept thirteen columns fixed and reassigned the elements of the remaining column optimally using the Hungarian algorithm. Each column was reassigned in turn and the process was repeated until no improvement was produced. This was similar to the approach of Parker, Parker and Proll [31] to the scheduling of parent-teacher evenings.

The author and colleagues adapted the process of Bennett and Potts for British bus driver problems, replacing the Hungarian algorithm by a heuristic which simply exchanged elements in the column being considered. This produced satisfactory solutions in terms of the specified constraints relating to the placing of shifts of particular types in particular positions of the roster. Unfortunately, the bus company for which this work was done frequently violated their own constraints, and following a change of personnel in the company it proved impossible to determine the circumstances in which such apparent violations might be acceptable. However, later work with a firm of consultants enabled the author to develop a partly interactive bus driver rostering system based on this work; this is now being used by many bus operators.

The author has also worked with a student [Townsend, 33] to develop a rostering system for London Transport Buses. This was a very specialised problem in which all shifts were paid for eight hours; the goal was to devise suitable positions in the roster for rest days and for particular types of shift, and then to fit the shifts in such a way that shifts on consecutive says had similar starting times. Unfortunately, the rostering rules in London were changed dramatically before the system could be implemented.

More recently, colleagues [Smith and Bennett, 34] have used constraint satisfaction techniques to produce a system to develop rosters for anaesthetists in a major Leeds hospital.

Although the rules are in general very different, rostering is perhaps closer to examination and class timetabling than is any other problem area treated here. The final result is a matrix of allocations formed to take account of the relationships between the objects allocated to the slots. Some of the processes developed by Bennett and Potts can be adapted to ensure that gaps in teaching loads or in student commitment are spread equitably through a timetable matrix, while both the Bennett and Potts use of the Hungarian algorithm and the author's improving heuristics can improve a first attempt at a timetable.

5. Review of Modern Methods

Other work in scheduling is far too extensive to review here, but we shall introduce some of the current methods, referring to a few applications, before introducing the author's own work on a number of transport scheduling problems.

Simulated annealing is analogous to the annealing of materials to produce sound low energy states (e.g., large crystals). The basic annealing model was developed in 1953 by Metropolis et al. [35], while simulated annealing as an approach to optimisation problems was developed by Kirkpatrick and colleagues in the early 1980's [e.g., 36], although claims have been made for its earlier discovery.

Simulated annealing addresses the problem of escaping from local optima by adopting a process controlled by a parameter known as the temperature. A heuristic designed for the problem in hand defines the neighbourhood of an initial solution, and a possible move within that neighbourhood is generated at random. The move is accepted if it produces a better solution; a worsening move is accepted with a probability governed by the cost of the move and the value of the temperature parameter. At a high temperature a given worsening move is more likely to be accepted, leading possibly to an escape beyond the contours of a local optimum. As the process continues, the temperature is reduced until at a very low temperature only non-worsening moves are accepted. The process is analogous to physical annealing in which at high temperatures the molecules are moving rapidly and may bring the material temporarily into a higher energy state; as the material cools, the molecules slow down until they subside into a smooth low-energy state; the energy is analogous to the function being optimised.

The success of simulated annealing depends on the starting temperature, the heuristic which gives the initial solution, the refining heuristic, and the cooling schedule (the rate of temperature decrease). The reasons for the success of simulated annealing are not generally well understood, but theoretical work by Sorkin for a PhD thesis has led to some interesting results [37].

A bibliography on simulated annealing was published in 1988 by Collins, Eglese and Golden [38]. Recent timetabling work using simulated annealing includes

Thompson and Dowsland [39] and Ross and Corne [40]. Osman [41] discusses simulated annealing with reference to the vehicle routeing problem.

Tabu search, due to Glover [42, 43], escapes from a current solution by applying a greedy heuristic, moving to the best neighbouring point. If the new solution is worse it is accepted (unless it has previously been defined as tabu). The search is prevented from falling back into local optima by a procedure which makes certain moves tabu if they would bring the search to a position similar to one recently visited. Tabu moves are accepted if they lead to a better solution than has previously been found, and certain steps may be taken to guide the search in apparently profitable directions. Ultimately, a decision is taken to terminate the search, and the best solution visited is chosen.

Tabu search has been applied to many scheduling problems, see Glover and Laguna [44].

One of the most exciting modern tools for scheduling and timetabling is the genetic algorithm [Goldberg, 45; Davis, 46; Michalewicz, 47]. This mimics the process of evolution and survival of the fittest to move from a population of (usually) randomly generated starting solutions through many generations until hopefully some population contains a near-optimal solution. Much theoretical work has been undertaken on genetic algorithms, and some authors have tried rather slavishly to follow very closely the natural processes. Some of the most productive work in the scheduling field has, however, been achieved when researchers have followed broad evolutionary principles while inventing new reproductive procedures. Although all such processes are often referred to as genetic algorithms, the term *evolutionary algorithm* is perhaps a better description which does not tie processes too closely to actual genetics. Of the texts quoted above, Michalewicz perhaps best recognises this.

Scheduling work involving evolutionary algorithms includes Fang, Ross and Corne [48], Wren and Wren [49] and Kwan and Wren [50].

Constraint logic programming which controls heuristic search by skilful use of the constraints of a problem is another method now being used in many scheduling problems. Mention has already been made of the rostering work of Smith and Bennett [34]. Much of the current success of constraint programming is due to powerful commercial packages which help drive user-provided heuristics.

All the above methods have been applied to timetabling problems as evidenced in the current volume. They have also been used successfully in various job shop scheduling problems, while the travelling salesman problem has often been used to illustrate their potential. They have so far been less successful in the problem areas discussed in Sections 6 to 8 below, although their application to driver scheduling is being heavily researched by the author and colleagues. It is understood that constraint programming is being applied to rail locomotive scheduling in France, but there is reason to think that the successes reported may owe more to the embedded heuristics than to the constraint formulation.

Finally, in this review of processes, we refer to the ant system [Dorigo et al.,51]. This follows the processes used by ants which lay down trails of pheromone as they move between the nest and food sites. Initial moves are random, but ants moving along short paths return to the nest sooner, thereby strengthening the pheromone on the short trails sooner. Other ants are more likely to follow the strongest trails, so that these become ever stronger. The effects of pheromone gradually wear off, so that those trails which are used infrequently quickly lose their attractiveness. Dorigo et al. apply the system in the quoted paper to the travelling salesman problem, comparing it favourably to simulated annealing and tabu search. They also quote applications to other problems. This approach would appear to be very promising, and the present author has a research student experimenting with it on driver scheduling problems.

Some of the author's own work on scheduling is now reviewed, together with work on similar problems by others.

6.   Rail Locomotive and Bus Scheduling

The simplest view of a locomotive scheduling problem is that a set of locomotives of a single class is to be allocated to a set of trains in such a way as to minimise the number of locomotives used, and subject to that minimum also to minimise the amount of light running (locomotives running on their own between arrival point of one train and the departure point of the next train allocated to the locomotive, or to and from a depot). The problem can be modelled in mathematical terms as a standard Assignment problem with a row and column for each train, and solved by the Hungarian algorithm. However, the number of trains in our first practical examples ranged up to 150, requiring cost matrices of 22.5K, well beyond our Ferranti Pegasus computer's capacity of 7K words for data and code together.

A heuristic [Wolfenden and Wren, 52] was therefore devised which had the merit of producing the optimal solution in all problems small enough to be checked against the Hungarian algorithm. In fact in the thirty years since the initial research, the heuristic has been applied to many thousand practical and often large rail and bus scheduling problems, and no better solution to real problems has ever been found. However, it is possible to construct artificial cases in which the constraint matrix of minimum journey times between points violates the triangular inequality and where the heuristic sticks in a local optimum. (Frequently bus companies have presented such constraint matrices to the system but have always agreed when the computer had checked them that they were illogical and have happily altered them.)

A strong lower bound to the required number of locomotives can easily be calculated based on the maximum number of simultaneously operating trains, where two trains are defined to be simultaneous if the locomotive used for the earlier finishing one cannot reach the starting point of any other train before the departure of the second. This bound mechanism was suggested by the author to Stern and Ceder who proved its validity [53]. A (possibly infeasible) solution is then developed using this bound as the number of locomotives; trains are taken in order of departure time and are assigned free locomotives rather arbitrarily; if no locomotive is free, then some locomotive is allocated infeasibly, and a penalty is assigned equal to the time needed to move the locomotive between the relevant points, minus the time available (which may be negative). The starting solution is then a linked list of activities (trains) for each locomotive where each link has either a cost equal to the time necessary to move between points or a penalty as above.

The heuristic then examines all pairs of links, exchanging their end points if this produces a reduction in total penalty, or a reduction in total cost for no increase in penalty. The process considers all possible pairs of links repetitively until two complete passes produce no improvement. An exchange is also made if no change in total cost or penalty results; this has the effect of kicking the current solution into a new pattern which can allow the heuristic to escape from a local optimum at the next pass.

Many experiments were carried out with different data sets and different starting solutions for each set, including some in which very large infeasibilities were present. All experiments, however bad the initial solution, converged for a given data set to the same total penalty and same total cost, apparently the global optimum. It may be noted, however, that without allowing exchanges which left penalty and cost unaffected, convergence would sometimes be to a local optimum.

Where a penalty remained after convergence, the original approach was to increase the number of locomotives by one and to try again. It was soon realised, however, that it was worth presenting the penalised links to the client, who would often find that it was possible to retime a train in order to remove the penalty. In the first practical exercise [52] implemented for British Railways (BR) in 1963 the number of locomotives was reduced from 15 to 12 (after two retimings) and the light running was reduced by 28%.

The first exercise had involved a set of freight trains ferrying traffic on the North London Line, principally between the docks and marshalling yards. These ran all round the clock (with similar work every weekday, and variations on Saturdays and Sundays), and the solution had to be adjusted to allow the locomotives to be returned from time to time to the depot for maintenance. This adjustment, which was carried out manually by the author, followed another heuristic which had been designed by him. The quality of the savings was preserved following the adjustment, although three additional locomotives were required to allow for maintenance, both in the "before" and "after" situations. Unfortunately, resources did not permit the coding (in Pegasus machine code) of the new heuristic which was quite complex.

It may be noted that the switching procedure is equivalent to pairwise swapping of the elements of a solution matrix for the assignment problem if the penalties are given precedence in the cost matrix. A major difficulty in having the process accepted by our peers in 1963 was the lack of a proof of optimality. The term "heuristic" was hardly known and the author was forced to use the term "trial and error" in presenting the process. By the time heuristics had become respectable, the method would have been classified as "eager but tedious" by Müller-Merbach [15].

The method was used by BR for several years, but was allowed to die when the Pegasus became obsolete, in favour of a system being developed in-house and based on linear programming. This was never fully implemented or published but was described by Wren [54] with the approval of its developers.

From 1970 the locomotive scheduling system became known as VAMPIRES and was adapted to bus operation, first in a simple single bus type, single depot situation (actually by separating out the work of different bus types from a single depot). The first trial was carried out for Yorkshire Traction in Barnsley where existing single decker and double decker work was treated separately and 23 buses were saved out of 107, partly by retiming as indicated by the system and partly by general improvements in efficiency (Wren [55]). Yorkshire Traction subsequently sponsored developments to allow more than one type of bus and more than one depot. Experiments for other companies followed, as outlined in [56] and [57]). The first regular user was however Greater Manchester Transport who installed the program in 1975 and used it as the basis of all their scheduling for several years. Buses are now scheduled in much smaller groups in response to competition, but the program is still used in Manchester on an occasional basis.

The consideration of more than one depot was relatively easy; an initial solution was built up as before, and the work of each bus was assigned to that depot providing the minimum cost links to the start of the first journey and from the end of the last journey. When a pair of links was then considered by the refining heuristic, the best depot after a prospective change was determined, and the total cost of links being exchanged and links to and from the depot was used to determine whether an exchange should be made. Special arrangements were made for buses that returned to the depot several times during the day. Although this process added to the computer time, the quality of the results was such as to make this acceptable.

The treatment of more than one vehicle type is too complex to consider fully here. The first tests were carried out on a problem involving nine basic types. A multi-stage process was devised wherein the best types of vehicle were considered when exchanges were examined. Several refining stages incorporating infeasibility of type as well as the earlier time infeasibilities were included. The solution of a classical Transportation Problem in which journeys were represented by columns and vehicle types by rows produced shadow costs which were used in subsequent phases to discourage the use of scarce bus types. The Transportation Problem was reformulated and solved again every time the heuristic converged, until either no bus had a journey for which its type was infeasible, or it could be concluded that there was no feasible solution, in which case either the number of buses was increased or management was invited to reconsider the constraints.

Although the results of this process were satisfactory where there were genuinely many types of vehicle, the increase in computer time was very great. Shortly after this development, there was a movement towards bus fleets consisting of a single vehicle type, and the multi-vehicle option was seldom used.

Although VAMPIRES was successfully used in many consultancy exercises, with considerable savings, its ability to explore all possible combinations of journey across a city or region was superfluous when routes were scheduled in relatively small groups, and operations were regular, so that the normal activity for a bus on reaching its destination was to turn and go back to its origin. A simpler system, called TASC [57], was developed in which dead journeys to other points were only considered if an arriving bus could not match a departure from the same point within a specified time.

A backtracking process was devised within TASC to try to ensure that where dead journeys were necessary, the most efficient set was used. TASC was installed for several bus operators in the early 1980's. It was easier to use than VAMPIRES, the data being specified as series of regular journeys on several routes, rather than as individual journeys, and was initially faster. However, users started to complain that sometimes the solution was not optimal, and the backtracking process was gradually made more complex to satisfy their complaints. Ultimately, a version of VAMPIRES was combined with TASC; a preliminary solution was found by TASC, and this was separated into blocks of continuous work with no long gaps or dead journeys; these blocks were then rescheduled by VAMPIRES as if they were individual journeys.

In 1983 the decision was made to convert the system for microcomputers, and after various trials were conducted it was determined that TASC had become so complex that VAMPIRES was now faster. Therefore the first microcomputer version contained a simple version of VAMPIRES which has since been made more complex. For example, a crude but fast method for dealing with more than one vehicle type was added at the request of a client; this incorporates a three-way swapping procedure. This micro version based on VAMPIRES is still in commercial use, although it has been suggested that it has become too complex, and that TASC should be resurrected, so that simple problems can be solved speedily!

7.   Heuristics for Bus Driver Scheduling

That the bus driver scheduling problem could be formulated as a set covering or set partitioning problem was known from the early 1960's. However, no practical solution could be obtained from such a formulation until much later. Some unpublished work by Deutsch around 1963 sought to develop an exhaustive tree search, but was defeated by problems of any reasonable size. Throughout the period 1967-1978 the author and his associates devoted much attention to seeking a good heuristic method [58], culminating in the TRACS system [59]. Others (e.g., Elias, [60]) devised other heuristics throughout the 1960's.

Bus driver scheduling is the problem of designing legal shifts fitted to a day's bus schedule in such a way that all buses have a driver assigned at all times of day. Shifts have constraints on their duration, on the position of meal breaks and on other features which may be negotiated locally. Drivers can only be changed at *relief opportunities* when buses pass suitable *relief points*. Most shifts in the UK consist of two stretches of work separated by a meal break. While each stretch would ideally consist of work on a single bus, it is often necessary in order to fit all the bus work together or to cope with short peaked work that a stretch should contain more than one *spell*, the spells being on different buses and separated by small paid breaks. Although manually created shifts have been found with up to six spells, the author has never found a situation in which more than three spells was necessary in an efficient schedule. (Manual schedulers often have difficulty in fitting all the work together, and find it necessary to cut the last pieces into small spells and to distribute these among several shifts.)

Wren [61] and Wren and Rousseau [62] have surveyed computer methods for bus driver scheduling, many of which are now in regular use by bus companies.

When the author was first presented with this problem he hoped that a similar approach to that used in locomotive scheduling could be devised, i.e., that it would be possible to construct an infeasible schedule and to refine this until eventually a good feasible schedule was obtained. Unfortunately in removing the infeasibilities the schedule was forced to become progressively more fragmented. The fragmentation introduced wasteful gaps between spells of work, and the schedule therefore required too many shifts. Attempts to devise processes to move from this inefficient result to a significantly better one were unsuccessful.

Several attempts were made to obtain better starting solutions, and to devise suitable refining heuristics. These latter consisted of routines which exchanged work between shifts in several ways. While the refining routines were often (indeed usually) successful in improving existing manual schedules, it became evident that they were not capable of moving from a really bad schedule to a good one. In particular, although some of the routines were designed to reduce the number of shifts, these were seldom effectual, and when successful often produced a more fragmented schedule which could not be significantly improved. The conclusion that it was unlikely that heuristics could move from a poor solution to a good one was borne out by observation of manual schedulers; when a trainee constructed a schedule it would be checked by a senior colleague who would try to improve it; unless the first attempt was reasonably good, the senior scheduler would find it easier to start again than to adopt the poor schedule as a basis for adjustment.

Much time was therefore spent in improving the starting routine, and several approaches were designed and abandoned. Although it proved impossible to get schedulers to explain the processes they used to construct schedules, they generally accepted that the refining routines were similar to the processes they used to improve their first attempts. Examination of the problem structure enabled the team to identify certain critical features which would lead to inefficiency unless properly addressed, and by about 1974 they had designed a process which would produce reasonably good initial schedules for three sample bus operators. This process incorporated techniques gleaned from human schedulers, and would nowadays be described as an expert system, both knowledge-based and rule-based. The initial schedules were refined by the heuristics designed several years earlier, resulting in solutions which were at least as good as manually produced ones.

Over the next few years feasibility studies were carried out for some dozen bus operators. The constraints on schedule construction (shift length, etc.) vary greatly between companies, as do the "shapes" of underlying bus schedules. Initial experience showed that the heuristics behind the starting solution had to be adapted to deal with new situations, but that the adaptations could be designed and accommodated within a general method after about three person-months of research. We were therefore hopeful that we should ultimately develop a general heuristic for the initial process which would be applicable with minor, if any, modifications to new situations.

During this time, several organisations had implemented schedules produced by the system, and one had used the programs to experiment in conjunction with the unions with many different sets of possible constraints in order to design a new mutually acceptable set of rules. This last company entered negotiations to buy the system, which ultimately broke down when its in-house computer group objected to operating a system which could not guarantee an optimal solution, despite its consistently achieving better schedules than those produced manually.

The last three organisations for whom tests were undertaken upset the earlier confidence in the system, and no acceptable schedule was obtained within the budgeted three months. In Glasgow the length of the working day was greater than had been previously met, and a desired percentage of "early" shifts was not achieved. In Dublin the times of the peaks were much later than elsewhere. In London the bus schedule had always been carefully designed to accommodate a good driver schedule, and there was generally only one acceptable solution. We therefore initiated in 1978 a search for a different solution method. It may be remarked that Glasgow and London are now both using the resulting new system, while Dublin is using a similar one supplied by a Canadian rival.

8. Mathematical Programming Methods for Bus and Rail Driver Scheduling

Advances in computer power led us in 1978 to examine again the possibility of basing a driver scheduling system on integer linear programming. The author and a colleague [63], [64] and [65] describe a new system which was first installed for London Transport in 1984 and for many other organisations later. The basis of the method is the generation of many thousand potential shifts followed by a specialised integer linear programming (ILP) process to select a subset of shifts which form a good schedule, and a final set of refining heuristics which are similar to those used in the earlier research and which are able to restore shifts rejected by earlier processes.

Vital parts of this process are the use of heuristics to restrict the size of the generated set and to drive the branch and bound part of the ILP. These are too complex to describe here, and readers are referred to Smith and Wren [63] and to Smith [65] for further details. It is sufficient to say that the generation process is restricted by two sets of heuristics based on knowledge of the problem structure. The first removes relief opportunities which are unlikely to contribute to a good solution. Typically a quarter to a third of opportunities are removed, leading to a better than proportional reduction in generated shifts. The shift generation consists of an initialisation phase in which only potentially sensible shifts are chosen and a refining phase in which combinations of generated shifts are inspected and shifts which appear to be redundant are discarded. The ILP which follows takes advantage of the fact that the continuous relaxation rounded up if necessary almost always yields the correct total number of shifts, and uses all the relief opportunities required in the final solution. The original system is fully described in a thesis by Smith [66].

This system, originally known as IMPACS but in later versions as TRACS II, is now installed for about thirty transport operators, including bus, tram and light rail systems, and with extensions has been used in a feasibility study for London Underground, as well as in other studies for British Rail (see below). It can solve directly problems which are of a size to satisfy most British operators, who tend to schedule relatively small operating units separately. (Up to about 150 shifts are regularly solved satisfactorily.) However, some organisations do have larger problems, and a decomposition heuristic has been developed and is described by Wren and Smith [64]. This analyses the bus schedule and forms sub-problems consisting of buses which fit well together in a driver schedule; there is a carry-forward of inefficient shifts from one sub-problem to the next.

Other systems which use different mixtures of heuristics and mathematical programming are HASTUS [67] developed in the University of Montreal and HOT [68] implemented by Hamburger Hochbahn.

The TRACS II decomposition process has had very good results in practice, always beating manually produced schedules and those produced by rival systems in test cases. However, users are suspicious of decomposition, seeing its potential drawbacks and believing wrongly that a system which attempts to tackle the whole problem simultaneously must be better; in practice such systems appear to be further from the optimum than the results of decomposition.

Rail driver scheduling is considerably more complex than bus driver scheduling. Distances are greater, and drivers operate out of several different depots. Individual shifts may cover more separate trains than buses, so that potentially, many more shifts have to be generated for a given size of problem. Drivers frequently have to travel quite long distances as passengers in order to return to their home depot.

Recently, the TRACS II model has been adapted to provide a very good estimate of the numbers of drivers needed to cover any given train schedule under a wide range of labour conditions. This model [69, 70] has been used frequently since 1991 by the Operational Research Unit of British Rail to test different strategies. The model uses most of the features of TRACS II, but stops after the linear programming processes has reached a continuous solution, from which the estimate is developed by some further processes.

In 1994 the author and a colleague were awarded a contract to research and develop a rail driver scheduling system. This is being based on TRACS II, and at the time of writing successful schedules have been produced for several British railway systems. One of the operating companies has used the prototype system to generate full schedules under a number of different depot closure scenarios. Current research is directed at new heuristics for shift generation which will be suitable for a wider range of bus and rail problems and will overcome the problems caused by shifts covering more different trains; these are already leading to better results for rail problems than the previous method.

9. Modern Heuristics for Bus and Rail Driver Scheduling

Another approach worth considering for driver scheduling is the use of genetic algorithms. A feasibility study is described by Wren and Wren [49] in which an optimal solution was found to a small problem of fifteen shifts. The GA starts with an initial population of schedules formed by selecting shifts at random from the set generated by TRACS II, and replaces the ILP. A later study [71] failed to find good solutions to considerably larger problems, but research is continuing to refine the methodology.

Kwan and Wren [50] are currently experimenting with another approach in which a GA is used to assist in determining the relief opportunities to be rejected in TRACS II or in any other driver scheduling system. A number of sample sets of chosen relief opportunities provide an initial population, each member of which is costed by applying the estimator described above. (A good set should provide a low estimate of shift numbers.) Mating of population members proceeds in a suitable way until hopefully a set of relief opportunities is obtained which yields an estimate equivalent to the optimum solution. It should be possible to generate from these a good set of shifts to provide the basis either for the ILP of TRACS II or for a GA approach as outlined above. As the set of relief opportunities obtained in this way should be much smaller than that currently used in TRACS II it should be possible to solve much larger problems, and initial investigations have proved encouraging.

Other methods being applied to bus and train driver scheduling in new research by the author and colleagues are tabu search (possibly to resolve certain combinatorial subproblems affecting the structure of shifts at certain times of day and therefore to cut down the number of potential shifts which need to be considered), constraint programming (for the same sub-problems), and a new approach based on the ant system [51].

10.   Conclusions

A large number of methods has been applied to a range of timetabling and scheduling problems, with varied success.   A common strand in these developments runs through simple heuristics in the 1960's and 1970's, with some mathematical models formulated but not applied, integer linear programming driven by heuristics through the 1980's and a range of modern metaheuristics in the 1990's.

Many problems are now being satisfactorily solved, but in some areas there is still a gap between theory and practice (relatively few large universities, for example, are committed to existing timetabling systems, although most are actively seeking good systems).

Although similar methods have been tentatively applied to all the types of problem discussed in this paper, their degree of success has varied considerably across the problem types. Frequently researchers have attempted to carry over approaches from one type to another, with little, if any, reported success.   However, the points of similarity between timetabling and staff rostering are such that there may be scope for cross-fertilisation. Driver scheduling (i.e. shift construction) and the various routeing problems appear to be very different structurally from timetabling.

While useful methods are regularly employed for some problem types, for example in bus driver scheduling where systems are being used in many hundred or thousand organisations, even then there is much scope for improvement, and developments in the methodologies itemised in Section 5 should lead to greatly improved systems over the next few years.

References

1.   A. Wren (ed.), Computer scheduling of public transport. North-Holland (1981).

2.   J-M. Rousseau (ed.), Computer scheduling of public transport - 2.   North-Holland (1985).

3.   J.R. Daduna and A. Wren (eds.), Computer-aided transit scheduling.   Springer-Verlag (1988).

4.   M. Desrochers and J-M. Rousseau (eds.), Computer-aided transit scheduling, 2. Springer-Verlag (1992).

5. J.R. Daduna, I. Branco and J.M.P. Paixao (eds.), Computer-aided transit scheduling, 3. Springer-Verlag (1995).

6. S. French, Sequencing and scheduling. Ellis Horwood (1982).

7. M. Carey, A model and strategy for train pathing with choice of lines, platforms and routes. *Transp. Research*, 28B, 333-353 (1994).

8. K. Wolfenden and A. Wren, Locomotive scheduling by computer. *In* Proceedings of the British Joint Computer Conference, *IEE Conference publication* 19, 31-37 (1966).

9. A. Wren, Bus scheduling, an interactive computer method. *Transportation Planning and Technology*, 1, 115-122 (1972).

10. P.D. Manington and A. Wren, Experiences with a bus scheduling algorithm which saves vehicles. *Pre-prints of* International Workshop on Urban Passenger Vehicle and Crew Scheduling, Chicago (25 pp.) (1975).

11. B.M. Smith and A. Wren, VAMPIRES and TASC: two successfully applied bus scheduling programs. *In* A. Wren (ed.) *Computer scheduling of public transport.* North-Holland, Amsterdam, 97-124 (1981).

12. S.M. Johnson, Optimal two- and three-stage production schedules with set-up times included. Nav. Res. Logist. Q., 1, 61-68 (1954).

13. J.M. Moore, An n-job, one machine sequencing algorithm for minimising the number of late jobs. Mgmt. Sci., 15, 102-109 (1968).

14. E.L. Lawler, Optimal sequencing of a single machine subject to precedence constraints. Mgmt. Sci., 19, 544-546 (1973).

15. H. Müller-Merbach, Heuristic methods: structures, applications, omputational experience. *In* R. Cottle & J. Krarup (eds.) *Optimisation Methods for Resource Allocation*, English Universities Press, 401-416 (1974).

16. S. Lin, Computer solution of the travelling salesman problem. *Bell System Technical Journal*, 44, 2245-2269 (1965).

17. G.B. Dantzig and J.H. Ramser, The truck dispatching problem. *Man.Sci.* 6, 80-91 (1959).

18. G. Clarke and J.W. Wright, Scheduling of vehicles from a central depot to a number of delivery points. *Opns.Res.* 12, 568-581 (1964).

19. T.J. Gaskell, Bases for vehicle fleet scheduling, *Opl.Res.Q.*, 18, 281-295 (1967).

20. N. Christofides and S. Eilon, An algorithm for the vehicle-dispatching problem. *Opl.Res.Q.*, 20, pp.309-318 (1969).

21. A. Wren, Applications of computers to transport scheduling in the United Kingdom, chapter 10, pp.70-75. West Virginia University Engineering Experiment Station Bulletin 91 (1969).

22. A. Wren and A. Holliday, Computer scheduling of vehicles from one or more depots to a number of delivery points. *Opl.Res.Q.* 23, 333-344 (1972).

23. B.C. Gillett and L.R. Miller, A heuristic algorithm for the vehicle dispatch problem. *Ops.Res.*, 22(2), 340-349 (1974).

24. B.A. Foster and D.M. Ryan, An integer programming approach to the vehicle scheduling problem. *Opl.Res.Q.* 27, 367-384 (1976).

25. G. Laporte, The vehicle routing problem: an overview of exact and approximate algorithms. Université de Montréal, Centre de Recherche sur les Transports, Publication 745 (1991).

26. R.S.K. Kwan, Co-ordination of joint headways. *In* J.R. Daduna and A. Wren (eds.) *Computer-Aided Transit Scheduling*. Springer-Verlag, Berlin, 304-314 (1988).

27. W. Keudel, Computer-aided line design (DIANA) and minimisation of transfer times in networks. *In* J.R. Daduna and A. Wren (eds.) *Computer-Aided Transit Scheduling*. Springer-Verlag, Berlin, 315-326 (1988).

28. R. Günther, Untersuchung planerischer und betrieblicher Maßnahmen zur Verbesserung der Anschlussicherung in städtischen Busnetzen. Schriftenreihe des Instituts für Verkejrsplanung und Verkehrswegebau der Technischen Universität Berlin (1985).

29. A.J. Cole, The preparation of examination timetables using a small store computer. *Computer Journal*, 7, 117-121 (1964).

30. D.C. Wood, A system for computing university examination timetables. *Computer Journal*, 11, 41-47 (1968).

31. A.W. Parker, M.E. Parker and L.G. Proll, Constructing timetables for parent-teacher interviews - a practical scheduling problem. Preprints of Combinatorial Optimisation 81 (CO81) 122-137 (1981).

32. B.T. Bennett and R.B. Potts, Rotating roster for a transit system. *Transpn.Sci.* 2, 14-34 (1968).

33. W. Townsend, Bus crew rostering by computer. University of Leeds MSc thesis (1985).

34. B.M. Smith and S. Bennett, Combining constraint satisfaction and local improvement algorithms to construct anaesthetists' rotas. Proc. Conference on Artificial Intelligence Applications (CAIA 92), 106-112 (1992).

35. N. Metropolis, A.W. Rosenbluth, M.N. Rosenbluth, A.H. Teller and E. Teller, Equation of state calculation by fast computing machines. *J. of Chem. Phys.*, 21, 1087-1091 (1953).

36. S. Kirkpatrick, C.D. Gellatt and M.P. Vecchi, Optimization by simulated annealing. *Science*, 220, pp.671-680 (1983).

37. S. Kirkpatrick and G.B. Sorkin, Simulated annealing. *In* M. Arbib (ed.), *Handbook of brain theory and neural networks.* MIT Press (1995).

38. N.E. Collins, R.W Eglese and B.L. Golden, Simulated annealing - an annotated bibliography. *AJMMS*, 8, 209-307 (1988).

39. J. Thompson and K.A. Dowsland, Variants of simulated annealing for the examination timetabling problem. *Annals of Operations Research* (1995).

40. P.M. Ross and D. Corne, Comparing genetic algorithms, stochastic hillclimbing and simulated annealing. *In* T.C.Fogarty (ed), *Evolutionary computing*, Springer-Verlag, 94-102 (1995).

41. I.H. Osman, Metastrategy simulated annealing and tabu search algorithms for the vehicle routing problem. *Annals of Operations Research*, 41 (1993).

42. F. Glover, Tabu search - Part 1. *ORSA J. Computing*, 1, 190-206 (1989).

43. F. Glover, Tabu search - Part 2. *ORSA J. Computing*, 2, 4-32 (1990).

44. F. Glover and M. Laguna, Tabu search. *In* C.R. Reeves (ed.) *Modern heuristic techniques for combinatorial problems.* Blackwell Scientific Publications, 70-150 (1993).

45. D.E. Goldberg, Genetic algorithms in search, optimisation and machine learning. Addison-Wesley (1989).

46. L. Davis, Handbook of genetic algorithms. Van Nostrand Reinhold (1991).

47. Z. Michalewicz, Genetic algorithms + data structures = evolution programs, second, extended edition. Springer-Verlag (1994).

48. H-L Fang, P.M. Ross and D.Corne, A promising genetic algorithm approach to job-shop scheduling, rescheduling and open-shop scheduling problems. *In* S. Forrest (ed.) *Proc. 5th International Conference on Genetic Algorithms.* Morgan Kaufmann, 375-382 (1993).

49. A. Wren and D.O. Wren, A genetic algorithm for public transport driver scheduling. *Computers Ops Res.* 22, 101-110 (1995).

50. R.S.K. Kwan and A. Wren, Hybrid algorithms for bus driver scheduling. *To appear in* L. Bianco and P. Toth (eds.) *Advanced methods in transportation analysis*, Springer-Verlag (1996).

51. M. Dorigo, V. Maniezo and A. Colorni, The ant system: optimization by a colony of cooperating agents. *IEEE Transactions on Systems, Man, and Cybernetics Part B*, 26, pp.1-13 (1996).

52. K. Wolfenden and A. Wren, Locomotive scheduling by computer. Proc. British Joint Computer Conference. *IEE Conference Publication 19*, 31-37 (1966).

53. H.I. Stern and A. Ceder, An improved lower bound to the minimum fleet size problem. *Transpn.Sci.* 17, 471-477 (1983).

54. A. Wren, *Computers in Transport Planning and Operation.* Ian Allen, London, 103-106 (1971).

55. A. Wren, Bus scheduling, an interactive computer method. *Transportation Planning and Technology*, 1, 115-122 (1972).

56. P.D. Manington and A. Wren, Experiences with a bus scheduliong algorithm which saves vehicles. *Preprints of* International Workshop on Urban Passenger Vehicle and Crew Scheduling, Chicago (25 pp) (1975).

57. B.M. Smith and A. Wren, VAMPIRES and TASC: two successfully applied bus scheduling programs. *In* A. Wren (ed.) *Computer scheduling of public transport.* North-Holland, Amsterdam, 97-124 (1981).

58. B. Manington and A. Wren, A general computer method for bus crew scheduling. *Pre-prints of* International Workshop on Urban Passenger Vehicle and Crew Scheduling, Chicago (49 pp) (1975).

59. M.E. Parker and B.M. Smith, Two approaches to computer crew scheduling. *In* A. Wren (ed.) *Computer Scheduling of Public Transport.* North-Holland, Amsterdam, 193-222 (1981).

60. S.E.G. Elias, The use of digital computers in the economic scheduling for both man and machine in public transportation. *Kansas State University Bulletin, Special Report* 49 (1964).

61. A. Wren, General review of the use of computers in scheduling buses and their crews. *In* A. Wren (ed.) *Computer Scheduling of Public Transport.* North-Holland, Amsterdam, 3-17 (1981).

62. A. Wren and J-M. Rousseau, Bus driver scheduling - an overview. *In* J.R. Daduna, I. Branco and J.M.P. Paixao (eds.) *Computer aided transit scheduling - 3*, Springer-Verlag, Berlin, 173-187 (1995).

63. B.M. Smith and A. Wren, A bus crew scheduling system using a set covering formulation. *Transpn.Res.* 22A, 97-108 (1988).

64. A. Wren and B.M. Smith, Experiences with a crew scheduling system based on set covering. *In* J.R. Daduna and A. Wren (eds.) *Computer-aided transit scheduling.* Springer-Verlag, Berlin, 104-118 (1988).

65. B.M. Smith, IMPACS - a bus crew scheduling system using linear programming. *Math Prog.* 42, 181-187 (1988).

66. B.M. Smith, Bus crew scheduling using mathematical programming. University of Leeds PhD thesis (1986).

67. J-M. Rousseau and J-Y Blais, HASTUS: an interactive system for buses and crew scheduling. *In* J-M Rousseau (ed.) *Computer Scheduling of Public Transport - 2.* North-Holland, Amsterdam, 45-60 (1985).

68. J.R. Daduna and M. Mojsilovic, Computer-aided vehicle and duty scheduling using the HOT programme system. *In* J.R. Daduna and A. Wren (eds.) *Computer-Aided Transit Scheduling.* Springer-Verlag, Berlin,133-146 (1988).

69. A. Wren, R.S.K. Kwan and M.E. Parker, Scheduling of rail driver duties. In T.K.S. Murthy et al. (eds.) *Computers in railways IV - Volume 2, Railway Operations*, 81-89 (1994).

70. M.E. Parker, A. Wren and R.S.K. Kwan, Modelling the scheduling of train drivers. *In* J.R. Daduna, I. Branco and J.M.P. Paixao (eds.) *Computer aided transit scheduling - 3*, Springer-Verlag, Berlin, 359-370 (1995).

71. R.P. Clement and A. Wren, Greedy genetic algorithms, optimizing mutations and bus driver scheduling. *In* J.R. Daduna, I. Branco and J.M.P. Paixao (eds.) *Computer aided transit scheduling - 3*, Springer-Verlag, 213-235 (1995).

Examination Timetabling in British Universities: A Survey

Edmund BURKE, Dave ELLIMAN, Peter FORD and Rupert WEARE

E.Burke@Cs.Nott.AC.UK
Department of Computer Science
University of Nottingham
Noxttingham, UK.

Abstract. This paper describes the results of a questionnaire on examination timetabling sent to the registrars of ninety five British Universities. The survey asked questions in three specific categories. Firstly, universities were asked about the nature of their examination timetabling problem: how many people, rooms, periods are involved and what difficulties are associated with the problem? Secondly, we asked about how the problem is solved at their institution and whether a manual or automated system is used. Lastly, we asked what qualities are required in a good timetable. We conclude by making some comments, based on the survey replies, as to what sort of criteria a general automated timetabling system must meet.

1 Introduction

There has been much literature on the subject of timetabling over a wide variety of subtly, and not so subtly, different problems. A great variety of algorithms have been proposed, employing heuristics and search methodologies, producing complete timetables or just helping the process along. One of the great questions for timetabling is whether it is unifiable, that is to say, can we find an algorithm or method, sufficiently general, that it will produce good timetables for all problems and for all constraints? The alternative, of course, is to continue developing isolated specialised algorithms each time the timetabling problem appears.

This survey is concerned with the University Examination Scheduling Problem. Its main aim was to discover how the requirements of each university differ and whether these differences are sufficiently small that a unified system may be produced? Specifically, the survey aimed to answer the following questions. How widespread is computer aided timetabling? Is a general timetabling package required at all? What functionality must such a package have? How big and complex is the timetabling problem and how does this vary between universities? What properties must an acceptable timetable possess before an institution will use it?

Fifty six out of ninety five universities (59%) replied to the survey of which 40 (71%) were former polytechnics. All universities, except one, returned a full questionnaire, two, unfortunately, being too late to be included in the results. One of the largest universities in the country, returned separate questionnaires for each faculty. These were incorporated, by the authors, into a single reply as seemed appropriate for each question.

Very few similar surveys have been carried out, none deal with examination timetabling as such. Comm and Mathaisel[1] surveyed 1494 U.S. college registrars to find out whether a computerised timetabling system existed. If not, whether one was needed and what characteristics it should possess. The study concluded that there was a large market for such a system and that, despite a high degree of automated assistance, most registrars were unhappy with their current systems.

Dowsland[2] and Junginger[3] both consider the school timetabling problem but provide alternative views on the usefulness of automated systems. Junginger states that "Even though the timetables produced required modification, the schools were content with the results. The time saved was remarkable, up to 75%." Dowsland, on the other hand, concludes that "It is very difficult to judge the present success of the mainframe packages for timetabling, but the very limited use to which they are put suggests that most consider the advantages to be limited." Clearly, no system designer may take for granted the idea that their product will be welcomed with open arms.

Pendlebury[4] surveyed British polytechnics with respect to course timetabling. Of the twelve from thirty that replied, seven utilised computer scheduling of which four were on a small scale and the others using the Amended SATS system as developed at DeMontford University. It is interesting to note that Pendlebury finds that most courses run are primarily class-based i.e. are largely independent of each other, and that, in most of the institutions surveyed, individual departments are responsible for producing their own timetable. Finally, Miles[5] and Schmidt and Strohlein[6] give useful bibliographies of early developments in computer-aided timetabling.

In this paper we only consider examination scheduling. Course scheduling is another subtly different problem again. We may hope to unify the processes of course and examination timetabling in which case, the bringing to together of all variations on the examination timetabling problem is a good first step.

2 The Timetabling Problem

Timetabling, the act of scheduling exams to periods, has long been known to be equivalent, and therefore as hard as, the general graph colouring problem. Graph colouring being one of a family of known computationally difficult problems. Often, we may make assumptions about the nature of the problem which may allow us to find a solution more efficiently. However, when trying to build a general system, we are obviously limited in that our assumptions must be the lowest common denominator of all possible scenarios.

One implicit assumption that has often been made is that of independence between separate academic units. One university schedules by asking its individual schools to come up with a timetable for their own exams. A central merging facility is then used to ensure that all relevant constraints are satisfied. In many cases, as at Nottingham University, this is still how the normal course timetable is produced, although some departments have developed their own course scheduling software.

Several of the universities surveyed indicated that students may take all of their courses outside the department with which they are registered (where such a concept was appropriate). Most quoted figures over fifty percent as the maximum allowed and only very few that quoted a figure said under fifty percent. Obviously independence should not be generally assumed, although there may well be a difference between the maximum allowed and the actual figure. At Nottingham, for example, the average probability of an exam conflicting with one not in the same department is 0.023 whereas the probablitiy of two exams conflicting in the same department is 0.281, a considerable difference, despite the degree scheme being modular for over two years. In Scottish Universities, students are assigned to faculties which encompass a whole range of different departments so these two figures may be closer and therefore, the problem more difficult.

2.1 Exams and Students

The size of a timetabling problem is essentially related to the number of events that are required to be scheduled, in this case exams. Clearly the size of the problem ranges considerably between universities, from small problems with around one hundred exams up to around two and a half thousand exams. This variation in size will obviously affect the time required to solve the problem. It may be possible to find the optimal solution for a small problem with just one hundred exams but at the other end of the scale, heuristics or other ways of cutting down the search space must be used for a solution to be found in a reasonable time.

It might be expected that the number of exams and number of students for each problem would be correlated (see figure 1 - each 'o' represents a different institution). While there is a certain pattern, it is clear that there are also many special cases where the ratios are considerably different giving a new complexion to the problem. The number of exams given, and therefore marked, by each member of staff may be calculated by extrapolating from the average ratio of full time equivalent staff to students in Britain (about 1:15) and is about one and a half exams per session. There may, of course, be many examination sessions per academic year. Whether it is more convenient for one member of staff's exams to be scheduled together or apart is unclear although if together they would need to be in the same hall according to normal rules.

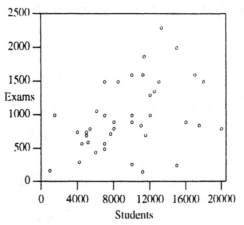

Fig. 1. Exams and students

Figure 2 gives some extra insight into the nature of the timetabling problem. It might be argued that on the left hand chart, the higher the number of exams, the more conflicting the problem and that, on the right hand chart, the higher number of students, the greater the problems of room assignment. These arguments have some value although there are many other factors to take into account. For example, no reference is made here to the inter-dependance of courses or to the amount of space available (see section 2.4) which may affect the difficulty of the problem at least as much.

In each graph, as in figure 2, only the institutions that fully completed all the relevant information could be included. In some cases, this has meant that the number of institutions represented is less than the number that actually returned surveys.

2.2 Exams and Departments

The average number of exams set by a particular department varies considerably between universities. The ratio, despite its variability, may still be seen as an indicator of the nature of the timetable conflict graph for the reasons given earlier.

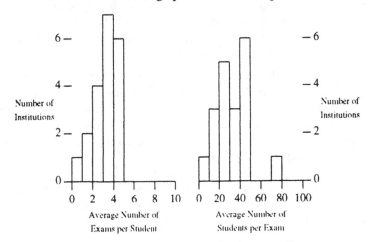

Fig. 2. Exams per Student and Students per Exam

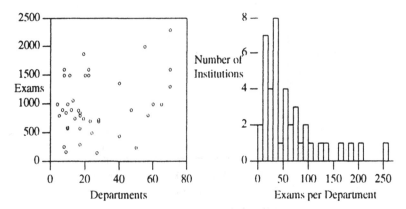

Fig. 3. Exams and departments

Figure 3 takes the academic unit which occurs most often within the institution. This we shall refer to as a department although it may be a faculty, school, department or a combination of these.

2.3 Exams and Periods

One of the assumptions of the survey, which may be seen as unrealistic with the advantage of hindsight, was that the exam timetable is periods based. That is to say, there are distinct timeslots in which exams take place and, generally, exams start only at the beginning of that time period. Most universities do use this system, however, there are some alternatives which may be worth considering given the pressure on resources most universities describe (see next section).

One university does not use the concept of periods at all. Instead exams may be scheduled at any time between 9.30am-12.30pm and 1.30pm - 6pm. Although potentially making the timetabling process considerably more difficult, it does allow rooms to be used a greater proportion of the time, especially where there is a large variation in exam lengths. Spread constraints must then be reformatted in terms of real time rather than a number of periods, for example, two hours may be required as a gap between two exams rather than one period.

Another university uses periods but is flexible about how many that are used on a particular day. This may be a reasonable compromise between the two ideas but relies partly on the assumption that exams of similar length may be scheduled at the same time because otherwise, the longest exams must be spread throughout the periods. Experience suggests that exam lengths are more likely to be uniform within a department than between them and therefore, those of similar length having a greater than average probability of conflicting.

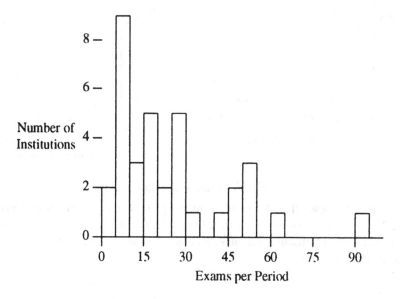

Fig. 4. Exams and periods

2.4 Exams and Rooms

Seventy three per cent of those universities that replied stated that accommodating exams is a major problem. This stems from two major problems. The first problem is the lack of halls available, many large lecture theatres being unsuitable for exams or possibly still being used for teaching. The second is the problem of splitting exams between more than one room. In many cases (86%), the size of an exam alone is enough to cause a split which may be into five, or more, different rooms.

Several universities overcome the problem of insufficient accommodation by hiring external halls. This solves the problem to a certain extent but, since the halls are also used for other functions, their availability is variable. These halls may also not necessarily be close to the university thus causing problems similar to that of split campuses where students must be allowed extra commuting time.

Splitting exams between rooms does not in itself seem to be a particular problem, though this may be because of the more important pressure on resources. Different universities vary greatly in terms of the number of halls they have available. Clearly, a timetabling problem with a small number of large halls on a single site is going to be markedly different to one with a large number of small halls spread across several sites. A number of universities have a very large number of exam rooms (in the order of sixty to seventy) and are not included in figure 5 for practical reasons.

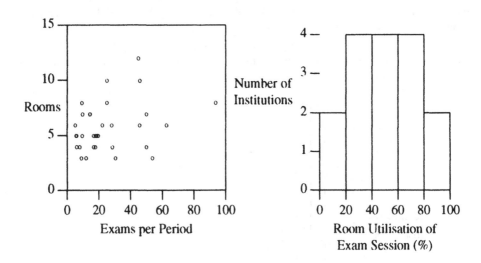

Fig. 5. Exams and rooms

Figure 5 (right) shows that the problem of assigning exams to rooms can vary in difficultly from almost being trivial to being of the upmost importance. Clearly, the greater the required utilisation, the more an algorithm must concentrate on efficiently placing exams into rooms.

2.5 Exam Lengths

In a fixed-length period-based timetable, the length of the individual periods is governed by the length of the longest exam. Where there are many shorter exams, periods of different lengths may be used which restrict the exams that may be scheduled then. Thirty two percent of universities said that there are some periods in which not all exams may be scheduled because of the exam length.

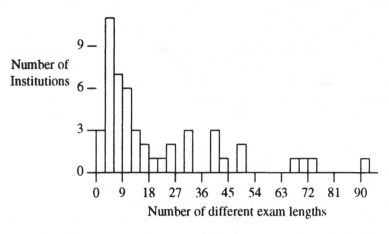

Fig. 6. Exam lengths

2.6 Scheduling Invigilators

Although this was not a major theme of the survey, we asked whether scheduling invigilators was a problem. Twenty nine percent of those universities that schedule invigilators centrally say this is a major problem. In some cases, professional invigilators are used, whereas in others, a specific department or member of staff is specified. In this latter case, it is generally required that the burden is spread evenly between staff and departments while at each exam, a member of the relevant department is present.

3 The Timetabling Process

The Timetabling Process encompasses every action that is required to create a final complete, correct timetable from the initial data input. This includes receiving, validating and formatting data, sending out draft versions and then making alterations and producing the final timetable. These are perhaps of less interest to us though, than the actual point when exams and rooms are assigned. It is this that is considered to be the computationally hard stage although it may not be the most difficult part of the process. That is dependent upon what resources are available. This section of the survey asks what computer based resources are used for timetabling, how much time is available to produce the timetable and why might timetables change from year to year as well as between draft and final versions.

3.1 Computer Usage

Fifty eight percent of those universities that responded use a computer at some stage in the timetabling process. Of these, eleven (21%) have a facility to perform scheduling, although these may, in some cases, still require a certain amount of manual input and previous knowledge of the particular timetabling problem. Two of the eleven scheduling systems are commercial and the rest have been developed in house. Four other universities stated that they are either currently developing their own or customising a commercial package.

Given the size of the timetables involved it is surprising that so many do not use any form of automation at all. This may, in some cases, be because the timetable does not change significantly from year to year. However, of those universities that do not schedule by computer, the split between those that use last year's timetable and those that construct a completely new timetable each year is exactly even. It is interesting to note, however, that in every case, those that do not use the previous year's or a computer take at least four weeks to produce a timetable (see figure 8). Where a scheduling system is used, virtually all (10/11) take no account of the previous year's timetable.

Two alternative timetabling approaches were given by those without scheduling aid. The first approach is to take draft examination timetables, as produced by each school or department, and then merge them centrally into a final timetable. This uses the assumption of independence between departments and is possibly a very good way of timetabling while the assumption holds. Many universities are however now heading towards modular schemes which make such an assumption very tenuous. The second approach is to *tweak* the teaching timetable. Since a working timetable using similar data is already in operation, why not use it to produce the examination timetable? To quote one institution, which is incidently developing a new system, "This, of course, doesn't work, since some lectures are repeated in different slots, or have more students in large lecture theatres than we can accommodate simultaneously in flat exam rooms." Obviously this approach depends on the nature of the associated course timetable.

3.2 Causes of Change from Year to Year

For a timetable to be usable year after year it must be sufficiently robust so that whatever changes occur in the input data, only a small alteration is necessary for the timetable. Whether it is possible to use the previous year's timetable depends on how robust the timetable is and also how much the exam data changes from year to year. One University, that has an automated system, reports that it has "highly volatile data". This means that constructing a completely new timetable is, for that University, the best option. Some other universities say that rather than completely rescheduling, part of the old timetable is reused, while part is reconstructed. Timetables will obviously exhibit similarities from year to year since their driving factor, the combination of courses on offer to the students, will remain the same in many, if not, most cases.

Figure 7 gives four possible reasons for changes in the timetable and the number of universities that consider them major causes of change.

New Exams	75%
Student Numbers	67%
Student Preferences	54%
Policy	21%

Fig. 7. Causes of change from year to year

Other causes given were: joint papers, modularisation/semesterisation, accommodation, departments' preferences and exams only being set in alternate years.

3.3 The Length of the Timetabling Process

The time it takes to produce a timetable may, in practice, often be measured in months and the actual scheduling may take much of this. Figure 8 (left) clearly shows that automated timetabling packages can reduce the time required to produce a timetable although this is not by any means guaranteed. This time may then be used to allow more extensive consultation, ease the pressure to rush the rest of the process or allow the timetables to be printed earlier. Figure 8 (centre) shows how much of the total time required to produce a final timetable from scratch is used for scheduling. Figure 8 (right) shows this as a percentage of the total amount of time available which may or may not be longer than the time taken. It is clear that although the time required by automated systems is less, the expected time to completion is also less.

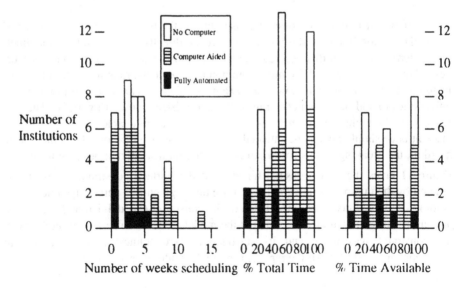

Fig. 8. Time required for scheduling

Generally, a draft timetable is first produced which, after consultation with departments, is turned into the final timetable. This may or may not include room or invigilator allocations which would be added after the draft version has been accepted. Some institutions quoted figures of up to 75% of the timetable being altered between draft and final versions. Reasons for these alterations were given as follows along with the number of universities that consider them the major reasons for amending the timetable.

Late Data	79%
Incorrect Data	65%
Poor Quality Timetable	17%

Fig. 9. Causes of change to the draft timetable

Incorrect data generally means that the students have filled in their registration form incorrectly or changed courses after the data was collected. The assessment of poor quality usually comes from Departments who notice that, for example, their students may have too many exams together at the beginning of the Examination Session or too short a gap between exams scheduled at different sites.

4. The Timetabling Solution

There are a vast number of possible constraints on the timetable produced, over and above those entirely due to resources. These relate directly to the quality of the timetable in terms of its usability and requirements on those who are subject to it. The survey asked about thirteen of the more common requirements, ranking each in terms of its usage, its importance and how many exams it affects. Space was also provided for universities to add their own constraints, these are listed below in figure 10. The survey assumed that the constraint that no student should be timetabled in more than one place at once should always be satisfied although, in some situations the authors have heard of, the breaking of this constraint is tolerated for a small number of students.

Figure 11 gives the survey results for each of the thirteen constraints, these being ordered by the number of universities that use them (given as a percentage under each graph). The x axis gives the importance of the constraint (rated 1-10) and the y axis, the number of exams it affects. x marks the modal value of those that replied, where the constraint was used, and its surrounding box defines a sixty-six percent confidence interval (66% of the replies, if plotted, would be inside the box).

The following extra constraints were given in no particular order.

Extra time/special rooms must be provided for disabled students
Foreign exchange students should have separate rooms
Religious convictions must be respected
Exams for the same department should be kept together
Students must be split in rooms according to end time
Students should be examined on their home site
Time must be provided for students to travel between sites
Finals/honours exams/those for external moderation should be early
Degree Exams must be scheduled in morning periods
Exams from same department should be kept together
No mix of different language exams on the same day
Availability of part time students should be respected
Close exams should not be at different sites
Take away exams should not be scheduled at the same time as other exams
Resit candidates are at different (global) locations
One exam must precede all others in a group
One exam must be the last in a group
Invigilators must be assigned fairly
Other specific departments' preferences

Fig. 10. More timetabling constraints

This demonstrates the wide variety of different factors that any general system would have to cope with. Many of these constraints will conflict either directly or indirectly. For many universities, due to the difficultly of the problem many are ignored altogether. The university that gave the constraint that no student should have exams in two different languages on the same day, went on to say that they were unable to enforce this.

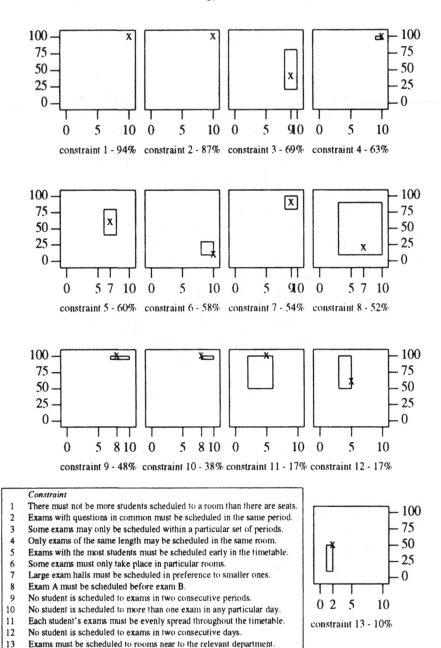

Fig. 11. Timetabling constraints

5. Conclusion

"There are so many variations within the timetabling schedule
- we could write a book really!" - One of the respondants.

It is clear that examination timetabling problems can vary greatly both between and within institutions (some have up to seven examination sessions per year spread across several sites). Certain themes have, however, occurred in the survey which lead us to the following comments on the nature of any future generalised examination timetabling system.

- The system must produce good quality timetables

Obviously, any new package, to be accepted must outperform the method currently used to produce timetables within an institution. This means that it must produce good draft timetables and then be able to alter the master timetable with minimal disruption to other exams to produce a generally accepted final timetable. It must then be able to take account of a wide variety of complex constraints and be sufficiently flexible to cope with special circumstances which fall outside the scope of the normal timetable.

- The users will not be computer experts

Although the users may be reasonably relied upon to have experience of the particular timetabling problem and other local knowledge, it is clear from the survey that many do not use any form of automation in the timetabling process. Where computers have been involved, it is often the case that only the results are seen by the examinations officer and that the actual computing is done by the University's main computing centre.

A requirement may therefore be placed on the system that it must be intuitive and easy to use, possibly using current practice as a model for development. The interface should also then provide at least as much functionality as previous systems, for example, giving clash lists or equivalent guides as to where exams may be moved. The examination department from one university said that they could "see the disadvantages in a fully automated system of examination timetabling. ... There is (dare it be said), also a case for working through the initial stages of timetabling with a chart and a pencil! This allows instant overview of the progress of timetabling in the whole of the examination session rather than reliance on a system of queries and scrolling almost inevitable on a computer screen."

- The system should be complete

Timetabling is concerned with the whole process from collecting registration to outputting results. Just to isolate the scheduling part may be interesting from a research point of view but cannot provide useful general systems. Requirements for a general timetabling package, as given in survey replies, are given below.

Schedule exams to periods or times
Allocate rooms for exams
Validate data
Assign invigilators
Print timetables for students, staff and departments
Print set up/set down requirements including stationary
Print desk cards, attendance lists and labels
Produce room layouts
Interact with other scheduling systems on semi-independent sites

Fig. 12.. Requirements for a complete general timetabling system

It must also be able to cope with other exam related events which fall outside the normal examination session, for example, take-away and language oral exams.

- The timetabling system should be compatible with present software

Many British universities have spent large amounts of time and money investing in computerised administration systems. The timetabling software must be able to download data from current systems and produce output in a form that these systems may accept.

- Real timetabling test data is required

Since timetabling problems vary so much, it is unrealistic to fully test a system without a range of real timetabling problem data. Even randomly generated data sets, while still useful in testing individual aspects of systems, may not provide the richness and complexity associated with real problems.

It seems appropriate to finish by passing on a comment by one university timetabler who has tried automating the timetabling process before.

"Having tried to do in the past what you are proposing now, I hope you have the time and resources to match your enthusiasm. Do **not** underestimate the complexity of the problem! Good luck anyway."

References

1. CL Comm and DFX Mathaisel, "College Course Scheduling. A Market for Computer Software Support," *Journal of Research of Computing in Education,*, vol. 21, pp. 187-195, 1988.

2. KA Dowsland and S Lim, "Computer Aided School Timetabling Part I: The History of Computerized Timetabling," *Computer Education*, pp. 22-23, Nov 1982.

3. W Junginger, "Timetabling in Germany - A Survey," *Interfaces*, vol. 16, no. 4, pp. 66-74, 1986.

4. J Pendlebury, *A Computer-Aided Timetabling System for use in FE/HE*, Department of Operational Research, University of Lancaster, UK, July 1989. PhD thesis

5. R Miles, "Computer Timetabling: A Bibliography," *Brit. J. of Educational Technology*, vol. 6, no. 3, pp. 16-20, Oct. 1975.

6. G Schmidt and T Strhlein, "Timetable Construction – an Annotated Bibliography," *The Computer Journal*, vol. 23, no. 4, pp. 307-316, 1979. Institut fr Informatik, Technische Universitt Mnchen, Ger many

Appendix - Universities that replied.

The authors are extremely grateful to all the following universities' Registrars and staff for replying to the survey.

University of Aberdeen, Aston University, University of Birmingham, Bournemouth University, University of Bradford, University of Brighton, University of Bristol, University of Buckingham, University of Cambridge, University of Central Lancashire, City University, Coventry University, De Montfort University, University of Derby, University of Dundee, University of East Anglia, University of East London, University of Edinburgh, University of Essex, University of Exeter, Glasgow Caledonian University, University of Greenwich, Heriot-Watt University, University of Hertfordshire, University of Huddersfield, University of Keele, University of Lancaster, University of Leeds, University of Liverpool, Liverpool John Moores University, Loughborough University, University of Manchester, University of Manchester Institute of Science and Technology, Manchester Metropolitan University, Napier University, University of Nottingham, University of Oxford, Oxford Brookes University, University of Plymouth, University of Reading, University of St Andrews, University of Salford, Sheffield Hallam University, University of Southampton, Staffordshire University, University of Sunderland, University of Surrey, University of Teesside, Thames Valley University, University of Ulster, University College of North Wales, University College of Swansea, Saint David's University College, University of Warwick, University of Wolverhampton, University of York.

Reasoning About Constraints

Employee Timetabling, Constraint Networks and Knowledge-Based Rules: A Mixed Approach

Amnon Meisels, Ehud Gudes and Gadi Solotorevsky

Dept. of Mathematics and Computer Science
Ben-Gurion University of the Negev
Beer-Sheva, 84-105, Israel, Tel.: 972-57-461627
Email: (am,ehud,gadi)@bengus.bgu.ac.il

Abstract. Employee timetabling problems (ETP) usually involve an organization with a set of tasks that need to be fulfilled by a set of employees, each with his/her own qualifications, constraints and preferences. The organization usually enforces some overall constraints and attempts to achieve some global objectives such as a just or equitable division of work. Examples for such problems are: assignment of nurses to shifts in a hospital, or assignment of phone operators to shifts and stations in a service-oriented call-center. One possible approach for solving ETPs is to use constraint processing techniques. Another approach is to model human knowledge into knowledge-based systems for timetabling. The present paper presents an approach to representing and processing employee timetabling problems (ETP) by a combination of *explicit representations* of some constraints in the network and *rule-based processing* in which specific heuristics for generic constraints of ETPs are embedded. The mixed-mode approach has been implemented in the form of a commercial software package for defining and solving real world ETPs. Example of a real world ETP is followed through the presentation and is used to experimentally compare standard CSP techniques with the proposed mixed-mode approach.

area: Constraint networks; Timetabling; Knowledge-based systems.

1 Introduction: Employee timetabling

Employee timetabling problems (ETP) form a very diverse family, arising in the diverse commercial world of today. ETPs usually involve an organization with a set of tasks that need to be fulfilled by a set of employees, each with his/her own qualifications, constraints and preferences. The organization usually enforces some overall constraints and attempts to achieve some global objectives such as a just or equitable division of work. Examples for such problems are: assignment of nurses to shifts in a hospital, assignment of workers to cash registers in a large store, or assignment of phone operators to shifts and stations in a service-oriented call-center. To clarify the problem further, we are interested in constructing the schedule for individual employees under various constraints and organizational needs, and not the optimal design of shifts.

ETPs can be represented as a constraint nerwork (CN) by representing activities as variables and representing the Employees as values, that have to be assigned to the variables (activities). Domains of variables consist of lists of employees that can be assigned to these variables. Specifically, the binary constraints that exclude employees from being assigned to more than one activity at a time, form constraint networks (CN) which are known to be equivalent to the *list coloring* problem and thus form a family of hard problems (cf. [2, 5]).

The above representation of employee timetabling enables the explicit representation of constraints by enumerating the allowed tuples in a suitable space of the cartesian product formed from the domains of the constrained variables. This is the standard representation of constraints in the CSP literature [11] and has been particularly well studied for binary constraints (for the definition of binary constraint networks see [11, 4]). Due to the form of the most common constraints of ETPs, such as limited weekly working hours for every employee, or uniform distribution of "weekends" among groups of employees, the constraint networks arising from these problems are almost never binary. Representing non-binary constraints in explicit form is usually very space and time consuming. In section 2 some typical non binary constraints of employee timetabling problems, together with explicit representations for these constraints, will be described.

In former studies we have looked at a knowledge-based approach to solving resource allocation problems (RAP) that incorporated rule-based structures for representing constraints [9]. The complete framework for specifying RAPs and strategies for solving them by the use of assignment rules and other control structures is described in [9]. The present paper describes a new approach to solving ETPs that uses a mixture of representations for constraints and as a result a mixture of processing techniques. The constraint networks (CN) of ETPs are processed by a mixture of explicit ordering heuristics and Knowledge-Based assignment rules. All explicit constraints are processed by heuristic techniques specifically suitable for employee timetabling problems (see section 3).

The mixed mode approach to solving ETPs was implemented as a software package for defining and solving a wide variety of employee timetabling problems. The experimental evidence for the efficiency of the present approach was accumulated over the last two years through the solving of real world problems by the software package we designed and implemented. The design of this software package is described in section 4. A family of real world ETPs is followed throughout the paper, that of timetabling nurses in typical departments of Israeli hospitals. These problems are then used for an experimental comparison of the performance of the proposed method with some standard CSP techniques (section 5). The family of Nurse timetabling problems is quantitatively described and the behavior of it's constraint network is experimentally tested. Our conclusions are summarized in section 6.

2 Constraints and Objectives of ETPs

Constraint-based processing typically uses explicit representation of constraints. Representing explicitly the domains of the constrained variables and the binary constraints among them (in the form of 0,1 matrices, for example) enables the use of constraint-based processing heuristics such as domain size ordering, constraint propagation and many forms of search strategies such as constraint-based backtracking (cf. [11, 7, 4]). The standard approach is to think of non binary constraints as admitting of an equivalent binary representation (see [8]). However, some of the generic non binary constraints of ETPs are not represented very well by explicit binary constraints. We will describe below typical constraints that can be represented explicitly in different ways.

Let us follow a simple example of a real world employee timetabling problem which will illuminate the concepts and techniques introduced in this report and will serve as the center of the experimental study of constraint processing and mixed-mode processing in section 4. The example is that of timetabling nurses in a department of a large Israeli hospital. The nurses of a department are of several different types and they can be assigned to different roles on several types of shifts. Each nurse has a list of preferred shifts for each week and a list of forbidden shifts, due to his/her personal constraints. This creates a constraint network with different domain sizes for different variables which is not typical to experimental work in the CSP literature (cf. [7]).

Generic constraints of ETPs fall into three simple families. Typical binary constraints are of the *mutual exclusion* form and can be represented explicitly in standard CSP format. Mutual exclusion binary constraints for ETPs arise from the fact that an employee can be assigned to one job at one time. This gives rise to complete subnetworks of shifts that overlap in time. representing these subnetworks explicitly as lists, enables a very fast procedure for propagating mutual exclusion constraints and supports a new ordering heuristic for variables *and* values involved in these binary constraints.

Another family of ETP constraints are non binary in nature and relate to the *finite capacity* of employees (i.e. a limited number of weekly working hours). All activities to which a particular employee can possibly be assigned are connected by this constraint, of limited number of working hours. The set of all activities to which an employee can be assigned is usually a large set. Representing *finite capacity* constraints by an additional variable with domain of values composed of tuples, denoting the allowed assignments, generates an impractical domain size. An efficient explicit representation for a finite capacity constraint turns out to be just a simple *counter*. This simple explicit representation for finite capacity constraints accommodates an efficient forward checking procedure that will be described in section 3).

The third family of constrains are many times called *objectives* and tend to constraint *all of the variables*. Typical objectives of the ETP, constraint the *distribution of employee assignments*. Complex non binary constraints are hard to express explicitly. Different types of nurses can be assigned to different types of roles but the assignment of each shift must contain some minimal numbers of the different types of nurses. At least two certified nurses, say, in any type of role, out of the total 10 nurses in a given shift. This constraints a large set of nurses and shifts, hence is a non binary constraint. Such non binary constraints can be implicitly represented in the form of relations or Prolog predicates. In this we continue our knowledge-based approach to representing and solving resource allocation problems (RAP) [9, 10]. The processing of these implicitly represented constraints is based on assignment rules and is described in subsections 3.2, 4.1.

3   Mixed mode processing of ETPs

There are two parts to the mixed mode representation and processing approach: one part addresses the set of explicit constraints, the other part utilizes knowledge-based techniques for extracting assignment rules from humans. This overall strategy generates a non exhaustive process of search (i.e. the assignment process). A non exhaustive mode of search avoids the complexity induced by the binary representation of complex non binary constraints. Being specifically designed for ETPs, backtracking is based on an *exchange principle* of employees among competing activities in case of a deadend.

The general rule-based processing strategy that is part of the mixed-mode approach follows our knowledge-based framework and language for resource allocation problems [9]. There are two kinds of rules: Assignment rules; and Constraint rules (expressing non binary complex constraints). Entities, like shifts and employees, have special fields that express their priorities. Selection of variables, values and their orderings take these priorities into account. The general control structure includes several contexts that enable the coding of different search strategies for different stages of processing a problem. All of these techniques are specialized for the domain of Employee Timetabling and are described in section 4 as part of our implementation.

Assignment rules typically use special features (of either activities or resources) in order to represent the human knowledge about the assignment process (see subsection 3.2). This is reminiscent of the "generalization" suggested by Faltings and Choueiry [2], in order to lower the complexity of the assignment procedure. Our knowledge-based processing techniques use additional fields for the description of activities and resources, that encode human knowledge, in order to achieve the exact same goal.

3.1   Search Heuristics and Strategies

The mixed mode processing strategy to solving employee timetabling problems includes two parts:

1. *Select classes of variables and values* by using knowledge-based rules that relate to implicit features of activities and employees.
2. *Order activities and employees of the above selected classes* (if they are non empty, i.e. if there are relevant assignment rules) by using the explicit part of the representation of the constraints of the ETP.

The central advantage of the mixed mode approach lies with the fact that for the family of Employee Timetabling Problems there is a nontrivial set of generic *explicit constraints* that can be used very efficiently for ordering heuristics and search strategies.

Mutual exclusion constraints The *meaning* attached to values in ETPs, that springs from the fact that they are employees, generates a new family of ordering heuristics for the binary *mutual exclusion* constraints, that mix variable ordering and value ordering [6] and is called *ordering by demand*:

1. Find the Value that appears in the *largest set of Variable domains*. Call it R_{max} (for Resource of maximal "demand").
2. Of all domains that include the Value R_{max} find the smallest domain. Call the Variable of this domain A_{min} (for activity with minimal number of possible Resources).
3. Assign R_{max} to A_{min}.

The above ordering heuristic is obviously a mixture of Variable and Value orderings. It also incorporates the *intrinsic meaning of Variables and Values* in an ETP. In a typical nurses timetabling problem, higher qualified nurses can in principle be assigned to all kinds of roles and certain roles need higher qualified nurses assigned to them than other roles. This is generic in many working places: Different (but hierarchical) qualifications to employees and different levels of need for different activities (i.e. roles). This necessarily creates the structure that is utilized by the above ordering heuristic, that takes into account the *demand for resources* (e.g. the higher types of nurses).

Finite-capacity and fair-distribution constraints The family of non binary "finite capacity" constraints relate to common working hours constraints and are represented explicitly by counters. Typical examples are the following:

- Limits on number of working hours of employees per day/week/month.
- Limits on number of special assignments (like night shifts), per employee.
- Limits on the *distribution* of assignments over time, for each employee.

The only additional data structure that is needed is a *counter for each finite-capacity constraint*. The ordering heuristics for the explicit non binary constraints are very intuitive. If a counter has a limit of n and it's current value is k, then it is $\frac{k}{n}$ full. This index orders values (i.e. employees) for assignment. This is an explicit realization of the "most constrained first" principle, applied to values in non binary constraints.

Propagation of non binary constraints Even though *finite capacity* constraints are non binary, their propagation is intuitively clear. Using the non binary representation of counters, the constraints are not propagated at all until a counter is full and when it is full, the value is erased from all the activities that are constrained by the non binary constraint. There is also an intuitive simple method of propagating global constraints of the *fair distribution* type. It is quite similar to the erasing of Values from domains of constrained activities that is performed for full counters. Here, the counters that are full (out of the array of constrained distribution) are propagated to their set of activities independently of the other, non full, counters.

Backtracking by exchanging resources A particularly suitable backtracking mechanism for problems of Employee timetabling (and resource allocation in general) is to perform an exchanges of resources between competing activities in case of deadend. This type of a backtracking mechanism, that consists of *exchanging resources among assigned and unassigned activities* whenever encountering a deadend in the search, has been described in detail in several former publications of the present authors (cf. [9, 10]). In a typical ETP assignment process, the arrival at a deadend (and the need to backtrack) arises from failure to locate an employee to assign to the next activity. The need to backtrack (i.e. to *deassign a formerly assigned employee*) is clear.

Ordering of constraint checking Solving the complex ETPs that arise in the real world needs the use (and processing) of non binary complex constraints, some of which are represented implicitly. This brings into the search procedure an additional set of entities that can benefit from ordering: the constraints that are being checked by the assignment process. Since many constraints are not binary, a simple count of 1's in the matrices representing them (as can be done for binary constraints) does not suffice for ordering heuristics. We have found in the past that the order of checking constraints is quite important for the search process (see [9]). One mechanism that we have found to be useful and is used in the mixed-mode approach to ETPs, is to order constraint checking by a *last failed - first checked* principle.

3.2 Knowledge-based processing

The knowledge-based part of processing includes assignment rules and structures for specifying preferences. Preferences can be specified and used for ordering several different entities. One important example is the set of preferences over some class of activities, such as preferring night-shifts to day-shifts. This imposes additional order on top of the order of activities by all of the explicit constraints. It is easy to specify such "order by preference" operations by using the additional fields in the description of activities, that are available for use with knowledge-based techniques. For the nurses timetabling example each nurse has a list of preferred shifts for each week. The nurses themselves have priorities for being assigned, that are attached by the scheduler (the head nurse) and are based on their relative importance or constrainedness.

Ordering the roles to be assigned in the processing of the problem and ordering the nurses to be assigned is composed of several parts. The constraint based part relates to domain sizes and to *demand* for certain types of nurses and/or individual nurses (see subsection 3.1). All of the personal constraints are accommodated by this constraint based ordering and this holds true for explicit non binary constraints (using the heuristics of subsection 3.1). However, the simplest way to accommodate the *preferences* of nurses is to assign an ordering index based on this special field and use it as part of the selection procedure, by assignment-rules (see section 4).

4   TORANIT - a software package for employee timetabling

In the last 3 years we have constructed a commercial software package for employee timetabling that is implemented in C and LPA Prolog on PCs, running under Microsoft Windows. The software package is called TORANIT for the Hebrew word TOR which is used for describing both queues and timetabling. TORANIT uses the mixed mode approach that is described in this paper to enable a user to define an ETP and to define the necessary parts of the solving strategy for it, which comply with the user's preferences and objectives. The use of a mixed mode approach is explicit in that the user defines assignment rules (out of a given library) and constraint rules (i.e. *implicit non binary constraints*). The explicit part of the constraint processing is based on the generic binary and finite-capacity constraints that the program extracts automatically from the problem definition.

The knowledge-based part of TORANIT includes a high level user interface by which the user can specify the problem characteristics, constraints and objectives in his or her own terms (see Figure 1 for typical windows for defining Employees and Shifts). The user can also encode a knowledge-based strategy for solving the problem, by constructing assignment-rules from a rich library of tokens. The high level user interface enables many forms of interactions with the data base of former instances of the same problem (i.e. former weeks or months). It provides a library of rules that code many common objectives of employee timetabling and many common constraints. In short, the user interface includes much knowledge accumulated over the years about defining ETPs and about the different strategies of performing assignments so that certain objectives are better achieved.

The result of the combination of assignment rules and explicit ordering heuristics is that search is not exhaustive in TORANIT and so enables a fast cycle of feedback for solving complicated ETPs. It enhances greatly the process of knowledge acquisition, both for the definition of the problem and it's objectives and for the extraction of strategies for achieving some of the global objectives of the problem.

4.1   Structure of the Allocation Engine (AE)

The Allocation Engine (AE) of TORANIT is the implementation of the mixed-mode, non exhaustive search and assignment mechanism that was described

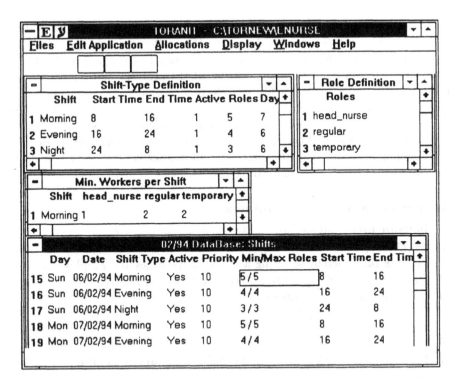

Fig. 1. A Typical Window of Toranit's User Interface: Definitions and Data base of Shifts

in section 3. It uses built-in data structures and propagation mechanisms for generic ETP constraints such as time-overlap of shifts, double role, or limits on consecutive assigned shifts per employee. The AE uses constraints propagation and updates lists such as: bad-shifts or not-available-shifts after each allocation. The lists of roles/shifts and employees to be assigned to these shifts are reordered at several points in the assignment process. These orderings are based on the constraints of the problem at hand and use the generic heuristics of section 2

The use of contexts The top level control of the AE's search and assignment procedure is implemented in the form of *contexts*. There are three built-in contexts: *Initial, Allocation, and Exchange*. Each context has a list of relevant rules. The purpose of each of these contexts is as follows. The Initial context uses employees preferences in it's ordering mechanism for employees. The *Allocation* context is the main context in which assignments are done. In the *Allocation* context the mixture of knowledge-based rules, fair-distribution rules and constraint-based heuristics that are described in section 3 are used for ordering shifts and employees for assignment and preferences are ignored. If all assignment rules are fired (and all selection done) in context *Allocation* and the assignment process is not complete, the *Exchange* context is entered. In the *Exchange* context resources (employees) are exchanged between different assignments. A series of transactions is performed, in each transaction only one (assigned) employee is exchanged for unassigned shifts. The order of exchanges is based on constraint-based attributes of the entities of the problem and on the state of partial allocation. Exchange rules, for selecting classes of unassigned shifts and employees, can be user defined. In principle each context can have a different set of constraints (i.e. different *implicit* constraint rules). This enables the relaxation of some global constraints that are expressed by constraint rules, while maintaining all of the explicit constraints automatically. The default mode has the same set of constraints in all three contexts.

Assignment procedure control flow

1. Initialize lists of all entities.
2. Select Assignment Rule.
3. Fire the rule, thereby selecting a set of Shifts/Roles and Employees.
4. Order the selected classes by the rule and by constraint-based heuristics.
5. For each possible assignment:
   Check validity of explicit constraints; Check validity of user-implicit constraints.
6. Perform all valid assignments.
7. Propagate the explicit constraints of the assignments to all relevant Shifts and Employees.
8. If there are no more unfired rules and there are unassigned Roles/Shifts, then change Context to Exchange (i.e. Backtrack).

The above control scheme leaves out many important details. One such detail concerns the order of choice of shifts and employees and the dynamic updating of constraints and propagation. All of these are user defined in TORANIT and are part of the configuration of each specific ETP and the user's knowledge about it's behavior. A major point that will not be discussed here is the interaction of the user with the assignment process. The control flow of the assignment procedure includes a preferred slot for user intervention. During any stage of the assignment process the user can change any of the assignments that are valid at that state, add assignments, delete assignments, etc. TORANIT's allocation engine enables these operations through the user interface and updates it's internal assignment state accordingly. This is achieved by the use of a default form of presentation which is called Allocation_Table (AT). The columns of the AT are the lowest-level time_periods, with higher-level periods as headers, and the rows of the AT are the hierarchy of shifts and roles. The entries in the table are names of assigned workers (see Figure 2). There are many other alternative tables for displaying the assignment information.

5 Exploring realistic ETPs

In order to be able to asses the complexity and behavior of typical ETPs we follow the example family of problems of this paper. This is a problem that

Day	6/2	7/2	8/2	9/2	10/2	11/2
Shift	Sun	Mon	Tue	Wed	Thu	Fri

Allocation Table (06/02/94-12/02/94)

		6/2 Sun	7/2 Mon	8/2 Tue	9/2 Wed	10/2 Thu	11/2 Fri
Morning	head_nurse	Amanda	Qian_N	Caren	Henia	Qian_N	Miriam	Henia
	regular	Glynn Francis	Francis Glynn	Edna Barbara	Francis Barbara	Ohana_N Rina	Laura Joan	Laura Joan
	temporary	Ohana_N Simonne_N	Nurith Irena	Francis Simonne_N	Diana Irena	Simonne_N Tina	Irena Tina	Diana Tina
Evening	head_nurse	Caren	Miriam	Qian_N	Caren	Henia	—	Miriam
	regular	Rina	Ohana_N	Laura	Laura	Barbara	—	Rina
	temporary	Karen Diana	Diana Karen	Philis_N Nurith	Nurith Karen	Karen Nurith	—	Simonne_ Irena
Night	head_nurse	Henia	Amanda	Miriam	Miriam	Caren	—	Caren
	regular	Edna	Henia	Rina	Edna	Edna	—	Glynn
	temporary	Philis_N	Joan	Tina	Joan	Philis_N	—	Philis_N

Fig. 2. Interacting with the Allocation process by a tabular interface

is solved routinely with TORANIT on a weekly basis in several departments of a large hospital. In the real world examples there are 14- 18 nurses of three hierarchical types to be timetabled and 60 weekly roles, belonging to 20 different shifts, each needing a different number of nurses of the three Types. Timetables are typically weekly and have a shift structure that varies over the days of the week (mainly changing in weekends). It is of interest to cast this problem in standard constraint network format and analyze the behavior of the network representing it.

Using the individual roles of the daily and weekly shifts as variables of the constraint network (CN), the number of variables is in the range of 60 - 100 and the domain of each variable is composed of nurses that are "assignable" to that Role/Shift. Domains are therefore of sizes that vary between 6 and 16. Variables that overlap in time are constrained to have non equal assignments (i.e. *mutual exclusion*) and these sets of overlapping variables (which form complete subnets) are of sizes between 3 to 5. Taking other binary constraints of the *mutual exclusion* type into account (such as forbidden *consecutive shifts* for all employees) the sets of mutually exclusive variables can go up to 8 in size. The constraint network that results from this ETP is non standard for CSP experimental papers in two major features. It has domains of variable of varying sizes and it includes several explicit non binary constraints.

The process of exploration of the ETP family of problems *starts from a definition of the ETP parameters*, the number of roles (variables), nurses (values) and an average number of unary (i.e. personal) constraints, that define the distribution of domain sizes. Adding mutual exclusion binary constraints of overlapping roles, a binary network representation is created for a variety of nurses timetabling problems. To this binary constraint network the typical finite capacity (non binary) constraints are added. The parameters that typically represent binary constraint networks in standard CSP experiments are then *measured* for the ETP.

One typical feature that can be measured on the network that is generated by the nurses ETP, is the probability of having a pair of variables connected by a constraint (p_1 in [7] for example). For the binary part of the nurses timetabling problem the typical value of p_1 is 0.10 which is a relatively sparse network. Another measure of constrainedness which is standard in random CSP tests is the average fraction of conflicts, out of all binary constraints (p_2 in [7]). The value of p_2 for the binary part of the Nurses timetabling problem is 2-4%, which is quite low. The generic finite capacity constraints generate conflicts during the run of the search process. Accumulating the average number of conflicts of the non binary constraints, during the assignment process, generates a new measure of the difficulty of the constraint network. We denote the fraction of conflicts, out of all non binary constraint checks, by p_3. Counting these finite capacity conflicts and averaging over many runs of the real world problem results in values of p_3 (for the Nurses timetabling problem) in the range of 20 - 70%. Another non standard parameter of these ETP CNs is the average size of domain sizes, expressed as a fraction of the total number of nurses and denoted $< r >$.

The constraint network of the Nurses' assignment problem was tested with several ordering and backtracking techniques that have been found to be very successful on random binary CNs [7] and the results of some preliminary runs are presented in Table 1. Only Back Jump and Forward Checking performed well enough to solve the problems in reasonable times. The last column of Table 1 presents the relevant processing times of TORANIT, for the equivalent problems. Note that the probabilities p_3 are *calculated* on the fly for the random Nurse problems. These probabilities, of failing non binary constraints, differ in different search strategies on the same problem. The family of randomly generated nurse timetabling problems has an equivalent value of $p_1 = 0.10$ and $p_2 = 0.04$. The average percentage of non binary constraint violations per run, p_3, is given in the third column of the table. The real parameters of the problem generator include the number of nurses, that is given in the first column of Table 1. All runs used the greedy mosy constrained first ordering heuristics and the initials BJ and FC (for search strategy) have their standard meaning - Back Jump and Forward Checking, respectively. The FC search strategy was implemented to include additional parts for treating finite capacity constraints, as described in section 3

Table 1 presents three set of runs on three different problems. The first one (19 nurses) is relatively difficult, the second one (14 nurses) is quite easy, and the third one (13 nurses) is over-constrained and has really no solution. In all three experiments Toranit has enforced more global constraints than the corresponding CSP method, and also run on a slower machine. Nevertheless, the results show the advantage of using Toranit in case of relatively hard and overconstrained problems over the CSP techniques which cause considerable amount of constraint checks and backtracking in these cases. This clearly demonstrates the advantages of the Mixed-mode approach.

It is important to note that the results of Table 1 are a lower bound on the real difficulty of the constraint networks of the Nurses timetabling problems we are exploring. The reason is that the finite capacity constraint are processed in the form of counters. This representational form is much simpler than the full binary form and leads to much smaller equivalent values of both p_1 and p_2. The non binary part of the constraint network can also explain the existence of difficult problems for relatively small values of the binary parameters. If the parameter p_3 would be taken face value, for example, then the values of p_1, p_2 would grow to approximately 0.15 and 0.3 respectively, for the 19 nurses run in the first line of Table 1.

No. of Nurses	p_3	$< r >$	Search Strategy	Cons.-Chcks (Binary)	Run Time CPU Sec.	TORANIT's run-time	TORANIT' non-bin Chcks
19	0.47	0.50	BJ	2,232,543	78.60	15.0	483
19	0.20	0.50	FC	297,357	44.09		
14	0.45	0.49	BJ	76,276	4.85	19.0	296
14	0.17	0.49	FC	6,891	4.0		
13	0.55	0.48	BJ	131,781,068	1087.2	23.0	198
13	0.10	0.48	FC	8,508,214	946.4		

Table 1. *Parameters of search on the Nurse Timetabling problem network*

6 Conclusions

Employee timetabling problems span a wide range of constraints, from binary to global. One part of the proposed mixed mode representation and processing for ETPs represents important families of generic non binary constraints in non standard explicit form. The non binary constraints and the variable sizes of domains create a constraint network that is interesting to explore experimentally, because it is different than random CNs in the CSP literature. Our preliminary results show that the explicit representation of finite capacity constraints, in the form of counters, and the ordering heuristics that were proposed in the present investigation are efficient in processing the complex networks of ETPs.

The major issues that need further investigation, to enable better use of the mixed mode approach and the construction of better selection mechanisms are the following:

- More complete exploration of the constraint networks of ETPs is needed, especially the creation of good measures for the degree of constrainedness (or expected difficulty) of the non binary part of these networks.
- The constraint-based part of processing of ETP constraint networks needs techniques for recognizing overconstrained problems and for fast recognition of deadends.
- The generic non binary constraints for employee timetabling and resource allocation problems (RAP) need more investigation. Some work is being done on this topic by several groups of investigators [3, 1].

Acknowledgement: We would like to thank Natalia Liusternik for programming and running all of the ETP constraint networks and for letting us use her preliminary results ahead of her Master Thesis publication.

References

1. D. Banks, A. Meisels, and P. vanBeek. Timetabling constraint networks - representation and processing, 1995. Submitted to Workshop on AI and OR, January 1995.
2. B. Y. Choueiry and B. Faltings. Temporal abstractions and a partitioning heuristic for interactive resource allocation. In *Notes of Workshop on Knowledge-based Production Planning, Scheduling and Control, IJCAI-93*, pages 59–72, Chambery, France, 1993.
3. T. Dackie, J. Adhikary, D. R. Gaur, and K. Jackson. Backtrack-free search for resource allocation problems, 1995. Submitted to CONSTRAINT-95, January 1995.
4. R. Dechter and J. Pearl. Network-based heuristics for constraint satisfaction problems. *Artificial Intelligence*, 34:1–38, 1988.
5. M. C. Golumbic. Algorithmic aspects of perfect graphs. *Annals of Discrete Mathematics*, 21:301–323, 1984.
6. A. Meisels, J. El-Saana, and E. Gudes. Decomposing and solving timetabling constraint networks. *Submitted to The AI Jou.*, 1994.
7. P. Prosser. Hybrid algorithms for the constraint satisfaction problem. *Computational Intelligence*, 9:268–299, 1993.
8. F. Rossi, C. Petrie, and V. Dhar. On the equivalence of constraint satisfaction problems. In *Proceedings of the 9th European Conference on Artificial Intelligence*, pages 550–556, Stockholm, Sweden, 1990.
9. G. Solotorevsky, E. Gudes, and A. Meisels. Raps - a rule-based language for specifying resource allocation and time-tabling problems. *IEEE Trans. DKE*, 6:681–698, 1994.
10. G. Trzewik, E. Gudes, A. Meisels, and G. Solotorevsky. Traps - time dependent resource allocation language. In *Proceedings of the ECAI Workshop on Practical CSPs*, pages 65–72, Amsterdam, 1994.
11. E. Tsang. *Foundations of Constraint Satisfaction*. Academic Press, 1993.

Automated Time Table Generation Using Multiple Context Reasonig with Truth Maintenance

Vevek Ram
Department of Computer Science
University of Natal
Private Bag X01
Scottsville 3209
South Africa
e-mail: vevek@compnt.cs.unp.ac.za

Chris Scogings
Computer Science Department
Massey University - Albany
Private Bag 102-904
North Shore Mail Centre
New Zealand
e-mail: C.Scogings@massey.ac.nz

Abstract

This paper describes the application of multiple context reasoning and truth maintenance to the automated generation of timetables. The reasoning system used is made up of a rule-based problem-solver which makes inferences and an assumption-based truth maintenance system that maintains a record of the justification of these inferences. While this method has been used for scheduling and planning applications before, the intention in this research is to investigate the practical feasibility of the method on readily accessible hardware. Various implementation prototypes were constructed and tested on a subset of a University Timetabling problem and the results obtained are discussed.

1 Introduction

Traditional approaches to the automated generation of time tables have great difficulties in overcoming the large search spaces which are created as a result of the number of variables that need to be considered in such problems. The use of Artificial Intelligence techniques allows much of the search space to be reduced through the use of advanced knowledge representation schemes and more informed search methods [9]. The application described in this paper is an example of such a technique and uses multiple context reasoning with truth maintenance. The traditional method of inference in many Artificial Intelligence problem solvers is monotonic reasoning. This assumes that axioms do not change and that conclusions drawn from them are always true even if assumed facts are later found to be false. Problem solving in the real world is characterised by making assumptions about uncertain information all the time and retracting these as they are subsequently unfounded. Nonmonotonic reasoning handles uncertainty by making the most reasonable assumptions and reasoning as if these assumptions were true. If these assumptions are proved untrue at a later stage, both the assumptions and all conclusions dependent on them must be retracted. Nonmonotonic by itself, however, is not enough to preserve the truth [7] and the monitoring of assumptions and their validity or justification is done by what is generally known as a truth maintenance system [3]. The reasoning system used in the time tabling system is made up of a rule-based problem-solver which makes inferences and a truth maintenance system which maintains a record of the justification of these inferences. The particular form of truth maintenance that is used is based on the work of De Kleer [2] and known as Assumption-based Truth Maintenance (ATMS). In this form of reasoning or problem solving, a set of related facts and assumptions constitutes a context or world. If an additional piece of information needs to be added to the context, all possible assumptions will spawn as many new contexts. Each of these new contexts will differ by the different assumption of the last piece of information. The ATMS will destroy contexts which are inconsistent when exact information is received and assumptions are justified. Only contexts with justified assumptions (beliefs) are preserved. In the time tabling application, contexts are created for a given unit of teaching time which reflect all the venue and course assumptions made in that time unit. When a context is consistent, that is, there are no constraints violated, the next set of contexts are generated. Constraints are propagated across contexts and invalid contexts in which some constraint is violated are immediately discarded. The process of generating contexts ends when there are no more remaining teaching units, in this case, the end of a teaching session. The partial solutions represented by each context can be merged to form a complete solution or timetable. The following section describes the procedure.

2 Implementation

At the University on Natal, an average sized campus, there are typically 10 lecture periods in a day, 80 venues of different size and approximately 450 courses. Currently, there are only four classes of constraints. The first, venue constraints arise out of size, as some venues can only accommodate small classes, or out of a special need for equipment for experiments or video projection which some courses require and only a few of the venues provide. Time constraints concern the avoidance of simultaneous scheduling of lectures which students take concurrently such Mathematics 1, Physics1, Chemistry 1 etc and also the minimum time, in lecture periods and tutorials, which courses require every week in order to effectively cover the curriculum. Location constraints concern the physical distance separating venues and teaching departments. Lectures offered by a department should be held close to the department and students should not be required to spend more than 10 minutes commuting between venues in consecutive lecture periods. The final constraint concerns teaching departments and requires that no more than two courses offered by one department are simultaneously scheduled.

The performance of the ATMS was investigated in three different prototypes on a subset of the problem consisting of 20 venues and 100 courses. The first prototype was constructed within a commercial knowledge engineering environment, the second prototype consisted of a hybrid object and prolog environment, and the third was a partial parallel implementation of the second using two machines. Each of these is described in more detail below.

In the first implementation, in the KEE shell (IntelliCorp), the knowledge base of the system consists of objects for each entity in the environment and rules that prescribe the procedure used for scheduling. In this case, the objects are venues, courses and a timerecorder. Every object contains slots which are used to store attributes of the object. The venue object contains slots for the venue identifier, location, size and special facilities. The course object contains slots for the course identifier, level, number of periods required per week, teaching department and class size. All venue and course objects inherit attribute types, default values and other values from parent objects in the same class. Rules are used to guide the scheduling process. The following rule is an example

IF   (venue is vacant) and
           (course is not complete) and
           (course_size < venue_size)
THEN   (assign course to venue) and
           (update course) and
           (update venue)

The system uses such rules to assign courses to venues in a given lecture period which is recorded by the timerecorder object. If no constraint violations arise, such as one student assigned to two venues at the same time or three simultaneous lectures for the same department, then the contexts at this level are preserved and the timerecorder moves the process into the next lecture period for a new level of contexts to be generated. In the first lecture period for example, course1 is assigned to venue1, course2 to venue2, etc. This is the first context. Not all possible combinations need to be considered since only certain venues can hold the large groups and this reduces the number of combinations. Also, heuristic rules such as "choose the closest venue which is just large enough to hold a group" allow many of the combinations to be disregarded. Generating the first context without any inconsistencies is a fairly simple task. It is the second and subsequent generations of contexts that give rise to inconsistencies that need to be detected and pruned from the whole search space. For example, suppose that the scheduler fires a rule that assigns course c_i to venue v_i in period p_i and a contradiction arises out of the fact that course c_i is taken by the same group who take c_j which was scheduled in period p_{i-1} in a venue v_j which is too far. A chronological backtracker would attempt to assign another course to venue v_i since course was the last choice made. While this may remove the contradiction, the problem solver loses the fact that the contradiction arose out of the venue choice rather than out of the course choice. Further, backtracking to the course choice node merely postpones the task of assigning c_i to a venue and which may lead to the same contradiction. The ATMS however, detects that the inconsistency in the context arises out of the venue choice and marks this context and all others which would generate the same inconsistency as invalid. Contexts are created until there are no lecture periods remaining. The chains of contexts created at this terminating stage are all consistent and thus represent a valid timetable. Contexts that are marked as inconsistent can be examined to investigate the cause of the inconsistency and to identify the constraint violation.

In the second implementation, a combination of SmalltalkV and Prolog V (Digitalk) was used. This forms an integrated environment in which smalltalk objects and a prolog interpreter interact. This is particularly useful because a context can be an object and methods can be used to detect inconsistencies and inheritance mechanisms can enable the automatic pruning of nogood objects. The same objects and slots as used in the first implementation were used and prolog rules were used to guide the process. In this environment, it is possible to send smalltalk messages from a prolog predicate and unify the results with prolog variables. Smalltalk object methods can be used to send clauses and queries to the prolog inference engine. This system was run on a 33MHZ 486 SX workstation.

In the third implementation, two separate identical personal workstations were used. One machine performed all the truth maintenance functions and the other performed the inferencing. Low level memory resident routines accessing the Novell LAN protocol were used on both machines as the basis for message handling and communication.

3 Discussion

The first and second implementations of the system were similar except that much of the TMS bookkeeping was handled intrinsically by the environment in the first. In fact, the only reason for constructing the second was to investigate the efficiency of the reasoning process without the overhead incurred by a large environment such as KEE. However, the additional programming required to maintain nogood environments and to update labels reduced the effectiveness of this approach. There is a difference in the approach that commercial programming shells use to implement truth maintenance and its original intended form [5],[10]. The use of state variables, explicit context generation and the recording of justifications are some examples of this difference. The main advantage of using such an environment is in the interactivity that it offers together with the facility to browse visually through contexts and examine them. The interactivity enables the user to simultaneously view two inconsistent contexts and relax some or other soft constraint in order for the problem solving to continue in a more promising direction. Also, since assumptions are the dominant representational mode, it is easy to compare sets of assumptions and to find the datum with the most or least assumptions.

The dual machine implementation was an attempt at increasing speed and efficiency. Sequential implementations are degraded severely by the addition of new assumptions and the generations of new contexts because most of the computational effort is spent on performing set unions and subset tests. In the parallel system, the nogood database is held and updated by a dedicated machine which also computes labels for every node generated by the problem solver. While real parallelism is not feasible, the inference mechanism can begin the generation of a new context (rule matching and firing etc) while the labels are being updated. Some waiting is inevitable but there is a considerable increase in efficiency. On a much larger scale, De Kleer suggests that the ATMS lends itself to parallelism if one considers that a separate processor could easily be assigned a single consistent viewpoint of the global problem [2].

The efficiency of an ATMS depends directly on the type of problem it is used to solve. Since it avoids all dependency directed backtracking and context switching, it is most suitable to problems with many solutions of which all are required. In the case of timetabling, this would be appropriate if all possible timetables were generated and some other method used to determine the optimal. If just a single valid timetable is required, other heuristic search methods would be more efficient, provided the level of dependency directed backtracking required remains relatively low. Label updating is the largest contributor to inefficiency in an ATMS and even though label update algorithms can be made extremely efficient, the size of the node labels remains a problem. Although some attention has been focused on the prevention of label explosion, [1][4], this is still a promising research area for improving efficiency. Theoretically, the efficiency of the ATMS is proportional to the number of environments that need to be considered but it is extremely rare that in a practical situation this actually occurs. Since timetabling applications do not share the temporal urgency of other similar applications like reactive scheduling, efficiency should not be a primary issue.

4 Conclusion

There are very definitive benefits that accrue from using a truth maintenance system [2],[6]. Although the addition of the truth maintenance to a problem solver does slow it down initially, it is not significantly slower than other pure search methods and offers a degree of interactivity from which can be gained useful insight into the nature and structure of the problem. Truth maintenance systems are extremely effective in reducing large search spaces, and is particularly useful when the rate of assumption changes is high, such as in time-tabling. The main deterrent of using an ATMS in time-tabling and scheduling problems generally is the overhead of computing and propagating labels. The high level of backtracking required in such problems however, makes it attractive. The advantage of the ATMS approach is primarily the possibility to work with inconsistent information and the avoidance of any form of expensive backtracking including dependency directed backtracking. There is no need for global constraint satisfaction and multiple contradictory solutions may exist and be compared. The initial cost of the approach is extracted early by making the initial propagation of an assumption more expensive because of label updating and updating the nogood database and in spite of De Kleer's assurance that the ATMS is practical even with 1000 assumptions (space size of 2^{1000}) [2], significant reductions in efficiency are evident with 20 contexts on a modest machine (33Mhz 486 workstation). Three prototype systems were developed to test the feasibility of this method. Of the three prototypes tested, the commercial knowledge engineering environment (KEE) was the slowest but offered the most facilities for the user to influence the problem solving process. Other commercial environments which also offer nonmonotonic reasoning with truth maintenance are available. A list and description of some of these may be found in [10]. The custom written systems can generate improvements in efficiency but are very rigid and cannot be used in other applications readily (planning for example). Further, if complex user interfaces and interactivity are to be added, this would slow these systems significantly. The partial parallel method showed the most promise as far as speed is concerned and it is intended that this is investigated further on truly parallel hardware.

References

1. Collins, J., and Decoste, D., CATMS: A ATMS which avoids label explosion, Proceedings of AAAI-91, 1991.

2. De Kleer, J., An Assumption Based Truth Maintenance System, Artificial Intelligence, Vol 28, No 2, March 1986, pp 127-162.

3. Doyle, J., A Truth Maintenance System, Artificial Intelligence, Vol 12, No 3, November 1979, pp 231-272.

4. Dressler, O., and Farquhar, A., Putting the Problem Solver back in the driver's seat: Contextual Control of the ATMS, Proceedings of the 2nd AAAI Workshop on Model-Based Reasoning, 1990, pp 106-112.

5. Filman, R., Reasoning with Worlds and Truth Maintenance, CACM, Vol 31, No 4, April 1988, pp 382-401.

6. Forbus, KD and De Kleer, J., Building Problem Solvers, MIT Press, Mass, 1993.

7. Kimborough, S.O. and Adams, F., Why Nonmonotonic Logic, Decision Support Systems, Vol 4, 1988, pp 111-127.

8. Martins, J., The Truth, the Whole Truth and Nothing But the Truth, AI Magazine, Vol 11, No 5, January 1991, pp 7-25.

9. Noronha, S.J. and Sarma, V.V.S., Knowledge-Based Approaches for Scheduling Problems: A Survey, IEEE Trans on Knowledge and Data Engineering, Vol 3, No 2, 1991, pp 160-171.

10. Stanojevic, M. et al, Using Truth Maintenance Systems, IEEE Expert, December 1994, pp 46-56.

Investigations of a Constraint Logic Programming Approach to University Timetabling

Czarina Cheng
Le Kang
Norrus Leung
George M. White

Computer Science Dept.
University of Ottawa,
Ottawa, K1N 6N5,
Canada

white@csi.uottawa.ca

ABSTRACT

The casting of university timetables is a problem which combines classical numerical scheduling techniques with important human considerations. It will be argued here that since the application involves the preferences of humans, the problem is qualitatively different than similar problems involving inanimate objects. The humane and profane facets are combined in this study by using the constraint logic programming approach. The constraints are hierarchical: the primary constraints are rigidly enforced and the secondary constraints are relaxed according to their priority if a solution cannot be found. We present a solution based on a Prolog description of the constraints and goals. Two working implementations are described, one using an IBM mainframe and one using a personal computer. Tests with synthetic data and real data from a university have shown that good timetables can be cast using this method in a reasonable amount of time.

1. Introduction

The casting of timetables is an activity which has been the source of a great deal of theoretical and practical work. Since the partitioning of resources among a set of competing processes is a universal problem arising in many different arenas, solutions to this problem are of interest in other domains.

One specialized area is the casting of *school* or *university* timetables *i.e.* finding suitable times and places for professors and students to meet for lectures, laboratories and other academic activities. This area is interesting because the problems are challenging, the results are immediately applicable and data is close at hand.[5, 11, 17, 23, 25, 26, 28, 29, 35]

The limited number of human and material resources available and the restrictions of use placed upon them means that the timetables have to be constrained so that certain conditions are met. Some of the constraints are absolute while others are relative, *i.e.* some constraints *must* always hold while others may be relaxed, if necessary, in order to cast the schedule.

The fact that humans, both students and teachers, are integral parts of the problem leads to the conclusion that the university timetabling problem is qualitatively different from other superficially similar types of timetabling and related problems such as stock-cutting[12] and decryption.[19] It also precludes the use of global optimization methods which may well lead to the "best" use of the resources available as calculated over some synthetic metric but at the cost of severely inconveniencing the personnel involved. It is the human consideration that has led to the approach that was adopted here. It is easier to incorporate human preferences into the formulation of the classical timetabling problem via the constrained logic approach than it is by most other methods. Thus considerations such as "classes should be scheduled only when their teachers are available" and "classes should be scheduled close to their home departments", constraints (7) and (13) of section 4, are easily incorporated into the problem, using the same formulation as that for the common numerical constraints such as no student can take two courses at the same time.

In addition, the constraint satisfaction approach permits the problem specification to be easily changed when constraints are added, removed or modified and allows easy portability among different institutions having different constraint sets.

The vocabulary of educational timetabling is fairly standard, at least within the English speaking world. Unfortunately the words used have ambiguous meanings, causing great confusion when scheduling matters are discussed. To clarify matters, a number of these words are defined below.

Rooms are places where teaching is done. Rooms have certain seating capacities which can be defined in a number of ways. They range from large amphitheatres to small seminar rooms. The rooms may have special furniture in them such as lab benches or pianos, obviously essential for chemistry labs or music lessons. In other cases furniture type is not important and all that is required is a regular lecture hall where everyone can sit down.

Time slots are the quanta of time into which the 24 hour day is divided. There is a great variety of ways in which this can be done. Often the day is divided into time slots of 1 hour each. The day starts in the morning at 8 or 9 am, ends at night at 10 pm and consists of 14 or 13 time slots of 1 hour in length. Often the time slot has a duration of 1.5 hours, 2 hours or 3 hours. The *repetition period* for timetables in usually a week, with successive weeks following each other for perhaps 3 months. Sometimes the repetition period lasts three days or two weeks. The timetable will not change during this repetition period.

A *course* is a body of subject matter which is taught by one or more teachers to one or more students in a room during one or more time slots. Courses usually have names and course codes such as "Introduction to Computing I, CSI1100". Often a single course is split into two or more parallel sections, distinguished from each other by a section letter. Thus CSI1100A and CSI1100B are two sections of the same course. The various sections are concerned with the same subject matter but the material is taught to different groups of students. Two or more sections may or may not have the same teacher but they do not have any students in common. Occasionally a course has more than one course code which enables administrators to refer to it in more than one way. All the sections of a course usually write a common examination. A course is taught at a rate of so many hours per week, three hours per week being very common. Such a course may occupy 3 time slots of 1 hour's length, 2 time slots of 1.5 hour's length or 1 time slot of 3 hour's length. Other divisions are possible as well and the length of the time slots used can be mixed according to the wishes of the institution. The exact format of the time slots used and the reasons for its choice are a matter of great concern in academic circles.

The *format* of a course's time slots is the pattern of the time slots over the days and hours of the timetable. A course requiring 3 hours per week may be taught in three time slots of one hour's length, each beginning at 9 am on Mondays, Wednesdays and Fridays. Another possibility is 8:30 on Monday, 10:30 on Tuesday and 9:30 on Thursday. Each of these patterns is a format. Often formats are required to lie completely in the morning or completely in the evening. Some commonly used formats can be found in[5, 11, 25]

A *program* of studies is a set of courses which students must follow. This program is broken down chronologically into *years* and *terms*. Students enrolled in Computer Science begin their studies by taking a certain set of courses offered in the Fall term. This is followed by another set of courses in the Winter term and so on for four complete years. The program for these first year students in the Fall session is a logically complete unit. However, this does not imply that this program is completely independent of other programs. Students have certain common required courses shared with students in other programs and certain other courses which they alone must take. These course requirements that spread across a number of different programs cause the greatest problems in the casting of the timetables.

Different institutions vary tremendously in programs, courses and formats. They differ also in the requirements that they impose on these items. This is the major cause of difficulty in using machine generated solutions in different institutions.

2. Problem Definition

Many techniques have been brought to bear on the timetabling problem but there are no generally accepted solutions in existence yet. Far more success has been obtained for various subsets, notably the *examination scheduling* problem.[2, 8, 18, 32, 33] and the *classroom assignment* problem.[9] The difficulty of casting timetables is complicated by the inherent complexity of the problem which is known to be NP-hard.[10] Solutions can involve thousands of values of 3 or more variables.

The university timetabling problem can be expressed as follows:

Let there be m time periods, $k = 1..m$; n_2 teachers, $j = 1..n_2$; n_1 classes, $i = 1..n_1$; and n_r rooms, $l = 1..n_r$. There is a requirements matrix $R = (r_{ij})$ and two vectors. E is an n_1-vector whose ith element is the enrollment in class i and C is an n_r-vector whose ith element gives the capacity of room i. Find a function

$$S = \{ x_{ijkl} \}: \{1..m\} \times \{1..n_1\} \times \{1..n_2\} \times \{1..n_r\} \rightarrow \{0,1\}$$

where $x_{ijkl} = 1$ iff teacher j meets class i in room l during period k such that:

$$\sum_l \sum_k x_{ijkl} = r_{ij} \tag{1}$$

$$\sum_j x_{ijkl} \leq 1 \tag{2}$$

$$\sum_i x_{ijkl} \leq 1 \tag{3}$$

$$\sum_l x_{ijkl} \leq 1 \tag{4}$$

$$\sum_j \sum_k e_i \, x_{ijkl} \leq \sum_j \sum_k C_l \, x_{ijkl} \tag{5}$$

(1) requires that the number of meetings of class i and teacher j conforms to the specifications of the requirements matrix;
(2) specifies that each period-class-room has at most one teacher involved;
(3) specifies that each teacher-period-room has at most one class in it;
(4) specifies that each teacher-period-class occupies at most one room;
(5) specifies that all rooms are large enough to contain the classes scheduled into them.

Any particular institution will likely have other requirements in addition to these basic ones. This is discussed in section 4.

3. Approaches

This problem has been studied for a long time, primarily by university based researchers and education administrators because the problem arises constantly and data is readily available. The solutions obtained to date have not been entirely satisfactory due to the complexity of the problem. To obtain a usable solution, researchers have generally had to simplify the problem, often to the point where the solved problem bears little resemblance to the real-life situation that originally spawned it. Several different approaches have been used to formulate solutions. A bibliography of some past explorations can be found in the review by Schmidt and Ströhlein.[26] Some of the approaches to solving the timetabling problem are discussed below.

The celebrated *graph colouring problem* requires that the nodes of a graph be coloured in such a way that no two adjacent nodes, *i.e.* those connected by an edge, have the same colour. The problem requires that the minimum number of colours be used. By identifying each of the nodes with a course and each pair of courses taken by a student as an edge, the minimum number of colours corresponds to the minimum number of periods required to timetable the courses. This problem has been studied both in its own right and because of its application to the timetabling problem.[4, 6, 13, 24, 33]

The timetabling problem considered as a problem of reducing the number of constraint violations becomes an *optimization problem*. Unfortunately a large number of variables and constraints are required in the description of realistic problems and this can cause the solution space to become unmanageably large. However several models have been studied and some good results have been obtained.[9, 15, 22, 27]

In the *interactive approach*, a semi-automated algorithm accepts data incrementally from an operator and builds a timetable piece by piece. Systems can be equivalent to electronic spreadsheets[29] or have some intelligence built in.[34] There are several methods in common use which do not use computers at all but rely entirely on humans with great stamina and long pencils.[5, 20, 28]

A new approach which has only recently been applied to the timetabling problem is that of *simulated annealing*, based on a Monte Carlo scheme. Courses are placed in the timetable at random and an initial cost is calculated for this initial placement. Random subsets of courses are then randomly re-arranged and for each new placement, a new value of the cost function is calculated. If the new cost is lower, the new placement is kept. If the new cost is higher, the new placement may still be kept based on chance and the value of the so-called temperature. The process continues with progressively lower values of temperature until either the cost is reduced to zero or a certain limiting number of iterations is reached.[1]

Another recent innovation is the use of the so-called *TABU* search family of algorithms.[16] An initial solution which may or may not satisfy all the constraints is formulated as the starting case and the initial value of an objective function is calculated. Values of the variables are changed and new values of the objective function are calculated. These iterations are halted when some stopping criterion is met. During the iterations, trial solutions which violate some of the constraints are encountered but provisionally accepted. Values of the variables are then changed in the hope that the new values will bring the solution back into the feasible region within a small number of iterations.

The *agent based* class of algorithms models human agents and attempts to mimic the procedures used by human beings, possibly using some of the strategies outlined above.[36] Very little is known presently about the quality of results generated by these procedures.

4. Constraint Logic Programming

Constraint programming is a relative newcomer to the area of timetabling although some work has been done in related areas by Carmel and Itzovitz[7] whose Comprehensive University Planner (CUP) is designed to support all administrative activities related to a university teaching system. As well, Feldman and Golumbic[14] have reported on a project of using constraint satisfaction algorithms for interactive student scheduling. The project was to determine which algorithms perform best in solving the student scheduling problem and under what conditions. They concluded that the order in which the variables were assigned values significantly affects the performance of the algorithms. After testing three algorithms, regular backtracking, forward checking and word-wise forward checking, they concluded that with large numbers of courses the word-wise algorithm was clearly better than the others, with regular backtracking the worst.

Yoshikawa *et al.*[37] have investigated the related problem of timetabling high schools using a general purpose constraint relaxation problem solver called COAS-TOOL. The method used was to create an internal relaxation assignment using the Really-Full-Lookahead Greedy (RFLG) algorithm, followed by a strongly biased optimization algorithm, the Min-Conflicts Hill-Climbing (MCHC) algorithm described by Minton *et al.*[21] These tools and techniques successfully produced timetables in three cases that were studied. The execution time reported varied between 26.2 minutes to 2.8 hours and the authors observed that the solution occasionally fell into an unacceptable local optimum. Otherwise the results were acceptable.

These results, while interesting, are not directly comparable to the results reported here because our problem is larger and the constraint set is different, making the granularity of our problem considerably different from theirs. This illustrates one of the differences between secondary school and university scheduling. In the schools, a group of students, typically called a *class* stay together for the entire week. These classes can then be timetabled independently apart from room considerations.

The rule base forming the non-volatile constraints used by the program described in this paper is divided into those rules which *must* be satisfied and those which *may* be satisfied. Any timetables produced will always satisfy the primary constraints and as many secondary constraints as possible.

4.1. Primary Constraints

1) No two or more required courses of a student program can be scheduled at the same time.

2) No recommended optional course of a student program can be scheduled at the same time as any required course of the same student program.

3) No two or more courses taught by professor can be scheduled at the same time.

4) Day courses must be scheduled during the day and evening courses must be scheduled during the evening.

5) The classrooms assigned to courses must have capacities equal to or larger than the enrollments of the courses scheduled into them.

6) Classrooms must not be scheduled during those times they have been reserved for other uses.

7) Classes cannot be scheduled when their professors are unavailable.

8) Preassigned courses must be scheduled into their preassigned classrooms at their preassigned times. There are three different kinds of preassignment. The first case occurs when a course's teaching time and classroom are all fixed before the scheduling; these are completely preassigned courses. The second case occurs when only the teaching time of the course is fixed; these are called time-preassigned. The final case preassigns a certain classroom to a course.

9) Certain courses must be taught in the same classroom at the same time. This is required when a course has more than one course code, as happens sometimes when a course is taken by students from different departments or faculties.

10) Certain courses must overlap in their teaching times.

11) Certain courses should have exactly the same teaching time but different classrooms. This constraint and the one above can be used to enforce course prerequisites.

12) If a course is held more than once a week, there will always be at least one day between any two lectures of the course.

4.2. Secondary Constraints

The following list of constraints will be imposed if it is possible to do so. Some of these have been added for improving the resource utilization and some are present for improving students' course choice. If it proves impossible to create a schedule with all secondary constraints, they are relaxed in groups in order to decrease the program's run time.

13) Courses should be scheduled into classrooms in the buildings as close as possible to a designated building. The first attempt will be the preferred building. If this is infeasible, then the next and succeeding buildings will be tried until a success is found.

14) Courses should be scheduled into rooms of the specified type. The *type* property of a room has three parameters: class type, furniture type and seating type. Any or all of the types can be specified. The system will first try to find rooms satisfying all three arguments. If they cannot be found, rooms which satisfy room type and furniture will be sought. If this fails, rooms satisfying only room type will be sought. If this fails, the constraint is abandoned.

15) Courses should be scheduled into classrooms whose size is large enough (but not too large) to contain them. The classroom should be in the smallest size range possible. Note that this is not the same as constraint 5.

16) Recommended optional courses of a student program should be scheduled in such a way that there are the fewest time conflicts among them.

17) Courses should be scheduled into the time zone specified by the department or the professor. The time slots available for day courses are partitioned into three time zones, morning, noon and afternoon. While evening courses are always scheduled into the evening time zone, a day course should be scheduled into the prescribed day zone if possible.

18) Friday afternoon shall be used only after all other scheduling possibilities are exhausted.

19) A professor should have at least one time slot free between any two teaching time slots.

Some of the constraints are at least partially in conflict with one another. This is particularly true with constraints 13 and 15 which deal with geography and room size. Constraint 15 will attempt to put a class of students into a classroom just large enough to hold them. This leads to efficient use of classrooms but may require that students and professors do a lot of walking between classes to get to those classrooms. Constraint 13 will minimize the amount of transportation (at least for professors) but may lead to an inefficient use of classrooms.

An analysis of the University of Ottawa's classroom size distribution yields the values shown in figure 1. The *Range* is a code assigned to a particular range of room and course sizes. As in many institutions, the room size distribution does not correspond well with the observed distribution of course sizes.

Room Size Distribution		
Room Size	Range	Number of Rooms
1-10	1	9
11-18	3	17
19-30	5	44
31-50	7	31
51-70	9	35
71-100	11	18
101-150	13	4
151-200	15	5
201-300	17	2
>300	19	2

Fig. 1. Classroom Size Distribution

As a result, in order to schedule all the courses offered, smaller courses must be scheduled into larger classrooms. The permitted difference between room size and class size is specified by a *size limitator*. Each size range is associated with a size limitator whose value indicates the largest classrooms into which courses whose enrollments fall into the size range may be assigned. A course with enrollment R whose size limitator is L can only be scheduled into classrooms whose size is no larger than range $R + 2 \times L$. A typical size limitator table is shown in figure 2.

Size Limitators									
Range	1	3	5	7	9	11	13	15	17	19
Size Limitator	1	1	2	1	2	1	1	1	1	0

Fig. 2. Size Limitator Table

This size limitator instance gives a value of 1 to rooms in range 1, a value of 2 for rooms in range 5 and a value of 0 for rooms in range 19. The larger the value of the size limitator, the greater the "flexibility" in the placing of a class whose size is in the specified range. Those ranges where the mismatch between class size and room size is the greatest have the largest values of size limitator. The size limitator has to be tuned for each institution and year in order to yield an efficient utilization of rooms.

The 19 constraints listed above are written as the conjunction of sub-rules and typically have the form shown in figure 3.

These rules are interpreted by a modified Prolog backtracking algorithm based on depth first search. The classical method is not efficient enough for our purposes and modifications were necessary to find good solutions within a reasonable execution

time. After much experiment, it was concluded that the order in which constraints should be considered is the following:
- select a time block in the specified time zone
- select a classroom with the proper room type
- verify whether this time-classroom pair violates any constraints

No required courses of a program may be scheduled at the same time
for all i,j,k

$\text{no\_common\_member}(T_j, T_k) \leftarrow$
$\quad \text{is\_a\_member}(sp_i(s_1, s_2), S) \quad \textbf{and}$
$\quad \text{is\_a\_member}(c_j, s_1) \quad \textbf{and}$
$\quad \text{is\_a\_member}(c_k, s_1) \quad \textbf{and}$
$\quad c_j \neq c_k \quad \textbf{and}$
$\quad \text{teaching\_time}(c_j, T_j) \quad \textbf{and}$
$\quad \text{teaching\_time}(c_k, T_k)$
where $i = 1, \ldots, m \quad j = 1, \ldots, n \quad k = 1, \ldots, n$
where
T_i is the time slot of *course*$_i$
sp_i is the set of courses of the ith program
s_1 is a list of required courses
s_2 is a list of optional courses

Fig. 3. One of the Constraints

If no constraints are violated, the course is scheduled into that classroom during that time block. If not, backtracking is performed with different classrooms and different time blocks. It may happen that no solution can be found even after attempts using all suitable time blocks and classrooms. The secondary constraints have been arranged in a constraint hierarchy[3] and if a course cannot be timetabled, these constraints are relaxed one by one and a new attempt is made. The highest numbered constraint, number 19, is the first constraint to be relaxed *i.e.* has the lowest priority. The lowest numbered of the secondary constraints has the highest priority and is the last to be relaxed.

There is a possibility that even after all secondary constraints are relaxed, a course is still not scheduled. If this occurs, the program enters a procedure that we call *equivalent reversing*, or ER. When a course becomes unschedulable, the ER first chooses an equivalent course which has already been successfully scheduled. It then deletes the latter's assignments and tries to reschedule it after first scheduling the former. If the former cannot be scheduled after deleting the latter's assignments, the ER will replace the latter's assignments and choose another equivalent course and repeat the procedure. Equivalent courses are those which:
- have enrollments in the same size range
- are in the same time zone
- require the same room type and
- request the same building

To avoid long search paths, nested equivalent reversing is forbidden *i.e.* there is no invoking an equivalent reversal from within an equivalent reversal. In addition, the number of equivalent reversals that can be selected for any course has been limited to 4. Of course, assignments to completely prescheduled courses cannot be deleted. If the program cannot schedule a certain course even after the equivalent reversing procedure, it is placed in a list of unschedulable courses to be manually placed later. The goal is to minimize the number of elements in this list.

5. Information Management

The information that is considered at different stages of the problem comes from different sources and has different degrees of volatility.

Some of the knowledge, such as the room inventory which contains lists of all the rooms available along with their sizes and facilities such as furniture type, overhead projectors and handicap access etc., is relatively stable while other blocks of knowledge, such as professor-course pairs, student program lists and professor unavailability lists, are quite volatile and change greatly from year to year, often changing several times within the same year. All this knowledge must be used by the system and if any of it changes, the changes must be accommodated without destroying the parts of the solution which are satisfactory. This is done by the three stage system described in detail later. All the data are gathered during the first stage when the system knowledge is created in the most up-to-date form possible. The constraint program is used during the second stage, taking the knowledge prepared by the first stage. Changes in the knowledge base are treated in the third stage. The timetable prepared by the constraint program is modified incrementally by hand as changes in the knowledge base arrive, keeping the constraints satisfied. Thus when a new academic session starts, the new timetable can be used immediately because it reflects the latest changes known to it.

Another aspect is the distributed nature of the knowledge.[36] This distribution not only reflects the different resources of the various parts of the university but also incorporates their different world views of the situation. Some faculties take the position that all their staff are available for duty during the whole week while other faculties wish their staff to be able to concentrate their teaching into two or three days of the week, leaving the other days free for other activities. There are, therefore, relatively few "universal rules" which can be applied across the entire problem. This is further complicated by the fact that students must take courses from a spectrum of disciplines and are therefore subject to different rules at different times. This problem is tackled by partitioning the domains of knowledge into a number of disjoint subdomains, each one of which is sufficiently homogeneous to be described into a small number of rules. In some cases this is best handled by incorporating a list of exceptions into the knowledge base. Typically, this exception list consists of professors and the times they do not wish to teach and a list of rooms and the times they are unavailable.

At the University of Ottawa, information is captured by the chief timetabling officer and by departmental administrative personnel. In this first stage, volatile data concerning academic staff and student programs is entered in a human readable format using any available word processor, the only requirement being that ASCII output, with no embedded formatting commands, can be produced. This data must be independently verified to make sure it is correct. One recurring problem is the over-specification of courses. In the rule base, there is a rule which tries to make optional courses available to as many students as want to take them. These courses have a tendency to appear in the optional course lists of many different departments, making them difficult to schedule.

In the second stage, this information is transformed into Prolog predicates. These predicates are entered into the main inference engine to produce the timetable.

The third part of the system consists of a perturbation module which allows the chief timetabling officer to modify the timetable based on knowledge updates. This part is required because the timetable must be generated during the month of March for the academic sessions which begin in the following September and January. Much can happen in the intervening period but the constraint resolving part cannot be re-executed. Thus the timetable is continually updated as new information is produced, in such a way as to keep most of the timetable intact. The perturbations are introduced manually and verification with the existing constraints is done by hand.

In cases where important changes take place, *e.g.* a professor leaves the university or a building burns down, the program can be rerun keeping everything the same except for the new variable value causing the perturbation. This permits changing the classrooms while keeping the times for all the courses the same as they were. An academic unit which already has a satisfactory timetable can keep it from year to year while other units can change to adapt to their changing resources.

6. Implementations

Two implementations of this system currently exist. The older one runs on an IBM mainframe under VM/CMS. The knowledge base and inference engine are written in a variant of the prolog language, WPROLOG.[30]

When the data has been prepared and checked, the main WPROLOG engine accepts it and generates the timetable. The output of this process is then input to other modules which generate human readable timetables that can be distributed to students, professors, resource administrators and printed in the official university timetable book. The information is classified in a number of ways:

• by course
• by department
• by room
• by professor.
The output can also be downloaded to other programs for further processing, if desired.

A newer implementation uses a stand-alone PC platform. Development of this version has been done using a 33 MHz - 80486 chip, using MS-DOS version 5.0 and the ALS Prolog[31] system. The data is captured in the same format. The timetabling officers can use any editor they wish, provided that it can produce ASCII output. The data transformations, the main prolog engine and the final data formatting and printing are done on the same PC. The user controls the system via a windows-like user interface using pop-up menus and mouse clicks.

The input and output are identical for the two systems.

7. Sample Results

One of the system goals is to produce timetables that use resources efficiently. A measure of room utilization efficiency is the *average seating usage*, ASU. The ASU is equal to the mean percentage of classroom space occupied by students during those time slots when the classroom is used.

A set of test data used in the production of the time table by traditional means was used as input data. There were 2147 course entries with 155 preassignments included. The room inventory included 167 classrooms whose sizes ranged from 4 to 474. The size distribution of the enrollments of the courses is shown in figure 4 in terms of the range values defined in figure 1.

Distribution of Enrollment										
Range	1	3	5	7	9	11	13	15	17	19
Number of Entries	156	160	871	387	267	189	63	30	21	3

Fig. 4. Size Distribution of Course Enrollments

Using the size limitators of figure 2, the results shown in the second line of figure 5 were obtained. An additional test run with more data is summarized on the third line of figure 5. These figures were obtained with the mainframe implementation. Note that the value of ES in line 2 differs from the number of course entries because of course numbering duplication, the phenomenon described by constraint 9.

Test Results				
CPU(secs)	PE	ES	UE	ASU
1402	155	2113	0	80.2%
9394	155	2244	24	88.8%

where:
CPU(secs) - CPU time in seconds
PE - number of preassigned courses
ES - number of courses scheduled
UE - number of unscheduled courses
ASU - average seating usage

Fig. 5. Test Run Results

The values of the average seating usage, ASU, for various room size ranges are shown on the histogram of figure 6. The shaded bars are the values corresponding to the traditional manual system and the clear bars show the ASU for the computerized

124

system. It is interesting to see that although the computerized system was not designed to minimize the ASU, it did produce substantially better values than did the manual system. Furthermore, this was done while simultaneously enforcing the constraints imposed on the timetable, not all of which were satisfied when the manual system was used.

With the size limitator of figure 2, all the courses were scheduled. This, however, says nothing about the location of the rooms. In order to minimize the amount of transportation, the size limitators have to have values larger than the minimum required for a successful timetable yet be small enough to improve the existing measures of efficiency. The balance between space efficiency and minimum transportation is one of the factors which must be weighed by the system operators.

A second measure of room utilization efficiency is the *average room utilization*, ARU, of a room calculated by dividing the total number of hours in the week avail-

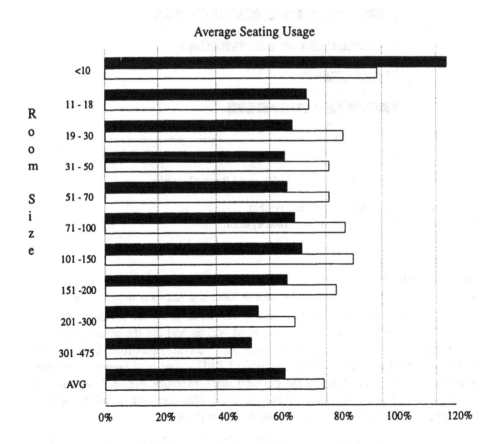

Fig. 6. Values of Average Seating Usage, ASU

Shaded bars are results with manual system.
Clear bars are results with computerized system.

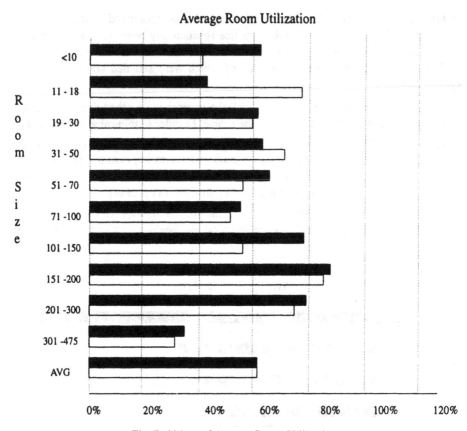

Fig. 7. Values of Average Room Utilization

Shaded bars are results with manual system.
Clear bars are results with computerized system.

able for use by the total number of hours in the week during which it was actually used. A histogram of these values for various room size ranges is shown in figure 7.

It can be observed that the manual system tends to use the smallest room size range more often than does the computerized version and use the next largest room size range less often than does the computerized version. Apart from this, the ARU values are about the same. This distribution of ARU values is of interest to planners who must make efficient use of the physical plant inventory. Figure 7 suggests that rooms in the capacity range 301 - 475 are used less often than others and that some of them might be converted into laboratories or offices if required.

One other timetable check that was made concerns the starting time of the courses. The manual method tends to schedule courses more heavily towards the early afternoon rather than in the early morning or late afternoon, reflecting the current professor preferences. One problem of computerized scheduling systems is that course starting times are weighted by the order in which the possible values are tried. This usually means that early mornings time slots will be more heavily used than the others since these time slots are tried first.

The inference engine used in this system chooses trial time slots according to a probability density function which approximates the one actually observed by the present manual system. Thus the distribution of course starting times is observed to be about the same in both the manual and the computerized versions.

8. Discussion

The system has been thoroughly tested with both artificial data and real data obtained from the university Registrar's office. Quantities of data representing departments, faculties and the entire university have been used to generate real timetables. In doing so, several additional problems had to be solved, in addition to the ones described earlier.

The manual timetabling method tolerated a number of different course formats. The traditional three hours per week was delivered as one 3 hour block, two 1½ hour blocks or three 1 hour blocks. Because other block formats were used by certain departments, a total of 15 different formats were identified in use at one place or another. In order to rationalize the use of classrooms a standard 1½ hour time slot is now used which can be doubled to make a single 3 hour time slot. A two hour time slot can be used if the professor wishes to begin at 8:00 in the morning. This will not interfere with the orderly allocation of 1½ hour time slots which begin at 8:30 am and continue throughout the day.

Another subtle but important aspect which must be considered is the political implication of the system. Unlike job shop scheduling, this program orders many aspects of the life of human beings. Fears of the "big brother" surface from time to time bedeviling relations between management and union, staff and timetabling officers, and humans and machines.

9. Conclusion

Our experience with these programs, spanning many years, leads us to conclude that:

1) All courses, both required and optional, of all programs in the university can be scheduled by machine with the resources available.
2) With the present room inventory, the size limitator can be adjusted such that all courses are scheduled without excessive movement between classes.
3) The number of recommended optional courses for students from different departments can been systematically increased. This was not generally attempted with the present manual system.

4) The former rate of seating usage, about 65%, has been increased to about 80%. Thus the efficiency of resource usage can be increased even while reducing movement between classes.

5) The large amounts of work required by the manual timetabling process can be greatly reduced.

6) The amount of CPU time used, less than 25 minutes for a typical run, is quite practical. It should be noted, however, that the time required may be increased by an order of magnitude as resources become scarce.

Work is continuing on improving rules corresponding to certain types of rather specialized requests made by the teaching staff and on improving the user interface.

10. Acknowledgements

We were greatly assisted in this work by the Registrar of the University of Ottawa, Mr. George H. von Schoenberg and by the timetabling officer, Ms. Pauline Bélanger. We wish to thank Prof. Clarence (Skip) Ellis for his hospitality at the University of Colorado during the drafting of this manuscript.

References

1. D. Abramson, "Constructing School Timetables Using Simulated Annealing: Sequential and Parallel Algorithms," *Management Science*, vol. 37, no. 1, pp. 98-113, Jan. 1991.

2. Nagraj Balakrishnan, Abilio Lucena, and Richard T. Wong, "Scheduling Examinations to Reduce Second-Order Conflicts," *Computers Ops. Res.*, vol. 19, no. 5, pp. 353-361, 1992.

3. Alan Borning, Bjorn Freeman-Benson, and Molly Wilson, "Constraint Hierarchies," *Lisp and Symbolic Computation*, vol. 5, pp. 223-270, 1992.

4. D. Brelaz, "New Methods to Color the Vertices of a Graph," *Comm. A.C.M.*, vol. 22, no. 4, pp. 251-256, 1979.

5. J.E. Brookes, *Timetable Planning*, Heinemann Educational Books, London, U.K., 1980.

6. J. Randall Brown, "Chromatic Scheduling and the Chromatic Number Problem," *Management Science*, vol. 19, pp. 456-463, 1972.

7. C. Carmel and M. Itzovitz, "A Comprehensive University Planner Implemented in a 5th Generation Language," *Proceedings of 33rd Annual College and Administrative Comptuer Users Conference*, pp. 418-428, Los Angeles, Calif., 1988.

8. M.W. Carter, "A Survey of Practical Applications of Examination Timetabling Algorithms," *Operations Research*, vol. 34, no. 2, pp. 193-202, Mar-Apr. 1986.

9. Michael W. Carter, "A Lagrangian Relaxation Approach to the Classroom Assignment Problem," *INFOR*, vol. 27, no. 2, pp. 230-245, 1989.

10. M.W. Carter and C.A. Tovey, "When Is the Classroom Assignment Problem Hard?," *Working Paper #89-03*, Department of Industrial Engineering, University of Toronto, 1989.

11. Richard A. Dempsey and Henry P. Traverso, *Scheduling the Secondary School,* Nat. Assoc. of Secondary School Principals, Reston, Virginia, U.S.A., 1983.

12. M. Dincbas, H. Simonis, and P. van Hentenryck, "Solving a Cutting-Stock Program in Constraint Logic Programming," *Proc. of Fifth Int. Conf. and Symp. on Logic Programming*, vol. 1, The MIT Press, Cambridge, Massachusetts, 1988.

13. F.D.J. Dunstan, "Sequential Colorings of Graphs," *Proceedings of the 5th British Combined Conference*, pp. 151-158, Aberdeen, England, 1975.

14. Ronen Feldman and Martin Charles Golumbic, "Interactive Scheduling as a Constraint Satisfiability Problem," *Annals of Mathematics and Artificial Intelligence*, vol. 1, pp. 49-73, 1990.

15. J.A. Ferland and S. Roy, "Timetabling Problem for University as Assignment of Activities to Resources," *Computers & Operations Research* , vol. 12, no. 2, pp. 207-218, 1985.

16. A. Hertz, "Tabu Search for large scale timetabling problems," *Eur. J. Op. Res.*, vol. 54, pp. 39-47, 1991.

17. Le Kang and George M. White, "A Logic Approach to the Resolution of Constraints in Timetabling," *Eur. J. Op. Res.*, vol. 61, no. 3, pp. 306-317, 1992.

18. Vahid Lotfi and Robert Cerveny, "A Final-exam-scheduling Package," *J. Opl. Res. Soc.*, vol. 42, no. 3, pp. 205-216, 1991.

19. Michael Lucks, "A Constraint Satisfaction Algorithm for the Automated Decryption of Simple Substitution Ciphers," *Lecture Notes in Computer Science*, vol. 403, pp. 132-144, Springer-Verlag, 1990.

20. Rick Mayoh, "Mission Impossible: Drawing up NHL Schedule," *Ottawa Citizen*, Ottawa, Canada, Jan. 15, 1992.

21. Steven Minton, Mark D. Johnston, Andrew B. Philips, and Philip Laird, "Minimizing Conflicts: A Heuristic Repair Method for Constraint Satisfaction and Scheduling Problems," *Artificial Intelligence*, vol. 58, no. 1-3, pp. 161-205, Dec. 1992.

22. J.M. Mulvey, "A Classroom/Time Assignment Model," *Eur. J. Op. Res.*, vol. 9, pp. 64-70, 1982.

23. J.E.L. Peck, R. Osterman, and D. De Werra, "Some Experiments with a Timetabling System," *OR Spektrum*, vol. 3, pp. 199-204, 1982.

24. J. Peemoller, "A Correction to Brelaz's Modification of Brown's Colouring Algorithm," *Comm. A.C.M.*, vol. 26, pp. 595-597, 1983.

25. Anthony Saville, *Instructional Programming: Issues and Innovations in School Scheduling,* Charles E. Merrill Publishing Co., Columbus, Ohio, U.S.A., 1973.

26. G. Schmidt and T. Ströhlein, "Timetable construction - an annotated bibliography," *Comp. J.*, vol. 23, no. 4, pp. 307-316, 1980.

27. S.M. Selim, "An Algorithm for Producing Course and Lecture Timetables," *Comput. Educ.*, vol. 7, no. 2, pp. 101-108, 1983.

28. Gardner Swenson, Donald Keys, and J. Lloyd Trump, *Providing for Flexibility in Scheduling and Instruction*, Prentice-Hall, Inc., Englewood Cliffs, N.J., 1966.

29. E.M. Timmreck, "Scheduler - A Program that Uses Instructor and Student Preferences to Form Timetables," *Comp. Sci. Tech. Report #3*, Univ. of Wisconsin, 1967.

30. R.G. Veitsch and J.C. Wilson, *An Introduction to PROLOG Programming with WPROLOG - Univ. of Waterloo PROLOG Interpreter for VM/SP CMS*, WATCOM Products, Inc., Waterloo, Canada, 1986.

31. Christopher M. White and Kenneth A. Bowen, *ALS Prolog User's Guide and Reference Manual* .

32. George M. White and Pak-Wah Chan, "Towards the Construction of Optimal Examination Schedules," *INFOR*, vol. 17, no. 3, pp. 219-229, 1979.

33. George M. White and Michel Haddad, "An Heuristic Method for Optimizing Examination Schedules Which Have Day and Night Courses," *Comput. Educ.*, vol. 7, no. 4, pp. 235-238, 1983.

34. George M. White and Simon K.S. Wong, "Interactive Timetabling in Universities," *Comput. Educ.*, vol. 12, no. 4, pp. 521-529, 1988.

35. W. Deane Wiley and Lloyd K. Bishop, *The Flexibly Scheduled High School*, Parker Publishing Co., West Nyack, N.Y., 1968.

36. Michael Woitass, "Coordination of Intelligent Office Agents - Applied to Meeting Scheduling," *Proc. of the IFIP WG8.4 Conf. on Multi-User Interfaces and Applications*, pp. 371-387, Elsevier Science Publishers, Sep. 1990.

37. Masazumi Yoshikawa, Kazuya Kaneko, Yuriko Nomura, and Masanobu Watanabe, "A Constraint-Based Appeoach to High-School Timetabling Problems: A Case Study," *Proc. Twelfth Nat. Conf. on Artificial Intellegence (AAAI-94)*, Seattle, WA, Jul. 31-Aug. 4, 1994.

Building University Timetables
Using Constraint Logic Programming

Christelle Guéret[1,2], Narendra Jussien[1], Patrice Boizumault[1], Christian Prins[1]
email: {Christelle.Gueret, Narendra.Jussien,
Patrice.Boizumault, Christian.Prins}@emn.fr

[1] École des Mines de Nantes
4 Rue Alfred Kastler, La Chantrerie, F-44070 Nantes Cedex 03, France.
[2] Institut de Mathématiques Appliquées
3 Place André Leroy, BP 808, F-49008 Angers Cedex 08, France.

1 Introduction

A timetabling problem can be defined as the scheduling of a certain number of lectures, which are to be attended by a specific group of students and given by a teacher, over a definite period of time. Each lecture requires certain resources (rooms, overheads,...) in limited number and must fulfill certain specific requirements. In particular, automatic building of timetables is extremely difficult because of the diversity of the constraints that must be taken into account.

The most usual methods to solve this problem are inherited from Operations Research such as graph coloring [14, 15, 19, 20] and mathematical programming [19, 20], from local search procedures such as simulated annealing and Tabu search [30, 31, 10, 11] or from Genetic Algorithms [13]. These well-known and widely used methods have given good results. But, OR inherited methods generally lack flexibility (i.e modifying the data may lead to the necessity of reconsidering the initial model); moreover it is difficult to find a model which includes all the constraints. For local search methods (where most of the constraints are put in the objective function) or for Genetic Algorithms (where the constraints are active in the fitness function), the user frequently obtains solutions by tuning rather than by defining his own search strategy dedicated to the problem.

Constraint Logic Programming is based upon the integration of Constraint Solving and Logic Programming. This combination helps make Constraint Logic Programming programs both expressive and flexible, and in some cases, more efficient than other kinds of programs.

Constraint Logic Programming over Finite Domains (CLP) is based upon the integration of CSP (*Constraint Satisfaction Problems*) approach in a Logic Programming scheme (Prolog). It benefits from the results obtained in the AI community in CSP (domains, consistency techniques, filtering algorithms, search strategies, ...) embedded in a Logic Programming scheme. Thus, the user is provided with a uniform framework in order to both model his problem (constraints) and develop his own search methods (labeling). It has already been proved that CLP is successful in tackling many combinatorial optimization problems such as planning, scheduling, resource allocation, assignment problems, ... [4, 7, 17, 21, 22, 23, 38, 39].

The aim of this paper is to show how CLP) is well suited for solving Timetabling Problems. Particularly, the declarativity of the CSP formalism improves the flexibility (heterogeneous constraints can be directly handled). Moreover, the CLP paradigm gives the ability to rapidly design efficient search procedures.

In this paper, we first present different approaches used for solving timetabling problems. Then, we describe the Timetabling problem of our institute in our University. After a brief description of the CLP programming language CHIP, we present our approach for solving timetabling problems. Finally, we give some hints on how to relax constraints.

2 Solving timetabling problems

General timetabling problems can be defined as the scheduling of a set of lectures which several groups of students must attend, over a preset period of time, using certain resources and satisfying a certain set of constraints. Many researchers [15, 20] have dealt with this problem since the fifties. And nowadays this problem continues to be studied because of its variety and its complexity [12, 46, 47]. In this section, we present OR solution techniques to solve this problem, the genetic algorithms approach, an example of Tabu search and some work in the CSP community.

2.1 OR approaches

Graph Coloring. The timetabling problem which consists in scheduling a set of lectures over p periods is equivalent to a graph vertex coloring problem [20, 15, 14, 19] where:

- Each lecture (a pair (*class, teacher*)) makes a vertex,
- Two vertices are connected if the associated lectures share a student or a teacher.

Then, we must find a vertex coloration using a maximum of p colors. Vertices colored with a same color are associated with classes which take place at the same time. We know that the problem of the existence of a graph vertex p-coloring (using atmost p colors) is $\mathcal{NP}$-Complete when $p \geq 3$.

We cannot introduce easily all types of constraints (e.g. precedence among lectures, allocation of a room to each lecture) in this modeling. Furthermore, crucial information about the nature of the constraints is lost. An edge can represent the fact that a student must attend two lectures, as well as the fact that two lectures must take place in the same room or that they need the same teacher.

Flow problems. Edge graph coloring problems can be solved with heuristics concerning max-flow problems [19, 20]. In this case, we assign to the problem a directed graph the vertices of which are the classes and the teachers. We create an arc (C_i, T_j) if the teacher T_j gives a lecture to the class C_i. We introduce a vertex s and arcs (s, C_i) for each C_i as well as a vertex t and arcs (T_j, t) for each T_j. A path from s to t is associated to a lecture.

Each arc receives a lower and an upper bound (see table 1) which change during the resolution of the problem. We have to solve p max-flow problems in this network (one for each period).

arcs	lower bounds	upper bounds
(s, C_i)	0	1 if all the lectures attended by class C_i are scheduled 0 otherwise
(C_i, T_j)	0	1 if the lecture given by teacher T_j to class C_i is scheduled 0 otherwise
(T_j, t)	0	1 if the lectures given by teacher T_j are scheduled 0 otherwise

Table 1. Lower and upper bounds for the flow modeling

Such a method is interesting because we know efficient algorithms for solving that type of problems. However, when solving a timetabling problem over T periods of time we must find T flows, one for each period. This problem is now again $\mathcal{NP}$-Complete. Furthermore, we cannot introduce all types of constraints (e.g. precedence constraints). Finally, this method demands the same duration for all lectures, which does not seem very realistic.

Mathematical programming. A third method that can be used is mathematical programming with integer variables [19, 20]. The main problem in this case is the number of data and constraints. Optimal resolution of an integer linear program is $\mathcal{NP}$-Hard in the general case, except if the constraint matrix is, for example, totally unimodular (rarely in real life).

For example, consider the timetabling problem which consists of m teachers and n classes. Each teacher T_j gives R_{ij} lectures to the class C_i. The lectures must be scheduled in ε periods of time. Let x_{ijk} be the variable whose value is 1 if the teacher T_j gives a lecture to the class C_i at time k and 0 otherwise. The timetabling constraints are:

$$\sum_{k=1}^{\varepsilon} x_{ijk} = r_{ij}, i =]n] \wedge j =]m] \tag{1}$$

$$\sum_{i=1}^{n} x_{ijk} \leq 1, j =]m] \wedge k =]\varepsilon] \tag{2}$$

$$\sum_{j=1}^{m} x_{ijk} \leq 1, i =]n] \wedge k =]\varepsilon] \tag{3}$$

Equation (1) models that *all the lectures must be scheduled*, and equation (2) that *a teacher cannot give more than one lecture at a time*. Equation (3) ensures that *a student cannot attend more than one lecture at a time*.

In order to reduce the problem size, it is possible to redefine the variables by grouping students, rooms or lectures. [41, 42] propose such a transformation. Next, they use a Lagrangean Relaxation method. However, this method which is quite complex only applies to the specific problem we want to solve, in spite of a certain reduction of the problem complexity. If we add constraints or modify the problem, we must reconsider the entire analysis.

2.2 Genetic Algorithms

We present here the works of [13]. In analogy with the reproduction of living beings, the process starts with an initial population of solutions.

A random population of feasible timetables is created thanks to a graph coloring algorithm [13]. Each timetable is evaluated according to a set of criteria e.g. the length of the timetable, how many students have to sit two exams in a row or how many unused seats there are. Each solution is coded with a chromosome: a vector of symbols whose length is $2N$ (number of exams), divided in N contiguous pieces containing two genes. The two genes of the ith piece represent the period and the room of the exam number i.

The mutation operator randomly changes the period and the room the exam is to be held in, still maintaining a feasible timetable. The cross-over operator takes a pair of timetables, selecting the early exams from one and the late exams from the other to produce a new timetable. A new population is thus generated. The process will be repeated until a good solution is found.

The fitness function includes three criteria: the length of the timetable, the number of conflicts (when a student must take two exams in a row), the spare capacity in each of the rooms.

Genetic algorithms can have good results [13] and find efficient solutions. However, all the parameters must be determined through experimentation. Furthermore, they do not have any guarantee of convergence.

2.3 Tabu search

Tabu search [30, 31] is an effective local search method which moves step by step from one initial solution of a combinatorial optimization problem towards a solution which is expected to be optimal or near-optimal. For each solution s, such a method requires the definition of a neighborhood $V(s)$, consisting of solutions which can be reached in one step from s. The basic step is to move from the current solution s to the best solution s^* of $V(s)$, even if it is not better than s. A tabu list T is used to avoid cycling. It acts as a short-term memory by storing a description of the NT last moves or solutions. When exploring $V(s)$ to find s^*, T is scanned to avoid the so-called tabu moves which could bring the search back to a previous iteration. The procedure stops after a maximum number of iterations and outputs the best solution found.

J.P. Boufflet [10, 11] implements such a method to solve a timetabling problem. He transforms his problem into a graph coloring problem in which the vertices are the lectures and the edges the constraints. A weight is assigned to each constraint. The problem is then to find a p-coloring which minimizes a multiobjective function. To do this, Boufflet uses a tabu search on a graph coloring problem inspired by de Werra's techniques [32]: each vertex is given one of the p allowed colors. This assignment may not be a coloring (if some adjacent vertices are assigned the same color). The idea is to minimize the conflicts (two adjacent vertices with the same color) by exploring the neighborhood of the initial solution (modification of the color of a node) .

2.4 Constraint Satisfaction Problems

A CSP (Constraint Satisfaction Problem) can be defined as: *a problem composed of a finite set of variables, each of which is associated with a finite domain, and a set of constraints that restricts the values the variables can simultaneously take. The task is to assign a value to each variable satisfying all the constraints.* [43]

Several methods are used to solve CSP, from filtering algorithms to hybrid algorithms [26, 43]. We will see in the following sections how to use CSP techniques to solve real timetabling problems.

3 Our problem

The IMA (Institute of Applied Mathematics) provides a five years training after the French Baccalaureate. The first three years require a weekly timetable whereas the last two are yearly organized. In order to simplify the presentation, we will only speak about the weekly timetables.

The first three years represent 160 students (60-50-50). Most of the taught subjects are divided into lectures, practical classes given by teachers (called TDE) and practical classes given by students (called TDM). A 4 hour period is reserved each week for examination. A few lectures are independent of our institute. Complete groups attend lectures, whereas half- or one-third groups attend TDE and TDM. Finally, all lectures take place in 8 different rooms with various capacities.

The whole problem can be stated according two types of constraints: general constraints and specific constraints.

General constraints are:

C_0 – A teacher can only give one lecture at a time.

C_1 – A room can only host one lecture at a time.

C_2 – A student can only attend one lecture at a time.

C_3 – Room capacities must be respected.

C_4 – A few lectures are fixed.

C_5 – Teachers have days or hours of non availability.

Specific constraints are:

C_6 – Two lectures about a same subject must not be scheduled the same day.

C_7 – Lectures can only begin after 8 am and must end before 8 pm.

C_8 – A teacher may not teach more than 6 hours a day.

C_9 – Lunches need one and a half hours and must begin between 11.45 am and 12.45 am.

C_{10} – TDMs must not be scheduled in parallel with third year student's lectures.

C_{11} – TDMs of a same subject must be scheduled at the same time for the one-third groups, also TDEs of a same subject must be scheduled at the same time for the half-groups.

C_{12} – As far as possible, all lectures of the same group must be scheduled in a same room.

C_{13} – Students must have a 15 min pause between lectures.

91 lectures involving 42 teachers have to be scheduled. Those lectures can be scheduled in 8 different rooms and their starting time can take 240 values. Our time unit is a quarter of an hour (48 quarters in a day beginning at 8 am and ending at 8 pm, for a five day week). At the present time, the manual resolution of this timetabling problem requires several days of work.

4 A brief overview of the finite domains in CHIP

CHIP (Constraint Handling In Prolog) is a Constraint Logic Programming language from ECRC and now developed and sold by Cosytec [18, 24, 44]. The CHIP language can handle constraints over three distinct domains: finite domains, booleans and rationals. We briefly present the finite domains which were used for our application.

4.1 Numerical and symbolic constraints

Each constrained variable has a domain (set of scalar values) which must be declared *a priori*. CHIP provides the usual numerical constraints: equality (#=), dis-equality (#\=), inequalities (#<, #<=,#>,#>=). Each one can be applied over linear terms built upon domain variables and constants.

Symbolic constraints are also handled. A very useful one is element(N, List, Value). It specifies, as an internal system constraint, that the Nth element of the list List must have the value Value. List is a non empty list of natural numbers and Value is either a natural number, a domain variable or a free variable.

The most interesting use of the constraint `element/3` is when `N` or `Value` are domain variables. Therefore as soon as the domains of `N` or `Value` change, a new constraint is dynamically added and inconsistent values are removed from the domains. The `atmost/3` (`atleast/3`) constraints state that at most (at least) `N` elements of a list `List` have the value `Value`.

The domain of the variables are reduced according to classical consistency techniques (Arc Consistency (AC)) and filtering algorithm (look ahead or partial look ahead).

4.2 The cumulative constraint

This constraint has been created [1] to solve scheduling problems difficult to solve with only the above presented constraints:

$$\text{cumulative([S1,...,Sn], [D1,...,Dn],[R1,...,Rn], L).}$$

where `[S1,...,Sn]`, `[D1,...,Dn]`, `[R1,...,Rn]` are non empty lists of domain variables and `L` is a natural number.

The usual interpretation of this constraint is a single resource scheduling problem. The S_is represent the starting times of the tasks, the D_is are the durations and the R_is the amount of resource needed by each task. L is the total amount of resource available at each instant of time. The cumulative constraint ensures that, at each instant of time i of the schedule, the consumed amount of resource cannot exceed the limit L. This is a simplified presentation of the cumulative constraint which owns in fact 8 arguments [18].

Let us consider three major uses of the cumulative constraint [1].

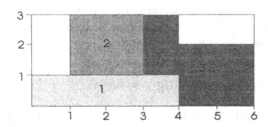

1. Considering figure 1, there are three tasks to schedule: the first task uses one unit of the resource during four consecutive periods; tasks 2 and 3 use two units during respectively two and three periods. At any time the total amount of resource used by the different tasks is always less than or equal to 3.

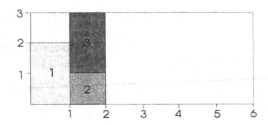

Fig. 2. cumulative([1,2,2],[1,1,1],[2,1,2],3)

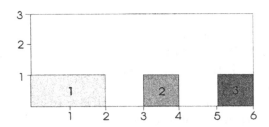

Fig. 3. cumulative([1,4,6],[2,1,1],[1,1,1],1)

2. For figure 2, all the tasks durations are equal to one. This particular case corresponds to the bin-packing problem [40]: m bins of fixed capacities and n objects of fixed size to put in these bins.
3. The third example (see figure 3) does not allow a cumulative amount of resource greater than 1. This corresponds in scheduling to the problem of tasks that cannot be executed at the same time because they share the same resource, the so called disjunctive tasks.

5 Solving our timetabling problem

The usual development of an application over finite domains consists of modeling the data and the domain variables, thus imposing the constraints, and finally defining the labeling strategy. We follow this pattern in our presentation.

5.1 Data representation

The domain variables are for each lecture: Room, Day, Hour and Qh (Quarter of an Hour), variables which domains are as follow: Room :: 1..8, Day :: 1..5, Hour :: 1..48, Qh :: 1..240 (the 5 days are decomposed in 5 × 48 quarters).

The hour of beginning of each lecture is then represented twice. The choice between these representations depends on their fitting to the expression of the corresponding constraint. The link between them is maintained by the constraint: `Qh = 48*(Day-1) + Hour`. To model breaks (a quarter of an hour) between lectures, we have chosen to *include* them at the beginning of each lecture. So, the length of each lecture is increased of a quarter of an hour.

5.2 Constraints modeling

In this section, we describe our problem in terms of CSP using the built-in constraints provided by CHIP.

The problem consists of 90 lectures and 500 constraints (110 of them are cumulative constraints).

Some constraints can be expressed directly:

C_{13} is taken into account in the data.
C_4 and C_{11} are expressed by an equality constraint.
C_5 and C_7 are expressed by domains restrictions.
C_9 is expressed by creating virtual lectures for lunches.

The other constraints are expressed by the symbolic constraints of CHIP, and especially by the cumulative constraint:

C_0 for each teacher, we set the disjunction of all his lectures by the cumulative constraint. Let `ListQh` and `ListLength` be respectively the list of the starting quarters of the lectures given by a teacher, and the list of the lengths of these lectures. The constraint is written:

$$\text{cumulative(ListQh,ListLength,ListOf1,1)}$$

where `ListOf1` is a list with the same length that `ListQh` but only composed of 1s. Thus, we consider each lecture as a task to perform with a resource (the teacher) whose capacity is of course one.

C_1, C_2, C_{10} The modeling of C_1, C_2 and C_{10} is based on the same principle as the one of C_0 by considering that each lecture is a task whose execution needs one unit of a resource of capacity 1. In C_1, this resource is a room, in C_2, a group of students and in C_{10} a student.

C_6 constraint claims, by the `alldifferent/1` predicate, that two lectures on a same subject cannot occur the same day.

C_8 is also expressed by the cumulative constraint: for each teacher, the length of the lectures he gives and the `Day` variables associated are collected into two lists. The constraint is then given by: `cumulative(ListOfDays, ListOf1, ListOfLength, R)`. The teacher is considered as a resource of capacity R=4*6 hours and the lectures are the elementary tasks that consume an amount of resource equal to their length.

C_3 is introduced by the `element/3` constraint. Let `Room` be the domain variable of a lecture and `ListCap` the list containing the rooms capacities. The constraint is then: `element(Room,ListCap,Cap), Cap #>= size of the group`.

C_{12} is taken into account during the labeling by the `indomain2/2` predicate which tries to assign a lecture into the room assigned to its group.

Notice that for C_0, C_1, C_2 and C_{10}, the cumulative constraint expresses disjunctive constraints but for C_8 it's a capacity constraint.

5.3   Labeling

We tried several enumeration strategies. We only present four of them to illustrate our work. The first two are basic strategies in the CSP community. The third and fourth, inherited from OR, apply the first-fit decreasing principle, a well known method for solving bin-packing problems [40].

naive1 : lectures are selected by the `first_fail` principle. The values of the variables **Day** and **Hour** are determined by the `indomain/1` predicate which chooses the smallest value of their domain (*i.e.* the lectures are assigned as early as possible in the week).

naive2 : at each step, the lecture chosen is the longest one (in case of equality, the `first_fail` principle is used). The values of the variables are selected by the `indomain/1` predicate.

first_fit1 : each lecture is selected by the `first_fail` principle. The day with the shortest length of lectures (for the corresponding group) is assigned to it. The hour is selected by the `indomain/1`.

first_fit2 : at each step, the lecture chosen is the longest one (in case of equality, the `first_fail` principle is used). The day and hour are selected as in `first_fit1`.

5.4   First results

The first two labeling strategies leave us without solution after 48 hours of computation time, whereas the last two first-fit strategies give us a solution in two seconds. This is due to the fact that a naive labeling places the lectures at the beginning of the week. Impossibilities appear then very late and cause a lot of useless backtracks. First-fit enumeration spreads lectures uniformly over the week. The resulting timetable is then well-balanced for the students.

The weekly timetable for the year 1993-1994 is computed in 2 seconds of cpu time thanks to the `first_fit2` enumeration. We tested the accuracy of our approach by lowering the length of a working day. Initially a working day begins at 8 am and ends at 8 pm. When we set the beginning time at 8.45 am and the finishing time at 7.30 pm, we still have solutions (in about 2–5 s - $\approx$ 100 backtracks). If we try to reduce the working day further, the program has not found any solution in less than 5 minutes (> 30000 backtracks).

Those results show the importance of a user defined labeling in the CLP framework. The CSP community is also aware of this view point. As quoted by E. Tsang [43], *one important issue is the ordering in which the variables are labeled and how the orderings could affect the efficiency of the search strategies significantly. The OR community is also aware of this conclusion: we can simply think about a graph coloring problem for which exists an ordering of the vertices which allows a simple coloration method to perform good results.*

5.5 Extensions

We have tested our approach upon another institute in our University for which we had to schedule about sixty lectures (the constraints are similar). A first-fit labeling strategy finds solutions in similar computation times (2–5 s).

These two institutes share common lectures, so, we tried a global solving of the timetabling problem, i.e. 165 lectures in 11 different rooms. Our program does not find any solution after 2 days of computing time for this problem. But, we are able to rapidly produce solutions by manually relaxing a few constraints (2–3) about teachers' availabilities.

The person who really builds the timetables in the two institutes considers that there is no *feasible* solution for the global problem under all the previously specified constraints. When he builds the timetables, he has to overcome several types of constraints and manually relax them depending on the lectures or teachers involved.

6 Constraint Relaxation

We said before that the global timetabling problem has no solution, thus, it seems very important to include a constraints relaxation system in an automated timetabling system. The fact that a solution exists in case of the manual relaxation of certain constraints (as we said above) and probably no feasible solution for the complete problem exists, comforts us in our position. We will, in the following sections, briefly survey about constraint relaxation in a logic programming environment and we will present our works.

6.1 Basic concepts

The majority of the concepts about constraint relaxation in a PLC scheme were introduced in [9], and [29] proposed a first theoretical framework.

In constraint relaxation problems, one must introduce a sort of hierarchy upon constraints. A weight is then proposed for each constraint. This weight allows the setting of a partial order relation between constraints. The lower the value of the weight, the more important the constraint is. Thus, constraints with weight 0 are called mandatory constraints, and those with a strictly positive weight are called preferred constraints.

A substitution (values for variables) which satisfies all the required constraints and which satisfies the preferred constraints in the best possible way with respect to a given comparator is called a solution. Thus, we are searching a maximal (to a given criteria) sub problem of the initial problem. This sub problem must have solutions.

To achieve constraint relaxation, one must answer three main questions:

- **when** exactly during the computation do we have to use constraint relaxation,

- **which** constraint do we need to relax in order to obtain a consistent sub problem,
- **how** do we have to perform the relaxation of the chosen constraint.

6.2 Former answers

As far as we know, no system is able to efficiently answer all the questions we raised above. In the literature, we identified two systems which fully answered the three questions but they were too simple for the kind of problems we want to solve [9, 33]. The others only answer one or two questions. In in [19, 35] the *who* is answered using responsibility between constraint or between variables to determine a *good* constraint to relax. In [19] the *when* ins asnwered using global consistency techniques. Nevertheless, those systems show good ways of works. Thus, it seems quite evident that before using a constraint relaxation module, we have to identify an inconsistency in the constraints system. Moreover, to choose the constraint that we have to relax to obtain a solution, we may try to identify the constraints responsible for the inconsistency.

Finally, we found a way to answer the *how* question in the ideas proposed in the dynamic CSP community [5, 6, 34, 37]. Let us recall that a dynamic CSP is a CSP in which constraints can be added or retracted during the computation. Besides, we think that the incremental system to interpret Prolog from [45] seems very interesting.

More global approaches were proposed in [25, 28]. Those approaches transform the original constraint relaxation problem into an optimization problem. This new problem is then solved with a classical branch and bound technique. We think this approach does not allow the intervention of the user during the process and thus seems unsatisfactory.

6.3 Our works

The aim of our work is to propose a complete constraint relaxation system. We started with a system which tried to make some of the above described propositions work together. We obtained a system which, when a Prolog fail occurred, used a constraint relaxation module using the identification techniques presented in [35] (The search of a dependence graph between constraints). This system, named FELIAC, has been implemented [8] above an incremental system which used ideas from [45].

We tried then to define a more unified system to solve the constraint relaxation problem. Thus, we worked on the ATMS (Assumption-based Truth Maintenance Systems) philosophy [27] to obtain a new system.

This new system associates a *justification* with each removal of a value from a variable during the computation. This justification will allow an easy identification of the causes of the removal of the value. Thus, in the case of an inconsistency, the recorded justifications lead to the identification of constraints responsible for the failed computation. We can then resume the computation erasing the effects of the removed constraint (to achieve this, we just have to state that the justifications depending on this constraint are no longer valid). We must add that all the preferred constraints are considered as ATMS *suppositions* and then can be added or removed easily. So the ATMS approach can provide a complete constraint relaxation system. We are currently working on more improvements in our new system.

7 Conclusion

Our experience shows how timetabling problems can be efficiently solved by the CLP approach. Our experience highlights the CLP scheme capability of combining both CSP and OR approaches. As shown in this paper, one can declaratively state the problem in terms of constraints and define efficient search strategies inherited from OR works. This declarative capability needs high level constraints. Defining such constraints is only possible by importing OR works and techniques in CLP [2, 3, 16, 36]. This illustrates the huge capacity of prototyping an implementation of real-life applications in constraint logic programming [38, 39]. Moreover, the conciseness of the programs and the short development times leads us to rapidly develop alternative versions. Indeed, various heuristics have been developed, tested and validated in a very short development time.

Our experience points out the importance of introducing Constraint Relaxation in CLP. Indeed, various timetabling problems (and other real-life problems) can be found to be over-constrained. The development facility of the CLP paradigm is not sufficient, it has to be extended for Constraint Relaxation. Thus, we are currently working on the embedding of Constraint Relaxation into CLP languages. At the moment, we are implementing our new general model based upon ATMS and validating it using timetabling problems.

References

1. Abderrahmane Aggoun and Nicolas Beldiceanu. Extending CHIP in order to solve complex scheduling and placement problems. *Mathl. Comput. Modelling*, 17(7):57–73, 1993.
2. P. Baptiste, C. Le Pape, and W. Nuijten. Incorporating efficient Operations Research algorithms in constraint-based scheduling. In 1st *Joint Workshop on Artificial Intelligence and Operational Research*, 1995. To appear.
3. N. Beldiceanu and E. Contjean. Introducing global constraints in CHIP. *Mathematical and Computer Modelling*, 20(12):97–123, 1994.
4. Jacques Bellone, André Chamard, and C. Pradelles. Plane : An evolutive system for aircraft production written in CHIP. In *Proceedings of the First International Conference on Practical Applications of Prolog*, London, 1992.
5. Christian Bessière. Arc consistency in dynamic constraint satisfaction problems. In *Proceedings AAAI'91*, 1991.
6. Christian Bessière. Arc consistency for non-binary dynamic CSPs. In *Proceedings ECAI'92*, 1992.

7. Patrice Boizumault, Yann Delon, and Laurent Péridy. Constraint logic programming for examination timetabling. To appear in Journal of Logic Programming, 1995.

8. Patrice Boizumault, Christelle Guéret, and Narendra Jussien. Efficient labeling and constraint relaxation for solving time tabling problems. In Pierre Lim and Jean Jourdan, editors, *Proceedings of the 1994 ILPS post-conference workshop on Constraint Languages/Systems and their use in Problem Modeling : Volume 1 (Applications and Modelling)*, Technical Report ECRC-94-38, ECRC, Munich, Germany, November 1994.

9. Alan Borning, Michael Maher, Amy Martindale, and Molly Wilson. Constraint hierarchies and logic programming. In Giorgio Levi and Maurizio Martelli, editors, *ICLP'89: Proceedings 6th International Conference on Logic Programming*, pages 149–164, Lisbon, Portugal, June 1989. MIT Press.

10. J. P. Boufflet and S. Negre. About planning an examination session. In *Proceedings ECCO VII, Conference of the European Chapter on Combinatorial Optimization*, Milan, Italy, February 1994.

11. J. P. Boufflet and S. Negre. A practical timetable problem. In *EURO XII, Operations Research Designing Practical Solutions*, Glasgow, United Kingdom, July 1994.

12. Bull SA. *AMPHI+ user's guide*, 1992.

13. Edmund Burke, David Elliman, and Rupert Weare. A Genetic Algorithm for university timetabling. In *AISB Workshop on Evolutionary Computing*, University of Leeds, UK, April 1994.

14. M. Cangalovié and J.A.M. Schreuder. Exact algorithm fro weighted graphs applied to timetabling problems with lectures of different lengths. *European Journal of Operations Research*, 1991.

15. M. W. Carter. A survey of practical applications of examination timetabling algorithms. *European Journal of Operations Research*, 34(2), 1986.

16. Y. Caseau and F. Laburthe. Improved CLP scheduling with task intervals. In 11th *International Conference on Logic Programming*, 1994.

17. André Chamard, Frédéric Decès, and Annie Fischler. Applying CHIP to a complex scheduling problem. In *JICSLP'92*, Washington, DC, November 1992. (Submitted).

18. Cosytec SA. *CHIP v4 reference manual*, 1993.

19. Xavier Cousin. *Application de la programmation logique avec contraintes au problème d'emploi du temps*. PhD thesis, Université de Rennes I, France, 1993. In French.

20. Dominique de Werra. An introduction to timetabling. *European Journal of Operational Research*, 19:151–162, 1985.

21. Mehmet Dincbas, Helmut Simonis, and Pascal Van Hentenryck. Solving a Cutting-Stock Problem in Constraint Logic Programming. In Robert Kowalski and Kenneth Bowen, editors, *ICLP'88: Proceedings 5th International Conference on Logic Programming*, pages 42–58, Seattle, WA, August 1988. MIT Press.

22. Mehmet Dincbas, Helmut Simonis, and Pascal Van Hentenryck. Solving the Car Sequencing Problem in Constraint Logic Programming. In *ECAI-88: European Conference on Artificial Intelligence*, Munich, August 1988.

23. Mehmet Dincbas, Helmut Simonis, and Pascal Van Hentenryck. Solving Large Combinatorial Problems in Logic Programming. *Journal of Logic Programming*, 8(1-2):74–94, January-March 1990.

24. Mehmet Dincbas, P. Van Hentenryck, H. Simonis, A. Aggoun, T. Graf, and F. Berthier. The Constraint Logic Programming Language CHIP. In *FGCS-88: Proceedings International Conference on Fifth Generation Computer Systems*, pages 693–702, Tokyo, December 1988. ICOT.

25. François Fages, Julian Fowler, and Thierry Sola. Handling preferences in constraint logic programming with relational optimization. In *PLILP'94*, Madrid, September 1994.

26. R. Feldman and M.C. Golumbic. Optimization algorithms for student scheduling via constraint satisfiability. *The Computer Journal*, 33(4), 1990.

27. Kenneth D. Forbus and Johan de Kleer. *Building Problem Solvers*. MIT Press, Cambridge, 1993.

28. Julian Fowler. Preferred constraints as optimization. In *Proceedings Journées Françaises de Programmation en Logique*, 1993.

29. Eugene Freuder. Partial constraint satisfaction. In *IJCAI-89: Proceedings 11th International Joint Conference on Artificial Intelligence*, pages 278–283, Detroit, 1989.

30. F. Glover. Tabu search. CAAI Report 88–3, University of Colorado, 1988.

31. F. Glover. Tabu search: a tutorial. *Interfaces*, 20:74–94, 1990.

32. A. Hertz and D. de Werra. Using tabu search techniques for graph coloring. *Computing*, 39:345–351, 1987.

33. Michael Jampel and David Gilbert. Fair Hierarchical Constraint Logic Programming. In Manfred Meyer, editor, *Proceedings ECAI'94 Workshop on Constraint Processing*, Amsterdam, August 1994.

34. Philippe Jégou. *Contribution à l'étude des problèmes de satisfaction de contraintes : Algorithmes de propagation et de résolution - Propagation de contraintes dans les réseaux dynamiques*. Thèse de doctorat, Université des Sciences et Techniques du Languedoc, Montpellier, France, January 1991. In French.

35. Francisco Menezes, Pedro Barahona, and Philippe Codognet. An incremental hierarchical constraint solver. In Paris Kanellakis, Jean-Louis Lassez, and Vijay Saraswat, editors, *PPCP'93: First Workshop on Principles and Practice of Constraint Programming*, Providence RI, 1993.

36. C. Le Pape. Programmation par contraintes : une nouvelle forme de débat entre recherche opérationnelle et intelligence artificielle. *Bulletin de l'AFIA*, (21), April 1995.

37. Projet CSPFlex., Gérard Bel, Éric Bensana, Khaled Ghédira, David Lesaint, Thomas Schiex, Gérard Verfaillie, Christine Gaspin, Roger Martin-Clouaire, Jean-Pierre Rellier, Pierre Berlandier, Bertrand Neveu, Brigitte Trousse, Hélène Fargier, Jérôme Lang, Philippe David, Philippe Jansenn, Tibor Kökény, Marie-Catherine Vilarem, and Philippe Jégou. Représentation et traitement pratique de la flexibilité dans les problèmes sous contraintes. In *Actes des Journées Nationales du PRC GDR Intelligence Artificielle*, Marseille, France, October 1992. In French.

38. Michel Rueher. A first exploration of Prolog-III's capabilities. *Software – Practice and Experience*, 23, 1993.

39. Michel Rueher and Bruno Legeard. Which role for CLP in software engineering? An investigation on the basis of first applications. In *Proceedings of the First International Conference on Practical Applications of Prolog*, London, 1992.

40. Smith and Shing. Bin packing. *Bulletin of the IMA*, 19, 1983.

41. Arabinda Tripathy. A lagrangean relaxation approach to course timetabling. *Journal of Operational Research Society*, 31:599–603, 1980.

42. Arabinda Tripathy. School timetabling - a case in large binary integer linear programming. *Management Science*, 30(12), 1984.

43. Edward Tsang. *Foundations of Constraint Satisfaction*. Academic Press, 1993.

44. Pascal Van Hentenryck. *Constraint Satisfaction in Logic Programming*. Logic Programming Series. MIT Press, Cambridge, MA, 1989.

45. Pascal Van Hentenryck. Incremental constraint satisfaction in logic programming. In *Proceedings 6th International Conference on Logic Programming*, 1989.

46. G. M. White and L. Kang. A logic approach to the resolution of constraints in timetabling. *European Journal of Operations Research*, 61:306–317, 1992.

47. M. Yoshikawa, K. Kaneko, Y. Yomura, and M. Watanabe. A constraint-based approach to high-school timetabling problems: A case study. In *Proceedings of AAAI'94 Conference*, 1994.

Complete University Modular Timetabling Using Constraint Logic Programming

Gyuri Lajos[1]

Division of Artificial Intelligence, School of Computer Studies, University of Leeds, England

Abstract. In preparation for the changeover to a new modular degree structure, at the University of Leeds, a new modular timetable for the 1993-94 academic session had to be constructed from scratch. This paper describes our experience in constructing a large scale modular timetable using Constraint Logic Programming techniques.

1   Introduction

The modularisation of degree schemes across the University of Leeds required the construction of a completely new timetable for the entire University from scratch for the 1993-94 academic session. Since an attempt to find a suitable "off the shelf" timetabling solution proved to be unsuccessful, a joint project between researchers in the School of Computer Studies, led by Professor Simon French, and the Registry Division of Planning and Management Information Systems was set up in 1992, charged with the task of delivering the new modular timetable for the 1993-94 academic session. The School of Computer Studies had been responsible for the design and maintenance of a database capable of holding the necessary data for central timetabling, and the development of a scheduling algorithm and program to compute the timetable.

The "in house" development of the new central timetable gave us greater control over decisions, and enabled completion of the task in a considerably smaller budget and shorter time scale than would have been required (or available) for an outside agency. The best candidate for this role was Scientia Ltd [13], [1], but their launch, in February 1993, of Syllabus Plus, a resource scheduling and timetabling program for higher educational institutions, came too late for us.

Timetabling in an educational setting covers a wide range of scheduling problems: the scheduling of students, staff and other resources in both time and space. It comprises two distinct phases:

1. The programmes of study are defined for each class or group of students. For each class appropriate resources both in terms of manpower and teaching space are designated.

* This research has been partially supported by the KCM (Knowledge and Constraint Management) Initiative of the University Funding Councils' Information Systems Committee, and the New Technologies Initiative (NTI) of the Higher Education Funding Councils' Joint Information Systems Committee.

2. Once an agreement has been reached concerning these requirements all the teaching activities are timetabled so that they are compatible with the previously identified requirements.

This paper deals only with the second phase of the overall timetabling process.

The techniques used to compute timetables on the basis of appropriate information sources are varied. The oldest, and most popular technique is based on graph colouring algorithms. [11] gives a good introduction to this approach. Graph colouring is an extensively researched approach with many refinements [18], [8]. Timetabling is known to be NP-hard precisely because, in its purest form, it is reducible to graph colouring. The main disadvantage of the graph colouring approach to timetabling, in practice, is the difficulty and sophistication required for incorporating practical constraints into the problem formulation.

Integer programming formulations of the timetabling problem can be given, but their major drawback is that the numbers of variables and constraints become intractably large for practical problems [4].

Interest in probabilistic search methods, such as Simulated Annealing, [2], [15], Genetic Algorithms [9],[6], [10] and Neural Networks [19] is growing. [12] compares simulated annealing with graph colouring. Although these techniques can be effective, they are still largely experimental, and their performance can be unpredictable. Furthermore, they require *all* the constraints to be incorporated into a single cost function. Because of the inherent difficulty of quantifying the relevant factors [17] the appropriateness of a cost function cannot be guaranteed. Minor changes in the cost function can result in large variation in performance and/or effectiveness. With genetic algorithms, this difficulty is compounded by the need to invent ad hoc, domain specific, genetic operators. Of course, if in the timetabling problem optimisation is important, than then stochastic methods come into their own.

Interactive algorithms like [7] are attractive for medium scale problems, but there is no human expertise available that can reasonably expected to make the right choices on the scale attempted here.

In contrast, Constraint Logic Programming (CLP) offers distinct advantages, with few of the drawbacks of other approaches [21], [22]. CLP generalises Logic Programming (LP) by replacing unification with constraint solving over a particular domain (e.g. finite sets, integers or reals, etc.). A CLP program is a set of clauses, as in LP, but each clause may now contain constraints in its body. The satisfiability of these constraints is then checked at each computation step. This, in turn, can lead to the removal of inconsistent values from the domains of the variables not yet instantiated. This process is known as *forward checking*. The gain in efficiency of program execution that this *a priori* pruning of the search space brings can make certain difficult combinatorial problems tractable. CLP supports a methodology for formulating combinatorial problems in terms of variables, their domains and the constraints that govern the assignment of values to variables drawn from their explicitly stated domains. CLP combines the declarativeness of LP with the efficiency of constraint solving techniques. It allows the separation of declarative information pertaining to the *logic* of the problem from *control*. The *logic* of the problem is stated in the form of variables, their domains and constraints between them. The *control* information is given in the form of *labelling* strategies which govern the order in which variables are chosen to be instantiated with appropriate values.

CLP is particularly well suited for timetabling problems. It allows the formulation of *all* the constraints of the problem in a more declarative way than other approaches. It shares one drawback, common to most approaches, that its performance can be greatly effected by even minor changes in problem formulation. One advantage still remains, that the alternatives in formulation are still within the bounds of logical equivalence.

A CLP formulation of a problem can also be submitted to an optimisation constraint. [14] reports on the construction of optimum timetables according to a given cost function. An advantage of this approach is that it enables the relaxation of certain constraints through appropriate modification of the cost function. Whether this approach would scale up (2000+ teaching periods) remains doubtful.[2] [5] rightly emphasises the importance of constraint relaxation in the context of timetabling. Because of the above advantages the decision was made early to use CLP, without optimisation but with some constraint relaxation, see Sect(s). 4.1 and 4.6.

In this paper we describe the main features of the CLP program that was used to compute the first modular timetable for the University of Leeds. The next section introduces the timetabling data model and all the constraints that a solution to the timetabling problem had to satisfy. Section 3 introduces the main features and the built-in constraints of DecisionPower Constraint (DPC) [3] that were used. Section 4 describes how the constraints of the problem were expressed in terms of DPC and the labelling strategy used. Section 5 gives an overview of the implementation. Section 6 presents the results and the conclusions drawn from comparisons with comparable attempts at solving the timetabling problem.

2 Timetabling Data Model and Constraints

Our Data Model of the timetabling problem is based on the concept of an *"offering,"* signifying a related set of teaching activities to be timetabled. Each offering comprises one or more *"blocks"* of contiguous periods of *"classes"* or teaching activities, such as lectures, tutorials, practicals etc. The timetable must satisfy the following constraints:

C1 *No-Clash Constraints:* for *academic* reasons certain offerings cannot be timetabled at the same time as others, e.g., there should be no clashes between: compulsory offerings of a given programme of study, offerings taught by the same lecturer and sections of the same offering. Of course, there should not be clashes between *classes* of the same *offering*.

---

[2] Timings in the range of 35 minutes for timetabling 37 subjects with a total of 135 teaching periods have been reported.

[3] DecisionPower is ICL's commercialised implementation of the Constraint Handling in Prolog (CHIP) system donated by ICL under the KCM Initiative

C2 <u>Space Constraints</u>: there must be enough teaching space (lecture theatres, seminar rooms, labs, etc.) for the blocks timetabled at each time period.

C3 <u>Smoothness:</u> decreasing the upper limit on the number n of teaching activities that can be timetabled in any given period improves the smoothness of the distribution of timetabled classes and can influence the utilisation of teaching space.

C4 <u>Time Constraints</u>: certain teaching is fixed in time. e.g. because it involves outside lecturers or certain ranges of periods are designated as particularly suitable. In addition, each department may require that no member of staff teaches at a particular time so that staff meetings/research seminars may be held.

C5 <u>Option Groups:</u> in a modular degree scheme students are offered option groups, groups of offerings (courses or modules) from which they have to choose a predetermined number. Unlike the case of compulsory modules of a degree scheme, some clashes are allowed within option groups, but their number is normally limited in some ways.

C6 <u>Spreading:</u> *blocks* of the same *offering* should be timetabled on separate days.

C7 <u>Contiguity:</u> *blocks* comprising more than one period should be timetabled contiguously.

In addition to most, if not all, of these types of constraint, timetabling systems in general may cater for others, such as: ordering of blocks within an offering (e.g. practical should follow lectures for the same course), geographic constraints, compactness requirements etc..

The feasibility study undertaken over the Summer and during the Autumn Term of 1992-93, using graph colouring techniques, identified large cliques: i.e. sets of offerings in which no pairs could be timetabled at the same time. These cliques pointed to bottlenecks in the modularisation plans and were used to target discussions on where plans needed be modified or modules *sectioned* (duplicated). The feasibility study also indicated the need to extend the working week to include "*marginal*" periods (Monday to Friday) in addition to "*core*" times. Figure 1 shows *core times* during the week shaded dark. This classification of periods was used in the labelling process, see Sect. 4.9.

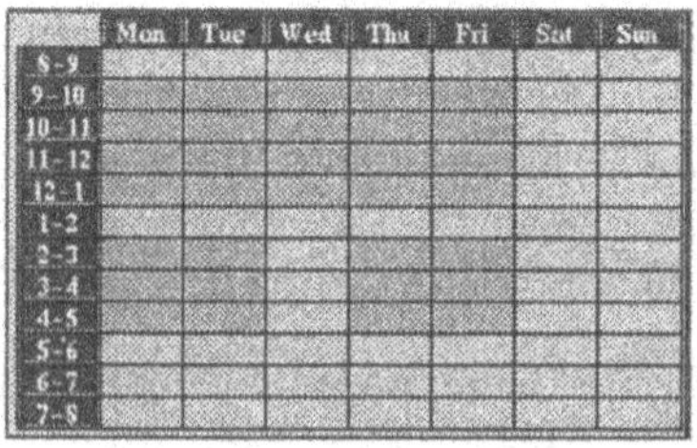

Fig. 1. Core Times

Subject to the above constraints the timetable had to meet several conflict-ing objectives: e.g. minimise the volume of teaching outside "core" hours and maximise the utilisation of space.

3 Constraint Logic Programming

A Constraint Satisfaction Problem (CSP), [20], is defined by a set of variables, and their associated domains together with a set of constraints that determines the combination of values that the variables can take. A solution to a CSP is an assignment of values to all the variables that satisfy all the constraints.

The beauty of CLP is that it provides a methodology for formulating con-straint satisfaction problems. The overall structure of CLP programs for solving CSPs is always the same:

1. State the domains of the problem variables.
2. State all the constraints.
3. Generate values.

This is reflected in the structure of the code one writes: [4]

```
solve(Variables) :-
    state_domains(Variables),
    state_constraints(Variables),
    generate_values(Variables).
```

Thus CLP supports the separation of *logic* and *control* as in LP. That is to say, in stating the domains and the constraints we can concentrate on describing the *logic* of the problem. In specifying how the values are to be generated in labelling, we can impart *control* information by concentrating on two issues: *variable ordering* – which variables to instantiate first, and *value ordering* – what values to choose from the domains of the chosen variables first. Devising different schemes for both is the way in CLP to introduce problem-specific *heuristics*.

As we shall see in the next section, the timetabling problem can readily be formulated in terms of finite (integer) domains, making use of the following built-in constraints:

$\mathrm{atmost}(N,L,V)$.   Atmost N variables in the list L can have the value V.

arithmetic constraints   equal (#=), non-equal (##), greater (#>), smaller or equal (#<=).

4 Problem Formulation and Constraints

This section describes how the university timetabling problem is modelled as a Constraint Satisfaction Problem, and discusses the main issues in formulating the constraints of the problem.

---

[4] or rather, in the structure of the program that is generated for a given instance of a problem.

4.1 Domain Variables

The decision on what the variables and their respective domains should be in a CLP formulation of a CSP can greatly influence the way constraints can be formulated and their computational effectiveness. Given our data model of the timetabling problem the task can be simply stated as: timetable each *class* of each *block* of each *offering* at some suitable period in the week respecting all the constraints. Looking at the problem in these terms it is natural to propose to introduce variables corresponding to each *class*. The domain of these "*class variables*" is then simply a set of integers representing periods in the timetable. We have chosen a simple consecutive numbering of periods running from 8 am on Monday to 8 pm on Saturday, giving 60 periods. We have also introduced additional, so called *virtual* periods, thus *relaxing* the constraint of feasibility. In this way we were able to pin point the most problematic offerings, candidates for *sectioning* and/or bringing forward consideration of problematic offerings in the labelling process.

This is by no means the only possible way of introducing domain variables for timetabling problems. For example, in [4] Azevedo and Barahona introduced problem variables corresponding to the *starting time* of each block and used a special coding scheme for these times. A clear advantage of their approach is that it involves fewer variables. The disadvantage is that the constraint that specific blocks should not overlap becomes complicated (they need to incorporate contiguity constraints) and presumably less efficient than simple disequations between class variables. In our model contiguity and spreading constraint can be formulated separately, but as will be shown in Sect. 4.9 can in fact be incorporated into the labelling process with substantial reduction in the use of virtual memory.

Boizumault *et al* in [5] also use variables representing the starting times of each lecture (in terms of quarters of an hour), but use *cumulative* constraints to express a range of timetabling constraints. Their formulation differs radically from ours or that of Azevedo and Barahona. In a future paper we intend to explore the "design space" of possible CLP formulations of the timetabling problem by attempting to solve one particular timetabling problem using different formulations.

4.2 No-Clash Constraints ($C1$)

Most of the constraints that the timetable has to satisfy are stated at the level of *offerings* and not that of *classes*. Each offering has a unique integer *Code* and a *Name* given in the form:

$$\texttt{offering}(Code, Name).$$

For each offering contiguity data is recorded in the following format:

$$\texttt{cdt}(Code, Length, Pattern).$$

Pattern is a list of integers giving the length of each *block* that makes up the offering

Length is the total length of the offering (i.e. the sum of the length of the blocks).

Class variables corresponding to a given offering are generated according to the following scheme: Let X be the name of an offering, let b_X be the number of blocks that make up that offering, let l_i be the length of the ith block, and let $X_{j,k}$ represents the domain variable corresponding to the kth period of the jth block; then the domain variables for an offering X are given as the list:

$$[X_{1,1}, \ldots, X_{1,l_1}, X_{2,1}, \ldots, X_{2,l_2}, \ldots, X_{b_X,1}, \ldots, X_{b_X,l_{b_X}}]$$

In the following the notation $\overline{X}$ will denote the sequence of domain variables separated by commas for offering named X.

The constraint that there should be no clashes between classes of an offering can be stated as:

$$\texttt{alldistinct([}\overline{X_i}\texttt{]),}$$

Thus the program generated for an instance of the timetabling problem, based on a given set of data, contains goals of this form for all offerings for $1 \leq i \leq$ *number of offerings*.

For each offering a list of offerings is given with which the given offering should not clash:

$$\texttt{data(}\textit{Code}, \textit{Length}, \textit{NoClashList}\texttt{).}$$

Code is an integer code for an offering

NoClashList is a list of *Codes* of offerings with which the given offering should not overlap.

A notable feature of this data format is that the codes in the no-clash list of offerings are strictly greater then the code of the offering for which they are given. E.g.

$$\texttt{data(139,5,[718,719,824,825,922,942]).}$$

This guarantees that symmetric information is not repeated.

The constraint that offering X should not clash with offerings Y_1, Y_2, $\ldots$, Y_k is stated as:

$$\texttt{listoutof([}\overline{X}\texttt{],[}\overline{Y_1}, \overline{Y_2}, \ldots, \overline{Y_k}\texttt{]).}$$

where $\texttt{listoutof}$ imposes the constraint that all class variables in $[\overline{X}]$ have values distinct from those in $[\overline{Y_1}, \overline{Y_2}, \ldots, \overline{Y_k}]$.

4.3 Space Constraints ($C2$)

The purpose of space constraints is to ensure that when a class is timetabled at a certain period appropriate teaching space is in fact available to accommodate it. To this end, all available teaching rooms are categorised according to their capacity:

$$Capacity_i \leq Capacity_j \quad for \ i < j \ and \ 1 \leq i,j \leq M \qquad (1)$$

where M denotes the number of such categories. The point of arranging these categories in this order is to allow for the possibility of assigning classes not only to rooms of just the right sizes, but if available, to any other rooms in *any* higher category of higher capacity.

For each category the number of teaching rooms in that category is given together with a list of codes of offerings that can just be accommodated in that category.

$$\texttt{space}(Category, Count, Codes).$$

> *Category* is an integer giving the accommodation category.
> *Count* is the number of teaching rooms in that category.
> *Codes* is a list of the codes of offerings that can be accommodated in the given category.

Based on this information space constraints are imposed as follows: Let C_i denote the list of class variables corresponding to the list of offerings that are designated for a given category i of teaching rooms. Let Q_i denote the result of appending all the lists of class variables of all C_k for $i \leq k \leq M$, giving a list of all class variables corresponding to classes that would fit into rooms of category i or higher. Let R_i denote the number of teaching rooms in category i. Then the constraint that at most X_i classes can be timetabled in period p of all classes that can fit into a room of category i or higher can be specified as:

$$\texttt{atmost}(X_i, Q_i, p). \quad \text{where } X_i = \sum_{k=i}^{k=M} R_k \qquad (2)$$

Constraints of this form are then imposed for all i and p for $1 \leq p \leq 60$. The above treatment of space constraint is comparable to the *size limiter* in [17, page 312-3].

4.4 Smoothness ($C3$)

Let V denote the list of all class variables. Then the constraint that atmost n number of classes can be timetabled in any period p can simply be stated as:

$$\texttt{atmost}(n, V, p).$$

Figure 2 shows the distribution of the number of timetabled classes for the parameter $n = 68$. In practice, smoothness may not even be an objective. The machinery, however, is there to limit the number of classes scheduled for each period.

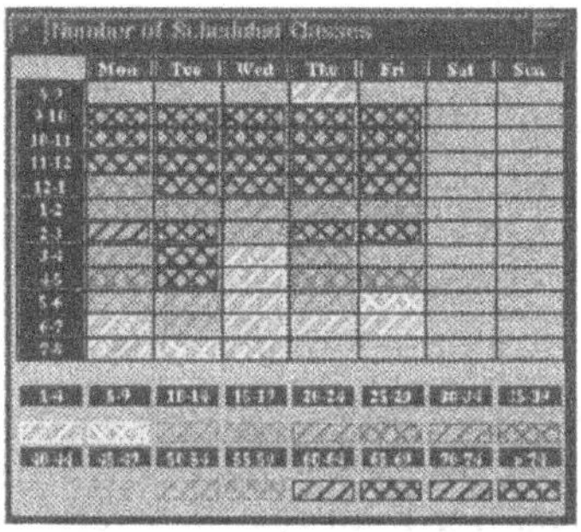

Fig. 2. Space utilisation

4.5 Time Constraints ($C4$)

There are two types of time constraints. The first designates certain periods that should not be used. These are termed "*avoid*" time constraints. The second type of time constraints are used to designate certain periods to be used. These are termed "*use*" time constraints. Time constraints can be imposed at either the level of offerings or blocks of an offering. Avoid time constraints stated at the level of offerings are used, for example, to reserve certain periods for departmental meetings/seminars. Time constraints stated at the level of blocks can be used to mark out certain periods to be used for each block of an offering. Although every "use" constraints can be stated equivalently as an "avoid" constraint, and vice versa, in any given circumstance one may be more natural to state than the other. The format of time constraint data is:

$$\texttt{timec}(\textit{Code}, \textit{Mode}, \textit{Duration}, \textit{Day}, \textit{Start}, \textit{End}).$$

Code	identifies the offering to which the time constraint is to apply.
Mode	is either u for *use* or a for *avoid* time constraints
Day	specifies the day of the week to be considered, **mf** designates Monday to Friday.
Start	specifies the starting time of the periods to be considered.
End	specifies the end time of the periods to be considered.
Duration	Length of contiguous periods to be used, (0 for avoid mode).

some examples are given below:

timec(3,u, 2, mf, 10, 0). *Use a two hour period, any day after 10*

timec(4,u, 2, mo, 14, 16). *Use a two hour period, Monday, from 14-16*

timec(30,a, 0, tu, 14, 19). *Avoid Tuesday between 14 and 19 hours*

Avoid constraints are imposed by generating appropriate inequalities for all the periods to be avoided. *Use* constraints are imposed as inequalities for the complement of the periods to be used.

4.6 Option Groups ($C5$)

In a *modular* degree scheme students are offered *option groups* from which to select a certain number, M, of modules. For each option group of O modules, there is a given integer c, which specifies the minimum number of offerings required to be clash free. Typically $O > c \geq M$.

The option group constraint is formulated as follows: Let $X^1, X^2 \cdots X^n$ be offerings (options) belonging to a given option group G. For each offering X^i let $\overline{X^i}$ be variables representing the classes for the given offering. Two offerings X^i and X^j are said to be clash free if all the class variables for both modules have different values.

In order to guarantee that at least a given number c of offerings are clash free in a given option group the following procedure is used:

INPUT: list of list of class variables $[[\overline{X^1}], [\overline{X^2}], \cdots , [\overline{X^n}]]$ corresponding to the offerings in the option group G and the integer c which specifies the minimum number of offerings required to be free of clashes.

STEPS:

1. A list of clash free offerings is initialised to contain the first offering in the option group (i.e. the list of class variables for the first offering).
2. The lists of remaining offerings are considered in turn as follows:
   - First the constraint is imposed that the offering currently considered should not clash with the offerings in the list of already accumulated clash free offerings. If the constraint is satisfiable the counter c is decremented and the list of class variables corresponding to the offering under consideration is added to the list of clash free offerings. The procedure is recursively invoked with the new counter, clash free list and the remaining offerings.
   - When the constraint imposed cannot be satisfied, (i.e. no assignment to the class variables of the currently considered offering can be found that would not clash with some class variable of the accumulated clash free offerings, due to time constraints already imposed, for example) the currently considered offering is skipped (i.e. it is not added to the list of clash free offerings) and the process is recursively entered with the remaining offerings (the counter and the clash free list are left unchanged).
3. The process is terminated when the counter is reduced to 1. The counter is one because by picking the first offering we already obtained, trivially, one clash free offering, so we need only to repeat imposing the clash free constraint successfully $c - 1$ times.

The above procedure is liable to over constrain the option groups. It may well be the case that there are sufficient numbers of clash free offerings further down the list which have not even been considered since the constraints of no clashes are imposed at least for the first c offerings, without ever needing to consider later ones. Given the nature of the task, that there should be as many options available as possible; this a desirable feature. Also, this procedure guarantees that, if possible, options that are listed earlier in the group will be timetabled clash free.

In order to avoid the clustering of all the unconsidered offerings into the same period we introduced the additional constraint that prevents more then a given number of classes to be timetabled at the same time. This parameter can be specified at the command line. Useful values are 2 or 3. In the case when this limit turns out to be too restricting an appropriate message is issued and the constraint is relaxed dynamically upon failure by increasing the parameter for the given option group before attempting to impose this constraint with the incremented parameter.

4.7 Spreading (C6)

Imposing the constraint that two blocks of the same offering should be timetabled on different days involves two steps:

1. Determine the day on which each block is timetabled.
2. Stating that they should not be equal. This can be expressed as constraints on class variables as follows:

```
onday_c(Var,Day) :-
    Day::1..7, Var + 12 #> 12*Day, Var #<=  Day*12.

not_on_same_day_c([]).
not_on_same_day_c([Block|Rest_of_Offerings]) :-
    B=[V1|Vs], onday_c(V1,Day1), not_on_day_c(Day1,Rest_of_Offerings),
    not_on_same_day_c(Rest_of_Offerings).

not_on_day_c(Day,□).
not_on_day_c(Day,[B|Rest_of_Offerings]) :-
    B=[V1|Vs], onday_c(V1,Day1), Day ## Day1,
    not_on_day_c(Day,Rest_of_Offerings).
```

Then it would be left up to the labelling process to awaken these constraints. The labelling process should ideally pick days at random so as to avoid the problem of always trying to fit everything on the same day to begin with. Since the labelling process is already required to make these choices, it turned out to be advantageous to make the labelling itself responsible for spreading, see Sect. 4.9.

4.8 Contiguity (C7)

Although contiguity constraints, like spreading, can readily be stated:

```
contig_c([P1]) :- !.
contig_c([P1,P2|Rest]) :-
    onday_c(P1,D1), P2 #= P1+1, onday_c(P2,D2), D1 #= D2,
    contig_c([P2|Rest]).
```

it again turned out to be beneficial to leave it up to the labelling process, as part of the *value ordering*, to ensure that contiguity constraints are not violated.

4.9 Labelling heuristics

The *variable ordering* we used in labelling relied on a static order determined by a measure of the difficulty of timetabling each offering so that the most difficult offerings were to be timetabled first. This measure took into account the number of offerings which could not be timetabled simultaneously and the lengths of each block. Our measure has worked well in most cases. Some manual adjustment were still required. When a run "timetabled" offerings into *virtual* times, our first line of attack was to select them to be timetabled earlier in subsequent runs. Offerings that could not be timetabled this way were *sectioned*, i.e. the group of students who were to take a given offering was broken up into smaller groups, thus reducing the scope of conflicts, and each group was timetabled separately.

For *value ordering* we have used a pseudo random generator to pick the days from a list from Monday to Friday so as to avoid timetabling everything on the beginning of the week. A minor modification to this procedure[5] was sufficient to do away with the need of stating spreading constraints altogether. Instead, we now had a labelling process, which by construction, guaranteed that the spreading constraints of the problem were not violated. Once a selection of the day to be tried was made, periods were chosen consecutively, first trying core periods, before marginal or virtual periods, so that contiguity constraints were satisfied. Spreading and contiguity can thus be said to have been interleaved with the labelling of variables. This interleaving had the beneficial effect of reducing nearly by half the otherwise quite excessive (over 600 Mb) virtual memory requirement of a typical run.

5 Implementation

The timetabling program had the usual components for a CLP program. One module was responsible for generating a CLP program that defined an instance of the the problem to be solved on the basis of appropriate data obtained from a data base. About 3000 lines of INGRES Embedded SQL code were used to extract this data. For each run of computing the timetable about 13000 lines of data (in 18 files around 500 Kb) were generated from the database. 300 Kb of this data related to option groups. These files were subsequently converted into Prolog data files, using Emacs code. All of this took 10 minutes of CPU time for a typical run on a Sun 10/20. Then this generated program (850 Kb) was run to obtain a solution to a particular instance of the problem, typically under 5 minutes of CPU time and required up to 1 Giga-byte of virtual memory in the worst case. The virtual memory requirement was substantially reduced

---

[5] Picking days at random and removing them one after the other from a list so that no day was to be picked twice.

once contiguity and spreading constraint were interleaved with labelling instead of being stated declaratively as constraints. The solution then was passed on to another module that interpreted the solution as required. Figure 3 shows the structure diagram for the timetabling system.

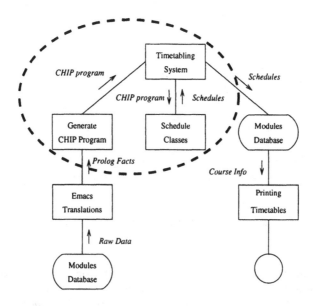

Fig. 3. Structure diagram for Timetabling Program

The scheduling program itself comprises about 2000 lines of Prolog. The bulk of this is concerned with bookkeeping and the generation of a CLP program from a given data. In the course of the project 2 to 3 times more code has been written: test harnesses, including a rudimentary constraint visualisation tool, using KHS 1.4 [6] and of course, as the means of exploring alternatives of CLP formulation of the timetabling problem.

The final timetable for the 1993/94 session timetabled around 2500 classes per week per semester involving over 1000 offerings. This comprised only first and second year offerings. Third year courses were not affected by modularisation in 1993/94 so their previous (non-modular) timetable was kept and was taken into account in scheduling the other years. The timetable for the the 1994/95 and 95/96 had been built on the basis of the timetable that we produced by adding a new modular timetable for third year and taught postgraduates using a commercial package Syllabus Plus by Scientia Ltd.

From the School of Computer Studies the following people have contributed to the timetabling project led by Professor Simon French. Stuart A Roberts and Tony Jenkins were responsible for the database with assistance from Jane Lewis.

---

[6] KHS (Knowledge Based systems HCI server) an object oriented graphics server which is part of DecisionPower.

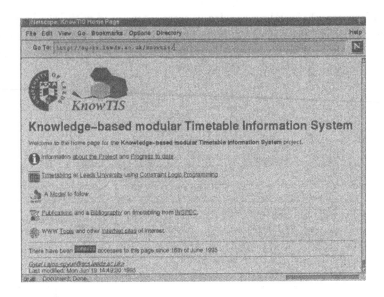

Fig. 4. World Wide Web Home Page

2. D. Abramson. Constructing school timetables using simulated annealing: sequential and parallel algorithms. *Management Science*, 37(1):98–113, Jan. 1991.
3. Eric Atwell and Gyuri Lajos. Knowledge and Constraint Management: Large Scale Applications. In *Knowledge at Work in Universities*, pages 21–25. Leeds University Press, 1993.
4. F. Azevedo and P. Barahona. Timetabling in constraint logic programming. In *Proceedings of World Congress on Expert Systems'94*, January 1994.
5. P. Boizumault, C. Gueret, and N. Jussien. Efficient Labelling and Constraint Relaxation for Solving Time Tabling Problems. In *Proceedings of the Workshop on constraint Languages and their use in Problem Modelling*, pages 116–130, Ithaca, New York, USA, 1994. International Logic Programming Symposium.
6. E.G. Burke, D.G. Elliman, and R.F. Weare. A Genetic Algorithm for University Timetabling. In *Proceedings of the 2nd East-West International Conference on Computer Technologies in Education*, pages 35–40, Crimea, Ukraine, September 1994.
7. E.K. Burke, D.G. Elliman, and R. Weare. A university timetabling system based on graph colouring and constraint manipulation. *Journal of Research on Computing in Education*, 27(1):1–18, 1994.
8. M. Cangalovic and J.A.M. Schreuder. Modelling and solving an acyclic multiperiod timetabling problem. *Discrete Applied Mathematics*, 35(3):177–95, 6 March 1992.
9. A. Colorni, M. Dorigo, and V. Maniezzo. Genetic algorithms and highly constrained problems: the time-table case. In R. Schwefel, H.-P.; Manner, editor, *Parallel Problem Solving from Nature. 1st Workshop,*, pages 55–9, Dortmund, West Germany, 1991. Springer-Verlag.
10. Dave Corne, Peter Ross, and Hsiao-Lan Fang. Fast Practical Evolutionary Timetabling. In T. Fogarty, editor, *Evolutionary Computing: AISB Workshop*

Willi Riha and Margaret West worked on feasibility studies. Margaret was also involved in checking the integrity of the database and the generated timetable. Allan Humphreys acted as a consultant in the early phases. Gyuri Lajos was the sole Prolog programmer on the project, and he is the Research Fellow in the follow-up project KNOWTIS (see below), directed by Eric Atwell and Tony Cohn.

6 Results and Conclusions

We have delivered successfully a new modular timetable which satisfied all the stated constraints and most importantly, gave cause for surprisingly few complaints. To our best knowledge, our use of a Constraint Logic Programming system like DecisionPower for constructing a complete modular timetable on the scale of a university as large as Leeds, is a first. In fact we did not know in advance if it would work. We took encouragement, however, from the work of researchers at the University of Ottawa [16], who have reportedly solved timetabling problems of comparable complexity to ours. Like us they formulated the problem as a Constraint Satisfaction Problem, but have used a mixture of C and WPROLOG. Expressing the problem directly in Prolog required them to code the domain manipulation and forward checking algorithm themselves. Working at a higher level of expressive power of a CLP language as opposed to plain LP, we certainly had an easier task, but presumably it would be easier to take our work as a model then theirs.

One important lesson that we have learnt is to consider the possibility of imposing certain constraints as part of the labelling process as a means of improving performance.

The project was driven by a practical need at Leeds University, but we realised that other Universities might also benefit from our experience. This has led to a follow-up project [3] to document fully the timetabler development and to integrate our successful timetabler and a taught module information server, into a Knowledge-Based Modular Timetable Information System (KNOWTIS) for online access by students and staff at Leeds, and also by planners at other HEIs seeking a model to follow. For further information visit the project's WWW home page at: (see http://agora.leeds.ac.uk/knowtis/).

In conclusion, we have demonstrated the practical utility of Constraint Logic Programming to timetabling on a much larger scale than attempted before. The only real difficulty that we have encountered relates to the the fact that the "search" space of possible logically equivalent formulations appears to be disconcertingly large. It requires some ingenuity and much perseverance to explore successfully. This we believe to be a research area requiring further investigation.

References

1. Syllabus Plus: A Management Aid to efficient Space and Resource Utilisation in Colleges. Scientia Ltd., St. Johns Innovation Centre, Cowley Rd. Cambridge CB4 4WS, Tel 01223 421221, 1993.

1994, Selected Papers, number 865 in Lecture Notes in Computer Science. Springer Verlag, 1994.

11. D. de Werra. An introduction to timetabling. In *European Journal of Operational Research* [17], pages 151–162.

12. K.A. Dowsland. A timetabling problem in which clashes are inevitable. *Journal of the Operational Research Society*, 41(10):907–18, Oct. 1990.

13. R. Everetsz, M. Dalgarno, G. Forster, and S. Watt. Syllabus: A Solution to the School Timetabling Problem. In *The First European Conference on the Practical Application of Lisp*, pages 301–308, 1990.

14. H. Frangouli and V. Harmandas P. Stamatopoulos. UTSE: Construction of Optimum timetables for University Courses - A CLP Based Approach. In *The Third International Conference and Exhibition on Practical Applications of Prolog*, 1995.

15. Alain Hertz. Finding a feasible course schedule using tabu search. *Discrete Applied Mathematics*, 35(3):255–70, 6 March 1992.

16. L. Kang, G.H. Von Schoenberg, and G.M. White. Complete university timetabling using logic. *Computers & Education*, 17(2):145–53, 1991.

17. L. Kang and G.M. White. A logic approach to the resolution of constraints in timetabling. *European Journal of Operational Research*, 61(3):306–17, 25 Sept. 1992.

18. L. Kiaer and J. Yellen. Weighted graphs and university course timetabling. *Computers & Operations Research*, 19(1):59–67, Jan. 1992.

19. M. Kovacic. Timetable construction with markovian neural network. *European Journal of Operational Research*, 69(1):92–6, 27 Aug. 1993.

20. Edward Tsang. *Foundations of Constraint Satisfaction*. Academic Press, 1994.

21. Pascal Van Hentenryck. *Constraint Satisfaction in Logic Programming*. Logic Programming Series. MIT Press, Cambridge, MA, 1989.

22. Pascal Van Hentenryck. Constraint logic programming. *Knowledge Engineering Review*, 6(3):151–194, September 1991. (Also available as Brown University Technical Report CS-91-05).

Using Oz for College Timetabling

Martin Henz and Jörg Würtz

German Research Center for Artificial Intelligence (DFKI)
Stuhlsatzenhausweg 3, D–66123 Saarbrücken, Germany
{henz,wuertz}@dfki.uni-sb.de

Abstract. In this paper, we concentrate on a typical scheduling problem: the computation of a timetable for a German college. Like many other scheduling problems, this problem contains a variety of complex constraints and necessitates special-purpose search strategies. Techniques from Operations Research and traditional constraint logic programming are not able to express these constraints and search strategies on a sufficiently high level of abstraction. We show that the higher-order concurrent constraint language Oz provides this high-level expressivity, and can serve as a useful programming tool for college timetabling.

1 Introduction

Constraint Logic Programming over finite domains is a rapidly growing research area aiming at the solution of large combinatorial problems. For many real-world problems the constraint logic programming approach (extended to the concurrent constraint approach) is competitive or better than traditional Operations Research (OR) algorithms. OR techniques lack flexibility and the effort to achieve customized solutions is often unaffordable.

The power of constraint logic programming has been proven by languages such as CHIP [DVS+88], Prolog III [Col90] or CLP(R) [JM87]. To solve real-world problems, several new constraints were added as primitives (like *atmost* or the *cumulative* constraint [AB93] for scheduling or placement problems importing experience from OR). This approach might be viable for well known problems but is not going to foster the exploration of new areas of applications. More clarity and flexibility for the programmer was achieved by clp(FD) [DC93] (inspired by [VSD91]). This approach is based on a single primitive constraint (called indexical) with which more complicated constraints may be defined. In terms of efficiency, clp(FD) is competitive with CHIP for certain benchmarks, and adds some flexibility. But still missing is one characteristic that we consider essential for solving certain constraint problems: *the flexibility to exploratively invent new constraints and search strategies*. While experimental languages such as cc(FD) [VSD95] and AKL(FD) [CCD94] provide flexibility in formulating constraints, their search strategies are still fixed.

Oz [Smo95b, SS94, SSW94, ST95] is a concurrent constraint language providing for functional, object-oriented and constraint programming. It is based on a simple yet powerful computation model [Smo95a], which can be seen as an extension of the concurrent constraint model [SR90].

In this paper, we describe how the unique features of Oz contribute to computing the timetable of a German college that we describe in Section 2. The problem contains a combination of complex constraints preventing the application of more standard timetabling techniques.

What can Oz offer to solve this problem?

Constraint Programming. The concurrent constraint language Oz allows to restrict the possible values of variables to finite sets of integers. In Section 3, we introduce some basics about concurrent constraint programming. Crucial for constraint programming is the ability to add constraints on variables concurrently and incrementally. In Oz, this is done by *propagators*, which can express several constraints of our timetabling problem as shown in Section 3.

Reified Constraints. A general scheme, called *reified constraints*, allows to express the remaining constraints of our timetable problem, as discussed in Section 4. Reified constraints allow to reflect the fact that a constraint holds into a 0/1-valued variable.

Constructive Disjunction. Disjunctive constraints (like resource or capacity constraints), can be used constructively in Oz, i.e. information common to different branches can be lifted out for active pruning. We describe constructive disjunction [VSD95] in Section 5 and show how it can be used for ovelap constraints in our timetabling problem.

Flexible Enumeration. In Oz, the programmer can invent customized search strategies for solving the timetabling problem and optimizing the solutions found. In Section 6, we develop a search strategy especially adapted to our problem, combining the first-fail heuristic for variable selection with a priority scheme for value selection. This strategy results in an efficiently computed first solution approximating an optimality criteria for the distribution of the college courses.

Optimization. This first solution can be further optimized using a branch-and-bound technique. Optimization can be achieved through an incremental process, allowing the user to inspect the current solution *any time* and to interrupt and resume the optimization at will, as described in Section 7.

Interoperability. The interoperability libraries of Oz allow convenient programming of graphical user interfaces, including the visualization of the computed timetables, as presented in Section 8.

In Section 9, we compare the described techniques with other approaches in constraint logic programming.

Due to space limitations we cannot further detail other aspects of Oz like conditionals and disjunctions, which have shown to be useful for other constraint problems. The interested reader is referred to the documentation of the Oz system (see concluding remark of the paper).

2 The Problem

Our goal was to find a weekly timetable for the Catholic College for Social Work in Saarbrücken, Germany, in the spring semester 95. The school offers a four year program for a degree in social work. Some courses are mandatory for and dedicated to students of a certain year while others are optional and open to all students. There are 91 courses, 34 instructors and 7 rooms of varying size. The assignment of instructors to courses is fixed. Each course needs to take place in a room of sufficient size. There are five school days, and the courses are being held between 8:15 am and 5 pm. They may start every quarter of an hour. There are short courses of 3 quarters and long courses of 6 quarters. There must be a break of at least one quarter after a short course and of at least two quarters after a long course.

In the following we state the additional constraints that a schedule must fulfill.

C1) Some courses are limited to certain time slots.
C2) Some instructors have times of unavailability.
C3) There are different lunch breaks for the different years in the program.
C4) Some courses must be held after others.
C5) There are sets of courses whose members must be held in parallel.
C6) To every course, a room of sufficient size must be assigned.
C7) An instructor can only teach one course at a time.
C8) Two instructors want to take turns in caring for an infant child and therefore cannot teach at the same time.
C9) The mandatory courses of each year must not overlap.
C10) Some optional courses must not overlap with courses of the first two years, and others not with courses of any year.
C11) Two mandatory courses of a year may overlap if they are split in groups.
C12) The instructors do not want to teach on more than 3 days a week.
C13) All members of some sets of courses must be held on different days.

3 Constraints and Propagators in Oz

Our goal is to assign to every course a starting time and a room. Note that the assignment of instructors to courses is fixed in our college. Here, we concentrate on the starting time and show in Section 4 how the room assignment is handled.

The courses are held between 8:15 am and 5 pm on five school days and may start every quarter of an hour. Thus, there are $36 * 5 = 180$ possible starting

---
[1] In Germany, several holidays in the spring semester fall on a Thursday.

times for each course. Since there are 91 courses, the overall search space contains 180^{91} elements. Instead of enumerating the whole search space and testing whether a valuation satisfies all the constraints (generate & test), the idea of constraint programming is to restrict the search space a priori through constraints. While the search space is being explored, more information on the starting times becomes known, i.e., the search space can be further pruned, while it is being explored. A programming language for constraint programming needs to provide flexible means to express pruning operators. In this and the following section, we concentrate on pruning operators, while the exploration of the search space is described in Section 6 and Section 7.

We represent a course, say "Psychology 101", by grouping together its start time, duration, instructor, room size, and its name in a record of the form

```
Psych101 = course(start     : _
                  dur       : 6
                  instructor: `Smith`
                  roomsize  : big
                  name      : `Psychology 101`)
```

The underscore _ indicates that no information on the **start** value is known. The starting time of a course is represented by an integer denoting the corresponding quarter of the school week. Because initially it is known that the course must start between quarter 1 and quarter 180 we can add the constraint

```
Psych101.start :: 1#180
```

expressing that this course can take values between 1 and 180, i.e., **Psych101.start** $\in \{1, \ldots, 180\}$ in a more mathematical notation. We say that the starting time is constrained to a *finite domain*.

Such constraints are stored in a *constraint store*. For the constraints residing in the constraint store Oz provides efficient algorithms to decide satisfiability. The largest set of integers satisfying all the constraints for a variable in the store, is called the *domain* of that variable. To distinguish the constraints in the store from more complex constraints, we often call them *basic constraints*.

The idea of constraint programming is to install constraints that further limit the possible **start** value for every course. For example, a constraint of type C1 may say that the course "Psychology 101" must be held on Monday morning or on Tuesday morning. This constraint is *imposed* on the constraint store by the expression **Psych101.start** ::[1#18 37#54][2] limiting the start value in the constraint store to satisfy **Psych101.start** $\in \{1, \ldots, 18, 37, \ldots, 54\}$.

Besides C1, the constraints C2 and C3 can be expressed by such constraints.

---

[2] The term [1#18 37#54] denotes a list consisting of the two pairs 1#18 and 37#54.

For more complex arithmetic constraints it is
known that deciding their satisfiability is not
computationally tractable (there are several
NP-complete problems on finite domains, e.g.

propagator   ···   propagator

graph coloring). Thus, such constraints are not contained in the constraint store
but are modeled by *installing* so called *propagators* inspecting the constraint
store, as depicted above.

A propagator inspects the store and when values are ruled out from the domain
of a variable, it may add more information to the store, i.e., it may amplify the
store by adding more basic constraints. Thus, we are replacing *global consistency*,
which is assured for the constraints in the store, by *local consistency* where
unsatisfiability may not be detected. It is important to allow propagators to act
concurrently since it is not statically known when they will be able to perform
their computation. This is one major motivation behind *concurrent* constraint
programming.

As an example consider a constraint of type C4, which states that the course
"Sociology 101" must be held after our course "Psychology 101". It can be
expressed by installing the propagator

`Psych101.start + Psych101.dur =<: Socio101.start`

For example, if `Psych101.start` is constrained as above to Monday morning or
Tuesday morning, and `Psych101.dur` to 6, then the propagator will add the basic
constraint

`Socio101.start :: 7#180`

to the constraint store. Vice versa, if later on it becomes known that `Socio101`
starts the latest at 10:30 am on Monday (`Socio101.start` $\in \{7, \ldots, 10\}$), then
`Psych101.start` will be constrained to start the latest at 9:00 am (`Psych101.start`
$\in \{1, \ldots, 4\}$). Note that the propagator remains active, waiting for more information on either `Psych101.start` or `Socio101.start` to come.

Observe that in the implementation we have to add the necessary break after
`Psych101` (depending on `Psych101.dur`) but we omit the breaks in this presentation for simplicity.

The constraint C5 is modeled by using the propagator `=:` expressing equality.
Note that `S=:T` is modeled by `S=<:T S>=:T`. Thus holes in the domains of `S` and
`T` as in `Psych101.start` are not considered for `=:`. It implements only partial
arc-consistency instead of full arc-consistency in the terminology of [Mac77].
Interval-consistency can be implemented efficiently since the propagator only
needs to watch the currently smallest and biggest possible values for the involved
variables.

4 Reified Constraints

We have seen in the previous section that propagators are crucial components in a constraint programming system, since they allow to prune the search space. A constraint programming language therefore must strive to easily express many kinds of propagators. In this section, we introduce *reified constraints* as a generic tool to express new propagators and show how the remaining constraints C6 - C13 of our college problem can be expressed with them.

The constraint C6 says that for every point in time the number of courses of a certain size must not exceed the number of rooms of that size. Assume that there are `NumberOfRooms` different rooms available of a given size. If we are able to compute for every quarter of an hour `Q` of the teaching week the number of courses `CoursesAtQ` of the given size being held in this quarter, then we only need to install the propagator

```
CoursesAtQ =<: NumberOfRooms
```

to express C6 for every quarter `Q` and every room size. To compute `CoursesAtQ` it would be convenient to be able to constrain a boolean variable `CAtQ` to 1 if a given course overlaps `Q` and to 0 if it does not. Then `CoursesAtQ` can be obtained simply by computing the sum of all `CAtQ` over all courses of the given size. To compute `CAtQ`, we use *reified constraints*, i.e. propagators that reflect the validity of a constraint into a variable. Reified constraints are also known in the literature as *nested constraints* [BO92, Sid93].

The constraint whose validity we want to reflect, has the form

```
Course.start :: Q-Course.dur+1 # Q
```

expressing that `Course` has started before or at quarter `Q`, but not finished at `Q`.

Now, we reflect the validity of this constraint into the variable `CAtQ`:

```
CAtQ = Course.start :: Q-Course.dur+1 # Q
```

First of all, every reified constraint always constrains the first variable to be either 0 or 1, i.e. `CAtQ` $\in \{0,1\}$. As in previous propagators, information flows either way. If the store logically implies `Course.start` $\in \{$`Q-Course.dur+1`$,\ldots,$`Q`$\}$, `CAtQ` is constrained to 1. If the store implies `Course.start` $\notin \{$`Q-Course.dur+1`$,\ldots,$`Q`$\}$, `CAtQ` is constrained to 0. Vice versa, if `CAtQ` is constrained to 1 or 0, the basic constraint `Course.start :: Q-Course.dur+1 # Q` or its negation `Course.start \:: Q-Course.dur+1 # Q` is imposed on the store. It is essential that while `CAtQ` is not determined to 0 or 1, the constraint on the right-hand side is used only for checking but not for pruning. If already `NumberOfRooms` courses are scheduled at `Q`, the remaining boolean variables `CAtQ` will be constrained to 0 by the propagator `CoursesAtQ =<:NumberOfRooms`.

Because we guarantee that at each time there are sufficiently many rooms available, it is straightforward to assign appropriate rooms to the courses. In particular, the room assignment can be performed after the timetable computation, which reduces the complexity of the problem considerably.

The constraints C7 - C11 express overlapping conditions on courses. Assume that Psych101 and Socio101 are mandatory courses for first year students. Then C9 says that they may not overlap. This constraint can be expressed with a disjunction of the following form

$$\text{Psych101.start} + \text{Psych101.dur} \leq \text{Socio101.start}$$
$$\lor\ \text{Socio101.start} + \text{Socio101.dur} \leq \text{Psych101.start}$$

If we are able to install a propagator stating that at least one of a given set of complex constraints is valid, we can express this disjunction. Thus, our problem is solved by reifying complex constraints:

```
B1 = Psych101.start + Psych101.dur =<: Socio101.start
B2 = Socio101.start + Socio101.dur =<: Psych101.start        (1)
B1 + B2 >=: 1
```

Let us consider the first reified constraint. If Psych101.start + Psych101.dur $\leq$ Socio101.start is logically implied by the constraint store, the basic constraint B1::1 is imposed on the store. If Psych101.start+Psych101.dur > Socio101.start is logically implied by the constraint store, the basic constraint B1::0 is imposed on the store. Vice versa, if B1 is constrained to 1, the propagator Psych101.start + Psych101.dur =<: Socio101.start is installed and if B1 is constrained to 0, the propagator Psych101.start + Psych101.dur >: Socio101.start is installed.

As an example consider now Psych101.start $\in \{8, \dots, 12\}$, Psych101.dur $= 6$, Socio101.start $\in \{10, \dots, 14\}$ and Socio101.dur $= 6$. The second reified constraint constrains B2 to 0 because the constraint store implies Socio101.start + Socio101.dur > Psych101.start. The constraint B2 ::0 in the store allows the propagator B1 + B2 >=:1 to constrain B1 to 1. This allows the first reified propagator to install the propagator Psych101.start + 6 =<:Socio101.start, constraining Psych101.start to 8 and Socio101.start to 14, the only possible values, if the two courses do not overlap.

Encoding the constraints C7 - C10 now becomes straightforward. For example, C7 says that no two courses of an instructor must overlap. Thus, for every pair of courses of an instructor, a propagator of the above form must be installed.

The constraint C11 boils down to the constraint that a certain course, say SplitCourse, may overlap with at most one of a list OtherSplitCourses of other courses. If we are able to install a propagator that constrains a variable Overlap to 1, if a course overlaps with the course SplitCourse and to 0, if it does not, we can build the sum Sum of these variables over OtherSplitCourses. Then, we only need to impose the constraint Sum =<:1, stating that at most one of OtherSplitCourses overlaps with SplitCourse.

So how can we constrain the `Overlap` variables? Two courses `SplitCourse` and `OtherSplit` overlap, if `OtherSplit` starts before `SplitCourse` is finished and vice versa, i.e. if both the constraints

```
SplitCourse.start+SplitCourse.dur >: OtherSplit.start
```

and

```
OtherSplit.start+OtherSplit.dur >: SplitCourse.start
```

hold. The variable `Overlap` must be constrained to 1, if these two constraints hold and to 0 otherwise:

```
B1 = SplitCourse.start+SplitCourse.dur >: OtherSplit.start
B2 = OtherSplit.start+OtherSplit.dur >: SplitCourse.start          (2)
Overlap = B1 + B2 =: 2
```

As usual, this constraint works also the other way around, e.g. if `Overlap` is known to be 1, then `B1 + B2 =:2` is installed. Thus, `B1` and `B2` are constrained to 1 and, hence, both propagators are installed. If `Overlap` is known to be 0, for example because another `Overlap` variable in `Sum` is already 1, the propagator `B1+B2 \=:2` is installed stating that only one of `B1` and `B2` may be constrained to 1. Thus, if, for example, `B2` is constrained to 1, then `B1` is constrained to 0 and the reified constraint for `B1` installs the non-reified version of its negation: `SplitCourse.start + SplitCourse.dur =<: OtherSplit.start`.

In a similar way, the constraint C12 can be expressed. Assume that all courses that a given instructor teaches are contained in the list `Courses`. For every instructor and every day, we compute the boolean value `TeachesOnDay` with

```
TeachesOnDay  = 1 =<: SumOfCoursesOnDay
```

where `SumOfCoursesOnDay` is the sum of the boolean variables obtained by reifying for every element of `Courses` a constraint that states that the course is taught on that day. For every instructor, we can express that she only teaches on three days with the propagator

```
TeachesOnDays =<: 3
```

where `TeachesOnDays` is the sum of all `TeachesOnDay` variables over the week. For example, if three courses have already been placed on different days, say Monday through Wednesday, then all the remaining courses are constrained to be held on Monday through Wednesday, thus, reducing the search space considerably.

The same technique can be applied for our last constraint C13. Assume that all elements of the list `DifferentDayCourses` with length `NumberOfDifferentDayCourses` must be held on a different day. Then the propagator

```
TeachesOnDays =: NumberOfDifferentDayCourses
```

does the job, where `TeachesOnDays` is defined as for C12.

5 Constructive Disjunction

In this section, we reconsider how to model the overlapping of two courses. Let us assume that the starting time of our two courses `Psych101` and `Socio101` is between (and including) 8:15 am (quarter 1) and 10:30 am (quarter 10), i.e., `Psych101.start, Socio101.start` $\in \{1, \ldots, 10\}$, and both durations are 6 quarters. Then the non-overlapping constraint of the courses expresses the disjunction

$$\texttt{Psych101.start} + 6 \leq \texttt{Socio101.start} \lor \texttt{Socio101.start} + 6 \leq \texttt{Psych101.start}$$

The left alternative of the disjunction constrains `Psych101.start` to $\{1, \ldots, 4\}$, i.e., `Psych101` must start before or at 9 am. Analogously, the right alternative constrains `Psych101.start` to $\{7, \ldots, 10\}$, i.e., it must start after or at 9:45 pm. Thus, independent of which alternative will succeed, we know that `Psych101` cannot start at 9:15 (quarter 5) am or at 9:30 am (quarter 6), i.e., `Psych101` $\in \{1, \ldots, 4, 7, \ldots, 10\}$.

The propagators in Section 4, however, do not extract this valuable information on `Psych101`. To obtain more pruning, there is a more active form of disjunction available in Oz, called *constructive disjunction* [VSD95]. It extracts the common information from the alternatives of a disjunction. We replace program (1) by constructive disjunction, supported in the following syntax:


```
condis Psych101.start + Psych101.dur =<: Socio101.start
[] Socio101.start + Socio101.dur =<: Psych101.start
end
```

As in (1), if one alternative is unsatisfiable, the propagator corresponding to the other alternative is installed. Additionally, common information is extracted as described above. While the pruning is enhanced by constructive disjunction, it is also potentially more expensive, since extraction of common information may be attempted relatively often. Thus it takes some experimentation to find out which form of disjunction is most appropriate for a given application. It is essential that propagators also take holes in the domains into account, because in our problem constructive disjunction cuts holes in domains of variables. This is the case for reified basic constraints like `B = X::9#10`. If, for example, the basic constraint `X::[1#8 11#15]` is added, `B` is constrained to 0. The use of constructive disjunction for all non-overlap constraints (C7 - C11) in our college problem resulted in a speed up of more than one order of magnitude.

For modeling constraint C12, we use a ternary constructive disjunction instead of program (2):

```
condis B=:1 SplitCourse.start+SplitCourse.dur >: OtherSplit.start
         OtherSplit.start+OtherSplit.dur >: SplitCourse.start
[] B=:0 SplitCourse.start+SplitCourse.dur =<: OtherSplit.start
[] B=:0 OtherSplit.start+OtherSplit.dur =<: SplitCourse.start
end
```

The common information is in this case extracted from all three alternatives (or two if one alternative is known to be unsatisfiable). If all but one alternative are known to be unsatisfiable, the propagators of the remaining alternative are installed (since the disjunction must be true).

6 Enumeration

To achieve maximal pruning of the search space, we allow the propagators to *exhaustively* amplify the constraint store. We call a store, together with all the propagators, *stable* if none of the propagators can add any more information to it. Typically many variables still have more than one possible values after stability of the store. Thus, we want to explore the remaining search space. We proceed in two steps. First, we compute a fairly good first solution as described in this section and then we optimize starting from this solution as described in Section 7.

To explore the remaining search space, one of the variables that have more than one possible value is selected and speculatively constrained to these values. In order to speculatively constrain a variable to a value, we impose this constraint on a copy of the current constraint store, including all the propagators. If later on, the computation fails, another value can be tried on another copy of the store.[3] We call this process *enumeration* (in the literature it is also known as *labeling*). Once a variable is speculatively constrained to an integer, some propagators typically become able to amplify the constraint store again. When the constraint store becomes stable again, the next variable is selected for enumeration, and so on. Thus, propagators allow to prune the search space, while it is being explored. This scenario makes clear why a sequential language is inappropriate for describing constraint problems. In a sequential language, the complex interaction between enumeration and propagation needs to be made explicit by the programmer, while concurrent constraint languages allow to conceptually separate propagation and enumeration. Sequential languages like ECLiPSe [ECR95] deal with that problem by introducing ad hoc concepts like freeze and demons.

The enumeration process has two degrees of freedom. Firstly, the variable to be enumerated next needs to be selected, and secondly, the order in which the remaining possible values are tried, needs to be fixed. It is an essential ingredient of Oz that both variable and value selection can be programmed in Oz achieving

---

[3] Instead of copying the store, as it is done in Oz, one can also trail the previous domain of the variable and restore it on failure.

a high degree of flexibility. For variable selection, we apply the first-fail strategy, in which a variable with the currently smallest domain is selected.

The simplest value selection beginning with the smallest possible value, does not lead to a solution of our problem after one day of computation on a Sun Sparc 20. The reason is a behavior we call "thrashing". This value selection tries to place courses in a compact timetable, which stands in conflict with the topology of our search space, in that constraints become violated quickly and the search strategy is not clever enough to find the repairable variable. An approach using intelligent backtracking could help here [BP84]. The so-called *first-fit* strategy, which tries to place a course in the day with the fewest already placed courses as described in [BGJ94], does not lead to a solution in reasonable time, either. Instead, we enumerate the courses of each year starting from a different time of the week. The domain from 1 through 180 is divided in 10 blocks representing mornings and afternoons of school days. These blocks can be individually ordered for each course (in the implementation we use the same ordering for each year). By carefully choosing these blocks, we can come to a first solution very fast.

We can make use of this additional flexibility to optimize the timetable according to the criteria in Section 2. We simply order the blocks such that the preferred times are tried earlier than others. The first solution is now more likely to be better with respect to the criteria.

7 Optimization

In the previous section we have seen how we approach the optimization criteria by choosing a suitable enumeration strategy. However, experimentation shows that enumeration alone cannot guarantee that the first solution will fulfill the criteria sufficiently well. A way to achieve optimal solutions in constraint logic programming is the use of branch-and-bound. Branch-and-bound starts out with one solution and imposes that every next solution must be better than the previous one using a suitably defined cost function.

Soft constraints, i.e., constraints which should hold, but might be dropped, if necessary, can be modeled by including their reified version in the cost function. As an example consider that Course should be scheduled on Monday. The cost function will use the result B of the reified constraint B = CourseNew::Monday >:CourseOld::Monday.

In timetabling, as in many constraint problems in the real world, there is rarely a unique cost-function to optimize. For example, the goals to achieve compact timetables for students and instructors may conflict with each other. Hence, we have chosen general criteria that students and instructors can agree upon, such as minimizing the number of courses being held after the lunch break.

After the first (fairly good) solution is found with customized first-fail, we use branch-and-bound search to further optimize starting from this solution. Since due to the topology of our search space, going for the globally best solution is not feasible, the user can define a limit on the number of enumeration steps leading to a resource-limited branch-and-bound search. The user can interrupt the optimization at any time and request the currently best solution. This solution can be inspected and the user can decide whether it is good enough or whether she likes to search for a better solution. This process can be continued arbitrarily often. In this sense, we can say that we implement an anytime algorithm.

8   Implementation Issues

Figure 1 shows the top-level graphical user interface to our timetabling program. By using the object-oriented features of Oz and the interface to the window programming toolkit Tcl/Tk [Meh94] it was straightforward to implement the interface. The interoperability features of Oz [Sch94] allow the integration of tools to display, type-set (using LaTeX) and print the resulting timetable.

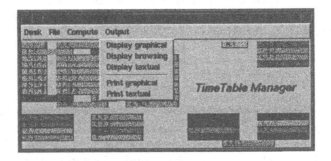

Fig. 1. Top-level graphical user interface

The visualization of the resulting timetable turned out to be extremely useful for the human user to judge the quality of the solutions during optimization. Figure 2 shows a program generated timetable visualization of a solution.

Other features of the language Oz, such as statically scoped higher-order programming and concurrent object-oriented programming, which are not available in other constraint logic languages, vastly facilitate coding and maintenance of programs.

The program deals with more than 25000 propagators. The first solution is found in less than a minute on a Sun Sparc20 with 60 MHz. A considerable optimization of 5 lectures less at afternoons is obtained after further 10 minutes.

9 Comparison to Constraint Languages

In this section we compare Oz with existing constraint systems for solving combinatorial problems.

CHIP [DVS+88] is the forerunner for most commercial constraint systems. It lacks flexibility for search strategies and constructive disjunction. Only a small set of predefined reified constraints are supported by an if-then-else construct. Nevertheless, it is a successful commercial tool because several OR techniques

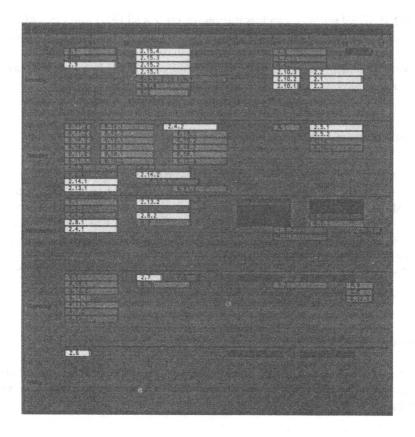

Fig. 2. Program generated timetable visualization

have been incorporated in operators dealing with disjunctive information. Disjunctive constraints not appropriate for these operators must be modeled by choice-points.

ECL^{i}PS^e[ECR95] is the research successor of CHIP enriched with features like attributed variables. By using attributed variables it is possible to program user-defined constraints.

clp(FD) [DC93] is a constraint language compiling to the C language. It is based on indexicals [VSD91] and is the fastest finite domain system freely available. Nevertheless it supports only basic ingredients for constraint programming (no reified constraints or conditionals).

The portation of the indexical approach to the concurrent constraint paradigm resulted in the experimental system AKL(FD) [CCD94]. It includes means to express reified constraints and constructive disjunction. Unfortunately, the maximal domain is limited to 255 and the system is not publicly available. The ability to invent new search strategies is not given.

cc(FD) [VSD95] served as an inspiration for both AKL(FD) and Oz. cc(FD) integrates for the first time reified constraints, realized by the cardinality operator (which can be expressed in Oz), with constructive disjunction. cc(FD) does not support the ability to invent new search strategies. There is no implementation of cc(FD) available for further comparison.

Acknowledgements

We thank the Prorektor of the Catholic College for Social Work at Saarbrücken, Peter Huberich, for explaining his timetabling problems to us. We thank Tobias Müller for implementing the constraint solver and Benjamin Lorenz for maintaining the timetable program. Martin Müller and Christian Schulte contributed comments on a draft of the paper. The research reported in this paper has been supported by the Bundesminister für Bildung, Wissenschaft, Forschung und Technologie (FTZ-ITW-9105), the Esprit Project ACCLAIM (PE 7195) and the Esprit Working Group CCL (EP 6028).

Remark

The DFKI Oz system and the documentation are available from the programming systems lab of DFKI through anonymous ftp from `ps-ftp.dfki.uni-sb.de` or through WWW from `http://ps-www.dfki.uni-sb.de/oz/`.

References

[AB93]   A. Aggoun and N. Beldiceanu. Extending CHIP in order to solve complex scheduling and placement problems. *Mathl. Comput. Modelling*, 17(7):57–73, 1993.

[BGJ94] P. Boizumault, C. Gueret, and N. Jussien. Efficient labeling and constraint relaxation for solving time tabling problems. Technical Report ECRC-94-38, ECRC, 1994.

[BO92]   F. Benhamou and W.J. Older. Applying interval arithmetic to integer and boolean constraints. Technical report, Bell Northern Research, June 1992.

[BP84]   M. Bruynooghe and L.M. Pereira. Deduction revision by intelligent back-
           tracking. In J.A. Campbell, editor, *Implementations of PROLOG*. Ellis Hor-
           wood Limited, 1984.

[CCD94]   B. Carlson, M. Carlsson, and D. Diaz. Entailment of finite domain con-
           straints. In P. van Hentenryck, editor, *Proceedings of the International Con-
           ference on Logic Programming*, pages 339–353. The MIT Press, 1994.

[Col90]   A. Colmerauer. An introduction to PROLOG III. *Communications of the
           ACM*, pages 70–90, July 1990.

[DC93]   D. Diaz and P. Codognet. A minimal extension of the WAM for clp(FD).
           In *Proceedings of the International Conference on Logic Programming*, pages
           774–790, Budapest, Hungary, 1993. MIT Press.

[DVS+88]   M. Dincbas, P. Van Hentenryck, H. Simonis, A. Aggoun, T. Graf, and
           F. Berthier. The constraint logic programming language CHIP. In *Proceed-
           ings of the International Conference on Fifth Generation Computer Systems
           FGCS-88*, pages 693–702, Tokyo, Japan, December 1988.

[ECR95]   ECRC. *ECL^{i}PS^e, User Manual Version 3.5*, December 1995.

[JM87]   J. Jaffar and S. Michaylov. Methodology and implementation of a CLP sys-
           tem. In *Proceedings of the International Conference on Logic Programming*,
           pages 196–218, 1987.

[Mac77]   A. K. Mackworth. Consistency in networks of relations. *Artificial Intelli-
           gence*, 8:99–118, 1977.

[Meh94]   Michael Mehl. Window programming in DFKI Oz. DFKI Oz documen-
           tation series, German Research Center for Artificial Intelligence (DFKI),
           Stuhlsatzenhausweg 3, D-66123 Saarbrücken, Germany, 1994.

[Sch94]   Christian Schulte. Open programming in DFKI Oz. DFKI Oz documen-
           tation series, German Research Center for Artificial Intelligence (DFKI),
           Stuhlsatzenhausweg 3, D-66123 Saarbrücken, Germany, 1994.

[Sid93]   G.A. Sidebottom. *A Language for Optimizing Constraint Propagation*. PhD
           thesis, Simon Fraser University, Canada, 1993.

[Smo95a]   Gert Smolka. The definition of Kernel Oz. In Andreas Podelski, editor,
           Constraints: Basics and Trends, Lecture Notes in Computer Science, vol.
           910, pages 251–292. Springer-Verlag, 1995.

[Smo95b]   Gert Smolka. The Oz programming model. In Jan van Leeuwen, editor,
           Computer Science Today, Lecture Notes in Computer Science, vol. 1000,
           pages 324–343. Springer-Verlag, Berlin, 1995.

[SR90]   V.A. Saraswat and M. Rinard. Concurrent constraint programming. In *Pro-
           ceedings of the 7th Annual ACM Symposium on Principles of Programming
           Languages*, pages 232–245, San Francisco, CA, January 1990.

[SS94]   Christian Schulte and Gert Smolka. Encapsulated search in higher-order
           concurrent constraint programming. In Maurice Bruynooghe, editor, *Logic
           Programming: Proceedings of the 1994 International Symposium*, pages 505–
           520, Ithaca, New York, USA, 13–17 November 1994. The MIT Press.

[SSW94]   Christian Schulte, Gert Smolka, and Jörg Würtz. Encapsulated search and
           constraint programming in Oz. In A.H. Borning, editor, *Second Workshop
           on Principles and Practice of Constraint Programming*, Lecture Notes in
           Computer Science, vol. 874, pages 134–150, Orcas Island, Washington, USA,
           2-4 May 1994. Springer-Verlag.

[ST95]   G. Smolka and R. Treinen, editors. *DFKI Oz Documentation Series*. Deutsches Forschungszentrum für Künstliche Intelligenz GmbH, Stuhlsatzenhausweg 3, 66123 Saarbrücken, Germany, 1995.

[VSD91] P. Van Hentenryck, V. Saraswat, and Y. Deville. Constraint processing in cc(FD). Technical report, Brown University, 1991. Unpublished.

[VSD95] P. Van Hentenryck, V. Saraswat, and Y. Deville. Design, implementation and evaluation of the constraint language cc(FD). In Andreas Podelski, editor, *Constraints: Basics and Trends*, Lecture Notes in Computer Science, vol. 910. Springer Verlag, 1995.

Genetic Algorithms

A Smart Genetic Algorithm for University Timetabling

David C. Rich[*]

149 E. Countryside Circle
Park City, Utah 84098-6102
USA
Dave_Rich@out.trw.com

Abstract

A software solution based on a genetic algorithm (GA) optimization has been designed for creating a university class timetable. The prototype program has demonstrated the capability to define an acceptable schedule within a maximum stress, minimum resource environment. The constraints imposed in such a complex environment are resolved by the GA assisted by a dynamic penalty function and greedy algorithms using domain knowledge. These techniques create an intelligent genetic algorithm for solving discontinuous, complex, and highly epistatic optimization problems.

1 Architecture

A steady-state, value-based GA is used to explore the large search space of potential university class timetables. The steady-state GA allows the new chromosomes to immediately become part of the population. The value of each gene is an integer representing the start time of the first period that the class meets each week. The prototype routine used eleven periods each day, five days per week, resulting in integer gene values between zero and fifty-four. The child is kept or discarded according to the results of a fitness tournament, with the fitness determined by a penalty function.

1.1 Fitness

The fitness of a chromosome is calculated using a penalty function. A penalty function not only pressures the search routine to move away from less desirable points in the search space but it also allows the opportunity to gain information from data points that are valid for the GA but not for the problem. Instead of discarding genes that do not satisfy the physical constraints, they are assessed a cost that causes the GA to move toward more acceptable results. This project addresses a set of three hard constraints and three soft constraints. Hard constraints are those constraints that can never be violated in an acceptable schedule. Instead of disallowing these data points during the processing, these points are assessed a high cost. All hard constraints have the same high cost, since a schedule is unacceptable if any hard constraint is violated. The high cost does not require an immediate repair of an unacceptable solution but causes evolutionary pressure to move the solution away from the hard constraints. This procedure transforms holes in the scheduling landscape to valid--but very undesirable--points, thereby making the landscape continuous although bumpy. The hard constraints addressed in this prototype are:

---

[*]

Dave Rich has worked in nuclear physics engineering and research for over twenty years, in which he currently works for TRW. This project represents a foray into artificial intelligence research, in which he works independently.

1)   An instructor cannot be assigned multiple classes at the same time.
2)   Multiple classes cannot be assigned the same room at the same time.
3)   All classes must be scheduled.

Soft constraints are those things that would be nice to have (or not have) but their lack (or existence) does not make a solution unacceptable. Soft constraints are restrictions that can be allowed but are not preferred. These are assigned a much lower cost than hard constraints, so that the hard constraints can take precedence over the soft constraints during evolutionary search procedures. The costs of the soft constraints can also be varied according to the relative value of each constraint. The soft constraints addressed in this prototype are:

1)   An instructor should not be assigned classes that meet back-to-back.
2)   Classes should be scheduled within preferred daytime hours.
3)   The distance that an instructor should walk to a classroom should be minimized.

The hard constraint costs are added to the soft constraint costs to calculate the total chromosome cost. The fitness of the chromosome is the inverse of the cost, which results in a fitness value for each chromosome that is in direct proportion to its value as a solution:

$$\text{fitness} = 1. / (1. + \text{cost})$$

The fitnesses of all chromosomes in the population are summed, and a fitness ratio is assigned to each chromosome. The fitness ratio for each chromosome is the chromosome fitness divided by the summation of all fitnesses, which identifies the value of each chromosome relative to the other chromosomes. The summation of all fitness ratios is 1.

1.2 Selection of Parent Chromosomes by Fitness Ratio

The parent chromosomes are selected for reproduction according to their fitness ratios. This method, applied to a steady state GA, will produce results similar to the roulette wheel selection method for a generational GA. That is, the more fit chromosomes are more likely to be selected as parent(s) of the new chromosome, but there is a finite probability that the less-fit chromosomes can also be selected. The probability of a chromosome being selected as a parent is greatest for the best fit chromosome and reduces to the lowest probability for the least-fit chromosome.

The procedure begins with a random real number between 0 and 1. To identify the selected chromosome, the fitness ratio of the best-fit chromosome is subtracted from 1. If the random number is greater than the result, the most fit chromosome is selected. If the random number is still smaller, the fitness ratio of the next-best-fit chromosome is subtracted. If that result is lower than the random number, that chromosome is selected. The process continues until the resultant fitness ratio is less than the random number. This can be expressed in psuedocode as:

```
order chromosomes by decreasing fitness ratio
get a random number between 0 and 1
for i = 0 through (population size - 1)
        sum the fitness ratios of all chromosomes number 0 through i
        if (1 - sum from above) is less than or equal to the random number,
                then use chromosome i and exit the loop
        otherwise, increment i to the next chromosome and continue
```

1.3 Dynamic Chromosome Operators

After the parent chromosomes are selected, one of two chromosome operators is used for child creation: fixed-point uniform crossover or mutation. In this implementation, crossover is accomplished by taking every other gene from one parent and the rest from the other parent. This crossover method was not selected for any specific reason, and a more effective crossover operation may be available. Mutation changes a gene value randomly within the allowed range (between 0 and 54). These two operators are used independently to observe the effects of each operator. Each operator selection rate changes during a run according to the success of each operator in improving the fitness of the best chromosome [12, 22].

The selection probability of both operators is initialized to 50%. For each increase in one operator selection probability, there is a corresponding decrease in the other operator selection probability. Each operator is assigned a base probability that it cannot go below. This maintains the integrity of always having a finite probability and not "losing" an operator. In the program prototype, this base probability was maintained at 20%.

Each operator has a success rate that keeps track of the fraction of the child chromosomes created by it that remain after each fitness competition. Each operator also has an integer credit that is incremented each time that the operator generates a chromosome with a fitness better than the previous best fitness. The "add-on" selection probability for mutation is calculated as the ratio of the mutation "credit for best" to the total "credit for best" plus the ratio of the mutation "success rate" to the total "success rate." The total mutation selection probability is the sum of the base selection probability plus the add-on selection probability:

$$
\begin{aligned}
\text{total credit} \quad &= \text{mutation credit for best} + \text{crossover credit for best} \\
\text{total success rate} \quad &= \text{mutation success rate} + \text{crossover success rate} \\
\text{mutation add-on probability} \quad &= \text{mutation credit for best} / (1. + \text{total credit}) \\
&\quad + \text{mutation success rate} / (1. + \text{total success rate}) \\
\text{mutation operator probability} \quad &= \text{mutation base probability} + \text{mutation add-on probability}
\end{aligned}
$$

The crossover operator selection probability is calculated as one minus the mutation operator selection probability:

crossover operator probability $= 1. - $ mutation operator probability

The dynamic operator selection probabilities were different in every run. In some runs, there would be large excursions in the selection probabilities, while in others the selection probabilities would be close to 50%. They would vary for each run as a different part of the scheduling landscape was explored through random selection of gene values. The dynamic selection rate, however, would progress toward the operator with the currently-best success rate. At the beginning of a run, the small numbers of successes for each operator would result in a few large changes before settling down to more gradual changes. Figure 1 displays a sample of the changing operator selection probabilities.

In this run, crossover dominated the selection probabilities for about one hundred chromosome generations. The dominance then changed to favor mutation for about three hundred chromosome generations. Crossover then dominated for a few dozen chromosomes, after which mutation dominated for the rest of the run. Of course, this graph is only one example. Other runs often resulted in graphs of operator selection probabilities significantly different from this one. However, by using

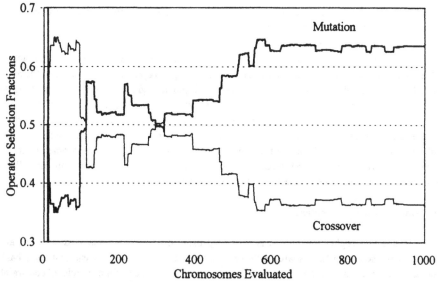

Fig. 1. Dynamic operator selection rates of mutation and crossover during the generation of 1000 chromosomes. The selection rates are adjusted according to the success of each operator to create chromosomes that improve the population fitness.

dynamic chromosome operators, no prior knowledge is necessary to determine when to manually modify the operator selection rate. Even if different operators were used, the automatic selection of the operator currently providing the best results would improve the overall optimization performance.

1.4 Tournament Selection with Local or Global Competition

Tournament selection determines which of the child chromosomes are kept and which chromosomes they replace. In a tournament selection, the fitness competitions are confined to a small subset of the chromosomes. After the operator and the parent(s) are selected, a new chromosome is created and evaluated. In this application, the fitness of the child is compared with either the fitness of the parents, for local competition, or the fitness of the worst-fit chromosome in the population, for global competition. Local competition replaces the worst-fit parent with the child if the child has better fitness. If the child has worse fitness, the child is discarded. Global competition replaces the worst-fit chromosome with the child if the child has better fitness. If the worst-fit chromosome has better fitness than the child, the child is discarded. Unlike the fitness ratio selection of the parents, the tournament selection does not allow any probability of selecting the least-fit chromosome; the least-fit of the chromosomes in the tournament is always discarded. As explained below when discussing the results, global competition works better than local competition in this project.

1.5 Convergence, Elitism, and Reinitialization

As the population of schedules evolves toward better and better schedules (chromosomes), there will come a point where the schedules are all equally good, or almost so. After convergence, there is very little improvement that can evolve through crossover, since the chromosomes are all almost alike. This point of almost-equal fitness values is called convergence. Beasley [5] defines convergence as, ". . . progression toward increasing uniformity." In this project, when the average chromosome fitness is within 95% of the best-fit chromosome, the population is said to have converged. Figure 1 implies that crossover is only effective for a few hundred chromosome generations. Since the operator selection rate is based on the success of each operator, the program could be left to continue to exploit mutation at an increasing rate. However, greater benefits can be achieved by having a break in the procedures after convergence.

When the population converges, all but the best-fit chromosome are reinitialized to random values within the legal gene range. Reinitializing a converged population allows almost the entire population to be randomly reassigned new gene values. It provides greater diversity in searching the landscape and improves the search process [16]. The best fit chromosome is not reinitialized but is kept, which is called elitism. Elitism provides some assurance that vital information already discovered is not lost through the reinitialization process. After reinitialization, the search continues with the new chromosomes blending their genes with those from the best chromosome previously discovered. This break in the search process not only expands the domain searched, but also allows for an operational point where penalty function costs can be made dynamic.

1.6 Dynamic Penalty Function

In this GA application, fitness is calculated using dynamic costs assessed for constraint violation. The scheduler begins with each constraint type associated with a basic cost and a basic cost increment. Each class and each instructor is assigned a personal cost for each related constraint. Each time the population converges and is reinitialized, the best-yet chromosome will (probably) have some constraints unresolved. The cost associated with each constraint violated by the best-yet chromosome is incremented by the associated cost increment. The increasing costs apply increasing pressure on the evolving scheduler to resolve the more difficult constraints. The greater the cost of an individual constraint, the greater is the pressure for that constraint to be resolved in the next evolution.

With the total costs dynamic, the important factor is the relative cost increment. Those constraints with the larger increments receive greater pressure more rapidly and will be resolved more quickly. As violated constraint costs are increased, those constraints will also be resolved until the best possible schedule is discovered. In the real world, the physical resources (rooms) rarely match exactly with the required resources. Typically, the physical resources are greater than the minimum required, and there may be multiple timetable configurations that have a lowest-cost, or almost-lowest-cost, class schedule.

Constraints that are difficult to resolve can generate very large costs through multiple convergence cycles. Sometimes, the cost of a constraint can be increased significantly but then become dormant and insignificant when the constraint is satisfied. If the constraints would stay satisfied, the large dormant costs would be irrelevant. However, as other constraints are satisfied, some previously-satisfied constraints may become violated again due to the highly interrelated, or epistatic, environment. The constraints forced into renewed violation when some other constraint is resolved, are immediately assessed the large dormant cost previously built up.

It is possible to avoid some of these down-the-road surprises by starting over. This program is designed to accept a seed chromosome as a member of the initial population. Therefore, the scheduling process can be run for a specified number of chromosome generations and then stopped. The best chromosome is then entered as a seed to a new run begun with all costs initialized to the basic costs. As a result, the scheduler begins working with a best-yet chromosome but at the beginning of the dynamic cost cycle.

Dynamic costs make it difficult to compare the best chromosome in one cycle with the best chromosome in another cycle after some constraint costs have increased. To overcome this difficulty, a "normalized cost" of the best-yet chromosome is calculated. The normalized costs used are the cost increments that have been entered relative to the importance of each constraint type. These increments do not change. The summation of cost increments of all violated constraints therefore provides a good comparative measure of each chromosome's value throughout the many cost-increasing convergence cycles.

The normalized costs can also increase as well as decrease. When one constraint is increased in priority with the increasing penalty costs, it may dislodge other less-penalizing constraints. This can actually result in an increase in the normalized cost even when the total cost decreases. This is described more fully below.

1.7 Greedy Room Scheduler

The room for each class is not determined by the GA but is determined by a knowledge-based selection procedure. With many rooms, it is assumed that any number of classes can meet at the same time, which makes it legal to have multiple copies of the same gene value on a chromosome.

The room scheduler is a greedy algorithm, sometimes called a graph-coloring scheme, that has been shown to provide good results in selection procedures [12]. A greedy algorithm begins at a specific point in the search space and works outward, selecting the first acceptable value found in the search space. It is called a greedy algorithm since it selects the first possible solution that meets the immediate, local requirements without any consideration for the complete solution. In this implementation as a room scheduler, the greedy algorithm not only selects the classrooms so no hard constraints are violated but it also minimizes the teachers' walking distances. Of course, this minimization must be considered with respect to the complete schedule optimization. Although the intent is to minimize the walking distances of the instructors, as the schedule is built, some options are removed from consideration in conjunction with some instructors. As a result, those instructors whose classes are added to the schedule later are less likely to have a minimized walking distance.

Each class is associated with an instructor, and each instructor is associated with the building where the instructor's office is located. The greedy algorithm room scheduler begins its search in the building of the instructor's office and looks for an available room at the time assigned to the class. If no room is available within the building, the next closest building is searched. This procedure continues until either an available room is located or all buildings have been searched. The room scheduler for those classes that are assigned "staff" as the instructor begins the search in the building of the department responsible for the class.

The order of the genes on the chromosome is correlated to the order of the classes on the class list. The genes, or classes, are processed sequentially. Because greedy algorithms make their selections based on local optimality, it is best to order the decisions made so the most important global decisions are made first [12]. This importance is the relative importance when using the GA automated search for timetabling and has nothing to do with the class subject. For scheduling purposes, the importance is based on the need to be assigned a room. This makes the larger classes more important than the smaller classes, since smaller classes can use larger rooms but not vice versa. The class list was therefore ordered according to expected enrollment, and the greedy algorithm finds the rooms in order of required size. No large class will be unassigned just because a smaller class has been assigned the room needed.

1.8 Greedy Time Search

Even the dynamic penalty function could not sufficiently increase the pressure to resolve all hard constraints in a minimum-resource environment. A greedy time search algorithm was implemented to resolve time conflicts quicker and to help the dynamic penalty function in difficult environments. Time conflicts are caused by the GA-evolved time assignment for a class overloading campus resources that are available at that time. A conflict is also created when the GA assigns a starting time too late in the week for the class to have the assigned number of meetings with the preferred time span allowed between meetings.

When the GA evolves a time conflict, a search begins to find a better time for that class. The search begins with the time identified as "prime time," since that time will eventually have the maximum number of classes. The first period in the week is currently used as the prime time, but the prime time could be set to any other period in the week. The greedy time search algorithm first finds a time for the class that does not result in a hard cost due to the instructor's time requirements. The greedy room scheduler then searches for a room. If no available room can be found, the greedy time search continues searching for the next available time.

The greedy time search can be turned on or off to evaluate the operation of the program with and without using it. The search can also be turned on part way through a run. For example, the program can evaluate 25% (or any other amount) of the maximum number of chromosomes to be evaluated without using the greedy time search and then turn on the search. The results of turning on the time search are very dramatic. A plot of the best fitness value versus the chromosomes evaluated shows that although the best fitness may slowly improve, when the time search is turned on, the best fitness value improves dramatically. (See Figures 2-7.)

Although a complete analysis has not yet been done, it is thought best to leave the time search off for the first part of the evolutionary process. This puts pressure on the scheduler to resolve the constraints as much as possible by juggling the assignments. It is thought that this initial juggling without the greedy time search will help in locating the best solution.

The program was also tested using the greedy time search without the dynamic penalty costs. The results were better than using only the dynamic penalty function without the greedy time search, but an acceptable schedule could not be found in a minimum-resource environment. The best results are achieved by using both the greedy time search and the dynamic penalty function.

2 Results

The program was written using the Borland C/C++ 3.0 compiler for an Intel 80486 DX 33 Mhz CPU. A run of 10,000 chromosomes without the greedy time search required about 17 minutes. A run of 30,000 chromosomes, using the time search after 7500, required approximately two hours.

The subset of a university class list used was the first 101 classes that identified a specific instructor. These classes were taught by 56 different instructors. Most of the runs testing the algorithms were made using 7, 8, or 9 classrooms. The week was divided into 11 one-hour periods per day for 5 days, which meant that each room made 55 room periods available. Some longer classes, scheduled late in the day, were allowed to extend into the "unpreferred" late evening hours, which were not included in the 55 periods.

Population sizes between 5 and 100 were tested during runs generating 8,000 chromosomes. An acceptable schedule could be evolved in short run times using 9 rooms. Therefore, much of the testing used 9 rooms. During this parametric analysis, the lowest-cost schedule was created using a population of 10 chromosomes.

When a larger population is used in this application, it results in more chromosomes generated during each convergence cycle, making the cycles longer. The longer cycles allow for greater exploration of the search space using mutation. However, reinitialization after convergence appears to provide even greater search opportunities than that of mutation in the extended cycle.

The dynamic penalty function also works better with smaller populations and shorter cycles which allow smaller cost increments that increase the pressure slowly, relative to each cycle, but still achieve large values due to repeated increases. The more opportunities there are for individual cost increments, the more gradual and steady the cost increments and pressure increases can be.

2.1 Local vs. Global Tournament Competition for Child Selection

Figure 2 shows the population progress in improved fitness using local competition for tournament selection of the children. Local competition results in extended convergence cycles, when compared to global competition (Figure 3), similar to the effect of larger population sizes. The population has converged only once during the last half of the run (1,000 chromosome generations), providing almost no opportunity for dynamic costs to increase the constraint pressures. Figure 2 also shows the significant improvement in the chromosome fitness due to the greedy time search. The search is left off during the first 1,000 chromosome generations, after which it is turned on. The time search results are discussed in more detail below.

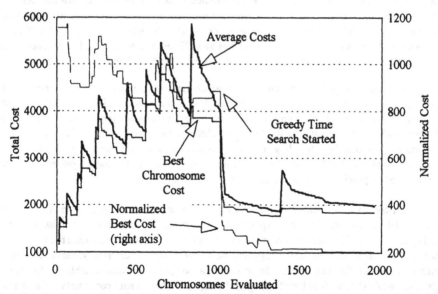

Fig. 2. Local tournament competition for child selection results in slower convergence and fewer reinitialization cycles than with global competition. As a result, the dynamic penalty function could not be as effective. This run left one hard constraint unresolved. This run used a population of 10 chromosomes with the classes assigned to 7 rooms.

Figure 3 shows the benefit of using global competition for tournament selection of the children. Global competition causes the population to converge more rapidly than local competition, causing more reinitialization and cost increasing cycles. There are 41 reinitialization cycles during the first half of the run compared with 9 cycles using local competition (Figure 2). The second half of the run

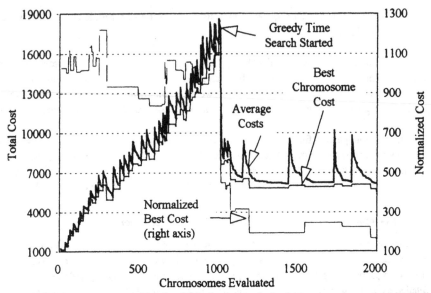

Fig. 3. Global tournament competition for child selection results in short convergence and reinitialization cycles. This run successfully found a schedule with no hard constraints. The drop in the normalized costs near the end suggests the last hard constraint may have been resolved just before finishing.

shows 6 reinitialization cycles with global competition versus 1 with local competition. Since the global competition converges more times than the local competition, it provides greater opportunity for the dynamic costs to increase the pressure on violated constraints. The 6 cycles of global competition allowed the costs to increase the pressure sufficiently to remove the last hard constraint, whereas the single reinitialization of local competition could not find an acceptable schedule.

Theoretically, global competition more rapidly removes the less-fit chromosomes from the population. Local competition removes the less-fit of 3 chromosomes, but those 3 could have a relatively high fitness. Local competition therefore provides a slower improvement in population fitness, with greater opportunity for the less-fit chromosomes to contribute. This provides more opportunity to explore the scheduling landscape. In practice, this more thorough exploration during each cycle does not contribute to a better solution. The more cycles and more rapid movement to a better schedule provided by global competition yields better results.

For comparison, Figure 4 displays a local competition run made without the reinitialization cycles and dynamic costs. Figure 5 displays a global competition run without reinitialization cycles and dynamic costs. Although the two graphs are very similar, the global competition has resolved the last hard constraint that the local competition could not resolve. Numerically, the differences are minor. However, the best schedule found with local competition is unacceptable due to one hard constraint while the schedule found with global competition has no hard constraints violated and is acceptable. Although a cost comparison would show only minor differences in the ending costs, the best schedule of Figure 4 is rejected while the best schedule of Figure 5 is accepted. These runs were made using 7 rooms for scheduling.

Figure 6 displays a local competition run made with the reinitialization cycles but without dynamic costs. Figure 7 displays a global competition run with reinitialization but without dynamic costs. These runs were both made using 7 rooms. These two figures show similar results as the

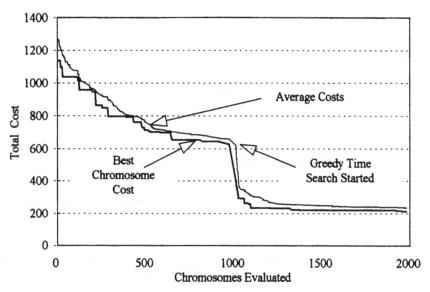

Fig. 4. Results using local competition without reinitialization and dynamic costs. The same data set that was used for Figures 2 and 3 was used here. One hard constraint was left unresolved.

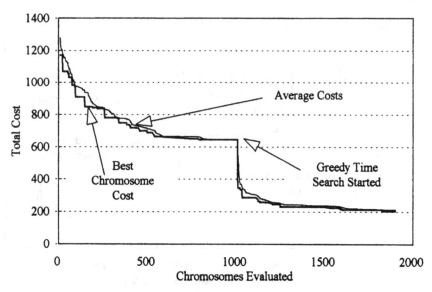

Fig. 5. Results using global competition without reinitialization and dynamic costs. The same data set that was used for Figures 2 and 3 was used here. All hard constraints were resolved.

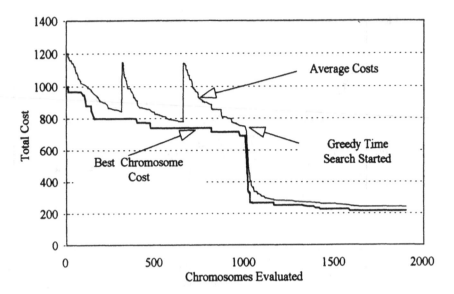

Fig. 6. Data from a local competition run with reinitialization but without dynamic costs. Although this run had only two reinitialization cycles. The lowest ending cost is very close to the lowest ending normalized cost with dynamic costs (Figure 2). However, the run still left one unresolved hard constraint, resulting in an unacceptable schedule.

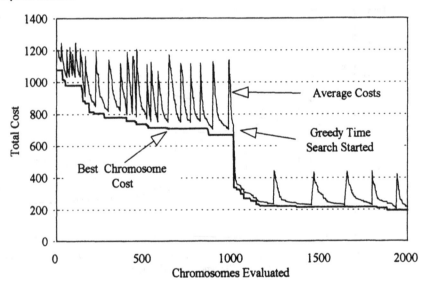

Fig. 7. Data from a global competition run without dynamic costs. There are about half as many reinitialization cycles as with dynamic costs (Figure 3). Numerically, the cost of the best final schedule in this run is close to the run with local competition (Figure 6), but this run represents an acceptable schedule without any unresolved hard constraints while that schedule was left with one hard constraint unresolved.

Figures 4 and 5. Numerically, the solutions from both local and global competition are very close. However, local competition has yielded an unacceptable schedule while global competition has yielded an acceptable solution. The runs could be made longer for local competition, which may result in an acceptable solution. However, the conclusion drawn from these comparisons is that global competition for tournament selection of the child chromosome is better than local competition. Additional comparisons of local and global competition runs are displayed below when discussing the benefits of the greedy time search algorithm.

2.2 Greedy Time Search

After the time search is turned on, the normalized best cost for both local and global competition drops almost immediately from near 900 to about 300. Such an immediate improvement in the solution is very dramatic. However, the time search may "overload" the front part of the week, or the prime time and those times immediately following, by seeking solutions in the early periods.

Figures 8 and 9 show what is possible without using the time search. Figure 8 shows the data from a local competition run, and Figure 9 shows the data from a global competition run. The number of evaluations has been extended to 10,000 chromosomes to allow a greater search of the schedule space and to allow the dynamic penalty function to significantly increase the pressure for a solution. Neither run discovered a schedule with a normalized cost below 600, and even the best solutions contain many unresolved hard constraints.

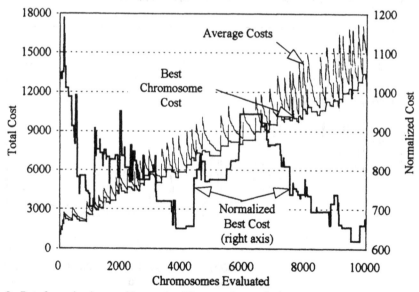

Fig. 8. Data from a local competition run that did not use the greedy time search. The run was extended to 10,000 chromosome evaluations to allow the dynamic penalty function more opportunity to force a solution. The best schedule found had a cost of 620, with many hard constraints still violated.

The schedule with a normalized cost of 620 from the local competition run was used to seed another local competition run of 10,000 chromosome evaluations. The lowest cost achieved was the beginning cost of 620, as displayed in Figure 10. The schedule with normalized cost of 600 from the global competition run was used to seed another global competition run of 10,000 chromosome evaluations. The lowest cost achieved was 599, as displayed in Figure 11.

order chromosomes by decreasing fitness ratio

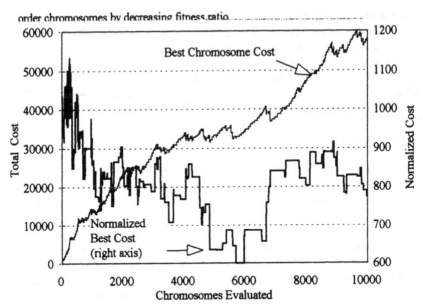

Fig. 9. Data from a global competition run that did not use the greedy time search. The run was extended to 10,000 chromosome evaluations to allow the dynamic penalty function more opportunity to force a solution. The best schedule found had a cost of 600, with many hard constraints violated.

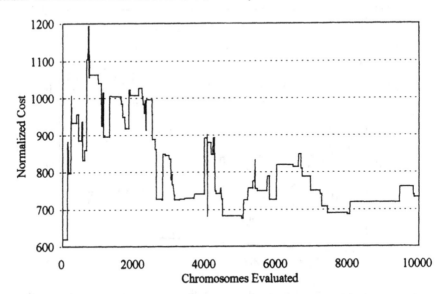

Fig. 10. The best schedule from the run displaed in Figure 8 was used as a seed for a second run using local competition but tithout the greedy time search. The normalized best cost of that run, shown here, never found a schedule with a normalized best cost below the original cost of 620.

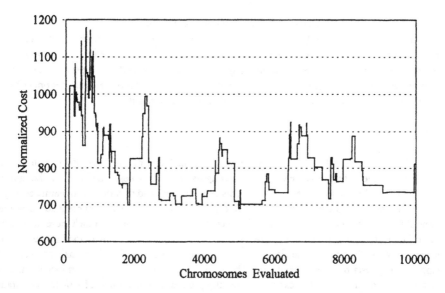

Fig. 11. The best schedule from the run displayed in Figure 9 was used as a seed for a second run using global competition but without the greedy time search. The normalized best cost of that run, shown here, never found a schedule with a normalized best cost much below the original cost of 600. The lowest cost found was 599.

2.3 Dynamic Penalty Function

The dynamic penalty function, or dynamic costs, has been discussed above in reference to tournament competition for child selection and in reference to the greedy time search algorithm. Figures above show data from runs that used the dynamic penalty function as well as data from runs that did not. As shown in Figures 5 and 7, acceptable solutions can be found using 7 rooms without dynamic costs. However, the scheduler was only able to identify an acceptable schedule in a minimum-resource environment when both the dynamic penalty function and the greedy time search were used. A minimum resource environment is defined to be one that contains the minimum number of rooms in which the classes can be mathematically scheduled. For these runs, 6 rooms left 26 room periods unused. Since each room provides 55 room periods in a week, 5 rooms would leave the schedule 29 room periods short. The minimum resource environment is therefore 6 rooms.

The surprising result of the dynamic penalty function is the many large excursions of the normalized best cost. The normalized cost of the best chromosome was expected to slowly decrease monotonically. Instead, there are peaks, valleys, and many significant excursions. The reason for the increases in the normalized cost of the best chromosome is found in the method used to define the best chromosome. The best chromosome is defined as the one with the lowest total cost. When the population is reinitialized and the cost assessments increase, a new "best chromosome" may emerge with lower total costs than the new assessment of the previous best chromosome but with constraints whose normalized costs are higher. For example, a repeated increase in the cost of a soft constraint with a low normalized cost may cause it to get resolved at the expense of a hard constraint with a high normalized cost but a low total cost that has not been increased. The highly interactive dependency of university classes causes such instability. This problem is expected to occur primarily in an environment of low resources where an acceptable schedule is difficult to define.

Adaptive programs augmented with domain knowledge can resolve even these difficult problems. The dynamic penalty function has helped resolve a minimum-resource schedule that could not be resolved without it. Theoretically, the dynamic penalty will provide pressure to find a better schedule, even when an acceptable schedule may be found without it. A dynamic penalty function may sometimes have only a minor numerical benefit on the resulting schedule costs, but under certain conditions, it may help locate an otherwise elusive acceptable schedule.

2.4 Final Schedule

The best schedule created using only 6 rooms had a normalized cost of 141 with no hard constraints violated. This schedule was created using two runs. The best schedule from the first run, with a cost of 176, seeded the second run. This reset all costs and restarted the dynamic cost cycle with a best-yet schedule while total costs were still at a minimum. The total costs accompanying some of the classes suggested that some of the constraints were in violation much more than others. For example, the classes with normalized instructor costs of 1 had a range of total instructor costs ranging between 62 and 264. The classes that had a normalized cost of 1 in the final schedule had a range of total costs between 29 and 184. These are the effects expected when an increase in costs resolves one constraint at the expense of another, causing an exchange of violated constraints periodically throughout the run. The large variation in the costs is evidence of the instability of this minimum-resource schedule. It also demonstrates the highly epistatic relationship among the classes.

An examination of the unused room periods during the week showed a range for the 6 rooms between only 2 and 8 unused periods for the entire week. A total of only 26 room periods were unused out of 330 available during the week. Some of the classes were allowed to extend into the "unpreferred" evening hours past 6:00 p.m., which were not included in the 55 periods per room. There was a soft constraint cost assessed to the schedule each time that this occurred. If done manually, such tight scheduling as this would be difficult even for an expert with many years of experience.

3 Summary

The design of this automated scheduler has taken an empirical approach to resolve a complex, epistatic, and time-consuming problem. The GA used steady-state population growth with integer-valued chromosomes. Chromosomes were selected as parents with a probabilistic selection in proportion to their relative fitness. The adaptive child creation operators used were independent mutation and fixed point uniform crossover. The fitness was determined by a dynamic penalty function, and the child chromosome was kept according to either a local or global fitness tournament.

The GA architecture was augmented with domain knowledge, using classes sorted by expected enrollment, a greedy room scheduler to improve the matchup of instructors and room assignments, a greedy time scheduler to improve the spread of class meetings during the week, and reinitialization, with elitism, after convergence for a more rapid exploration of the scheduling landscape.

The application has demonstrated that combining a GA search with domain knowledge can resolve a complex, highly epistatic optimization problem even in a minimum-resource environment. Dynamic operator selection optimizes the use of the evolutionary operators. Global tournament competition has outperformed local competition. A knowledge-based list ordering improved the results of sequentially processing the genes. Using domain knowledge, greedy algorithms improve the selection of rooms and times. A dynamic penalty function adds just enough pressure on the GA to resolve an acceptable schedule when the resources are limited to the mathematically-minimum resources possible to resolve the problem. The scheduler was challenged with the minimum resource, maximum stress environment of 6 rooms for 101 classes of varying lengths and meeting times and it successfully defined an acceptable schedule. The final schedule using 6 rooms left only 26 room periods unused out of 330 room-periods available.

References

1. Abramson, D. and Abela, J. A Parallel Genetic Algorithm for Solving the School Timetabling Problem. Presented at *15th Australian Computer Science Conference*, Feb. 1992, and *IJCAI Workshop on Parallel Processing in AI*, August, 1992.

2. Alander, J. *An Indexed Bibliography of Genetic Algorithms: Years 1957-1993 (Draft)*. Department of Information Technology and Production Economics, University of Vaasa, Finland. Feb. 13, 1994.

3. Bäck, T., Hoffmeister, F., and Schwefel,H.P. Applications of Evolutionary Algorithms. Technical Report No. SYS-2/92. Systems Analysis Research Group, Department of Computer Science, University of Dortmund, Germany. August, 1993.

4. Bäck, T. and Schwefel, H.P. An Overview of Evolutionary Algorithms for Parameter Optimization. Department of Computer Science, University of Dortmund. (No date).

5. Beasley, D, Bull, D.R., and Martin, R.R. An Overview of Genetic Algorithms: Part 1, Fundamentals. In *University Computing*. 15, 2 (1993), 58-69.

6. Beasley, D, Bull, D.R., and Martin, R.R. An Overview of Genetic Algorithms: Part 2, Research Topics. In *University Computing*. 15, 4 (1993), 170-181.

7. Beasley, D. Hitchhiker's Guide To Evolutionary Computation. Internet: comp.ai.genetic::FAQ (Frequently Asked Questions). ftp alife.santafe.edu::/pub/USER-AREA/EC/FAQ/hhgtec-2.2.ps.gz. (Other source locations available outside the United States.)

8. Colorni, A., Dorigo, M., and Maniezzo, V. A Genetic Algorithm to Solve theTimetable Problem. Submitted to *Computational Optimization and Applications Journal*.

9. Colorni, A., Dorigo, M., and Maniezzo, V. Genetic Algorithms: A New Approach to the Timetable Problem. NATO ASI Series. Vol. FS2. Combinatorial Optimization, edited by M. Akgui, et. al., Springer-Verlag, Berline Heidelberg, 1992.

10. Colorni, A., Dorigo, M., and Maniezzo, V. Genetic Algorithms and Highly Constrained Problems: The Time-Table Case. Politecnico di Milano, Dipartimento di Elettronica. via Ponzio 34/5, 21033 Milano, Italy. dorigo%ipmell.polimi.it@iboinfn.bitnet and maniezzo%ipmell.infn.it@iboinfn.bitnet.

11. Corne, D., Fang, H.L, and Mellish, C. Solving the Modular Exam Scheduling Problem with Genetic Algorithms. Research Paper No. 622. Department of Artificial Intelligence, University of Edinburgh.

12. Davis, L. *Handbook of Genetic Algorithms*. Van Nostrand Reinhold, New York, 1991.

13. Goldberg, D.E. *Genetic Algorithms in Search, Optimization & Machine Learning*. Addison-Wesley, Reading, Mass., 1989.

14. Goldberg, D.E. Sizing Populations for Serial and Parallel Genetic Algorithms. In *Proceedings of the Third International Conference on Genetic Algorithms, 1989 (ICGA89)*, 70-79. Morgan Kaufmann Publishers, Inc., San Mateo, California.

15. Goldberg, D.E. and Deb, K. A Comparative Analysis of Selection Schemes Used in Genetic Algorithms. In *Foundations of Genetic Algorithms, 1991 (FOGA-91)*, 69-93. Morgan Kaufmann Publishers, Inc., San Mateo, California.

16. Karr, C.L. Air-Injected Hydrocyclone Optimization via Genetic Algorithm. In *Handbook of Genetic Algorithms*, by L. Davis, 222-236. Van Nostrand Reinhold, New York, 1991.

17. Khuri, S., Bäck, T., and Heitkotter, J. An Evolutionary Approach to Combinatorial Optimization Problems. *Proceedings of the Computer Science Conference, 1994*. March 8-10,1994. ACM Press.

18. Richardson, J.T., Palmer, M.R., Liepins, G., and Hilliard, M. Some Guidelines for Genetic Algorithms with Penalty Functions. In *Proceedings of the Third International Conference on Genetic Algorithms, 1989 (ICGA89)*, 191-197. Morgan Kaufmann Publishers, Inc., San Mateo, California.

19. Saravan, N. and Fogel, D.B. A Bibliography of Evolutionary Computation & Applications. Technical Report No. FAU-ME-93-100, Revision 1.3. Department of Mechanical Engineering, Florida Atlantic University. October, 1993.

20. Smith, A.E. and Tate, D.M. Genetic Optimization Using a Penalty Function. In *Proceedings of the Fifth International Conference on Genetic Algorithms, 1993 (ICGA93)*, 499-505. Morgan Kaufmann Publishers, Inc., San Mateo, California.

21. Syswerda, G. Schedule Optimization Using Genetic Algorithms. In *Handbook of Genetic Algorithms*, by L. Davis, 332-349. Van Nostrand Reinhold, New York,1991.

22. Tate, D.M. and Smith, A.E. Dynamic Penalty Methods for Highly Constrained Genetic Optimization. Submitted to *ORSA Journal on Computing*, (Aug. 1993).

23. Whitley, D. A Genetic Algorithm Tutorial. Technical Report CS-93-103. Colorado State University. March 10, 1993.

A Genetic Algorithm Solving
a Weekly Course-Timetabling Problem

Wilhelm Erben and Jürgen Keppler

Department of Computer Science, Fachhochschule Konstanz, D-78462 Konstanz
(e-mail: erben@fh-konstanz.de, jkeppler@fh-konstanz.de)

Abstract. In this paper we describe a heavily constrained university time-tabling problem, and our genetic algorithm based approach to solve it. A problem-specific chromosome representation and knowledge-augmented genetic operators have been developed; these operators 'intelligently' avoid building illegal timetables. The prototype timetabling system which is presented has been implemented in C and PROLOG, and includes an interactive graphical user interface. Tests with real data from our university were performed and yield promising results.

1 Introduction

The course-timetabling problem essentially involves the assignment of weekly lectures to time periods and lecture rooms. Because there are quite a lot of versions of the timetabling problem, differing from one school to the next, we focus on constructing course timetables at our own university rather than on trying to develop a universal program.

Faced with increasing student numbers, with new courses introduced, with shortage of lecture rooms and laboratories and with growing numbers of lessons open for students of different departments, and hence with a large number of conflicting constraints, timetables which can be largely accepted by teachers and students are very difficult to schedule at our university.

We present a prototype of a system for the automated construction of timetables which is based on genetic algorithm techniques. It therefore aims not only at finding a feasible solution to the problem, but it also searches for timetables people can be happy with in that as many nice-to-have constraints as possible are satisfied.

A 'natural' chromosome representation was chosen, and the genetic operators we developed make use of knowledge specific to the particular problem. In that way we avoid building illegal timetables, and are not in need of any 'repair algorithm'. This is in contrast to approaches described in other papers (see e.g. [4], [5] and [13]).

The initialisation of a population, the evaluation, and the genetic operators were implemented in PROLOG. These procedures are controlled by a program written in C, which is combined also with an interface enabling the user to interact and modify various parameter settings.

In section 2 our special timetabling problem is depicted in full detail. The genetic algorithm, the underlying chromosome representation, the genetic operators, and the evaluation function are presented in section 3. Some implementational aspects of our timetabling system are described in section 4. Finally, section 5 presents computational results and conclusions.

2 The Weekly Course-Timetabling Problem

Our weekly course-timetabling problem involves scheduling *classes*, *teachers*, *course modules* and *rooms* to a number of *periods* (or *time slots*) in a week.

Each day of the week is divided into 6 periods (of 90 minutes' duration). There are 5 working days per week. Hence, the set P of *periods* consists of 30 elements. We denote these elements by *mon1, mon2, ..., mon6, tue1, tue2, ..., fri6*.

Our university offers a number of *courses* (e.g. Business Computing, Architecture, Civil Engineering, ...) in different departments, and each course lasts eight semesters. A *class* consists of all students studying a given course in the same semester. We denote by C the set of all classes. For each class $c \in C$ the (estimated) maximum number of students must be given as part of the input to our system.

T is the set of all *teachers* (lecturers, tutors, etc.). Each lecturer requires a number of free-time slots (or even one or two free days) where he or she is unavailable. These data must also be present.

R is the set of all *rooms* available in the university. A room can be a laboratory (e.g. for chemistry, or computing) or a lecture theatre. Some rooms can only be used by the department to which they belong. Each room has a maximum capacity which must be given.

Each department offers a number of *course modules*. A course module may be taken by students of one or more classes. It may either be compulsory or optional.

A course module consists of one or more *lessons*. A lesson may be a lecture, a laboratory or a group exercise class, and it has a duration of 90 minutes. The lessons belonging to one course module may be taught by different teachers. The set of all lessons is denoted by L. For each $l \in L$ the type of the lesson, its unique teacher and the coordinate list of classes must be present.

The input data also specifies those lessons for which particular requirements exist: Some lessons must be taught in special rooms, for instance in a computing lab. Some lessons must be scheduled to more than one room (for instance, a lecture theatre and a lab; this enables a teacher to decide each week in which of the two differently equipped rooms his or her lesson should take place). Some lessons are prescheduled, i.e.

must appear in a specified period in the timetable. Some lessons must be blocked, i.e. scheduled to consecutive periods.

A timetable is *feasible* if and only if the following *hard constraints* are satisfied:

- Each lesson $l \in L$ is scheduled to exactly one period.
- There are no clashes at all: Neither a class nor a teacher nor a room is assigned to more than one lesson in the same period.
- Teacher unavailabilities are considered.
- All allocated rooms are large enough to hold the students.
- Specific room requirements are taken into account.
- Lessons marked as prescheduled are scheduled to the specified time.
- Lessons are blocked, if so required.

There is also a huge list of *second-order* (or: *soft*) *constraints* which should be taken into account if possible. Here are some examples:

- Students, as well as some teachers, do not like to have many 'holes' (empty periods between two lessons) in their timetables.
- Lessons should be spread uniformly over the whole week, in general.
- Some teachers, by contrast, wish to have all their lessons scheduled to consecutive periods.
- Some teachers wish to have a special equipped classroom.
- In order to avoid much movement, lecture rooms should be close to the host department.
- Some lessons should not take place late in the evening.
- Each student may select a certain number of optional course modules; in order to give a real choice, conflicts where 2 modules chosen by a student are scheduled at the same period should be avoided.
- Rooms should be *just* large enough to hold the students.

We decided not to separate room assignment from time scheduling because one of the main goals consists in achieving efficient room utilization rates. This is accomplished in a more promising way by trying to do (or modify) time and room assignments simultaneously.

3 The Algorithm

3.1 Chromosome Representation

In a 'classical' genetic algorithm chromosomes are represented as bit strings. However, we believe that problem-specific knowledge should be incorporated in the representation of solutions to our timetabling problem, and the *chromosome representation* should be 'natural': It should contain all the relevant information and be close to the original problem.

In this sense it is straightforward to define a timetable to be a map

$$f: C \times T \times L \times R \times P \rightarrow \{0,1\},$$

where $f(c,t,l,r,p) = 1$ if and only if *class c* and *teacher t* have to meet for a *lesson l* in *room r* at *period p*. Such a mapping is easily translated into PROLOG facts of the form

timetable(Class, Teacher, Lesson, Room, Period).

A fact is either a member of the timetable database and therefore *true*, or it simply does not exist. A *gene*, in this representation, may also be considered as an element of a 5-dimensional matrix, with an allelic value of 0 (*false*) or 1 (*true*).

Recall that the input data of our system specifies for each lesson a unique teacher. Therefore, we can simplify the definition of a chromosome slightly:

$$f: C \times L \times R \times P \rightarrow \{0,1\}.$$

Different classes, by contrast, can share common lessons. Let us denote by L_c the set of all lessons which are offered to class *c*. Then, for a timetable *f* to be feasible it is necessary that

$$f(c,l,R,P) = \{0\}, \text{ if } l \notin L_c,$$

and

$$f(c,l,r,p) = f(c',l,r,p), \text{ if } l \in L_c \cap L_{c'}.$$

Similarly, some lessons must be scheduled to more than one room (see section 2). In order to take into account this requirement, actually, we deal with *lists* of rooms instead of single elements $r \in R$. For the sake of simplicity, however, we do not describe this in further detail.

Given an arbitrary timetable *f* and a subset π of the set *P* of periods (a 'time window' cut out of the week), we denote by $L(f;\pi)$ the set of all lessons which are scheduled in the timetable *f* to a period $p \in \pi$. For a $c \in C$, the set

$$L_c(f;\pi) = L(f;\pi) \cap L_c$$

contains only those lessons of $L(f;\pi)$ which are attended by students of class *c*. Clearly, $L(f;P) = L$ and $L_c(f;P) = L_c$.

Figure 1 shows a timetable *f* restricted to a specific class *c* (which is identified by the symbolic name *WI2*). *algoA*, *wengA*, etc. are unique identifiers of lessons. Let π, for instance, be the time window made up of the periods *mon2*, *mon6*, *wed2*, *thu2* and *fri5*; then

$$L_c(f;\pi) = \{bwl2A, anis2C, anis2A, bwl2B\}.$$

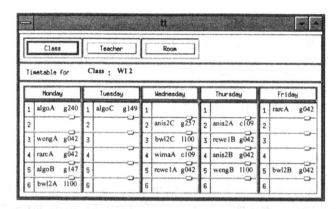

Fig. 1. Part of a Randomly Generated Timetable

3.2 Initialisation

The *initialisation procedure* creates at random a population of feasible solutions (as defined in section 2). Our objective, valid for the whole algorithm, is to start with legal timetables and never leave this search space. Otherwise, in a highly constrained problem like ours, "one runs the risk of creating a genetic algorithm that spends most of its time evaluating illegal individuals" [8], and the chances of an effective search for good solutions would be very low.

The price we have to pay for this is that initializing a population (and defining advanced genetic operators) is not a simple task. In fact, the timetable problem is known to be NP-hard [11]. Nevertheless, our PROLOG-based assignment procedure succeeds in producing an initial population. The members of this population, however, suffer from very poor *fitness*, in general: They may contain a large number of 'holes', or courses are allowed, for example, to run on Friday late evening, even though this would not be accepted in practice. This is because the initialisation routine does not care at all about soft constraints; otherwise the procedure would not have enough degrees of freedom and would frequently fail. Handling soft constraints is left to the evolutionary process that follows. Figure 1 shows part of a timetable which was generated by the initialisation procedure.

Of course, a number of necessary conditions for the existence of solutions must have been checked before we start the initialisation process. For a timetable to be generated, those lessons that are fairly limited as to their possible allocation are considered first: Having processed the (normally few) items which are marked as 'prescheduled', the set of lessons requiring a special laboratory, or having to appear in the timetable in consecutive periods, has preference to the set of those lessons which are almost entirely free in this respect. Apart from this obvious strategy, lessons are selected in random order, and each lesson is assigned to a randomly chosen period and lecture room without violating any hard constraint. The rooms are selected according to a list of priorities: rooms should be close to the home department if possible.

3.3 Evaluation

Our *evaluation function* is made up in the form

$$eval(f) = \frac{1}{1 + cost(f)}$$

where $cost(f)$ is a sum of weighted penalty values:

$$cost(f) = \sum_{i=1}^{k} w_i \cdot n_i(f)$$

(see [7], e.g.). Here, $n_i(f)$ is a penalty value imposed to the violation of a specific soft constraint, and w_i an attached weight. $n_1(f)$ may count, for instance, the number of undesirable 'holes' in the timetable f. $n_2(f)$ could be the component measuring the costs of having scheduled lessons so that some classes have to attend more than four lectures during a day. $n_3(f)$ could be the number of large rooms allocated to lessons attended by only a few students; etc. Note that we do not need to impose penalties on violated *hard* constraints because the concept of our domain-specific genetic operators is to produce only feasible solutions.

The values of the evaluation function range from 0 to 1, and our genetic algorithm aims at finding a timetable which maximizes this function. We are still experimenting with different settings $\{w_1, w_2, \ldots, w_k\}$ of weights for the components of the cost function. Often it is hard to decide which soft constraints should be considered to be more important than others. Students, for example, may be exhausted after 3 hours of maths, whereas a teacher might insist in having his lectures in consecutive periods. Some teachers are happy if all their lectures take place within two days of the week, others might prefer to spread them over the whole week.

3.4 Mutation

Having selected a timetable f for *mutation*, a natural number m and a set $\pi \subseteq P$ consisting of m (not necessarily contiguous) periods are chosen at random and the set $L(f; \pi)$ (see section 3.1) is formed. A mutated timetable f' is produced by assigning new periods or rooms only within the 'time window' π and by leaving the rest unchanged. Taking π and $L(f; \pi)$, instead of P and L, as input, the initialisation procedure described in section 3.2 does the job.

The window size m ranges between two values m_{min} and m_{max} which are parameters of this mutation operator. Clearly, if m is too small, the mutation operator might fail in finding a solution f' different from f. This is because even slight modifications of period or room assignments are likely to produce invalid timetables, and some points in the search space may be 'isolated', i.e. there might be no feasible timetable in a neighbourhood local to the given one. On the other hand, if m is too large, f' may lose similarities to f.

We have tested mutation with different parameter settings and have seen best results for random numbers m between 4 and 15. As special cases of mutation we get operations like swapping time assignments between teachers or classes, shifting a lesson into an empty slot, permuting the order of some lessons, or merely changing rooms, as long as the feasibility conditions are not violated. In general, however, combinations of these elementary operations arise.

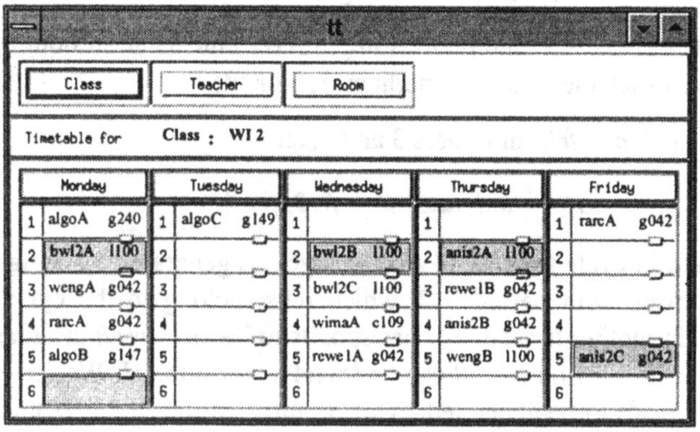

Fig. 2. Timetable of Figure 1 After Mutation

Figure 2 shows, as an example, part of a timetable f' which is a mutation of timetable f from Figure 1. The set π includes the periods *mon2, mon6, wed2, thu2* and *fri5*. The lesson *bwl2A* was shifted from *mon6* to *mon2*. For the lesson *anis2A*, scheduled to *thu2*, only the room number was changed, from *c109* to *l100*. The time assignments of the lessons *anis2C* and *bwl2B* were swapped.

The kernel of our mutation algorithm could also be used if we wanted to modify a given timetable slightly, rather than develop a new one from the scratch. We feel that this is what a mutation in our timetabling problem should look like: It is a stochastic operator which introduces new solutions into the population without destroying information which belongs to 'good' timetables and which has already been accumulated.

3.5 Crossover

Having selected two parent timetables f and g, let us call them *mother* and *father* respectively, we build offspring in such a way that each lesson and its time and room assignment comes from one of the parents. This is done by generating, for each class $c \in C$, a set $\pi_c \subseteq P$ of periods such that the timetable defined by

$$h(c,l,r,p) = \begin{cases} f(c,l,r,p), & \textit{iff } p \in \pi_c \\ g(c,l,r,p), & \textit{else} \end{cases}$$

is feasible. h is an offspring which has inherited some properties from mother f, others from father g (see figures 3 to 5 for an example). A second offspring is simply established by changing the roles of f and g.

In order to explain the mechanism in more detail we have to introduce the notion of a *cycle*: Given a class $c \in C$ and a period $p \in P$, *a cycle for c generated by p (with respect to the parents f and g)* is a minimal set $\zeta_c(p) \subseteq P$ containing p such that

$$L_c(f; \zeta_c(p)) = L_c(g; \zeta_c(p)),$$

i.e. the lessons of class c at the periods in $\zeta_c(p)$ are the same in both mother timetable f and father timetable g (though perhaps permuted).

Take $c = WI1$ and $p = fri2$ in figures 3 and 4, and

$$\zeta_c(p) = \{tue1, tue2, fri1, fri2, fri3\}$$

as an example of a cycle for class $WI1$. This cycle is generated by using the following algorithm: Starting with period $fri2$, which must belong to the cycle, we see that lesson $anis1B$ in mother timetable f corresponds to lesson $bwl1B$ in father timetable g. In timetable f again, lesson $bwl1B$ can be found at period $tue1$. We therefore add $tue1$ to the list of periods to be generated. This, in turn, implies that $fri1$ must also belong to the cycle: lesson $anis1A$, scheduled to $tue1$ in father timetable g, is found at period $fri1$ of mother timetable f. Proceeding in this way, the next step consists in looking at period $fri1$ in timetable g: Because this is an empty time slot, we randomly choose an empty period in timetable f which could be, for instance, $fri3$. In that case $tue2$ would be the next period to be added. Finally, we return to period $fri2$ which is already on the list. Hence, we have completed the cycle.

The crossover operator starts with a class c_0 and a period p_0, both chosen at random, and generates a cycle $\zeta_{c_0}(p_0)$. This cycle will be part of the set of periods π_{c_0} which we aim to construct: $\zeta_{c_0}(p_0) \subseteq \pi_{c_0}$. Hence all assignments for class c_0 within the time window $\zeta_{c_0}(p_0)$ will be taken from the mother timetable f, in order to build the offspring h. If all other parts of timetable h were taken from father g, no conflicts would arise as long as only the restriction of h to class c_0 is considered: All lessons for class c_0 would have been scheduled then, and no student of class c_0 would have to attend more than one lesson in a period.

But, suppose now that there exist a period $p_1 \in \zeta_{c_0}(p_0)$ and a teacher t with the following property: At period p_1, t has to meet class c_0 for a lesson l_0, according to mother timetable f; according to father g, on the other hand, teacher t is scheduled to meet class c_1 ($\neq c_0$) for a lesson l_1 ($\neq l_0$) at period p_1. In that case, the crossover procedure will generate a cycle $\zeta_{c_1}(p_1)$.

See figures 3 and 4 for an example: The lesson $l_0 = bwl1B$ for class $c_0 = WI1$ is scheduled by f to period $p_1 = tue1$. In timetable g the lesson $l_1 = bwl2B$ for class $c_1 = WI2$ appears in the same period. Suppose, both lessons have the same lecturer.

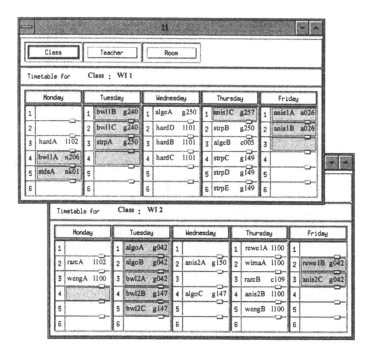

Fig. 3. Mother Timetable *f*

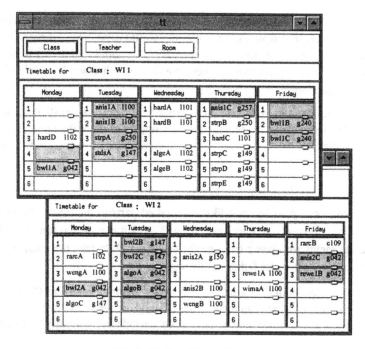

Fig. 4. Father Timetable *g*

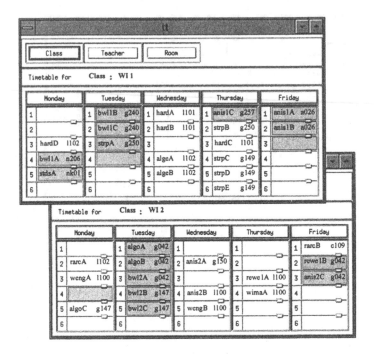

Fig. 5. Offspring Timetable h

Then, if we took the assignments for *WI1* on early Tuesday morning from mother, and those for class *WI2* from father, a conflict would arise. Thus, if *tue1* belongs to a cycle which was already generated for class *WI1*, we should mark this period also for class *WI2* as to be taken from the mother timetable; in other words, we should generate the cycle $\zeta_{WI2}(tue1)$.

Similarly, cycles have to be generated in order to avoid *room* conflicts, or in order to have regard to lessons which are attended by students of more than one class. Then, if for a class c disjoint cycles ζ_c, ζ_c', ζ_c'', ... have been produced, the set π_c is defined by

$$\pi_c = \zeta_c \cup \zeta_c' \cup \zeta_c'' \cup \dots$$

Time windows π_c typically look like the marked parts in the timetables of figures 3 to 5. For some classes c we may have $\pi_c = P$, which means that timetable h inherits all the assignments for class c from mother. If $\pi_c = \varnothing$, to take the other extreme, the offspring looks exactly like father in this respect.

Note that cycles generated by a period may contain empty time slots ('holes'). That is why they are not necessarily unique. Also, even if mother and father are totally different timetables, cycles consisting of only a few periods can normally be found.

Let $|C|$ denote the number of elements of the set C. In the worst case, the crossover procedure had to process all $|C| \cdot (|C| - 1)$ pairs *(c,c')* of classes in the way described above. However, in practice the complexity is much lower because classes from different departments, such as architecture and telecommunication, rarely share common teachers or lessons. Therefore the search for potential clashes can be restricted to pairs of classes belonging to the same or to related courses.

4 Implementation

Before we could start the implementation of our timetabling program, some fundamental considerations had been necessary. We wanted the system to be equipped with a hardware independent graphical user interface, in order to be able to use it on different workstations. We further desired that it should be easily possible to manage the input data, consisting of the facts and rules out of which feasible timetables are produced. Constraints often have transitive dependence; therefore to have an inference mechanism seemed to be worthwhile.

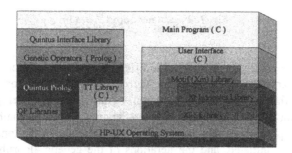

Fig. 6. Program Library Model

For the realization of the graphical user interface we use the X Window system which is available on our HP workstations. The X and Motif libraries, however, exist only for the C programming language. On the other hand, we are in need of a programming language like PROLOG which is useful for solving problems that involve objects and relationships between them; with the power of logic programming constraints are easily handled. In order to be able to combine these completely different languages we use Quintus Prolog, which provides an interface to foreign programming languages and is also available for HP workstations.

The main program of our timetabling system interacts with all layers of the windowing system, the operating system, and the Quintus interface library. The user interface, by contrast, is restricted to the Motif, Xt, and Xlib libraries (see figure 6), in order to support its portability. It is implemented in C, whereas the genetic operators are written in PROLOG.

The genetic operators can be reached by the main program only by using functions of the Quintus Interface Library. They can interact with the main program using our TT Library which is written in C, and use Quintus Prolog and its libraries.

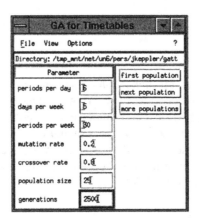

Fig. 7. Parameter Input Window

We designed the user interface with two different windows, one for the input of parameters and starting the program (see figure 7), and the other for the output of a timetable (see figures 1 to 5). In the input window, among other parameters, the crossover and mutation probabilities, the population size and the number of iterations can be set. By pushing certain buttons, the generation of a random population of timetables can be initiated, and the iterations of the genetic algorithm can be controlled.

It is possible to look at each timetable produced by the system from different views: A given lecturer's timetable can be displayed, as well as the timetable of a specific class or room. A view can be selected by pushing the corresponding button.

5 Results and Conclusions

We have been testing our system using a large data sample and incorporating all types of possible constraints. The results are promising, but a number of refinements still have to be made during the next few months. In particular, we still have to find the optimal parameter settings.

In figure 8, results from a test run with a crossover rate of 0.8 and a mutation rate of 0.2 are shown. The run was stopped after 2500 generations. It took almost 30 minutes to generate the initial population of 25 chromosomes, and about 8.5 hours were needed for the iterative process.

Recall that our evaluation function takes values between 0 and 1, and has to be maximized. The fitness values of the initial population range from 0.36 to 0.48, whereas after 2500 generations values between 0.91 and 0.93 have been achieved. These figures have to be compared with a value of approximately 0.91, which has been calculated for the hand-made timetable of the last year.

Next steps will be tests with full data (about 300 teachers, more than 80 classes, approximately 1500 lessons, nearly 100 rooms) and will include experimentation on parallelizing the algorithm. We shall have to improve and extend the heuristics used in our genetic operators. The effect of incorporating local search and/or elitism will be investigated. In order to get accepted by a timetabler at our university, the algorithm has to be made more transparent. The user should be able to modify, to a certain extent, the evaluation function according to his own understanding of a 'good' timetable. Finally, we shall expand the graphical user interface such that basic input data, including second-order constraints, is entered or modified easily.

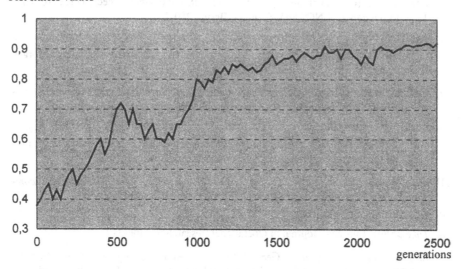

Fig. 8. Results from a Test Run

References

[1] Abramson, D. (1991): *Constructing School Timetables Using Simulated Annealing: Sequential and Parallel Algorithms*. Management Science 37/1: 98-113

[2] Burke, E.K.; Elliman, D.G.; Weare, R. (1994): *A Genetic Algorithm for University Timetabling*. Proceedings of the AISB Workshop on Evolutionary Computing, Leeds

[3] Burke, E.K.; Elliman, D.G.; Weare, R. (1995): *A Genetic Algorithm Based University Timetabling System*. In: Proceedings of the 2nd East-West International Conference on Computer Technologies in Education, Sep. 19-23, Crimea, Ukraine, Vol. I: 35-40

[4] Colorni, A.; Dorigo, M.; Maniezzo, V. (1990): *A Genetic Algorithm to Solve the Time-table Problem*. Technical Report No. 90-060, Politecnico di Milano, Italy

[5] Colorni, A.; Dorigo, M.; Maniezzo, V. (1991): *Genetic Algorithms and Highly Constrained Problems: The Time-Table Case*. In: Schwefel, H.-P.; Männer, R. (eds.): Parallel Problem Solving from Nature. Proceedings of the First Workshop PPSN I, Dortmund, Oct. 1-3. Springer, Berlin: 55-59

[6] Corne, D.; Fang, H.-L.; Mellish, C. (1993): *Solving the Module Exam Scheduling Problem with Genetic Algorithms*. In: Chung; Lovegrove; Ali (eds.): Proceedings of the Sixth International Conference on Industrial and Engineering Applications of Artificial Intelligence and Expert Systems: 370-373

[7] Corne, D.; Ross, P.; Fang, H.-L. (1994): *Fast Practical Evolutionary Timetabling*. In: Fogarty, T.C. (ed.): Evolutionary Computing. AISB Workshop, Leeds, U.K., April 11-13. Selected Papers. LNCS 865. Springer, Berlin: 250-263

[8] Davis, L.; Steenstrup, M. (1987): *Genetic Algorithms and Simulated Annealing: An Overview*. In: Davis, L. (ed.), Genetic Algorithms and Simulated Annealing. Morgan Kaufmann Publishers Inc., Los Altos, CA: 1-11

[9] East, N. (1995): *Genetische Algorithmen für Stundenpläne*. Final Year Project Dissertation, University of Nottingham, U.K., and Fachhochschule Konstanz, Germany

[10] Erben, W. (1995): *Timetabling Using Genetic Algorithms*, in: Pearson, D.W.; Steele, N.C.; Albrecht, R.F. (eds.): Artificial Neural Nets and Genetic Algorithms. Proceedings of the International Conference in Alès/France. Springer, Wien: 30-32

[11] Evan, S.; Itai, A.; Shamir, A. (1976): *On the Complexity of Timetable and Multicommodity Flow Problems*. SIAM Journal of Computing vol. 5, no.4: 691-703

[12] Kang, L.; White, G.M. (1992): *A Logic Approach to the Resolution of Constraints in Timetabling*. European Journal of Operational Research 61: 306-317

[13] Ling, S.E. (1992): *Integrating Genetic Algorithms with a Prolog Assignment Program as a Hybrid Solution for a Polytechnic Timetable Problem*. In: Männer, R.; Manderick, B. (eds.): Parallel Problem Solving from Nature, Proceedings of the Second Conference on PPSN, Brussels, Sep. 28-30. North-Holland, Amsterdam: 321-329

[14] Michalewicz, Z. (1992): *Genetic Algorithms + Data Structures = Evolution Programs*. Springer, Berlin

[15] Werra, D. de (1985): *An Introduction to Timetabling*. European Journal of Operational Research 19: 151-162

GA-Based Examination Scheduling Experience at Middle East Technical University

Ayhan Ergül[1,2]
Department of Computer Engineering
Middle East Technical University, Ankara, Turkey.
e-mail: ergul@ceng.metu.edu.tr

Abstract

In this paper, the development and implementation of a university examination scheduling system, based on a genetic algorithm, is described. The system has been used for scheduling examinations in two real instances so far at Middle East Technical University, involving 682 exams in one case and 1449 exams in the other. The methods employed are described including two adaptive mutation operators that yielded a more robust genetic search, a proximity matrix for efficient computation of the fitness function, a scaled conflict matrix and temporal suspension of highly conflicting exams resulting in schedules with better patterns.

1 Introduction

Middle East Technical University (METU) is a large state university with around 20,000 students, 40 departments offering graduate/undergraduate degrees in more than 50 fields. Every semester, roughly 2,000 courses are offered with 75% having final examinations at the end of the semester. The preparation of the final examination schedule normally requires considerable amount of paperwork and an uncountable number of phone calls between the Registrar's Office and the departments. Programme Chief (of the Registrar's Office) responsible for the examination and course schedules devotes 4 weeks of hard work to obtain an acceptable final exam schedule every semester.

Although exam scheduling is a tedious task for the Programme Chief, he has always been able to come up with quite satisfactory schedules for he has been

---

[1]Most of the work described in this study was carried out as part of the author's master's thesis and the author thanks the thesis supervisors Dr. Göktürk Üçoluk and Dr. Halit Oğuztüzün for their contributions and motivation.
[2]The author was the project manager of Registrar's Office Automation System at Middle East Technical University's Computer Center during this study.

performing the same task since 1983. However, several factors have made this task increasingly difficult through the years:

(i) expansion of the university's student capacity,

(ii) steady growth in the number of courses opened each semester,

(iii) introduction of double major/minor programmes enabling students with outstanding academic performance to get an additional degree in another field by completing extra courses,

(iv) revision of programmes in order to keep pace with world standards and accreditation issues, resulting in more freedom for students in choosing courses,

(v) amnesty laws enforced by the government enabling dismissed students to re-join their programmes, almost always taking courses irregularly and creating new conflicts.

In the Fall'93 semester, the Administrative Board of METU has decided to de-centralize the scheduling of examinations by delegation of the task to departments. Large courses opened to several departments were pre-scheduled by the Programme Chief and the departments had to schedule their courses around them. This approach has lifted the critical load from the Programme Chief but resulted in more people being involved in the scheduling activity around the university and the Programme Chief still spending a lot of time for coordinating independently produced schedules. In the meantime, there was another effort initiated by the Administrative Board to support the Registrar's Office that has been facing increasing loads and tighter deadlines. A project called "Registrar's Office Automation System" has been undertaken by the Computer Center of METU, led by the author since May 1994, to replace the existing hardware, software and data model hosting METU's student information system. As part of this project (also as his master's thesis), the author has decided to develop an examination scheduling system on computer.

A survey in the field revealed that there has been various approaches to the solution of this problem mainly using graph colouring [3, 7, 16, 20, 13, 5, 2] and integer programming [10, 1, 15]. However, the author's background in evolutionary algorithms suggested that a genetic algorithm might be a good choice for the solution of examination scheduling problems. In fact, this idea is supported by the trend towards genetic algorithms in recent works [8, 17, 4]. A system called GUNES (Genetic UNiversity Examination Scheduler) has been developed based on a genetic algorithm.

GUNES was tested on actual data from the Amnesty Examinations at METU held in September 1994. This problem involved 682 exams, 1179 students, 2893 sittings and 15 slots over 5 days. The best schedule obtained by GUNES in 3,000 generations contained no direct conflicts, 72 students sitting consecutive exams and 104 students having two exams in the same day. The schedule was well received by the Registrar's Office and was announced as the official schedule without any change.

Satisfactory results for amnesty examinations provided motivation for applying GUNES to a full-scale problem, the scheduling of final exams in Fall'94 semester. This problem involved 1467 exams, around 16,000 students, 70,000 sittings and 39 slots over 13 days. However, the problem had several constraints that GUNES did not handle at the time such as pre-set courses, control over load distribution and restricted slots. Hence, during Fall'94 semester, only test runs were performed discarding these constraints. Actually, the problem is much harder when all the constraints are enforced.

In the next section, we describe the essential implementation details of GUNES. In Section 3, further enhancements to GUNES are described which were implemented to handle all the requirements of a semester's final examination schedule at METU. The results of our work, used as the official schedule for Spring'95 semester at METU, are also presented in Section 3. Then in Section 4, we go on to compare the manually prepared schedule of Fall'94 semester with schedules generated by GUNES.

2 Implementation

A basic steady-state genetic algorithm has been developed with rank-based selection, elitism, 1/2-point crossover operators, inversion operator, and mutation operator. The algorithm is outlined in Figure 1.

Step 1: Construct the initial population
Step 2: Evaluate the chromosomes and report progress. If an acceptable solution is found or a pre-set number of generations have passed, then stop.
Step 3: Select pairs of chromosomes and apply crossover operator generating one child chromosome for each pair.
Step 4: Apply inversion operator to child chromosomes.
Step 5: Apply mutation operator to child chromosomes and replace bad chromosomes in the population by the mutated child chromosomes.
Step 6: Go to step 2.

Fig. 1. Operation of the genetic algorithm

The timetable is represented in the chromosome by allocating one gene to each exam. Every gene holds the slot number to which the exam corresponding to that gene has been scheduled. This is a common scheme called "direct representation".

None of the genetic operators make use of domain-specific information, in contrast with previous work employing genetic algorithms [8, 9, 4]. Burke, et.al. [4] also use a mutation operator that randomly mutates genes, however, they make sure that the resulting chromosome still corresponds to a feasible schedule. Ross, et.al. [17] use a scheme that they call "violation directed mutation" where they search for a value that will result in fewer violations while mutating a gene. Our mutation operator modifies the values of genes with a probability assigned to the chromosome. However, the mutation operator differs from the classical mutation operator [14] in the way these probabilities are determined.

Crossover and inversion operators work in the classical sense. Crossover operator swaps a portion of one chromosome with genes from its mate. Inversion operator inverts (puts in reverse order) the values of a sequence of genes in the chromosome.

2.1 Adaptive Mutation Operators

Most implementations of genetic algorithms have a fixed value as the mutation probability that determines the number of chromosomes/genes that will be mutated and this value does not change through generations. Some researchers have suggested alternatives to this scheme. Fogarty [12] employs a method where mutation probability decreases exponentially through generations. Whitley& Starkweather [19] decide the mutation probability of a chromosome during crossover as a function of the Hamming distance between its parents where children of similar parents are assigned higher mutation probabilities to retain genetic diversity. Davis [9] suggests monitoring the performance of the genetic operators and adapting their probabilities according to how good they are doing. Cobb&Grefenstette [6] describe a mechanism that they call "triggered hypermutation" where they monitor the performance of the GA and temporarily raise mutation probability to a very high value if performance deteriorates. Srinivas&Patnaik [18] describe an adaptive mutation scheme where chromosomes with better-than-average fitness values get a linearly interpolated probability value between 0 and a pre-defined upper limit depending on their fitness and chromosomes with sub average fitness values get a pre-determined constant value as mutation probability.

We employ two techniques that we call "linear mutation" and "quadratic mutation" that are conceptually similar. In linear mutation, chromosomes are sorted in decreasing order of their fitness values. A value obtained by linear interpolation between pre-determined lower and upper mutation limits is assigned to each chromosome depending on its rank in the pool of chromosomes. Quadratic mutation follows from this scheme: The values are obtained by quadratic interpolation this time. In every generation, each chromosome is re-assigned a mutation probability before the application of genetic operators. Figure 2 illustrates the difference between constant, linear and quadratic mutation operators. In the figure, constant mutation assigns 0.07 as the mutation probability to all chromosomes independent of their ranks. Linear mutation assigns linearly-interpolated values between 0.03 and 0.20, whereas quadratic mutation assigns quadratically-interpolated values between 0.00 and 0.30. As illustrated in Figure 2, chromosomes that are ranked high (or, equivalently, that are more fit) receive a low mutation probability and those that are ranked low (that have low fitness) receive a high mutation probability.

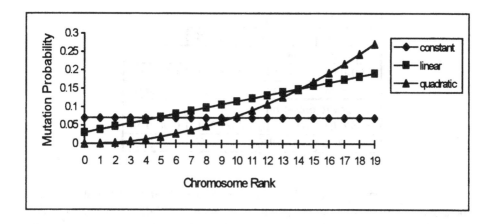

Fig. 2. Mutation Probability Assignments for a Population of 20 Chromosomes

Experiments with mutation operators have shown that linear and quadratic mutation exhibit less sensitivity to GA parameters while preserving robustness across problems of different scales in the domain of examination scheduling. All the experiments have been performed 5 times with a different random seed at each run. In this section, only the results of median runs are used for the purpose of comparison. The GA employed 2-point crossover with a rate of 0.75, mutation operators at a rate of 1.00, no inversion and 1 chromosome as elite throughout these experiments.

Table 1 illustrates the sensitivity of constant, linear and quadratic mutation schemes. These experiments were performed on a problem with 682 exams to be scheduled into 15 slots over 5 days, which is the problem of scheduling amnesty examinations held at METU in September'94. Each mutation scheme is tested with different parameter values and their performance is recorded in Table 1. It is observed that variations in mutation probability within a small range can lead to serious performance degradation when constant mutation is used. Although mutation probabilities lie in a wide range in the case of linear mutation, degradation in performance is not as serious as in constant mutation. For example, in the marginal case of linear mutation in the range 0.00 to 0.50, mutation probability results in 25% of the genes to mutate which is equivalent (in terms of the number of genes to mutate) to constant mutation with 0.25 probability. Although constant mutation of such a high probability would end up with a totally unacceptable performance, linear mutation performs close to its best configuration. Performance of quadratic mutation is more interesting. The performance difference between the best and worst configurations is less than that in the cases of constant and linear mutation.

Table 1. Sensitivity of Mutation Schemes to Parameter Values[1]

constant mutation			
0.001	0.01	0.1	
0%	33%	192%	
linear mutation			
0.00-0.01	0.00-0.10	0.00-0.30	0.00-0.50
80%	0%	22%	58%
quadratic mutation			
0.00-0.01	0.00-0.10	0.00-0.30	0.00-0.50
0%	18%	34%	34%

Experiments described above have shown that linear and quadratic mutation operators are less sensitive to variations in mutation probability. However, this does not make much sense if these new operators cannot perform comparable to the classical constant mutation operator. In order to compare these operators, the following three configurations were selected:

- *constant:* constant mutation with probability 0.001
- *linear:* linear mutation with probability in the range 0.00 to 0.10
- *quadratic:* quadratic mutation with probability in the range 0.00 to 0.10

Experiments using these configurations were performed on the following three real-world problems of different scales:

- *Small-scale problem:* A high school problem with 30 exams and 11 slots over 2 days (from the PGA package developed at University of Edinburgh).
- *Medium-scale problem:* METU amnesty examinations held in September'94 with 682 exams and 15 slots over 5 days.
- *Large-scale problem:* METU Fall'94 semester final examinations with 1449 exams and 39 slots over 13 days (with some constraints left out since some features were not implemented at the time).

For the small-scale problem where there are only 2 slots in a day, the sameday and within24hours conflicts were not used. Table 2 contains the results

---

[1]In this paper, the fitness values are expressed as "percent worse than best" where "best" is the fitness of the configuration that achieved lowest penalty scores in the set of experiments under consideration. "Best" is distinguished with the value 0%.

obtained in terms of conflicts that remained at the end of 1000 generations (300 for the small-scale problem). These results illustrate that the adaptive operators perform comparably well to the classical mutation operator on problems of different scales. When combined with the fact that the adaptive mutation operators we propose are much less sensitive to mutation probability, one can employ these operators without extensive experimentation with mutation probability values. Through the use of adaptive mutation operators we overcome, to some extent, a common problem in GA research: determination of good mutation probability values.

Table 2. Performance of Mutation Operators on Problems of Different Scales

		Fitness	**Cl**	**Con**	**Sam**	**Bb**	**24h**
Small-Scale	constant	16%	1	45	na	59	na
Problem	linear	0%	2	44	na	27	na
	quadratic	5%	4	37	na	32	na
Medium-Scale	constant	18%	0	24	53	44	81
Problem	linear	0%	0	26	40	17	96
	quadratic	32%	0	39	42	26	129
Large-Scale	constant	0%	59	801	521	643	1951
Problem	linear	3%	72	838	503	709	1731
	quadratic	24%	112	827	803	766	2082

Further experiments with other GA parameters/operators and penalty weighting are described in [11].

2.2 Fitness Evaluation

The fitness function records pre-determined penalty points, for every pair of exams, proportional to the number of common students taking those exams if they violated any of the following conflicts:

(i) clash: exams are scheduled to the same slot
(ii) consecutive: exams are scheduled to consecutive slots in the same day
(iii) sameday: exams are scheduled to non-consecutive slots in the same day
(iv) back-to-back across night: one exams is scheduled to the last slot in one day and the other to the first slot of the next day
(v) within24hours: exams are scheduled to slots within 24 hours and do not cause one of the conflicts above

The fitness function makes use of a symmetric matrix that we call the "proximity matrix"; a simple and efficient, yet generalizable tool for computing penalties accrued for conflicts between every pair of exams. A sample proximity matrix for an exam period of 2 days with 3 slots per day is given in Table 3 and the description of its entries is given in Table 4. However, schedules are flexible in the number of days and the number of slots per day. Proximity matrix is generated automatically when the total number of slots, the number of days and the conflict penalties are given.

Table 3. A Sample Proximity Matrix

	Slot 1	Slot 2	Slot 3	Slot 4	Slot 5	Slot 6
Slot 1	250	100	75	0	0	0
Slot 2	100	250	100	30	0	0
Slot 3	75	100	250	50	30	0
Slot 4	0	30	50	250	100	75
Slot 5	0	0	30	100	250	100
Slot 6	0	0	0	75	100	250

Table 4. Proximity Matrix Entries for a Total of 6 Slots Over 2 Days

	Slot 1	Slot 2	Slot 3	Slot 4	Slot 5	Slot 6
Slot 1	clash	consecutive	sameday			
Slot 2	consecutive	clash	consecutive	within24hours		
Slot 3	sameday	consecutive	clash	backtoback	within24hours	
Slot 4		within24hours	backtoback	clash	consecutive	sameday
Slot 5			within24hours	consecutive	clash	consecutive
Slot 6				sameday	consecutive	clash

The fitness function is calculated according to the following formula:

$$\sum_{i=1,2,\ldots,|E|} \sum_{j=i+1,\ldots,|E|} conflict\left[e_i, e_j\right] \times proximity\left[slot(e_i), slot(e_j)\right]$$

where E is the set of exams, $|E|$ is the number of exams in E and the notation $slot(\bullet)$ represents the slot number to which its parameter, an exam, is scheduled. Hence the fitness function evaluation is a summation of the product of a conflict matrix entry with the corresponding proximity matrix entry over all exam pairs. The conflict matrix records the number of common students between every pair of exams as usual.

3 Enhancements

GUNES had been extended to support previously unavailable features by the time when exam scheduling activity for the Spring'95 semester was due to start. Pre-setting, exclusion and load distribution control were implemented to handle the fundamental constraints of a semester's final examination schedule. These were: (i) Sunday is used only for 3 large courses, (ii) two Saturdays should be used at half capacity and never for large must courses, (iii) student and exam distribution over slots should be controlled with preference to morning slots against evening slots, (iv) 24 courses have to be pre-scheduled to their accustomed slots. There were 1449 exams, more than 70,000 sittings and, again, 39 slots over 13 days (from Monday of one week to Saturday of the next week). There were more than 40 courses conflicting with at least 100 other courses. There was even an elective course ("History of Jazz") conflicting with 375 other courses. The total number of conflicting course pairs was 21,818. Initial run of GUNES favoured decreasing conflicts and a schedule having less than 10 direct conflicts (some caused by pre-scheduled courses) was generated. However, this schedule was regarded as completely unusable by the Programme Chief who, only then, explained that top priority is given to the comfort of regular students, meaning that must courses of every department at each class level should be distributed evenly over the exam period. A new conflict type, *within48hours* conflict, was implemented in GUNES to force empty days in-between must courses. Also two techniques (a scaled conflict matrix and temporal suspension of highly conflicting exams) were employed which are described below.

3.1 Scaled Conflict Matrix

In order to discriminate must courses from electives, GUNES employed a simple look-up technique where courses with high conflict rates (i.e., nodes with a high 1-degree in graph theory terms) are considered electives and those with low conflict rates are considered must courses. Hence, new fitness evaluation scheme takes the conflict rates of both courses into account while penalizing a conflict caused by a pair of courses. However, we needed to implement a "scaled conflict matrix" in order not to waste time calculating the degree of each course every time a chromosome's fitness needs to be evaluated. The following formula was used to calculate the entries of the scaled conflict matrix:

$$conflict'[e_i, e_j] = conflict[e_i, e_j] \times \left(1 - \frac{degree(e_i)}{|E|}\right) \times \left(1 - \frac{degree(e_j)}{|E|}\right) \times \sqrt{|e_i|, |e_j|}$$

$$i, j = 1, 2, \ldots, |E|$$

where $|e|$ is the size of the exam e and the notation $degree(\bullet)$ represents the number of exams conflicting with its parameter. Then, the only thing to change in fitness function is to replace the $conflict[\bullet, \bullet]$ term with the $conflict'[\bullet, \bullet]$ term. It should be noted that the formula also takes the sizes of the exams into account (the square-root term) in addition to conflict rates of the exams. While the conflict values of hard-to-schedule courses are dampened by the conflict rate terms, large exams are favoured by the exam size term. This combination has yielded a satisfactory compromise for the scheduling taste of METU.

3.2 Temporal Suspension of Highly Conflicting Exams

In order to further dampen the undesirable effects of problematic elective courses and large must courses taken by several departments, another technique has been implemented. This technique also makes use of conflict rates: Exams with high conflict rates are temporarily scheduled to predetermined slots and then released after other exams have been stabilized to some extent (after a predetermined number of generations). When combined with the use of scaled conflict matrix, this technique results in schedules with better patterns. In order to make sure that temporal suspension does not result in a performance deterioration we have conducted two series of experiments. First, exams with a conflict rate higher than 0.08 in a 1190 exam problem were temporarily suspended and the performance of GUNES was recorded for different release times of 100, 300, 500 and 1000 generations. In the next series of experiments, the release time was fixed at 300 generations while the conflict rate for temporal suspension was realized as 0.06, 0.08 and 0.10. It has been observed that, in both sets of experiments, the progress tends to converge very quickly to that of the experiment with no suspended exams. The numerical results achieved at the end of the experiments (in 4000 generations) are also presented in Table 5 and Table 6.

Table 5. Release Time Varied as Conflict Rate for Temporal Suspension Fixed at 0.08

	Fitness	Cl	Con	Sam	Bb	24h	48h
not suspended	2%	176	1067	635	903	3230	14845
100	1%	137	1152	471	736	2810	15913
300	2%	171	1049	535	659	2757	16665
500	0%	158	1026	512	810	3109	15371
1000	2%	185	1019	624	673	2629	16315

Table 6. Conflict Rate for Temporal Suspension Varied as Release Time Fixed at 300 Generations

	Fitness	Cl	Con	Sam	Bb	24h	48h
not suspended	2%	176	1067	635	903	3230	14845
0.10	0%	180	1096	460	754	2402	16172
0.08	2%	171	1049	535	659	2757	16665
0.06	5%	148	1008	608	977	2476	16084

The rule of thumb for choosing the conflict rate for temporal suspension has been as follows: The exams to be scheduled are sorted in decreasing order of conflict rates and a conflict rate is chosen such that there does not exist any exam with a lower conflict rate taken by at least 3 departments. The exams are usually suspended for 300 generations.

Proving the claim that temporal suspension helps the generation of schedules with better patterns is not trivial and only an expert eye can differentiate best schedules from others when there are more than a thousand courses since the fitness function is only a rough reflection of what is expected from a schedule. We believe the decision to use a GUNES-generated scheduling in Spring'95 semester at METU supports our claim more than anything else. However, we will try to illustrate how close GUNES has come to a manually prepared schedule in Section 4.

3.3 Final Examination Schedule for Spring'95 Semester

After several revisions, GUNES generated schedules that were better in terms of the relaxation periods between must courses, decreased loads on Saturdays and distribution of the number of exams and the number of sittings to slots. Indeed, the schedule generated by GUNES in the end was considered worthy of further study by the Programme Chief although the number of clashes was increased to 330. The total number of conflicts that remained after 3450 generations is given in Table 7.

Table 7. Results for Spring'95 Semester

Cl	Con	Sam	Bb	24h	48h
330	1713	940	926	4356	24145

Of the 1449 exams scheduled, 46 were moved to new slots, mostly to Saturdays where the load was lighter than ever. The modified schedule has been approved by both Registrar's Office and the Administrative Board as the final examination schedule for Spring'95 semester at METU.

4 Comparison With a Manually Prepared Schedule

In order to illustrate how GUNES performs, we present the properties of GUNES generated schedules and compare with the manually prepared schedule. The manual schedule is the one used as the official schedule in Fall'94 semester at METU. However, only 1190 of 1467 exams were scheduled manually and the rest were left out probably because these courses were not yet defined in the main database at the time when the listings for conflicting courses were printed. GUNES was presented with the data of those 1190 exams to have a fair basis for comparison. There were 19,317 conflicting exam pairs yielding a conflict matrix density of 2.73%. GUNES employed 2-point crossover with a rate of 0.75, mutation operators at a rate of 1.00, no inversion and 1 chromosome as elite throughout these experiments. The mutation operator was quadratic mutation in the range 0.001 to 0.30. In fact, this configuration is an exact replica of the configuration that was used to obtain Spring'95 semester schedule.

The results, in terms of the remaining conflicts at the end of 4000 generations, are presented in Table 8. It is seen that GUNES achieves far fewer number of conflicts than the manual schedule, both first order and also of higher orders. In fact, GUNES outperforms the manual schedule in under 500 generations (or equivalently in one hour of computer time).

Table 8. Results for Fall'94 Semester

	Fitness[1]	Cl	Con	Sam	Bb	24h	48h
manual	398%	685	2303	1787	2175	3894	20183
GUNES w/o enh.	5%	127	1037	726	711	3359	15389
GUNES w. enh.	0%	171	1049	535	659	2757	16665

One may argue that enhancements in GUNES has lead to more first and second order conflicts. However, this is in return for higher gains in the quality of the overall schedule. Table 9 summarizes the total number of constraints violated, by the three methods, in the schedules of second year must courses of all departments on the basis of exams. Second year schedules were preferred because first year students generally take common courses many of which are pre-scheduled, third year students take many courses from other departments or from upper/lower levels and fourth year students specialize in a field by taking courses from various sets of courses. Furthermore, second year courses are scheduled early in the manual process and, hence, have a higher chance of conforming to constraints. If GUNES can do better on this part of the schedule, one can be quite sure that it will also be good on other parts. Indeed, the manual schedule has several serious violations that GUNES-generated schedules do not have and has more instances of less serious violations. It is also observed that GUNES with enhancements has done better when compared to GUNES without enhancements.

Table 9. Constraints Violated in the Schedules of Second Year Must Courses

	Clashing exams	2 exams in 1 day	Sunday exams	Saturday exams	4 exams in 4 days	3 exams in 3 days	2 exams in 2 days
manual	1	6	1	8	1	4	18
GUNES w/o enh.	-	-	-	12	-	3	25
GUNES w. enh.	-	-	-	11	-	1	21

GUNES employs load distribution control to make sure that no slot is swamped by too many exams or too many sittings. Limits on the number of students and exams for every slot is read from file. Exceeding the limits result in an added

---

[1]The fitness function employed by GUNES with enhancements was used to obtain these figures.

penalty proportional to the amount of excess. The figures in Table 10 illustrate the extent to which desired student and exam load distributions are exceeded. It is observed that GUNES-generated schedules conform to the desired distributions better than the manual schedule does.

Table 10. Excess of Limits on Student and Exam Load Distribution

	Student	Exam
manual	4.85%	5.89%
GUNES w/o enhancements	0.37%	0%
GUNES w. enhancements	2.12%	0%

5 Runtime Platform

GUNES is written in C++ using only ANSI-92 C functions, hence is very portable. It has been compiled on IBM AIX, DEC OSF/1, Sun Solaris and MS Windows operating systems. The work described in this paper was carried out on IBM ES590 and IBM SP2 systems with 66 MHz RISC processors and 64MB main memory running AIX 3.2.5 operating system. GUNES was compiled using GNU C++ 2.6.1 with optimization turned on.

GUNES runs in $O(g \times c \times e^2)$ time where e is the number of exams, g is the number of generations to run and c is the number of chromosomes. In all experiments, populations of 50 chromosomes were used. A run on Fall'94 data which had 1190 exams, for example, lasts 8.5 hours of user time on a single processor for 4000 generations. The problem of scheduling 200 exams would take under 15 minutes (assuming the run lasts 2000 generation which is more than enough for a problem of this size). It should be noted that an identical run on Fall'94 data takes 5.6 hours when GUNES is compiled using IBM C Set ++ Compiler (available on the systems used) with optimization turned on.

6 Conclusions

We have presented the details on the course of the implementation and development of GUNES, a GA-based examination scheduling system, that has gone into continual use at METU. Although GUNES has not gotten mature enough to be used by a novice, its use does not require much expertise on genetic algorithms. We have shown that the configuration of GUNES that yielded the official schedule for the Spring'95 semester can be used to obtain a satisfactory schedule for the Fall'94 semester without any change in GA parameters.

The promising and proven results of GUNES deserves further work, at least in order to wrap it up as a general-purpose exam scheduler. Room considerations will have to be taken into account. We have left out that part since METU, being located on a large campus, does not fall short of rooms as long as load distribution is controlled. Other practical features like orderings between certain exams, pre-setting to or excluding from more than one specific slot may be added.

The adaptive mutation operators of GUNES promise a satisfactory outcome on different instances of examination scheduling problems without changing GA parameters. The proximity and scaled conflict matrices are efficient and effective tools in obtaining good schedules considering the fact that not all exams should be treated the same. Temporal suspension of highly conflicting exams, on the other hand, helps the GA engine to concentrate on the more useful activity of scheduling the must courses first so that they have a neater examination schedule.

References

[1] Arani T., Karwan M.H., Lotfi V., "A Langrangian Relaxation Approach to Solve the Second Phase of the Exam Scheduling Problem", *European Journal of Operational Research*, Vol. 34, No. 3, pp. 372-383, 1988.

[2] Balakrishnan N., "Examination Scheduling: A Computerized Application", *Omega*, Vol. 19, No. 1, pp. 37-41, 1991.

[3] Broder S., "Final Examination Scheduling", *Communications of the ACM*, Vol. 7, 494-498, 1964.

[4] Burke E.K., Elliman D.G., Weare R.F., "A Genetic Algorithm Based University Timetabling System", East-West Conf. on Computer Technologies in Education, Vol. 1, pp. 35-40, Crimea, Ukraine, 19-23 Sept. 1994.

[5] Carter M. W., Laporte G., Chinneck J.W., "A General Examination Scheduling System", *Interfaces*, Vol. 24, No. 3, pp. 109-120, 1994.

[6] Cobb H.G., Grefenstette J.J., "Genetic Algorithms for Tracking Changing Environments", Proc. of the Fifth Int. Conf. on Genetic Algorithms, pp. 523-530, Morgan Kaufmann, San Mateo, CA, 1993.

[7] Cole A.J., "The Preparation of Examination Timetables Using a Small-Store Computer", *Computer Journal*, Vol. 7, pp. 117-121, 1964.

[8] Corne D., Ross P., Fang H.-L., "Fast Practical Evolutionary Timetabling", *Lecture Notes in Computer Science*, Vol. 865, pp. 250-263, Springer-Verlag, 1994.

[9] Davis L., editor, *Handbook of Genetic Algorithms*, Van Nostrand Reinhold, New York, 1991.

[10] Descroches S., Laporte G., Rousseau J.M., "HOREX: A Computer Program for the Construction of Examination Schedules", *INFOR*, Vol. 16, No. 3, pp. 294-298, 1978.

[11] Ergül, A., "A Genetic Algorithm for University Examination Scheduling", Unpublished M.Sc. Thesis, Dept. of Computer Eng., Middle East Technical University, 1995.

[12] Fogarty T.C., "Varying the Probability of Mutation in Genetic Algorithms", Proc. of the Third Int. Conf. on Genetic Algorithms, pp. 104-109, 1989.

[13] Foxley E., Lockyer K., "The Construction of Examination Timetables by Computer", *Computer Journal*, Vol. 11, pp. 264-268, 1968.

[14] Goldberg D.E., *Genetic Algorithms in Search, Optimization and Machine Learning*, Addison-Wesley, Reading, MA, 1989.

[15] Lotfi V., Cerveny R., "A Final-Exam-Scheduling Package", *Journal of the Operational Research Society*, Vol. 42, No. 3, pp. 205-216, 1991.

[16] Peck J.E.L., Williams M.R., "Algorithm 286: Examination Scheduling", *Communications of the ACM*, Vol. 9, No. 6, pp 433-434, 1966.

[17] Ross P., Corne D., Fang H.-L., "Improving Evolutionary Timetabling with Delta Evaluation and Directed Mutation", *Parallel Problem Solving from Nature III*, Y. Davidor ed., Springer-Verlag, 1994.

[18] Srinivas M., Patnaik L.M., "Adaptive Probabilities of Crossover and Mutation in Genetic Algorithms", *IEEE Trans. on Systems, Man and Cybernetics*, Vol. 24, No. 4, pp. 656-667, 1994.

[19] Whitley D., Starkweather, D., "GENITOR-II: A Distributed Genetic Algorithm", *J. Expt. Theor. Artif. Intell.*, Vol. 2, pp. 189-214, 1990. (As cited in Srinivas&Patnaik, 1994)

[20] Wood D.C., "A System for Computing University Examination Timetables", *Computer Journal*, Vol. 11, pp. 41-47, 1968.

Peckish Initialisation Strategies for Evolutionary Timetabling

David Corne[1] and Peter Ross[2]

[1] Parallel Emergent & Distributed Architectures Laboratory,
Department of Computer Science, University of Reading, Reading RG6 6AY, UK
Email: D.W.Corne@reading.ac.uk
[2] Department of Artificial Intelligence, University of Edinburgh,
80 South Bridge, Edinburgh EH1 1HN, UK, Email: peter@aisb.ed.ac.uk

Abstract. Some evolutionary algorithm (EA)/timetabling researchers find benefit from combining an EA with graph-colouring based greedy algorithms, while others opt for a simpler but faster method. We consider a combination of the two approaches, largely retaining the speed of the simpler method while adopting the greedy method to bootstrap the process. In this combination, the initial population is produced by a 'peckish' timetable construction algorithm, similar to a greedy algorithm, but less concerned with finding a best timeslot for an event at each step. We find peckish population initialisation more effective than either greedy or random initialisation on non-trivial problems. Peckish initialisation is shown to aid a simple hill-climbing approach in a similar way. Finally, we add to the growing observation that hill-climbing often outperforms an EA on timetabling problems, but that this effect is reversed on problems of particular overconstrainedness or difficulty.

1 Introduction

A number of researchers have applied Evolutionary Algorithms (EA)s to various kinds of timetabling problems [4, 6, 9, 7, 2]. In particular, some find benefit from the combination of an EA with graph-colouring based greedy or similar algorithms [2, 8]. We shall call this as the 'greedy' method. In such work, a greedy algorithm builds a timetable piece by piece, gradually assigning times (and perhaps rooms, and so on) to events in such a way as to avoid conflicts which may arise from previous assignments. Paechter et al [8] use this approach, employing an evolutionary algorithm to essentially search through a space of choices in this process; these choices concern the order in which events are considered and which conflict-free time or room assignments to use at each step. Burke et al [2] employ a similar strategy, also using such techniques during the genetic recombination and mutation steps.

In contrast, Abramson and Abela [1], Colorni et al [4], Ling [6], Corne et al [5], and others, rely on a much simpler timetable-building technique in which time and/or room assignments are taken directly from an ordered string of assignments. Random strings typically lead to timetables with a great many conflicts;

the onus is then on the EA to search the space of such strings for good timetables. This is usually aided by the use of fast local hill-climbing operators [10], or 'genetic repair' or 'filtering' operators [6] . We shall refer to this as the 'direct' method.

Clearly, a standard EA using the direct method starts with a very weak population of timetables. On non-trivial problems, very many generations will pass before the artificial evolution of acceptable timetables. When using the greedy approach, however, the initial population is far healthier than in the direct case, and the path towards acceptable timetables is consequently shorter. Nevertheless, the effectiveness of the direct method then seems to vie with that of the greedy method [3]. This is largely because the evaluation of a candidate timetable is much faster in the direct approach; the longer route towards good timetables is mitigated by the speed of steps along that route.

It is worth considering ways in which the two approaches can be effectively combined, so as to promise an overall improvement in speed and/or solution quality. Herein we report on a simple such combination, in which the initial population of an EA is produced via 'peckish' timetable construction algorithms, with ensuing search using the direct method. A peckish algorithm is similar to a greedy algorithm, but not quite so concerned with finding a (or the) best timeslot (or room) for an event at each step. The general class of such peckish algorithms spans various degrees of greediness ranging through random time assignment (just as in the direct approach) through to 'best' time assignment (as in the greedy method).

In section 2, greedy and peckish algorithms are presented in detail. We then discuss population initialisation strategies in general terms in section 3. Section 4 then presents the test problems we will use for the experiments reported in section 5. Some concluding discussion then appears in section 6.

2   Greedy and Peckish Algorithms

Assume a timetabling problem involving a set E of events, and a set T of potential non-overlapping timeslots. Assume further that just two kinds of constraint are involved: first, there is a set P of pairs of events such that no two events in a pair can be assigned the same timeslot. Any such assignment will be called a 'clash', Second, no such pair of events should be assigned adjacent timeslots. Any such assignment will be called a 'too-close'. A greedy algorithm for building a timetable works in the following typical manner:

start: set $i = 1$.

assign : Find the set of times S in T, such that for each time s in S, event i can be assigned time s without introducing clashes or too-closes in respect of events assigned earlier (that is, events with index smaller than i.)

---

[3] As yet the two approaches have not been directly compared on a common set of problems;however , at least it is known that both approaches have been used to successfully solve large, real-world problems.

If S is non-empty, assign event i a timeslot randomly chosen from S.

If S is empty, construct the set M of slots which introduce minimal conflict when assigned to event i. Assign event i a slot randomly chosen from M.

next: Increment i. If $i > |E|$ stop; else go to **assign**.

The main dimensions of variation among different greedy algorithms are within the assignment step. In the above example, after identifying a set of potential timeslots S which can lead to a conflict-free assignment for the current event, the choice of slot to use is made randomly. A different approach, known as 'first-fit', would be to simply place i in the earliest such slot in S. The 'next-fit' strategy, on the other hand, would assign the earliest slot in S which has so far not been assigned to any event. Many other variations can be imagined. Similarly, a host of strategies are available for the case where S is empty.

Greedy algorithms of this kind can also be used to initialise the population for any population-based search algorithm, such as EAs. Being 'greedy', all such variations still share the characteristic that an event is never assigned a timeslot which would introduce conflict if an alternative assignment would avoid it. As such, timetables built by the greedy algorithm will represent a 'skewed' sample from their cost band (the collection of possible timetables with similar cost). To avoid this, we can relax the idea of 'always avoiding conflicts if possible', and use a peckish algorithm.

A peckish algorithm differs from the greedy algorithm described above in the **assign** step., which is replaced by the following procedure, involving a new parameter k.:

peckish-assign: Choose k members of T uniformly at random. Assign each of these k times a score representing the number of conflicts which would be introduced by assigning that time to event k. Choose a time from these k with a minimal such score, and assign event i to that time.

Clearly, $k = 1$ corresponds to random initialisation, while in the limit as k gets large this becomes equivalent to greedy initialisation. In between, the peckish algorithm resembles a greedy algorithm which occasionally makes mistakes, assigning conflicting times to events when non-conflicting times are possible. In this way, by varying the parameter k, populations of timetables can be generated which vary in the degree to which mistakes are made.

Clearly, variations on the above to cope with room assignments, teacher assignments, and so on, can be readily imagined. Certain other points of variation are of particular interest however; these concern differential ways of treating hard and soft constraint violations. Here we will investigate use of the following four styles of algorithm for the population initialisation step.

greedy-feasible (GF) : This is the greedy algorithm described earlier, but only attempting to satisfy hard constraints. At any step, S may therefore contain timeslots which would lead to violation of soft constraints.

This variant would seem to promote diversity in the initial population without sacrificing the general degree of feasibility in the resulting timetables.

The price paid is that quality in terms of soft-constraint violations will tend to be initially poor.

greedy-uniform (GU) : The greedy algorithm described earlier, but attempting to avoid both hard and soft constraint violations at each step. Overall quality of the initial population should be generally fitter than with GF, but at the cost of generally reduced diversity and a degree of skewedness (see next section).

peckish-feasible (PFk) A peckish-feasible algorithm with 'pressure' (or 'greediness') k. As with GF, in this case the k randomly sampled timeslots are assessed only in respect of avoiding hard constraint violations.

peckish-uniform (PUk : As PFk, except that sampled timeslots are assessed in terms of avoiding both hard and soft constraint violations.

Note that PF1 and PU1 are equivalent to random initialisation. Also, though at first sight it may seem that PFT and PUT, where T is the number of timeslots available, are respectively equivalent to GF and GU respectively; this is not the case, however, since the T timeslost are sampled with replacement.

We later investigate a hybrid EA which uses the direct method along with 'event-freeing mutation' [5], but incorporating one of the above four techniques to produce each member of the initial population.

3 Aspects of Population Seeding

Population seeding is an interesting and generally important aspect of EA research. Essentially, the idea is that solution speed, final solution quality, or both, may be improved by inserting non-random chromosomes (seeds) into the initial population. Generally, these non-random chromosomes are rather fitter than the average random chromosome. It is worth considering the following two aspects of seeding: *how* fit should these seeds be? And, what proportion of the initial population should contain seeds?

If only a small proportion of the initial population contained seeds, and these were considerably fitter than the average random chromosome elsewhere in the initial population, then this may clearly lead to convergence to a peak close in some sense to one of these seeds. If we were to be able to ensure that one or more of these few initial seeds was in the basin of attraction of a global optimum, then we would probably know enough not to require the EA at all, and certainly not to require the random portion of the population. So, a small proportion of highly fit seeds seems like an unwelcome idea. As we reduce the fitnesses of the seeds, we give more chance for the rest of the population to play a role. Also, as we increase the proportion of the seeds, especially if we can do so without sacrificing diversity, there seems to be less chance of falling into local traps. So, something towards the area of a high proportion of slightly fit seeds seems most preferable.

Greedy and similar algorithms provide a convenient way of seeding populations in genetic timetabling applications. Considering how they generally work, however, a further important issue is brought to light. It is not, of course, just the fitnesses of the seeds that might count, but the region of the solution space they generally occupy. For example, the application of a greedy algorithm to a certain 100-event problem may tend to assign times conflict-free to about the first 90 events. The remaining 10 or so events will then usually find themselves assigned times in conflict with earlier ones. For the purpose of illustration, we shall assume a simple measure of cost which we wish to minimise, namely the number of events involved in any conflict. In the situation described, costs might tend to be around 10—15. That is, repeated attempts at using a particular greedy algorithm on this problem, given a pre-specified (but perhaps heuristically chosen) ordering of the events, will tend to produce timetables with costs between 10 and 15. The point to note here, however, is that *none* of these timetables will involve conflicts between any pair from the first 90 or so events. Presumably, the region of the space of timetables containing points in the cost band 10—15 is rich in examples involving conflicts between the first 90 events; the subregion without such conflicts is probably only a small portion of this. The greedy method, when applied as described in this example, will simply never visit most of this region, and hence leads to a considerably skewed and restricted sample from the 10—15 cost band.

If the greedy algorithm in question is presented with a randomised ordering of events each time it is used, then the skewness referred to above is alleviated to some extent. However, considerable skewness is retained simply in the fact that the timetables produced still sample a relatively thin cost band. It may be useful to sample a wider band, providing more varied material for the EA to use. The potential problem is essentially the fact that greedy population initialisation offers us initial populations of a characteristic nature; for present purposes we can simplify matters by identifying this characteristic nature with the average cost of the initial population. Standard random initialisation offers us a low average cost; greedy initialisation offers an initial population with a much better average cost. However, general considerations concerning the likelihood of being trapped in local optima, and the population's general skewedness, suggest that different initial population characteristics would be worth considering. In particular, those with average fitness somewhere between that of random and greedy populations. A 'peckish' timetable construction algorithm, as described above, allows us to access such a range of initial populations.

4 Test Problems

Several experiments were performed to examine the effect of these different population initialisation strategies. Experiments are centred on the examination timetabling problem faced by the University of Edinburgh Department of Artificial Intelligence (EDAI) for the first semester of 1995. In this problem, a mixture of 231 postgraduates and undergraduates each sat a varying number of examinations from a pool of 67. Seven days were available for the examinations, with four timeslots per day, and available seats in each slot were limited to 80 (seating arrangements were more complex than this, but are simplified for the purpose of this study). Also, many of the examinations were restricted to occur in certain time windows. Full details of the problem are available from the authors.

Results are considered in terms of four main indicators of timetable quality, as follows:

Clashes: In any given timetable, the number of clashes refers to the number of situations in which a student has to be in two places at once. This is evidently a hard constraint, since a timetable which contains clashes is infeasible. Hence, for example, the greedy-feasible and peckish-feasible initialisation strategies tried hard to avoid clashes.

Extra Seats: 80 seats were available in each timeslot; if a given timetable required $s > 80$ seats in a given slot, then this contributed to a need for $s - 80$ extra seats. Summed over all slots, this becomes the 'extra-seats' score of the timetable. Avoiding any such extra seats is considered a hard constraint, and hence taken firmly on board by the greedy-feasible and peckish-feasible initialisation strategies.

Too-Closes: In the given problem, we wished students to have a break of at least 100 minutes between any two examinations on the same day. If we number a day's slots in temporal order from 1 to 4, this constraint effectively meant that exams (taken by the same student) in consecutive timeslots were too close. Minimising the number of such too-closes was a soft constraint, and hence ignored by the greedy-feasible and peckish-feasible initialisation strategies.

Penalty: A timetable's penalty score is simply a linear weighted sum of its clashes, extra-seats, and too-closes.

Two further measures we look at relate to the diversity of solutions produced. The end-result of an EA run is typically that a number of different solutions of equal quality exist in the final population; we can measure this diversity simply in terms of the number of different solutions with an equal penalty score to the best found, and the average Hamming distance between pairs of these solutions. In cases where hill-climbing (see below), for example, performs roughly equally to an EA in other senses, such extra diversity offered by the EA may often make it the preferred algorithm.

Experiments are performed on three different versions of the underlying EDAI-1995 examination timetabling problem, in which the examinations are respectively restricted to occur within a 7-day, 6-day, and 5-day period, all other conditions being the same.

5 Experiments

5.1 Algorithms

In all, we test thirteen different initialisation strategies. These are: GF, GU, R (random), PF5, PF10, PF15, PF20, PF25, and PU5, PU10, PU15, PU20, PU25.

Each of these is examined in the context of initialising the population of an EA, and also in the context of producing the starting point of a Stochastic Hillclimber (SH). Hence, a total of 26 different algorithms were tested on each of the three problems.

The EA always had a population size of 50, set out spatially on a 10 × 5 grid. Local mating selection [3] was used with a random walk size of 2, and a steady-state reproduction strategy. The only operator was 'event-freeing mutation' [9] applied at a pressure of 0.2; in event-freeing mutation, an exam is chosen at random, and then a sample of potential new timeslots is considered for this even; the best of that sample (causing least conflicts) is chosen as a the new timeslot for the exam.

The SH algorithm used event-freeing mutation at the same pressure, but was otherwise a standard hillclimber: maintaining a single current timetable (ie: a population of one), any mutation equal or better in fitness replaced it as the new current timetable, while worse mutants were always discarded.

In both EA and SH trials, computation was stopped after 20,000 timetable evaluations.

5.2   Results on the 7-Day Problem

Each of the 26 algorithms was tested for 20 trials on the 7-day problem. Figure 1 shows the average best penalty scores emerging from the 20 trials for each method.

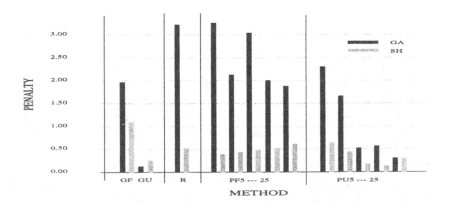

Fig. 1. Average best penalties for each method on the 7-day problem.

Evidently, SH was markedly better than EA on this problem as a whole for the same initialisation strategy. Other indications from this figure are: peckish-uniform is generally better than peckish-feasible; greedy-uniform was much better than greedy-feasible. All other methods (except possibly peckish-feasible at low values of greediness) were superior to random initialisation. The performance of the peckish methods generally improves with greediness; and, finally, best results on this problem seem to come from greedy-uniform, and peckish-uniform at relatively high pressure.

In the 7-day case, the number of extra-seats and clashes at the end of any run of each of the algorithms was always zero. Hence, figure 1 is identical to the 'average too-closes vs method' graph for the same set of experiments, which is therefore not shown. Also, the best over the 20 trials, for each algorithm, was always a perfect zero-penalty timetable.

5.3 Results on the 6-Day Problem

Figure 2 shows average best penalty results on the 6-day problem. The same

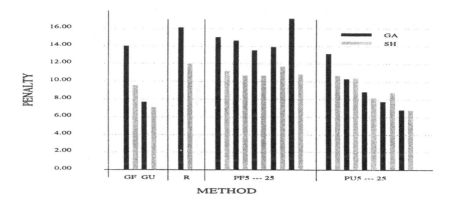

Fig. 2. Average best penalty for each method on the 6-day problem.

general trends seen in the 7-day case are also exhibited in the more tightly constrained 6-day case, except that the relative superiority of SH over GA is much less marked.

Figure 3 shows average clashes on the 6-day problem. Most notable here is the fact that SH almost always delivered a clash-free (and hence feasible solution), while the GA was often lacking in this respect. Also, it is notable that GF's and PF's extra concentration on avoiding clashes in the initial population did not significantly affect the end result. Despite starting with fewer clashes (see section 6) GF and PF failed to shine over GU and PU in terms of timetable feasibility.

Average best too-closes for the 6-day problem are almost identical to average penalty, while extra-seat scores were almost always zero for each algorithm.

Figure 4 shows the best penalty result achieved for each method on the 6-day problem; this is almost identical to the best too-closes result graph (which is therefore not shown).

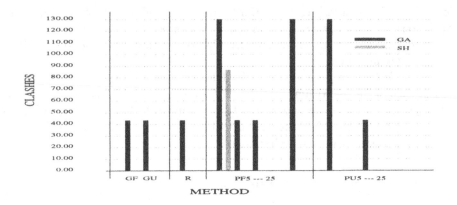

Fig. 3. Average best clashes for each method on the 6-day problem.

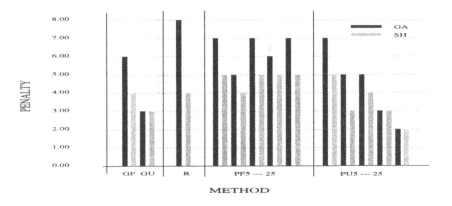

Fig. 4. Best penalty for each method on the 6-day problem.

From figure 4, we can see that the best overall result arose from using PU with high pressure. Otherwise, trends are generally similar to those we have seen earlier, with SH generally doing better than EA, 'uniform' generally outperforming 'feasible', and all 'uniform' initialisation methods outperforming random initialisation.

5.4   Results on the 5-Day Problem

Figure 5 shows average penalty per method on the 5-day problem. Trends remain familiar, except that now that the problem is even more constrained we find that the GA results consistently beat the SH results.

Figure 6 shows average best clashes per method on the 5-day problem. We can again see familiar trends repeated, as well as again observing that the feasible

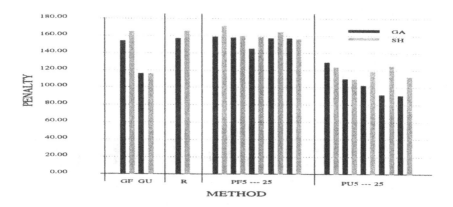

Fig. 5. Average best penalty for each method on the 5-day problem.

methods seem unable to gain advantage from their extra avoidance of clashes in the initial population.

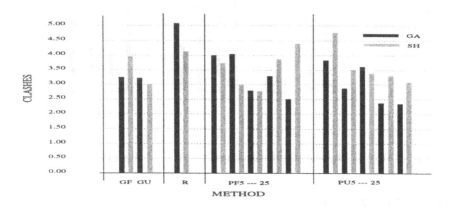

Fig. 6. Average best clashes for each method on the 5-day problem.

Average best too-closes per method on the 5-day problem is again very similar to the average best penalty graph, and is therefore not shown. On this problem, however, timetables with numbers of extra seats required were fairly common. Figure 7 shows average best extra-seats per method on the 5-day problem.

Here it seems that the peckish strategies are particularly helpful, with peckish-uniform at medium pressure offering perfect results every time. Meanwhile, figure 8 shows best overall penalty per method on the 5-day problem, and we again see familiar trends.

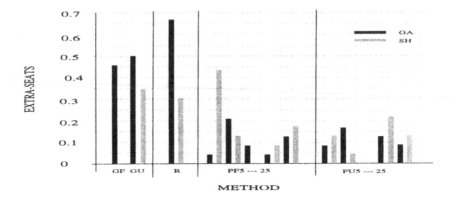

Fig. 7. Average best extra seats for each method on the 5-day problem.

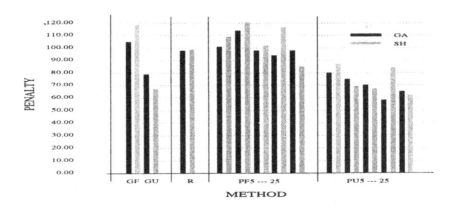

Fig. 8. Best penalty for each method on the 5-day problem.

5.5 Diversity Results

Figure 9 shows multiplicity and average Hamming distance results for each of the EA methods on the 5-day problem; these results were typical of those on the 6-day and 7-day problems too.

As figure 9 indicates, peckish-uniform methods tended strongly to show higher overall diversity than the other methods, although we can see no clear relation between levels of diversity and increasing greediness.

6 Discussion

In summary, we argue that one way in which the two more prominent current approaches to EA-based timetabling research can be combined is by using greedy

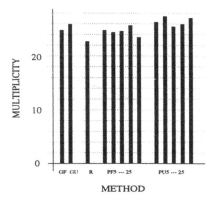 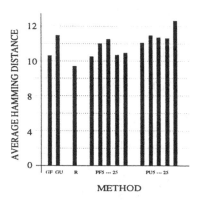

Fig. 9. EA Diversity on the 7-day problem.

or similar algorithms to form the initial timetable population, followed by genetic search using the simpler direct method. Further, by considering some intuitions concerning the general idea of population seeding, and the skewedness of the timetable samples generated by a typical greedy algorithm, we present 'peckish' algorithms as a flexible alternative. Some variations on this general theme are presented.

Experiments described bear out the intuition that peckish initialisation helps significantly. In particular, best results seem to come from using the peckish-uniform initialisation strategy. Results suggest that, independently of the general constrainedness of the problem, there is nothing to be gained from 'feasible' initialisation strategies which concentrate on finding initial points sparse in hard-constraint violations. In constraint, many of the GF and PF results suggest that the consequent skewedness of the starting point handicaps future search progress. Figure 10 aids us in these intuitions; with timetables considered as points on a 2D clashes/too-closes space, this figure shows typical start and end points of search as encountered when solving the 5-day problem. Concentrating on the 'too-closes' axis, the difference in starting points between the random and 'feasible' strategies, and those of the 'uniform' strategies, is clearly vast, reflecting the fact that the latter ignore too-close constraints at initialisation. GF and PF25 make up for this with a strong low initial average number of clashes; the figure shows, however, that this fails to be true compensation. In the course of search, the effort expended in clawing back the too-close score renders eventual results unimpressive. Both GU and PU begin with a far more impressive overall score, with much less distance to traverse clash/too-close space towards the optimum. End results show that GU and PU both take advantage of this good start. Note also that the figure 10 hints at the disadvantage of starting with a 'skewed' sample in clash/too-close space. Taking random initialisation as a guide to avoiding skew, it appears starting-points with around 50% more

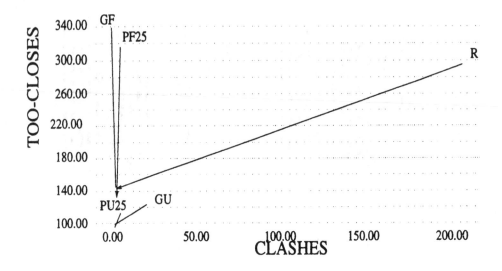

Fig. 10. Typical trajectories in clash/too-close space for the four initialisation methods.

too-closes than clashes are most representative of the space. Both GU and PU are far nearer this mark than GF and PF.

In summary, we have found evidence for the following conjectures:

Peckish-uniform population initialisation significantly aids an evolutionary algorithm or hillclimber on timetabling problems.
All reported results suggest this. Best results on average, or overall best result found, was always via (or equaled by) a PU initialisation strategy, usually at a fairly high pressure.

'Feasible' strategies, which concentrate on initially promoting the satisfaction of hard constraints, tend to be counterproductive.
'Uniform' strategies always outperformed 'feasible' strategies in the experiments described. As figure 10 displays, despite starting off 'nearer' to feasible timetables, it seems such skewed locations in clash/too-close space are more difficult to progress from.

Unlike other algorithmic variants, the superiority of peckish-uniform seems maintained across wide variation in problem constrainedness.
Peckish-uniform was the best strategy in all three problem cases, although between the 6-day and 5-day case there was a shift in relative performance between EA and SH.

Various interesting areas of future work are heralded. First, we need to delve more into the effect of the 'greediness' parameter on peckish-uniform performance, as well as generally test these ideas more thoroughly on a wider range of problems. Other work already under way is also looking more deeply into the nature of cases where SH defeats an EA. Finally, many further variations on the peckish algorithm itself are worth studying, such as examining the effect of heuristic or variable ordering of the events, and incorporating multiobjective Pareto-optimisation based methods for determining between timeslot choices. In conclusion, it seems that this simple combination of ideas from different 'camps' in the EA/timetabling research community has led to promising results, which in itself bodes well for further such inter-camp collaboration.

Acknowledgements

We are grateful to the EPSRC for support of the first author via an award with reference GR/J44513, and to anonymous referees for their suggestions on an earlier draft of this paper.

References

1. D. Abramson and J. Abela, 'A parallel genetic algorithm for solving the school timetabling problem', Technical report, Division of Information Technology, C.S.I.R.O., (April 1991).
2. Edmund Burke, David Elliman, and Rupert Weare, 'thm for university timetabling', in *AISB Workshop on Evolutionary Computation*. Workshop Notes, (1994).
3. Robert J. Collins and David R. Jefferson, 'Selection in massively parallel genetic algorithms', in *Proceedings of the Fourth International Conference on Genetic Algorithms*, eds., R.K. Belew and L.B. Booker, pp. 249–256. San Mateo: Morgan Kaufmann, (1991).
4. Alberto Colorni, Marco Dorigo, and Vittorio Maniezzo, 'Genetic algorithms and highly constrained problems: The time-table case', in *Parallel Problem Solving from Nature*, eds., G. Goos and J. Hartmanis, 55–59, Springer-Verlag, (1990).
5. Dave Corne, Peter Ross, and Hsiao-Lan Fang, 'Fast practical evolutionary timetabling', in *Proceedings of the AISB Workshop on Evolutionary Computation*, ed., Terence C. Fogarty, Springer-Verlag, (1994).
6. Si-Eng Ling, 'Intergating genetic algorithms with a Prolog assignment problem as a hybrid solution for a polytechnic timetable problem', in *Parallel Problem Solving from Nature II*, eds., R. Manner and B. Manderick, 321–329, Elsevier Science Publisher B.V., (1992).
7. B. Paechter, H. Luchian, A. Cumming, and M.Petruic, 'An evolutionary approach to the general timetable problem', in *Proceedings of the 9th Romanian Symposium on Computer Science*, (1993).
8. B. Paechter, H. Luchian, A. Cumming, and M.Petruic, 'Two solutions to the general timetable problem using evolutionary methods', in *Proceedings of the First IEEE Conference on Evolutionary Computation*, pp. 300–305, (1994).
9. Peter Ross, Dave Corne, and Hsiao-Lan Fang, 'Improving evolutionary timetabling with delta evaluation and directed mutation', in *Parallel Problem Solving from Nature III*, ed., Y. Davidor, Springer-Verlag, (1994).
10. Peter Ross, Dave Corne, and Hsiao-Lan Fang, 'Successful lecture timetabling with evolutionary algorithms', in *Proceedings of the 11th ECAI Workshop*, Springer-Verlag, (1994).

A Memetic Algorithm for University Exam Timetabling

E. K. Burke, J. P. Newall and R. F. Weare

Department of Computer Science, University of Nottingham, University Park, Nottingham, UK

Abstract. The scheduling of exams in institutions of higher education is known to be a highly constrained problem. The advent of modularity in many institutions in the UK has resulted in a significant increase in its complexity, imposing even more difficulties on university administrators who must find a solution, often without any computer aid.

Of the many methods that have been applied to solving the problem automatically, evolutionary techniques have shown much promise due to their general purpose optimisation capabilities. However, it has also been found that hybrid evolutionary methods can yield even better results. In this paper we present such a hybrid approach in the form of an evolutionary algorithm that incorporates local search methods (known as a *memetic* algorithm).

1 Introduction

1.1 The Timetabling Problem

Many constraints involved in exam scheduling vary from institution to institution. However it is generally accepted that the following two constraints are fundamental to any timetabling problem:

- No entity must be demanded to be at more than one place at a time. In exam timetabling this would mean that no student can sit more than one exam at any one time.
- For each period in the timetable, the resource demands made by the events scheduled for that period must not exceed the resources available. In exam timetabling it is important not to schedule more exam sittings in a room than there are desks.

These two rules define a *feasible* timetable, and were the objective merely to find a feasible timetable, the problem could be solved using a variety of methods such as heuristic assignment [10]. However, we are usually interested in finding *good* feasible timetables, which can be defined as timetables that are practical and with which the user is happy. It follows that many different institutions will have differing views on what constitutes a good timetable [2] and therefore the engine of any automated timetabling system must be capable of satisfying the wide range of constraints that may be specified. Common constraints that may be demanded by users include:

- No students should have to take two exams in adjacent periods.
- No student should have to take two exams on the same day.
- Exam A must be scheduled before exam B

- Exam A must be scheduled at the same time as exam B (as they contain same or similar material).
- An exam must be conducted in a particular room (as it requires special resources only available in that room).

It is unlikely that, given the length of the average exam period and the number of suitable rooms available for exam sittings, that all of the above constraints could be satisfied completely. The optimisation capabilities of Genetic Algorithms [12] have been found to work well on various timetabling problems [4] [6], usually by first ensuring satisfaction of the conditions for a feasible timetable, and then optimising the number of desirable but not essential constraints that are satisfied. It has further been suggested that some amount of local search within evolutionary algorithms may enhance the quality of final solutions [14].

1.2 Genetic Algorithms

Genetic algorithms are a general purpose optimisation tool based on Darwin's theory of evolution. They have the capability to produce optimised solutions even when the dimensions of the problem increase and for this reason they have been successfully applied to a wide variety of problems [5].

Genetic Algorithms operate on a population of solutions represented by some coding. Each member of the population consists of a number of *genes*, each of which is a unit of information. New solutions are obtained by combining genes from different population members (*crossover*) to produce offspring or by altering existing members of the population (*mutation*). For our purposes we will also define light mutation as any small alteration and heavy mutation as any large scale alteration. A simulation of 'natural selection' then takes place by first evaluating the quality of each solution and then selecting the fittest ones to survive to the next generation.

1.3 Memetic Algorithms

The concept of a *memetic algorithm* was first introduced by Moscato and Norman [8] to describe evolutionary algorithms in which local search is used to a large extent. This idea has further been formalised by Radcliffe & Surrey [7] and a comparison between memetic and genetic algorithms made. A *meme* can be thought of as a unit of information that reproduces itself as people exchange ideas. A meme differs from a gene in that as it is passed between individuals, each individual adapts the meme as it sees best whereas genes are passed unaltered.

The main advantage gained from the use of memetic algorithms is that the space of possible solutions is reduced to the subspace of local optima. To illustrate this, consider a single variable function $f(x)$ described by the curve in figure 1. The solution initially produced by mutating an existing solution is outside the space of local optima, but by then using the information available about the height of the curve immediately to either side we can navigate an upward path until the local peak is found.

The addition of local search to the normal genetic operators inevitably has some computational expense but this can be justified by the reduction in search space that must be explored in order to find the optimum solution.

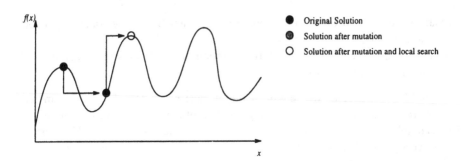

Fig. 1. An Example Memetic Operation

2 The Memetic Timetabling Algorithm

The algorithm presented below deals exclusively with fixed length timetables. This approach was chosen because, for most timetabling problems, an upper limit on the number of periods is specified which should not be exceeded under normal circumstances. If at any time an exam cannot be scheduled in any of the available periods it is placed in a list of unscheduled events. This has the effect that the population may contain timetables that are feasible but incomplete. However, given sufficient time and an adequate number of periods these should evolve into complete good quality timetables. The main techniques used in the algorithm are a combination of both light and heavy mutation followed by hill-climbing.

2.1 Solution Representation

Each solution in the population is represented as a number of memes. Each meme contains information on what exams are scheduled in which rooms for a particular period. A further meme is used to hold exams which could not be scheduled in the prescribed periods. Figure 2 shows an example of an encoded solution, where e_i is exam number i.

Period 1			Period n		Unscheduled
Room 1	e1, e2, e4		Room 1	e5, e22, e24	e53, e49
Room 2	e3, e7	O O O O	Room 2	e37, e57	
Room 3	e11, e36		Room 3	e45	
Room 4	e90, e27		Room 4	e63, e52	

Fig. 2. The Problem Encoding

2.2 Initial Population Generation

The initial population is generated using a weighted roulette wheel to choose which period to place each exam (based on the exams already placed). The routine to generate a member of the initial population can be summarised as:

1. Remove an event e at random from the list of unscheduled exams. If all exams have been scheduled then finish.
2. For each period in the timetable, determine if it is legal to place e in that period. If so, calculate a measure of how 'good' it would be to do so using the function:

$$\frac{numCommon + Size + 1}{penalty + 1} \quad (1)$$

where $numCommon$ is the number of neighbours that e has in common with the exams already scheduled in that period, $Size$ is the number of exams already scheduled in the period and $penalty$ is the cost (as used in the evaluation function) of placing e in that period. This heuristic measure is intended to, firstly, schedule events that have similar sets of neighbours together. This is a graph colouring heuristic that is often, but not always, a characteristic of a good timetable. Secondly, it tries to minimise the penalty caused by scheduling e by biasing the roulette wheel to those periods which can accommodate e with lesser penalties.
3. Construct and execute a roulette wheel based on the values calculated to choose a period in which to place e.

This mix of random and heuristic assignment was chosen in order to produce a higher quality initial population than the normal purely random generation while still keeping the degree of diversity that is desirable in Genetic Algorithms generally.

2.3 The Evolutionary Operators

There has been some debate as to whether crossover should be the main operator in a Genetic Algorithm. It has also been suggested that maybe local search has a part to play [7][8], this approach being known as *memetics*. A directed mutation approach has also been found to achieve good results[6].

The algorithm presented here has been found to work well (see section 4) using a combination of light and heavy random mutation, followed directly by application of hill climbing techniques. Figure 3 shows the cycle of evolution for the algorithm.

The Light Mutation Operator A random mutation operator is used to perform light mutation on population members. This chooses a number of events at random from any point in the timetable and reschedules them at some other legal period. This is then directly followed by an application of the hill-climbing algorithm shown below.

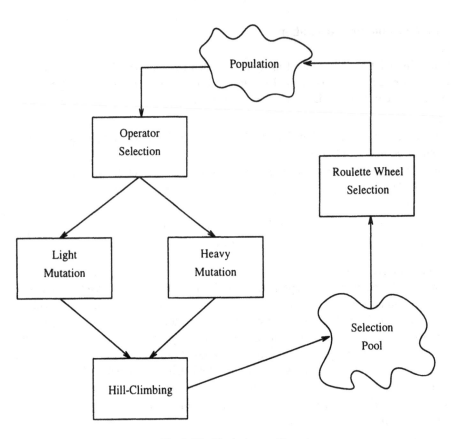

Fig. 3. The Evolutionary Operators

The Heavy Mutation Operator In order to find good solutions quickly a heavy mutation operator is used. This operator disrupts one or more whole periods in a timetable.
This preserves well constructed periods in a timetable while randomly rescheduling
exams in the remaining periods in order to find new higher quality solutions. The procedure for determining whether or not a period is to be preserved can be summarised
as:

- Take each period i in the timetable in turn.
    - Calculate the *penalty* arising from the events in period i assuming the events
      scheduled in period j (where $j > i$) will remain fixed.
    - If this penalty is lower than the *average penalty* in the population then give the
      period a probability of being disrupted of

$$P(disrupt) = \frac{penalty + 0.2}{2.average} \qquad (2)$$

- Else, if the last period was not disrupted then do not disrupt this period but instead
  disrupt the next period.
- Otherwise disrupt this period.

Once it has been decided which periods will be disrupted the exams contained within these periods are grouped together. Each exam in this group is then removed at random and rescheduled in the first legal period. This operation alone rarely produces any substantial improvement but when followed by an application of the hill-climbing algorithm to reach the new local optimum substantial improvements can be made.

The Hill-Climbing Operator As Hill-Climbing techniques generally require a great deal of evaluations, this operator uses a technique of calculating the penalty incurred by scheduling an event in a particular period, given that the other events are fixed. This has the advantage that when attempting to reschedule each individual event, the improvement can be found in a fraction of the time that it would take to perform a full evaluation. This is essential in the case of this algorithm due to the sheer number of times that the operator is applied.

A deterministic Hill-Climbing algorithm is used at present. While it is considered generally better to incorporate as much non-determinism as possible in Hill-Climbing methods, the deterministic approach can be justified in this case as it only forms part of the solution finding mechanism. The algorithm can be summarised as follows:

– Take each period in order
  • Take each event e in this period in order
    * For each period p in the timetable, calculate the penalty that would arise from scheduling event e in period p if no hard constraints are broken.
    * Schedule e in the period causing least penalty.
  • Try to schedule events from the list of unscheduled events.

The Evaluation Function In order to ascertain the value of a solution the evaluation function is applied to it to calculate its *fitness*, and therefore its ability to survive in the total population. For the trials shown below the objective was to schedule all events in the given number of periods such that if a student has two exams on the same day then there should at least be a full period between them. The evaluation function can be expressed as:

$$\frac{10 numEvents}{2000 numUnscheduled + \sum_{i=0}^{numPeriods-1} NumConflicts(period_i, period_{i+1})} \tag{3}$$

where *numEvents* is the number of events in the timetable, *numUnscheduled* is the number of events not scheduled in a period yet, and *NumConflicts* is a function returning the number of conflicts, weighted by student numbers, between two periods on the same day.

The Selection Method After application of the operators the population expands to a specified size. In order to reduce the population to its original size individuals are chosen from the pool to join the new population. This is achieved by using classic roulette wheel selection, which involves creating a roulette wheel where each individual is assigned a section that is proportional to its fitness relative to the competition. The wheel is then spun a number of times equal to the population size to select each individual member of the new population.

3 Results

The algorithm has been tested on a range of real data in order to ascertain its potential. Furthermore in order to ascertain the value of combining local search with the mutation operators in a population a multi-start random descent algorithm was run on the Nottingham data.

3.1 Nottingham University 1994/95 Data

The algorithm has been tested on the Nottingham University 1994/95 Semester one examinations data. This consists of 805 exams with 10,034 student conflicts between them, 7,896 students and 34,265 different enrolments. These exams must be scheduled into 32 periods or less such that the following constraints are met:

1. No student is scheduled to take two exams at any one time.
2. The maximum number of seats is 1550 and cannot be exceeded.
3. If a student is scheduled to take two exams in any one day there must be a complete period between the two exams.

The first two are, of course, the fundamental constraints that a timetable must satisfy in order to be at least feasible.

While this data is not as conflicting as it could potentially be, the scale of the problem presents a challenge to find a complete solution within a reasonable number of trials. The problem is also particularly compounded by the number and size of rooms available for each period. The algorithm was run with a population size of fifty on the same data varying the number of periods the timetable had to be scheduled in. The tests range from 23 periods (the minimum length given rooms constraints) to 32 periods (the time usually allocated by Nottingham University). Table 1 shows the results obtained. To give an idea of the CPU time involved the algorithm ran at a rate of about 1500 evaluations an hour, with the perfect solutions to the full 32 and cut down 31 period cases being found within one and two hours respectively.

To give some comparison the Nottingham data was also used to test how well the algorithm compared against a straight-forward random descent algorithm.

This consists of randomly generating a timetable then making random improvements until a number of tries have elapsed in which no improvements could be found. A new timetable is then generated and the process repeated, keeping the best timetable found throughout the process. Table 2 shows the results of this when run on the Nottingham data for various numbers of periods for 8000 trials.

The Nottingham data is freely available over the Internet from

`ftp://ftp.cs.nott.ac.uk/ttp/Data/`.

Table 1. Results on Nottingham 1994/95 Data

Periods	Evaluations	Num Unscheduled	Violations of (3)
32	1300	0	0
31	2900	0	0
30	6500	0	4
26	10100	0	53
23	7500	0	269

Table 2. Results of Applying Multi-Start Random Descent

Periods	Num Unscheduled	Violations of (3)
32	0	14
31	0	33
30	0	66
26	0	214
23	3	752

3.2 Other Data Sets

The following results are from data that is also freely available over the Internet from `ftp://ie.utoronto.ca/mwc/testprob`. The same constraints that were applied to the Nottingham data were applied to all of these problems, with the exception of varying the maximum number of seats per period to represent the real life maximum. Tables 3 and 4 list the characteristics of each of the data sets while Table 5 lists the results when the algorithm was applied to each.

Table 3. Code for each Data Set Used

Code	Institution
cars91	Carleton University 1991
carf92	Carleton University 1992
kfu	King Fahd University
tre	Trent University
utas	University of Toronto, Arts & Science

These data sets provide a reasonable range of benchmark problems for comparison with other methods.

Table 4. Characteristics of Data Used

Data	No. Exams	No. Students	No. Enrollments	Max Students per Period
cars91	682	16926	56242	1550
carf92	543	18419	55189	2000
kfu	461	5439	25113	1955
tre	261	4362	14901	655
utas	638	21329	59144	2800

Table 5. Results on Data Sets

Data	Periods	Evaluatrions	Unscheduled	Violations of (3)
cars91	51	8800	0	81
carf92	40	10100	0	331
kfu	20	10100	0	974
tre	35	4500	0	3
utas	38	10000	0	772

4 Conclusion

This algorithm offers an interesting approach to evolutionary timetabling. The addition of the Hill-Climbing operator after each mutation operator greatly increases the speed at which better solutions are found above the evolutionary operators alone. While the application of Hill-Climbing after each operation does involve some computational expense, this is reduced by the use of delta-evaluation[1] and can be compensated for by the simplicity of the mutation operators, with any remaining net increase being justified by the reduction in total evaluations required.

Comparing the results on the Nottingham data with those obtained by applying multi-start random descent it appears that even though the random descent method was given significantly more CPU time it could not achieve equal results. Particularly notable is the fact that random descent could not find a perfect solution even when given the full 32 periods. This significant difference in results offers justification for the use of the memetic algorithm and the operators within it.

Although the initial results are promising, the results have shown that the algorithm does not perform quite as well on the more highly constrained problems as some other methods [4]. This is probably due to the local search operator being less effective on these sorts of problems. Therefore further research will be directed at refining the existing operators and introducing new ones. Experimentation with various methods of recombining different solutions found by the existing operators is of particular interest. This may include hybrid heuristic recombination operators such as those presented in [4]. Effort will also be directed at applying the algorithm to the lecture timetabling problem in order to investigate its potential on more general timetabling problems.

References

1. Peter Ross, Dave Corne: Improving evolutionary timetabling with delta evaluation and directed mutation. Parallel Problem Solving in Nature **III**, Ed. Y. Davidor, Springer Verlag, (1994)
2. E. K. Burke, D. G. Elliman, R. F. Weare: Examination Timetabling in British Universities - A Survey. Proceedings of the 1st International Conference on the Practice and Theory of Automated Timetabling, (Napier University, Edinburgh, UK) (1995)
3. E. K. Burke, D. G. Elliman, R. F. Weare: Specialised Recombinative Operators for Timetabling Problems. Lecture Notes in Computer Science 993 (Evolutionary Computing), Springer-Verlag, Ed. T. C. Fogarty, 1995, pp 75–85
4. E. K. Burke, D. G. Elliman, R. F. Weare: A Hybrid Genetic Algorithm for Highly Constrained Timetabling Problems. 6th International Conference on Genetic Algorithms (Pittsburgh, USA), 15-19 July 1995
5. Peter Ross, Dave Corne: Applications of Genetic Algorithms. AISB Quarterly **89**, Ed. T.C. Fogarty, (1994), 23–30
6. Dave Corne, Peter Ross, Hsiao-Lan Fang: Fast Practical Evolutionary Timetabling, Lecture Notes in Computer Science **865** (Evolutionary Computing), Springer-Verlag, Ed T. C. Fogarty, (1994), 250–263
7. Nicholas J. Radcliffe, Patrick D. Surry: Formal Memetic Algorithms. Lecture Notes in Computer Science **865** (Evolutionary Computing) Springer-Verlag, Ed. T. C. Fogarty, (1994), 250–263
8. Pablo Moscato, Michael G. Norman: A "Memetic" approach for the travelling salesman problem – implementation of a computational ecology for combinatorial optimisation on message-passing systems. Proceedings of the International Conference on Parallel computing and Transputer Applications, IOS Press (Amsterdam)
9. E.K. Burke, D.G. Elliman, R.F. Weare: Extensions to a University Exam Timetabling Systems. IJCAI '93 Workshop on Knowledge-Based Production Planning, Scheduling and Control (1993)
10. E.K. Burke, D.G. Elliman, R.F. Weare: A University Timetabling System Based on Graph Colouring and Constraint Manipulation, Journal of Research on Computing in Education, (1993)
11. EK Burke, DG Elliman, RF Weare: A Genetic Algorithm based University Timetabling System. 22nd East-West International Conference on Computer Technologies in Education (Crimea, Ukraine, 19th-23rd Sept 1994) (1994) 35–40
12. Davis L.: Handbook of Genetic Algorithms. Van Nostrand Reinhold, (1991)
13. Dawkins R.: The Selfish Gene. Oxford University Press, (1976)
14. Paechter B., Cumming A., Luchian H.: The Use of Local Search Suggestion Lists for Improving the Solution of Timetabling Problems with Evolutionary Algorithms. Lecture Notes in Computer Science 993 (Evolutionary Computing), Springer-Verlag, Ed. T. Fogarty, (1995), 86–93

Extensions to a Memetic Timetabling System

Ben Paechter
Andrew Cumming
Computer Studies Dept.
Napier University
219 Colinton Road
Edinburgh
Scotland
EH141DJ
benp@dcs.napier.ac.uk
andrew@dcs.napier.ac.uk

Michael G. Norman
Makespan Ltd.
Bonnington Mill
72 Newhaven Road
Edinburgh
EH6 5QG
mgn@makespan.demon.co.uk

Henri Luchian
Faculty of Computer Science
"Al. I. Cuza" University
Iasi
Romania
hluchian@uaic.ro

Abstract

This paper describes work in progress to increase the performance of a memetic timetabling system. The features looked at are two directed mutation operators, targeted mutation and a structured population that facilitates parallel implementation. Experimental results are given that show good performance improvements with directed and targeted mutation, and acceptable first results with the structure population.

1. Introduction

Paechter et al. have proposed, in [1], [2] and [3], a method of producing good timetables of the lecture and tutorial type using evolutionary methods as described in for example [4], [5] and [6]. The approach differs from other work in the field such as [7], [8], [9], [10] and [11] in that the timetables are produced indirectly by working from a set of coded instructions. These instructions describe a point in the space of all possible timetables by encoding a start point and a local search from that start point to a point which represents a more feasible timetable. The production or good timetables can then proceed by a search through the space of all possible sets of instructions. This use of an indirect representation of the timetable has been shown in [2] to greatly increase the efficiency of timetable production over simple direct methods. The system can be thought of as a memetic algorithm (described in section 3. below).This paper describes work in progress to improve the system. It looks at directed and targeted mutation and a new population structure which facilitates a parallel implementation.

2. The Problem

The lecture and tutorial timetable problem can be thought of in the following manner: a number of events (classes) must be timetabled by associating them with timeslots. If there are m events and n timeslots, then the number of ways of associating events with timeslots is n^m. However, there are hard constraints on where events can be placed in the timetable, making the vast majority of "possible" timetables *infeasible*. These constraints are due to resource (room, lecturer or student) limitations. Most events will require a certain number of resources, and these resources may not be available at all times. Further to this, many events will require the same resource and so will be prevented from taking place at the same time. There are also hard constraints which are due to inter-event temporal considerations. Two events may need to take place, for example, at the same time or with a particular time interval between them.

In addition to hard constraints there are soft constraints, which make particular timetables undesirable rather than infeasible. Soft constraints can be split into two types, those which relate directly to events, known as "direct soft constraints" (for example *"Lecture A Must Come Before Lecture B"*), and those which relate only indirectly to events, known as "indirect soft constraints" (for example *"All Lecturers Must have a Teaching Free Day"*).

3. Memetic Algorithms

Evolutionary algorithms (as defined in [5]) are firmly rooted in the ideas of biological evolution. There are however things other than biological organisms that are capable of evolution. In particular, ideas and behaviours tend to evolve. By analogy with the gene of genetics, Dawkins [12] described a unit of cultural transmission known as the meme, which can be viewed simply as an idea.

The evolution of memes is different from the evolution of genes. In some respects the process is similar. Ideas are created, good ideas are more likely to survive than bad ones, ideas can be combined together to form new ideas, and ideas can mutate through misunderstandings. The important difference between genes and memes is that a meme can be improved by the individual holding it before it is passed on. This process of evolution of ideas has inspired the development of a strand of evolutionary algorithms known as memetic algorithms which can be described in terms of the metaphors of cultural transmission. The difference between a memetic algorithm and an evolutionary algorithm is that a memetic algorithm allows the meme to be improved as it is evaluated. A basic memetic algorithm, is then, an evolutionary algorithm with some local optimisation technique.

A description of the application of memetic algorithms and can also be found in [13], [14], [15], [16] and [17]. The theory of memetic algorithms was explored by Radcliffe et al. in [18].

The work described here takes things a stage further, by having details of how the search is to be carried out encoded in the memetic material.

4. The Searchspec

In this system the specification for the local search, or *searchspec*, consists of a number of suggestion lists, one for each event, along with a permutation of the events. A suggestion list is a list of timeslots into which the event might possibly be placed. Suggestion lists do not contain duplicate timeslots. The length of the suggestion lists is a parameter to the algorithm. Initial searchspecs are produced filling each suggestion list with timeslots randomly chosen from the list of possible timeslots for that event (those timeslots where the event could be placed if no other event was taking place). Searchspecs can be regarded as chromosomes.

4.1 Executing a Searchspec

Timetables are produced from a searchspec in the following manner: the events are considered in the order specified by the permutation and an attempt is made to place each into the timetable. The first timeslot considered for an event is that at the head of the suggestion list. The event may not be assigned to this timeslot because hard constraints might be broken, for example, a previously placed event may be using a required resource at that time. If placement in the timeslot is not possible then the next suggestion in the list is considered. When all timeslots in the list have been considered then any remaining timeslots are tried in timetable order (starting immediately after the timeslot at the head of the list). If no timeslot can be found for the event then it is considered unplaced and the next event is considered.

The local search also considers direct soft constraints. Two search passes occur for the placement of each event. In the first pass direct soft constraints must not be broken. If this pass is not successful then a second pass occurs which ignores these constraints.

The local search of the space of timetables, starts from the point collectively specified by the head of each suggestion list, and progresses in a manner collectively specified by the tail of each list and the permutation.

4.2 Ordering of Placement Permutation

The order in which an attempt is made to place the events is important as events placed first have a better chance of receiving the resources they require. In the current system, the initial ordering permutation for all searchspec is determined by a heuristic. The heuristic looks at the number of possible timeslots for the event and places those with fewer possibilities first. The permutation for a searchspec may subsequently be altered by directed mutation (see section 6 below).

4.3 Writeback

The results of the local search can be written back into the search specification. This can be achieved by placing a successful timeslot for an event at the top of the event's suggestion list and pushing other suggested timeslots down in the list. Writeback can be made to occur in only a percentage of cases, either by writing back to the suggestions lists of a percentage of events, or by writing back to the suggestion lists of all events in a percentage of searchspecs. In the system described in this paper the results of the local search are always written back to the searchspec.

5. Recombination of Searchspecs

A class of recombination operators was defined by Paechter et al. [3] and the most successful of these is used here. The operator complies with the concepts from Forma Theory of *respect* and *assortment* [19].

The base operation is a "zipping together" of two parent suggestion lists to produce a child suggestion list, (see Figure 1). This involves taking the first element of the child list from the top of the first parent's list, then the second from the top of the second parent's list. The next element is taken from the second element of the first parent, and so on, with elements being taken alternately from each parent. Duplicates are not allowed in suggestion lists and when building the child's list, if the next element to be inserted is already in the list then it is discarded and consideration continues (continuing to alternate between parents rather than searching through the same parent for an unused timeslot suggestion). The parent which contributes the first element of the list is considered to be dominant in this particular operation.

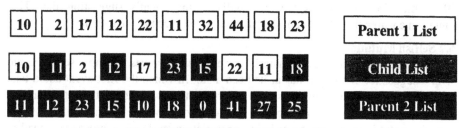

Fig. 1. Zipping Together Suggestion Lists

When producing a searchspec from two parents, each suggestion list in the child is produced by zipping together the corresponding suggestion lists (i.e. the ones for the same event) in the parents. At the searchspec level the recombination is a single point crossover. A point is chosen in the searchspec, any suggestion list before this point is zipped with the first parent as dominant, while any suggestion list after the point is zipped with the second parent as dominant. The permutation of the child is taken entirely from the first parent.

5.1 Ancestral Memory

An interesting and possibly important aspect of this recombination operator is that a child suggestion list will normally have at its head the head of its dominant parent, and in its second position the head of its non-dominant parent (unless the heads are the same or mutation has occurred). So if the slot suggested by the first parent is no good then the second parent's suggestion is tried. These two suggestions came however from each of the parents' dominant parent - two of the child's grandparents. The third and fourth items in the list will however be the second suggestions from each of the parents, which they in turn will have inherited from their non-dominant parent - the other two of the child's grandparents. We can quickly see that as time goes on traversing the suggestion list becomes a breadth first search of the ancestral tree of suggestions. When writeback is used, each suggestion list makes direct use of the information gained by its ancestors' searches.

6. Mutation

Mutation of searchspecs occurs by the memetic material for each event having a certain probability of mutation. The probability of mutation is independent for each event and is normally set at 1/(number of events) so that the expected number of mutations per searchspec is one. When memetic material mutates this can happen in three different ways: Blind Mutation, Selfish Mutation and Co-operative Mutation. Which mutation occurs is determined randomly, with the relative probabilities being a parameter to the algorithm. The selfish and co-operative operators are types of directed mutation. Other directed mutation operators for timetabling have been defined by Ross et al. in [20].

6.1 Blind Mutation

Blind mutation simply involves reinitialising the event's suggestion list. This mutation ensures that all parts of the suggestion list space are reachable.

6.2 Selfish Mutation

Selfish mutation of the genetic material for an event involves finding a second event with a suggestion list which has at its head a slot in which the first event could take place. The event then steals the slot by inserting it at the head of its suggestion list. To ensure that the event has priority over the second event in the allocation of that slot, the event is moved in the ordering permutation so that it is processed ahead of the second event. This mutation is unfair on the second event which may then be unable to place its event in the slot specified by the head of its suggestion list.

6.3 Co-operative Mutation

Co-operative mutation of the memetic material for an event involves finding a second event such that each event could take place in the slot at the head of the other's suggestion list. The heads are then swapped and the two events are placed in the first and second positions of the ordering permutation. This mutation has the potential of benefits for both events.

7. Targeted Mutation

Some events cause particular problems in a timetable. For example, an event might take place on the only day on which a lecturer has no other teaching, so breaking the soft constraint that all lecturers have at least one teaching free day. When targeted mutation is used, the probability of mutation of the memetic material for an event is increased for these problem events.

During evaluation of a timetable each of the events is given a penalty score based on its contribution towards problems in the resultant timetable (see section 11 below). The probability of an event's memetic material being mutated is then increased by an amount proportional to the square of its penalty, the total increase being 1/(number of events).

8. Standard Population Strategy

Two population strategies have been implemented; the first is a standard steady state evolutionary strategy.

In this strategy a pool of searchspecs is kept. Parents are selected from the pool by binary tournament selection. To select a parent two searchspecs are chosen at random from the population. The best of the two is chosen to be a parent with some probability ps greater than 0.5.

After choosing two parents, two children are produced, these children will either be identical to the two parents or recombination will occur to produce two new children. Whether of not recombination has occurred, mutation may then occur. These children are then inserted into the population.

Binary tournament replacement strategy with elitism is used to decide which two searchspecs are removed from the population to make room for the new children. To select a searchspec for replacement two searchspecs are chosen at random from the population. The worst of the two is chosen to be replaced with some probability pr greater than 0.5. The best individual in the population cannot be replaced.

9. Structured Population Strategy

The second population strategy extends the memetic algorithm to include further features of the behaviour of natural memes. Firstly, individuals have memory, and can recall ideas from long in the past to combine with new ideas they have heard about. Secondly, ideas often develop in small isolated pockets of opinion, before being accepted as common currency by the population as a whole.

The approach is based on a population of a number of distinguishable individuals called *agents* (following Huberman's glossary [21] and [22]), which are involved in periods of independent optimisation interspersed with periods in which they interact. The agents are arranged in a tree structure, with communication possible between adjacent nodes. The approach is similar to that used by Muhlenbein [23], [24], and [25], Brown et al. [26], Gorges-Schleuter [27] and work performed by the Dynamics of Computation Group at Xerox PARC [21].

Agents are arranged in an inverse k-ary tree of depth n, where k and n are normally in the range 2 to 4. Optimisation is performed in generations in which recombination, local optimisation, and searchspec migration are performed in sequence across all agents in the population. Interactions between agents are local and so the generations could be implemented loosely synchronously if the agents were to be physically distributed across parallel hardware platforms. Having only local interactions considerably eases parallel implementation and the associated communications overhead.

Each agent maintains two searchspecs: the *pocket* and the *current*.

9.1 The Pocket Searchspec

The searchspec in the pocket of an agent is (roughly speaking) the best solution found so far by agent, after local optimisation. The pockets of the agents are initially seeded with searchspecs which have suggestions lists for each event produced randomly from the list of possible slots for that event.

9.2 The Current Searchspec

The current searchspec is the one being considered by an agent at any time. At each generation each agent replaces its current searchspec with the result of recombining its pocket with the pocket of another agent (followed by local optimisation). The root agent of the tree always recombines with the pocket of its fittest child; the leaf agents always recombine with their parent. Internal agents perform recombination in alternate generations with their parent in the tree or the fittest of their children. If the new current searchspec is better than the agent's pocket then it is copied into the pocket.

9.3 Signatures

This population strategy uses the concept of *signatures*. A signature is used to estimate the identity of a searchspec in order to compare it with another searchspec without time-consuming comparisons. If two searchspecs have the same signature then they are assumed to be equal. The signature is determined from a combination of the attributes of the searchspec and the attributes of the timetable it produces.

9.3 Lateral Inhibition

There is one exception to the replacement of pocket searchspecs by fitter current searchspecs. An agent will never replace its pocket if a searchspec with the same signature is present in a pocket in the branch of the tree in which the agent is found. Branches are defined starting at the root, along the path from the root to the agent, and fanning out recursively to the leaf agents via the children of the agent.

9.4 Pocket Propagation

After each wave of recombination, searchspecs can explicitly propagate up the tree towards the root. The pocket of an agent is swapped with the pocket of its best child if that child's pocket searchspec is fitter than the agent's pocket searchspec. At the same time, a copy of the agent's original pocket searchspec is copied into the pocket of the least fit child, and subjected to mutation. Swapping is performed at all levels in the tree except that a pocket that has been swapped into at a given generation is not considered for another swap at the same generation. Thus pockets can only be moved one level at each generation.

9.5 Avoiding Diversity Loss

Each agent has a *briefcase* into which it puts the signatures of all new current searchspecs produced by itself and the agents adjacent to it. If an agent has added nothing new to its briefcase for a certain amount of time, (*b* generations) it takes action to reverse the loss of diversity. It empties its briefcase, applies a large mutation to its pocket and instructs its children to do likewise. An exception is made for the root agent which does not mutate its own pocket (thus providing elitism).

The briefcase can hold $b(k+2)$ unique signatures. When the briefcase is full the least recently inserted signature is removed.

10. Test Problem

The system was tested with a standard data set which is the timetable problem for the Computer Studies Department at Napier University, semester one 1994. This data has been used in previous experiments and has been successfully processed by a previous system [2] into a working timetable.

There are 525 events over several courses within the department. Each event has a number of lecturers and student groups who must all attend. Each event must be assigned a room from a list of available rooms, the room must have sufficient capacity and must support the features (such as having certain equipment) demanded by the particular event. Each event must be timetabled in one of 45, one hour long slots. The availability of staff, students and rooms is limited. In many cases, such as with events involving day release students or part time staff, this is a severe restriction. The pressure on rooms is particularly high.

The test data contains over 8000 hard constraints due to lecturer and student availability and further hard constraints due to room availability. There are 525 events, 45 timeslots, 54 lecturers, 28 rooms and 77 student groups.

11. Evaluation

Candidate timetables from this test data set are evaluated in the following way.

Hard Constraints:

> For each event that cannot be placed without breaking a hard constraint 200 penalty points are assigned.

Soft Constraints:

> Timetables are also assessed according to various soft constraints which are derived from user criteria:

> - For each class which takes place between 5.00 p.m. and 6.00 p.m., 60 penalty points are assigned.

> - For each lecturer who does not get a teaching free day 30 penalty points are assigned.

> - For each occurrence of a student group having more than three hours in a row penalty points are assigned: 10 for 4 hours, 20 for five hours, 30 for six hours and so on.

> - For each occurrence of a student group having a gap of more than 3 hours between classes on the same day penalty points are assigned: 1 for four hours, 2 for five hours, 5 for six hours and 6 for seven hours.

> - For each occurrence of two events not taking place one directly after the other, where it is considered desirable (but not essential) that they

should, 5 or 25 penalty points are assigned depending on the degree of desirability (as defined by the user).

- For each occurrence of two events not taking place in a particular order, where is it considered desirable (but not essential) that they should, 2 penalty points are assigned.

12. Experimental Strategy

Experiments were designed to test the new features of directed mutation, targeted mutation, and the new population structure. Each test run was allowed 100,000 evaluations. This figure was chosen because it is approximately equivalent to an overnight run on a low specification PC, and experience shows that this is about the number of evaluations that the main user is prepared to wait for. Each test was run 25 times and the results given here are averages over all the runs.

All runs used blind mutation, some used one or more directed mutation operator. Where more than one mutation operator was used each had an equal chance of being applied.

The standard population used tournament selection parameters (*ps* and *pr*) of 0.9 and a population size of 50.

The structured population strategy was tested using a binary tree of depth four, with directed and targeted mutation. The time that a briefcase is allowed to remain unchanged (*b*) was set to 2. The large mutation that occurs is the event of diversity loss was the standard mutation operator applied three times.

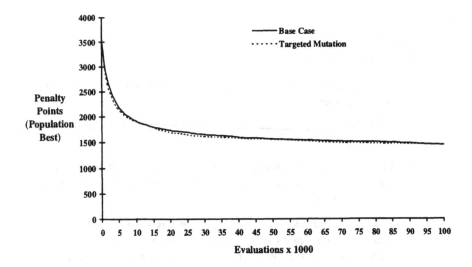

Fig. 2. The Base Case and Targeted Mutation

13. Experimental Results

13.1 The Base Case with Targeted Mutation

A base case test was run in order to act as a control. In this test neither directed or targeted mutation were used, and the standard population structure was employed. The result can be seen in Figure 2.

Timetables with less than about 2000 penalty points would normally be considered satisfactory, and so it can be seen that the base case system produces acceptable results.

Figure 2 also shows the effect of targeted mutation when used without either of the directed mutation operators. It can be seen that this has no significant effect.

13.2 Selfish Mutation

When selfish mutation was added the system was significantly improved as can be seen in Figure 3. The addition of targeted mutation to selfish mutation significantly improved the performance in the initial stages. This improvement is important as it halves the time taken to reach an acceptable timetable. However, all of the improvement is lost by the end of the 100,000 evaluations. It is not clear whether this simply means that targeting selfish mutation becomes less useful as time goes on, or whether targeting the mutation is actually impairing performance in the latter stages. Further work is required in this area, to determine the best policy for adapting targeted mutation as applied to selfish mutation as the run progresses.

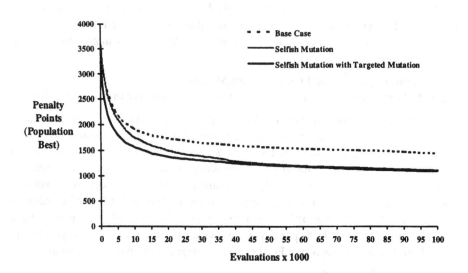

Fig. 3. Selfish Mutation and Targeted Mutation

13.3 Co-operative Mutation
Figure 4 shows the effect of co-operative mutation with and without targeted mutation.

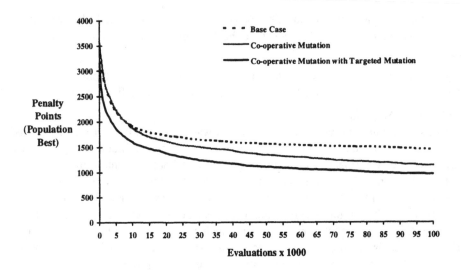

Fig. 4. Co-operative Mutation and Targeted Mutation

Here we see a significant improvement with the addition of co-operative mutation. With the further addition of targeted mutation there is another significant improvement. Unlike selfish mutation, co-operative mutation is improved by being targeted throughout the run.

13.4 Combining Selfish and Co-operative Mutation
Figure 5 shows the effect of using both selfish and co-operative mutation together.

It can be seen that the combined effects of the directed mutation operators has a marked effect on performance over the base case. When targeted mutation is added, the effect is greatly increased in the early stages, giving acceptable timetables in approximately a quarter of the time. In the longer term targeting the mutation has little if any beneficial effects, possibly suggesting that the improvement seen with co-operative mutation is being counteracted by some detrimental effect of combining selfish and targeted mutation in the latter stages. Alternatively, there may be a natural limit at around 1000 penalty points which is difficult for any algorithm to cross, however well it starts out. Further work is required to investigate this area.

13.5 Structured Population
The results of the experiments with the structured population can be seen in Figure 6. It can be seen that while results were not as good as with the standard population, they were in the same region. This can be considered a success for two reasons.

Firstly, these are initial trials, and no attempt has yet been made to optimise the system parameters. Secondly, there is no necessity for this population structure to perform better than the standard system on a sequential machine; its real power will come about when implementing the system in parallel.

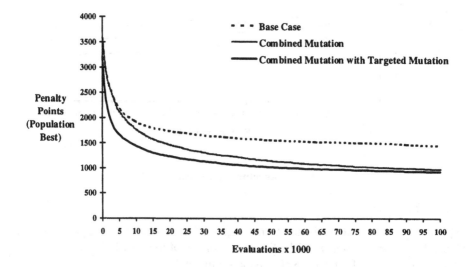

Fig. 5. Combined Mutation and Targeted Mutation

14. Conclusion

A memetic timetabling system has been described which encodes local search specifications into the memetic material. A recombination operator has been described which results in an interesting ancestral memory. This paper has defined two directed mutation operators and a method of targeting mutation to those events which are causing problems in resultant timetables.

Selfish and co-operative mutation have been found to be very useful in increasing the performance of this memetic timetabling system. Targeted mutation has been found to have no effect when used with blind mutation, but to increase performance when used in conjunction with the directed mutation operators, particularly in the initial stages.

This paper has also described a structured population which extends the memetic metaphor and facilitates a parallel implementations. It has had initial trials and has shown reasonable results without optimisation of its parameters. Its real power would be tested if the system were implemented in parallel.

Further work is required on many parts of the work presented here, and is currently in progress.

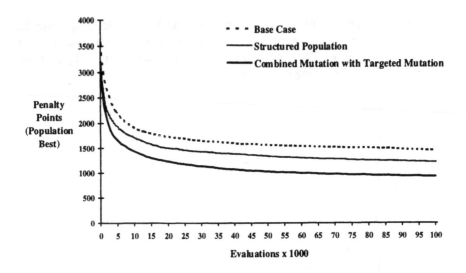

Fig. 6. Structured Population

15. References

[1] Paechter, B., Luchian, H., and Cumming, A., "An Evolutionary Approach to the General Timetable Problem", The Scientific Annals of the "Al. I. Cuza" University of Iasi, special issue for the ROSYCS symposium 1993.

[2] Paechter B., Luchian H., Cumming A., and Petriuc M., "Two Solutions to the General Timetable Problem Using Evolutionary Methods", The Proceedings of the IEEE Conference of Evolutionary Computation, 1994.

[3] Paechter, B., Cumming, A., Luchian, H., "The Use of Local Search Suggestion Lists for Improving the Solution of Timetable Problems with Evolutionary Algorithms.", Proceedings of the AISB Workshop in Evolutionary Computing, Springer-Verlag Lecture Notes in Computer Science Series No 993, Heidleberg, 1995.

[4] Goldberg, D. E. Genetic Algorithms in Search, Optimisation and Machine Learning, Addison Wesley, Reading, 1989.

[5] Michalewicz, Z., Genetic Algorithms + Data Structures = Evolution Programs, Springer-Verlag, Heidelberg, 1992.

[6] Davis, L., Handbook of Genetic Algorithms, van Nostrand Reinhold, London, 1992.

[7] Colorni, A., Dorigo M., Maniezzo, V. "Genetic Algorithms and Highly Constrained Problems: The Time-Table Case". Parallel Problem Solving from Nature I, Goos and Hartmanis (eds.) Springer-Verlag, Heidelberg, 1990.

[8] Corne, D., Ross, P. and Fang, H., "Fast Practical Evolutionary Timetabling" Proceedings of the AISB Workshop on Evolutionary Computing, Springer-Verlag Lecture Notes in Computer Science Series No. 865, Heidelberg, 1994.

[9] Burke, E., Elliman D., and Weare, R., "A Genetic Algorithm for University Timetabling" AISB Workshop on Evolutionary Computing, Leeds, 1994.

[10] Ross, P. and Corne, D. "Comparing Genetic Algorithms, Simulated Annealing, and Stochastic Hillclimbing on Several Real Timetable Problems", Proceedings of the AISB Workshop in Evolutionary Computing, Springer-Verlag Lecture Notes in Computer Science Series No 993, Heidleberg, 1995.

[11] Burke, E., Elliman, D. and Weare, R., "Specialised Recombinative Operators for Timetabling Problems", Proceedings of the AISB Workshop in Evolutionary Computing, Springer-Verlag Lecture Notes in Computer Science Series No 993, Heidleberg, 1995.

[12] Dawkins, R., "The Selfish Gene", Oxford University Press, 1976

[13] Moscato, P. "On evolution, search, optimization, genetic algorithms and martial arts: Towards memetic algorithms." Technical Report 826, Pasadena, CA, 1989.

[14] Moscato, P. and Fontanari, J. F., "Stochastic versus deterministic update in simulated annealing." Physics Letters A, 146(4):204-208, 1990

[15] Norman, M.G. and Moscato, P. "A competitive-cooperative approach to complex combinatorial search". In Selected Work for the Proceedings of the 20th Joint Conference on Informatics and Operations Research (20th JAIIO), pages 3.15-3.29, Buenos Aires, Argentina, August 1991.

[16] Moscato, P. "An introduction to population approaches for optimization and hierarchical objective functions: The role of tabu search". Annals of Operations Research, 41(1-4):85-121, 1993.

[17] Moscato, P. and Norman, M.G., "A memetic approach for the travelling salesman problem. implementation of a computational ecology for combinatorial optimization on message-passing systems". In Proceedings of the International Conference on Parallel Computing and Transputer Applications, pages 177-186, Amsterdam, IOS Press, 1992.

[18] Radcliffe, N. J. and Surry P. D., "Formal Memetic Algorithms", Proceedings of the AISB Workshop on Evolutionary Computing, Springer-Verlag Lecture Notes in Computer Science Series No. 865, Heidelberg, 1994.

[19] Radcliffe, N. J. "Forma Analysis and Random Respectful Recombination" Proceedings of the Fourth International Conference on Genetic Algorithms", Morgan-Kaufmann, 1991.

[20] Ross, P., Corne, D., and Fang, H., "Improving Evolutionary Timetabling with Delta Evaluation and Directed Mutation", Parallel Problem Solving from Nature III, Springer-Verlag, Heidelberg, 1994.

[21] Huberman, B.A. and Hogg, T., "Complexity and adaptation." Physica D, 22:376-384, 1986.

[22] Huberman, B.A. and T. Hogg, T.. "Phase transitions in artificial intelligence systems." Artificial Intelligence, 33:155-171, 1987.

[23] Muhlenbein, H., "New solutions to the mapping problem of parallel systems: The evolution approach." Parallel Computing, 4:269, 1987.

[24] Muhlenbein., H., "Evolution algorithms in combinatorial optimization". Parallel Computing, 7:65, 1988.

[25] Muhlenbein., H. "Parallel genetic algorithms, population genetics and combinatorial optimization". In J. D. Schaffer, editor, Proceedings of the Third International Conference of Genetic Algorithms, page 416, San Mateo CA, Morgan Kaufmann, 1989

[26] Brown, D., Huntley, C. L., and Spillane, A., "A parallel genetic heuristic for the quadratic assignment problem." In J. D. Schaffer, editor, Proceedings of the Third International Conference of Genetic Algorithms, page 406, San Mateo CA, Morgan Kaufmann, 1989.

[27] Gorges-Schleuter, M., "ASPARAGOS an asynchronous parallel genetic optimization strategy". In J. D. Schaffer, editor, Proceedings of the Third International Conference of Genetic Algorithms, page 422, San Mateo CA, Morgan Kaufmann, 1989.

Automatic Timetabling in Practice

R.C. Rankin

Department of Computer Studies
Napier University
219 Colinton Road
Edinburgh EH14 1DJ
Scotland
rcr@dcs.napier.ac.uk

Abstract

This paper describes the experience of using an automatic timetable generation system, based on a memetic algorithm, to produce working timetables for a large department that offers a range of undergraduate and postgraduate courses attended by some 500 students. The automatic algorithm is supported by a records system which permits manual data collection and editing, viewing and printing of timetables.

The paper outlines the operation of the department as far as it affects timetabling, the method developed to use the system and discusses the benefits and difficulties arising from its practical application.

The author is responsible for timetabling in the department.

1 Introduction.

The department of Computer Studies at Napier University is the parent department for five courses at undergraduate and postgraduate levels, and participates in teaching of modules on several courses offered by other departments. A logical semester system operates in which the two semesters are mapped on to three terms, with an inter-semester week occurring during the second term. An automatic timetabling system is used to schedule classes. It consists of a graphical interface and records system supporting a memetic algorithm. Both the graphical interface, "Neeps", and the memetic algorithm, "Tatties", were developed in the department by Ben Paechter and Andrew Cumming [1], [2] and [3].

Before the introduction of the automated system, manually produced timetables were often incomplete at the start of teaching; frequently one lesson from a module could not be placed, and lecturers were required to make adjustments to find solutions for the lessons to which they were assigned. Although course leaders attempted to incorporate "goodness" into draft timetables, their initial success was eroded after several alterations to place outstanding lessons.

In recent years both institution and department have grown substantially. The number of courses, the number of students enrolled on each, and the accommodation base have all doubled. Institutions in more stable circumstances can maintain a similar timetable from year-to-year. This has not been possible at Napier, and the difficulties of managing the timetable had reached the point where a better solution was needed. This level of change will continue for some years yet as new accommodation becomes available on another site and the pattern of use alters.

About 80% of the lessons to be timetabled come from the five courses for which the department is the parent. These five courses are made up of nine year groups with between 12 and 80 students per group.

Course	Stage	No. of Students	No. of Groups	Comments
BSc Computing/ BSc Information Systems	1	80	7	
	2	70	6	
	3	60	-	Industrial Placement
	4	60	6	Optional routes
	5	35	3	
HNC/D Computing.	1	48	6	Options & day release
	2	36	3	Options
PGDip/MSc Information Systems.	1	60	8	Options & part-time students
PGDip/MSc Software Technology.	1	36	5	Options & part-time students
MSc Object Oriented Software Engineering.	1	12	2	

Table 1 - Structure of Courses.

Each year group attends lectures together, but is divided into groups of about 12 to 16 for practical and tutorial sessions, although some variants exist. A typical small module might require every student to attend one lecture and one other lesson (tutorial or practical) per week. This could create between two and eight events: one lecture and one other lesson for each of between one and seven groups. A larger module could double these figures. Additionally, some practical modules require unsupervised events to reserve laboratory space for self-study by students. The worst case has been a single module with 26 events per week. On a course where no options are offered, these tutorial groups are distinct, with each student attached to exactly one group. In courses with options a student may belong to more than one logical group and care has to be taken in specifying which groups attend which lessons. In total there are about 60 separate student groups to be timetabled.

In any semester over 60 individual members of staff service these events. Only 30 of these are permanent lecturers in the department, and a further 20 are part-time lecturers. About 10 come from other departments. While the permanent departmental staff does not change significantly from semester to semester, there is a higher rate of change in the other categories.

Courses are taught in three types of accommodation: University general purpose teaching rooms, University computing facilities, and specialist departmental computing laboratories. General purpose rooms and theatres, holding from 15 to 200 persons, are managed by a central room-allocation service. Bids for accommodation are made in competition with other departments. There are some general computing laboratories managed by the University's Computer Services Unit on the site, and these are used mainly for lower-level modules. While access to these is also competitive, the Computer Studies department is by far the largest user and conflict is rare. Some of the computing laboratories managed by the department are also used for lower-level modules, while others are specialised, and provide support for the higher-level modules. When account is taken of the different facilities available in laboratories there are six different accommodation sub-types.

At the heart of the system is a *lesson* - a one-hour event. In total, there are over 500 lessons per week taught by the department, with more than half of these changing at the start of the second semester. A typical lesson, or event, is an intersection of a staff member, a room and one or more student groups. Some exceptions exist: more than one lecturer may be assigned to lessons to share teaching; no staff are assigned to unsupervised practical lessons. Finally, some lessons take place on other sites; in these cases the room and the students are under the control of the external department, therefore the lesson only requires to have lecturer(s) assigned. As each lesson is created in the system, the student groups who must attend are attached. Lecturer(s) are attached, where appropriate after decisions about teaching duties have been made. The task of the memetic algorithm is to select, for each lesson, a time slot in the week when that lesson can be placed in suitable accommodation.

The window showing a typical lesson is illustrated below (Figure 1). This also shows one lecturer (CG), and two groups of students (LSSD-a and LSSD-b) attached to this lesson. Finally, a classroom from the general purpose accommodation is required; there are 25 students in total (box, bottom left) so this will be the minimum room size allocated.

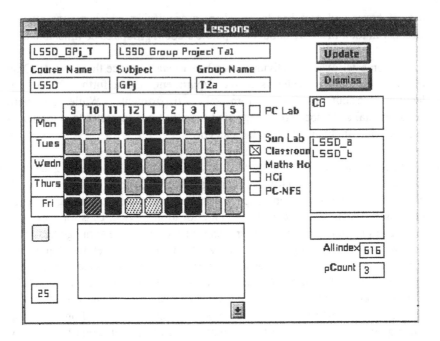

Figure 1 - Window of Typical Lesson

The tiles representing the timetable are colour-coded to show the status of each timetable slot. The colour codes are explained in table 2, below:

Colour (as printed)	Status of Timetable Slot
Red	The event has been placed in the timetable slot manually, or fixed in the slot from an earlier semester. (N/A in Fig. 1)
Blue (striped)	The event has been placed in the timetable slot by the algorithm. (e.g. Friday at 10am in Fig. 1)
Yellow (speckled)	All of the components of the intersection (staff, students and accommodation) are available at this timetable slot. (e.g. Friday at 12 noon and 1pm in Fig. 1)
Grey (grey)	At least one of the components is unavailable at this timetable slot. e.g. Monday at 10am and 3pm in Fig. 1)
Black (black)	Another event involving at least one of the components has been timetabled in this slot. e.g. Monday at 9am in Fig. 1)

Table 2 - Colour Coding of Timetable Window

2. Timetabling Constraints.

A system of allowances operates in the department to release time for approved academic and administrative tasks. New lecturers are given lower workloads in their first year. The total workload of the department is taken to be the sum of the contact hours to be serviced, plus the allowances allocated, and this is divided equitably across the lecturing staff.

Lecturers may be restricted in the times when they are available for teaching: unrestricted implies that the person has no particular preferences, while highly-restricted indicates that there are few points in the week when they are available to teach. Departmental lecturers with high allowances, part-time lecturers with external commitments, and lecturers from other departments are generally more restricted. Examples of such restrictions include:

- lecturers from other sites can reduce their apparent availability to force clustering of Computer Studies lessons and reduce inter-site travel;
- lessons given at other sites require travelling time before and after, making the Computer Studies lecturer unavailable for longer than the actual lesson;
- part-time staff may wish to specify times when they are not available;
- lecturers with allowances for administrative or research activities want to create substantial blocks of time free of teaching.

Figure 2, below, illustrates the window of a member of staff showing the availability map. All other resources in the system, i.e. students and accommodation, have similar windows.

Student groups can impose restrictions also. Senior students usually have one day per week free of conventional lessons for project work, and this can be recorded on a student-group basis by marking the group unavailable for that day. This is more flexible than defining a day-long event, because different groups can be made available on different days to reduce peaking of demand on resources. Part-time students also require to be unavailable on days when they cannot attend. The availability maps of student groups are logically 'AND'ed together to determine the availability of the whole class. Thus lessons to be attended by both small groups of part-time students, and larger groups of full-time students can be constrained to those days when all groups can attend.

Some events are fixed by other departments because they are internally subject to constraints similar to those described.

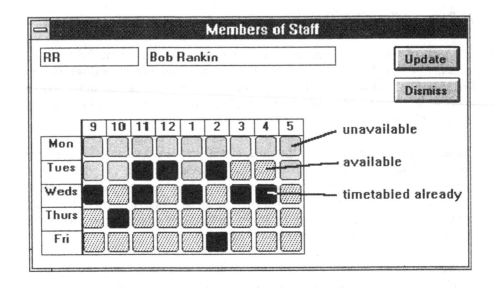

Figure 2 - Window of Resource Availability

The University operates a room-allocation service in which each department requests general purpose rooms at times indicated on manually prepared course timetables. If no suitable room is available for a lesson it is moved to a time when a room is available. For automatic generation this method has required adaptation, because no timetable can be generated until room availability is known. A block of rooms is now requested and this availability map is entered into the system. Because competition for centrally managed laboratories is low on the site where the department is located, it has not yet been necessary to initiate similar arrangements, although in principle the allocation of these resources would be the same. The specialist laboratories are totally under the department's control, but utilisation levels have until now been very high.

3. The Method.

This section describes the method which has been developed to make use of the memetic algorithm and its recording and reporting system. In essence it consists of the following steps:

- Course leaders prepare a list of all the weekly lessons necessary for each year of their courses for the next semester, and a list of all student groups participating. This list is annotated with the student groups who should attend each event, and any constraints or relationships between lessons. For example some lessons must coincide with others. Some lessons must follow others. For a large proportion of events this is simple, but for optional subjects it can become difficult. Each event specifies the type of accommodation needed and the minimum size is determined from the student groups involved. Table 3 summarises the constraints used:

Constraint Code	Meaning - "The event to which the code is attached...."
CO x	.. must coincide with named event x."
UC x	.. must not coincide with named event x."
FI x	.. should follow immediately after named event x."
FW x	.. should follow named event x."

Table 3 - Constraint Codes.

- From this events list an estimate is made of the minimum set of general purpose classrooms which will be needed. The room-allocations unit is then asked to nominate hours in the week for specific rooms, plus a suitable margin for flexibility. The margin is returned to the pool of rooms as soon as the timetables have been generated. Ideally, the greater the margin the better. There is a question about how well the system would cope with the last department on a site to be timetabled, when the margin of unallocated rooms would be very small.

- A staff loading grid is prepared which details the allowances and contact hours per week for all lecturers under the control of the department. This "load-balancing" activity is central to the process. When the grid is agreed by the head of department lecturers are attached to the lessons. At present loading is measured crudely in terms of contact hours. This measure is not ideal because it does not take account of the other factors which contribute to workload such as preparation of materials, the number of students attending the lessons, and the nature of the assessments. A move to more accurate measures of staff loading is planned, based on a variable number of points for each lesson depending on circumstances. This will be fairer for staff, but will make integrating timetables and loadings a little harder, because at present the mapping is fixed at 1:1.

- When the final list of events has staff members and student groups attached, then the availability of all staff, student groups and accommodation is checked. At this point the data is complete, and the memetic algorithm is used to generate the timetable. The formats of the input and output data used by the algorithm are essentially the same, and therefore the Neeps interface used to create the input data can also be used to view and manipulate the timetables produced.

4. Discussion.

4.1 The Success of the Algorithm.

The first point to note is that the memetic algorithm used has been highly successful. In the two semesters of the 1994/95 session it produced complete working timetables, with no lessons unplaced and acceptable measures of fitness or "goodness".

Two types of constraints exist in the system, classed as "hard" or "soft". Failure to satisfy a "hard" constraint prevents generation of a timetable. They are:

- No clashes, i.e. staff, student groups and accommodation cannot be double-booked;
- All staff and students have at least one hour free between 1200 hrs. and 1400 hrs;
- Coincidence and Uncoincidence of events must be obeyed;
- Unavailability of a lecturer, student group or accommodation cannot be altered automatically.

Failure to satisfy a "soft" constraint does not prevent generation of a timetable, but the number of constraints breached determines the "goodness" of the timetable produced. In practice there is a *cost* associated with each constraint. The cost is a number of penalty points and the best timetable of a run has the lowest number of points. These points were decided empirically following discussions with members of staff and groups of students about what constituted a "good" timetable. Table 4 below lists the constraints used and the number of points attached to each breach (the Cost Criteria). The table also shows typical scores from the first and final evaluations of an overnight run of the Tatties algorithm; initial scores can be significantly higher (in some runs over 3,000 points) if there are any unplaced lessons initially. The final score shown was after 113,527 evaluations. The search had not yet converged. Some runs have been allowed to continue for four days after which the score had reduced to about 800 points.

There is some evidence that the system has dealt successfully with difficult problems embedded in the detail of the timetabling. For example, some part-time students on day-release from employment are required to attend 8 lessons in 9 available hours. This was successfully timetabled. In another instance, a tutorial group of 12 students was placed in a 200-seat lecture theatre - an extensive manual effort to change this to a smaller room, (even at another time slot) was unsuccessful, suggesting that the algorithm had found a rare solution. On another occasion it was noticed after a timetable had been produced that it included a room which was no longer available. Some 25 events had been placed in this non-existent classroom. These lessons were all freed (changed from blue to yellow in terms of table 2) and the room removed from the system. All other events were left in place. The algorithm was rerun and a usable solution was found in a few minutes.

Cost Criterion	Penalty Points	Initial Count	Initial Score	Final Count	Final Score
Lesson unplaced.	200	0	0	0	0
Lecturer with no day free of teaching	30	9	270	5	150
Event placed between 1700-1800 hrs.	30	26	780	9	270
Supervised lesson not following immediately.	25	12	300	12	300
Unsupervised lesson not following immediately.	5	10	50	10	50
Three events in a row.	5	95	475	50	250
Lesson not following another in week.	2	9	18	1	2
Gaps of 7hrs. between events.	6	0	0	0	0
Gaps of 6hrs. between events.	5	2	10	0	0
Gaps of 5hrs. between events.	2	1	2	1	2
Gaps of 4hrs. between events	1	21	21	7	7
Total Fitness Score			1926		1031

Table 4 - Cost Criteria Used.

Thus, from the point of view of evolutionary algorithms, this memetic program has been highly successful. However, the data for the exercise and the timetables produced are for use in a live situation, and the measures of success there relate to the effectiveness of the timetables and the amount of editing and correction needed after their production.

4.2 Causes of Change in Timetables.

Three types of imperfection have been noted in the timetables produced.

The first type of imperfection is unavoidable unless student numbers can be predicted accurately in advance. If there were no options, and every session a course team were able to choose a cohort of constant size from a larger pool of prospective students, it would be possible to create a precise number of events in advance. For many courses, either because the numbers of students can vary, or optional streams have yet to be chosen by students, the exact number of events cannot be accurately set in advance of enrolment. Course leaders define a set of events on the basis of anticipated student numbers, and adjustments must be made once exact numbers are known. It is easier to adjust the timetables by removal of redundant events, than it is to insert additional events, so over-estimation of numbers is preferred. However, when the resource base is fixed, over-estimation reduces the "headroom" available to the algorithm, and the timetables produced will usually be a less good fit than would have been possible if there had been fewer events.

The second type is due to mistakes in the original event list. On the scale of operations of the department it is impossible to be 100% accurate. Up to 10% of the lessons contain errors. The most common errors have been:

- The wrong accommodation type was specified, (for example, a UNIX laboratory specified instead of a PC laboratory). If appropriate accommodation is free at the selected time change is easy; where utilisation of specialist laboratories is high this is not often the case and manual adjustment of the timetable is needed.
- The availability of accommodation has been incorrectly recorded. This may be inevitable in some degree, and has similar problems to the previous error.
- Failure to specify the availability of staff correctly. This can result in lessons being placed when staff are not in fact available, or in poorly clustered teaching for visiting staff. It is usually those with the lowest teaching loads who require most adjustment, because commitments outside the department or the institution are less easily altered.
- Where students take options and virtual groups are specified to deal with this, the constraints on lessons are not always correctly specified. For example, if two events must not coincide and the appropriate constraint code is omitted, the adjustments needed to repair the timetable can be non-trivial.

The third type arises directly from the nature and weightings of the soft and hard constraints written into the algorithm. The cost criteria tabled above have been chosen after experiment and debate, and represent a balance between staff and student interests. The algorithm appears to be willing to sacrifice anything to obtain a lower score. Careless adjustments to the penalty points can have bizarre effects, which are not always predictable when setting the scores; what seemed reasonable in discussion may be unsatisfactory in use. Some of our criteria have caused conflict, for example:

- Staff who fail to obtain a day free of teaching feel strongly that they have been mistreated by the automatic system. However, these lecturers are usually carrying a high teaching load, and it is relatively much harder to free them for a day. Simply raising the penalty for this criterion could result in a poorer timetable for everyone.
- It was widely believed that a timetable that had no more than two consecutive lessons and avoided long gaps between lessons (i.e. a well-distributed timetable)

would be much appreciated by students. The algorithm has chosen, for example, to avoid the five-point penalty of three consecutive lessons on Thursday by placing a single lesson on a Friday for which there is currently no penalty; the students who have to attend only for that lesson are unconvinced that this is a "better" timetable.

- Five o'clock lessons are universally unpopular. The example given in table 4 shows these reducing from 26 to nine in an overnight run. The persons involved in these nine lessons do not acknowledge the improvement.

- At present the system only deals temporal proximity, i.e. events can be made to happen simultaneously or not. At the time of its development no need was seen for including geographical proximity as a constraint. Coincident lessons are often required to take place in adjacent laboratories to allow tutors to move easily between them. On a site where facilities are widely separated this fault caused disproportionate trouble until manually altered.

- A serious omission from the original system was flags to show that a student group contained a person with special needs, and that accommodation could meet such needs. Difficulty of access for wheelchairs is one such example. This resulted in a timetable which scored well, but was unworkable for a particular student group. This case highlights the fact that the cost of the timetable is measured by the criteria defined in the algorithm, but its workability depends on how complete and realistic those criteria are.

All types of imprecision cause the generated timetables to require change. Even where data describing lessons have been correctly specified and the resulting timetable is technically accurate, lecturers or student groups request changes for personal reasons. These can be significant or trivial, and the decision to adjust the timetables for them is of necessity a local one. Nevertheless, changes will be unavoidable unless one adopts a rigid rule of non-compliance. There is an irony in the fact that software professionals demand this kind of change; it is not something which we tolerate readily in users of software which we develop. To date, changes have been dealt with manually, because it has not proven beneficial to deal with them through the memetic algorithm.

4.3 Operational Tactics.

As indicated above changes to a correctly-generated timetable are inevitable. The most common forms of change can be described as:

- swapping two lessons or components of two lessons;
- finding another timeslot when a lesson can take place.

The current version of Neeps indicates via its coloured tiles when all the components of a lesson are free (the yellow tile). Frequently no alternative slots appear to exist. However, it is not unusual for another room to be available into which the event can be moved. To automate this search fully is not possible because some accommodation is not under the control of the department and its availability apart from our allocation is unknown. To facilitate the search, a "what-if" facility has been developed which uses a dummy room which is always available. Attaching this room to the event eliminates the slots when other components are unavailable. It is relatively simple then to check with the Room Allocation Service for the availability of a suitable room at any of the possible slots.

One particular difficulty arises when the students in a year do not all attend the same events. this occurs when a course offers options, or when a course has both full and part-time students. When a course offers options a number of student groups is created. These groups are attached to the option and to any core modules. In the diagram below the larger circle represents a set of core modules, and the superimposed semi-circles represent two options, A and B. All four student groups are attached to the core modules, and groups 1 and 2 to optional module A, groups 3 and 4 to optional module B.

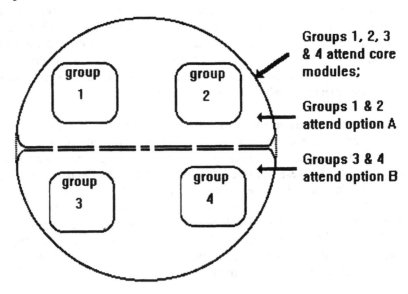

Figure 3 - Dealing with Options.

Two variants have been used: in one the students are polled for their choices, and negotiations and assignment to groups concluded before the events are created; in the second the events are created and students assigned to groups to match the events. The former always yields coherent groups, i.e. a student will always be in one named group. The latter can be more efficient but the coherence of groups is lost i.e. a student may be in one group for one module and a different group for another.

Some courses have part-time students who complete their studies over two or three years by attending on one or two days per week. Student groups are created for such part-time students, and the group is marked as available only on the appropriate day(s). The part-time group is attached to lessons, along with any full-time groups taking the module. The lecture and at least one practical/tutorial lesson will then be timetabled into the day when the part-time students attend:

Groups A & B are full-time students, x & y are part-time students, attending on different days. Module P is taken by Groups A, B and y. Module Q is taken by Groups A, B and x.

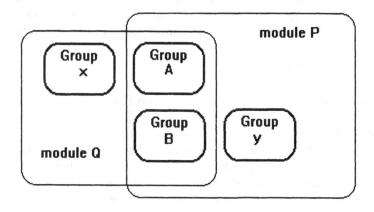

Figure 4 - Dealing with Part-time Students.

In the example above the lecture for module P will be forced into the day when group Y attend, while that for module Q will be forced into the day when group x attend. The tutorial lessons for those groups will be likewise constrained. Tutorials for groups A and B will not be so constrained.

It was stated above that some events are fixed. These are either set by external departments or are carried forward from the first semester of the session. In the first semester of a session about 25% of lessons are fixed. In the second semester over 50% are fixed. The algorithm places fixed events in a mask at the start of a run. This mask reduces the available slots into which the algorithm can place unfixed events. Fixed events are not otherwise involved in the evolutionary part of the system. They are counted in the cost score when any timetable is evaluated. The Tatties algorithm has worked successfully with fixed events in the proportions noted. In the original version, when the same approach was used to make small scale changes, such as those discussed in 4.2 above, the algorithm converged prematurely with relatively poor scores. However, in its most recent form, which includes targeted and directed mutation, it has successfully dealt with low proportions (<10%) of unfixed events.

4.4 Future changes.

The scoring system for evaluating cost has been derived empirically, and a more sophisticated approach is needed to develop values which provide the best possible timetables. A more detailed investigation of all criteria is needed, together with experimentation using known data to examine the effects of altering the values.

Some of the cost criteria concern the temporal relationships between lessons. Two of these require one event to follow directly after another. They are a consequence of using uniform events of one hour duration. Many practical lessons are two or even three hours in length and ideally should be timetabled as a block. From the scores shown in table 4 it is clear that the algorithm has been unable to meet this need fully, and relatively little improvement is seen in a typical run. A later version of the system will include variable length events to address this problem.

5. Conclusion.

In environments where change in accommodation, staffing and student numbers is slow there would be little need for a system like that described. The phase through which this new University is passing is unlikely to be repeated. However, any organisation whose timetables require significant change from year-to-year could benefit from the approach taken here. The Neeps and Tatties system has altered the nature of departmental timetabling. The emphasis has moved from the task of producing a working timetable to that of workload management, generating the correct data for the algorithm, and managing the necessary changes. This implies that a successful automatic algorithm alone is insufficient for producing "real" timetables; a comprehensive records system is also needed. The former removes the tedium of producing an acceptable timetable, and the latter provides the means of recording events, managing timetables and reporting staff and resource utilisation,

6. References.

[1] Paechter, B., Luchian, H., and Cumming, A., "An Evolutionary Approach to the General Timetable Problem", The Scientific Annals of the "Al. I. Cuza" University of Iasi, special issue for the ROSYCS symposium 1993.

[2] Paechter B., Luchian H., Cumming A., and Petriuc M., "Two Solutions to the General Timetable Problem Using Evolutionary Methods", The Proceedings of the IEEE Conference of Evolutionary Computation, 1994.

[3] Paechter, B., Cumming, A., Luchian, H., "The Use of Local Search Suggestion Lists for Improving the Solution of Timetable Problems with Evolutionary Algorithms.", AISB Workshop in Evolutionary Computing, Sheffield, April 1995.

Complexity Issues

The Complexity of Timetable Construction Problems

Tim B. Cooper and Jeffrey H. Kingston

Basser Department of Computer Science
The University of Sydney
Australia

Abstract. This paper shows that timetable construction is NP-complete in a number of quite different ways that arise in practice, and discusses the prospects of overcoming these problems. A formal specification of the problem based on TTL, a timetable specification language, is given.

Specifically, we show that NP-completeness arises whenever students have a wide subject choice, or meetings vary in duration, or simple conditions are imposed on the choice of times for meetings, such as requirements for double times or an even spread through the week. In realistic cases, the assignment of meetings to just one teacher (after their times are fixed) is NP-complete. And although suitable times can be assigned to all the meetings involving one student group simultaneously, the corresponding problem for two student groups is NP-complete.

Keywords: timetable construction, specification, complexity.

1. Introduction

The timetable construction problem is to assign times, teachers, students and rooms to a collection of meetings so that none of the participants has to attend two meetings simultaneously. This basic requirement is often augmented with others concerning limits on the workload of teachers, constraints on the way a meeting's times are spread through the week, and so on.

Many different techniques have been applied to the timetable construction problem. Previous work by the authors and others has attempted to break it into subproblems, in the hope that each will be efficiently solvable. In such work a detailed understanding of the inherent complexity of timetable construction is needed; a broad statement that the overall problem is NP-complete gives no guidance on the prospects of solving any particular subproblem. This paper fills in some of these details by identifying five independent NP-complete subproblems, and discussing the prospects of solving each in practice.

2. Specification of the Timetable Construction Problem

In this section we present a specification of the timetable construction problem based on a *timetable specification language* called TTL. This language is formal yet flexible enough to specify instances encountered in practice. An earlier version of TTL appeared in [1].

A TTL instance consists of a *time group*, some *resource groups*, and some *meetings*. A formal grammar appears in Figure 2.1. Here is a typical time group:

timegroup *Times* **is**

>*Mon*1; *Mon*2; *Mon*3; *Mon*4; *Mon*5; *Mon*6; *Mon*7; *Mon*8;
>*Tue*1; *Tue*2; *Tue*3; *Tue*4; *Tue*5; *Tue*6; *Tue*7; *Tue*8;
>*Wed*1; *Wed*2; *Wed*3; *Wed*4; *Wed*5; *Wed*6; *Wed*7; *Wed*8;
>*Thu*1; *Thu*2; *Thu*3; *Thu*4; *Thu*5; *Thu*6; *Thu*7; *Thu*8;
>*Fri*1; *Fri*2; *Fri*3; *Fri*4; *Fri*5; *Fri*6; *Fri*7; *Fri*8;

>*conditions* (*omitted*)

end *Times*;

It lists the names of the times available for meetings, followed by *conditions* (see below). Here is a typical resource group:

group *Teachers* **is**

>**subgroups** *English, Science, Computing*;

>*Smith* **in** *English, Computing*;
>*Jones* **in** *Science, Computing*;
>*Robinson* **in** *English*;

end *Teachers*;

This group contains *resources* (*Smith, Jones*, and *Robinson*) which are available to attend meetings, and *subgroups* which are subsets of the set of resources defining functions that the resources are qualified to perform: teach English, etc. A resource may be in any number of subgroups. Typical instances have *Teachers*, *Rooms*, and *Students* resource groups.

After the groups come the meetings, which are collections of *slots* which are to be assigned elements of the various groups, subject to certain restrictions. For example, here is a typical meeting expressing five Science classes which meet simultaneously for six times per week:

instance	→	*timegroup* { *resourcegroup* } { *meeting* }
timegroup	→	**timegroup** *timegroupname* **is**
		{ *timename* ; }
		end *timegroupname* ;
resourcegroup	→	**group** *resourcegroupname* **is**
		[**subgroups** *subgrouplist* ;]
		{ *resourcename* [**in** *subgrouplist*] ; }
		end *resourcegroupname* ;
subgrouplist	→	*resourcegroupname* { , *resourcegroupname* }
meeting	→	**meeting** *meetingname* **is**
		{ *timeselect* | *resourceselect* }
		end *meetingname* ;
timeselect	→	*number timegroupname* [: *timeconditionlist*] ;
	→	*timename* ;
resourceselect	→	*number resourcegroupname* ;
	→	*resourcename* ;
number	→	*integer* | **all**

Fig. 2.1. Grammar of the TTL language. { ... } means zero or more of, [...] means optional. Time conditions and some unimportant extensions required in practice have been omitted.

meeting 10-*Science* **is**
    *Year*10;
    5 *Science*;
    5 *ScienceLab*;
    6 *Times*: *TwoDouble*;
end 10-*Science*;

There is one slot which must contain the *Year*10 resource from the *Students* group; five slots which must contain resources from the *Science* subgroup; five resources from the *ScienceLab* subgroup of the *Rooms* group, and six times from the *Times* group, which must satisfy the *TwoDouble* condition, defined as follows: there must be at least two double times (i.e. two pairs of adjacent times), the times must be spread over as many days of the week as possible, and all but one of the times must be nice (i.e. not last on any day). These conditions are defined in the time group, but lack of space prevents us from explaining them in detail here. Formally, the meaning is that the eleven selected resources will all be occupied together for the six times; in fact, it is clear that the Year 10 students will be split into five groups.

Although most meetings are similar to 10-*Science*, there are some exceptions, for example Faculty meetings:

meeting *EnglishFaculty* **is**
    all *English*;
    1 *Times*;
end *EnglishFaculty*;

and meetings which ensure that each teacher teaches at most 30 out of the 40 possible times each week (say):

meeting *SmithFree* **is**
    Smith;
    10 *Times*: *TeacherFree*;
end *SmithFree*;

The *TeacherFree* condition is defined to mean that at least one time from each day must be included. Real instances may have two hundred or more meetings altogether.

This completes the presentation of the TTL language. It has been used successfully by the authors, with some unimportant extensions, to specify high school instances [1, 2], and it can easily be extended to accommodate the multiple sections needed in university timetabling, and to express preferences in selections. Requirements that do not seem amenable to expression in TTL include relations between meetings (must not be consecutive, etc.), and conditions on the set of meetings assigned to some resource (at most two Senior courses per teacher, minimize walking distance, etc.).

We will denote by TIMETABLE CONSTRUCTION (TTC) the decision problem of determining whether an assignment of times and resources to all the slots exists which satisfies the various conditions and is such that no resource is assigned to two meetings which share a time. This is polynomial-time equivalent to the problem of actually producing such an assignment: given TTC, one can construct a solution if it exists by trying each possible assignment to the first slot until TTC indicates that a solution exists, then repeating on the other slots in turn.

3. NP-Completeness Results

In determining the complexity of the TTC problem defined in Section 2, formally it is sufficient to prove TTC $\in$ **NP** (obvious) and to demonstrate one transformation from any known NP-complete problem to TTC. But we wish to show that TTC is NP-complete in several independent ways, all of which arise in practice. For this it is necessary to find transformations which construct TTC instances that resemble special cases of the TTC problem that arise in real instances.

The well-known formulation of the timetable construction problem given by Gotlieb [6] assumes that each meeting contains exactly one nominated student group, one nominated teacher, and any number of times which may be freely chosen. Csima [3] showed that Gotlieb's problem is in **P** if the teachers are initially available at all times, and Even, Itai, and Shamir [4] showed that it is NP-complete if each teacher may be assumed initially unavailable at an arbitrary subset of the times.

More relevant in practice was the work of Karp [7] showing that graph colouring is NP-complete. At that time the connection between graph colouring and timetable construction (revisited below) was already well known [8, 9].

3.1. Intractability Owing to Student Choice

We begin with a well-known result relating timetable construction to graph colouring. It shows NP-completeness when each student is granted a free choice from a wide range of subjects, as is characteristic of university timetable construction.

Theorem 1. GRAPH K-COLOURABILITY $\propto$ TTC.

Proof. Recall that the NP-complete GRAPH K-COLOURABILITY problem asks whether it is possible to assign a colour to each vertex of a graph G in such a way that no two adjacent vertices have the same colour; at most $K \leq |V|$ distinct colours are allowed. Let $G = (V, E)$ with $V = \{v_1, \ldots, v_n\}$ and $E = \{e_1, \ldots, e_m\}$. Construct the TTC instance

> **timegroup T is**
> $t_1; \ldots; t_K;$
> **end T;**
>
> **group R is**
> $r_1; \ldots; r_m;$
> **end R;**
>
> **meeting M_1 is**
> $1\,T;$
> $c_{1,1}; \ldots; c_{1,k_1};$
> **end M_1;**
>
>   ...
>
> **meeting M_n is**
> $1\,T;$
> $c_{n,1}; \ldots; c_{n,k_n};$
> **end M_n;**

where the resources $c_{i,1}, \ldots, c_{i,k_i}$ selected by meeting M_i are exactly those resources r_j such that e_j is adjacent to v_i in G.

Suppose a K-colouring $f : V \rightarrow \{1, \ldots, K\}$ exists for G. Assign t_k where $k = f(v_i)$ to M_i for all i. The condition $f(v_i) \neq f(v_j)$ whenever $\{v_i, v_j\} \in E$ guarantees that meetings which share any resource receive different times, so the TTC instance is solved. Conversely, a successful time assignment defines a successful graph colouring. $\square$

Taking each r_i to represent one student, this transformation shows that assigning times to university classes such that all students can attend their choices is NP-complete even when each meeting occupies only one time, each student chooses just two meetings, and teacher and room constraints are ignored. It also demonstrates that university examination timetable construction is NP-complete.

Universities avoid this problem by publishing the timetable in advance and requiring students to choose only combinations of subjects permitted by the timetable. Large classes are divided into *sections* (alternative offerings of the same subject) which run at different times. Choosing appropriate sections for just one student after times are fixed is NP-complete (Section 3.3), but sections provide sufficient freedom in practice to make solutions fairly easy to find.

In high schools known to the author, student choice is limited by deciding in advance that certain groups of meetings will occur simultaneously, and inviting students to choose one meeting from each group. The decision as to which meetings to group in this way is often influenced by a preliminary survey of student preferences, which of course makes it into an NP-complete graph colouring problem too.

3.2. Intractability Owing to Varying Meeting Size

Meetings occupy more than one time each. A typical pattern in high schools might be six times for English and Mathematics, five for Science, three for Sport, and so on. When meetings of such varying sizes are assigned to teachers, it can be difficult to assign exactly the 30 (say) times that comprise each teacher's workload. Overloading is forbidden by industrial agreement, and underloading one teacher implies overloading another. This leads to NP-completeness even disregarding restrictions imposed by teachers' qualifications and the need to avoid clashes:

Theorem 2. BIN PACKING (with unary encoding) $\propto$ TTC.

Proof. Recall that the NP-complete BIN PACKING problem asks whether a set of items $U = \{u_1, \dots, u_n\}$, each with a positive integer size $s(u_i)$, can be packed into B bins each of capacity C in such a way that no bin is overfull. We assume that these numbers are encoded in unary rather than binary; since BIN PACKING is NP-complete in the strong sense [5], this version is NP-complete. We transform to the TTC instance

timegroup T **is**
   $t_1; \dots; t_C;$
end T;

group R **is**
   $r_1; \dots; r_B;$
end R;

meeting M_1 **is**
   $s(u_1) T$;
   $1 R$;
end M_1;

...

meeting M_n **is**
$s(u_n)\,T$;
$1\,R$;
end M_n;

Given the initial unary encoding, this transformation clearly has polynomial complexity.

Suppose that the BIN PACKING instance has solution $f : U \rightarrow \{1, \dots, B\}$. Assign r_k where $k = f(u_i)$ to meeting M_i for all i; then, for each r_j in R, the total time requirements of all meetings containing resource r_j will be at most C, and we may assign any disjoint sets of times to these meetings. Conversely, from any solution to the TTC instance we may deduce a bin packing by assigning $f(u_i) = k$ where M_i contains r_k. $\quad\Box$

In high schools known to the author, some meetings in the junior years are split into two in the following way in order to create small fragments to fill the bins:

meeting M_i^1 **is**
$(s(u_i) - k)\,T$;
$1\,R$;
end M_i^1;

meeting M_i^2 **is**
$k\,T$;
$1\,R$;
end M_i^2;

for some k, allowing two teachers to share the meeting. This is called a *split assignment*, and it is the major form of compromise permitted in high school timetable construction. Universities are not subject to this problem, because face-to-face workloads are lighter and more flexible.

3.3. Intractability Owing to Time-Incoherence

The bin packing NP-completeness just explained would vanish if all meetings were of equal size, they were aligned in time, and each teacher's workload were a multiple of the meeting size. Meeting sizes and workloads are not under the control of timetable construction programs, but the alignment of meetings in time is. It was called *time-coherence*, and shown to be a powerful heuristic in practice, in [1]; and so the question naturally arises, is it possible to guarantee a time-coherent solution when meeting sizes vary? We now show that the answer is no.

There are several ways to define time-coherence formally. One simple way is to define the time-incoherence $i(M)$ of a set of meetings M to be the number of pairs of meetings from M that share at least one time. We can then define the decision problem TTC-TC to be TTC augmented with the requirement that $i(M)$ not exceed a given bound K. Unfortunately, TTC-TC is NP-complete even when the underlying TTC instance is trivial:

Theorem 3. BIN PACKING (with unary encoding) $\propto$ TTC-TC.

Proof. We remind the reader that the purpose of this theorem is not just to prove the result (we have already done so in Theorem 2) but to construct a TTC instance which establishes an independent source of NP-completeness.

As previously described, the NP-complete BIN PACKING problem asks whether a set of items $U = \{u_1, \ldots, u_n\}$, each with a positive integer size $s(u_i)$, can be packed into B bins each of capacity C so that no bin is overfull. Transform to a TTC-TC instance whose groups are

> **timegroup T is**
> $t_1; \ldots; t_{BC};$
> **end T;**

> **group R is**
> $r;$
> **end R;**

and whose meetings are $X_1, \ldots, X_n$ and $Y_1, \ldots, Y_B$ where the X_i are

> **meeting X_i is**
> $r;$
> $s(u_i)\, T;$
> **end X_i;**

and the Y_j are

> **meeting Y_j is**
> $t_{(j-1)C+1}; \ldots; t_{jC};$
> **end Y_j;**

and the bound on $i(M)$ is $K = n$.

Suppose that the BIN PACKING instance has solution $f : U \to \{1, \ldots, B\}$. For each meeting X_i, choose any $s(u_i)$ times (not already chosen) from the set $S_k = \{t_{(k-1)C+i}, \ldots, t_{kC}\}$ where $k = f(u_i)$. This is possible because f guarantees that at most C times will be chosen from S_k. All requirements are satisfied, and each X_i overlaps with exactly one Y_j, so $i(M) = n$.

Conversely, suppose that the TTC-TC instance has a solution with $i(M) \leq n$. We must have $i(M) \geq n$ since each X_i must overlap at least one Y_j, so $i(M) = n$ and each X_i overlaps exactly one Y_j. Setting $f(u_i) = j$ then defines a bin packing for the u_i. $\square$

Any reasonable definition of time-coherence would permit the same transformation. In practice then, when meeting sizes vary we cannot expect to maintain time-coherence.

This inevitable loss of time-coherence causes severe problems in practice. To illustrate this, we present a transformation which shows that, in the absence of time-coherence, the problem of assigning meetings to just one teacher is NP-complete:

Theorem 4. EXACT COVER BY 3-SETS $\propto$ TTC.

Proof. Recall that the NP-complete EXACT COVER BY 3-SETS problem is as follows. We are given a set $X = \{x_1, \ldots, x_{3q}\}$, and a collection of 3-subsets of X called $C = \{C_1, \ldots, C_n\}$ with $n \geq q$. The problem asks for an exact cover of X, that is, a subcollection $C' \subseteq C$ such that every element of X lies in exactly one element of C'.

Let $C_j = \{c_{j,1}, c_{j,2}, c_{j,3}\}$ for $1 \leq j \leq n$, where each $c_{j,k} = x_i$ for some i such that $1 \leq i \leq 3q$. We transform an instance of EXACT COVER BY 3-SETS to a TTC instance whose groups are

timegroup T is
   $x_1; \ldots; x_{3q};$
end T;

group R is
   $r_1; \ldots; r_{n-q}; z;$
end R;

and whose meetings are $A_1, \ldots, A_{n-q}$ and $B_1, \ldots, B_n$ where the A_i are

meeting A_i is
   $(3q - 3) T;$
   $r_i;$
end A_i;

and the B_j are

meeting B_j is
   $c_{j,1}; c_{j,2}; c_{j,3};$
   $1 R;$
end B_j;

Now suppose X has exact cover C'. Assign z to each B_j such that $C_j \in C'$. This is feasible since no time x_i appears in two elements of C', and it takes care of q of the n meetings B_j. To each of the remaining $n - q$ meetings B_k assign one of the r_j. This leaves r_j free at all times except $c_{k,1}, c_{k,2},$ and $c_{k,3},$ so we may assign the $3q - 3$ times $T - \{c_{k,1}, c_{k,2}, c_{k,3}\}$ to A_j. The converse is similar: in any solution to the TTC instance, z must be assigned to exactly q of the B_j, and these define an exact cover for X. $\square$

The constructed instance amounts to assigning meetings to a resource z (after their times have been fixed) so as to maximize the number of times that z is used. The importance of this was discussed in relation to bin packing (Section 3.2), but now we find that time-incoherence makes the problem NP-complete even when bin packing problems are absent.

3.4. Intractability Owing to Conditions on Times

As explained in Section 2, the choice of a meeting's times is often constrained by requirements for double times, an even spread of times through the week, and so on. The authors have experimented with a method of specifying these time conditions in TTL that is sufficiently general that it permits a transformation from the archetypal NP-complete problem, SATISIFIABILITY, containing exactly one meeting with no resources but with a complex condition on the choice of times. At present, however, we use a simpler method which provides a fixed finite list of allowed time conditions. In any case, in real instances the difficulty arises not from complex time conditions, but rather from the need to satisfy the simple time conditions of several meetings simultaneously. The following transformation establishes this NP-completeness:

Theorem 5. EXACT COVER BY 3-SETS $\propto$ TTC.

Proof. Once again we remind the reader that the purpose is to construct independent NP-complete instances of TTC, not merely to prove the result (which has been done before in Theorem 4). As previously described, the NP-complete EXACT COVER BY 3-SETS problem is as follows. We are given a set $X = \{x_1, \ldots, x_{3q}\}$, and a collection of 3-subsets of X called $C = \{C_1, \ldots, C_n\}$ with $n \geq q$. The problem asks for an exact cover of X, that is, a subcollection $C' \subseteq C$ such that every element of X occurs in exactly one element of C'.

Let each $C_j = \{c_{j,1}, c_{j,2}, c_{j,3}\}$ where each $c_{j,k} = x_i$ for some i. We transform an instance of EXACT COVER BY 3-SETS to a TTC instance whose groups are

> **timegroup T is**
> $\quad x_1; \ldots; x_{3q};$
> **end T;**
>
> **group R is**
> $\quad r;$
> **end R;**

and whose meetings are $M_1, \ldots, M_q$ where each M_j is

> **meeting M_j is**
> $\quad 3\,T;$
> $\quad r;$
> **end M_j;**

In addition, we impose on each M_j the time condition that the three times chosen must be $\{c_{k,1}, c_{k,2}, c_{k,3}\}$ for some k such that $1 \leq k \leq n$.

First suppose that the initial instance of EXACT COVER BY 3-SETS has a solution $C' = \{C_1', \ldots, C_q'\}$. C' must have exactly q elements. For all j, assign the times of C_j' to meeting M_j. The collection of all these sets of times is pairwise disjoint, as required by the presence of r in each meeting, and each meeting's times satisfy the time condition.

Conversely, any solution to the TTC instance defines a collection of disjoint sets of times, each of which satisfies the time condition, and from this we obtain a solution to the EXACT COVER BY 3-SETS instance. □

The TTL instance constructed here has small meetings, all with the same time condition, which is a simple list of alternative time patterns as often occurs, for example, in university timetabling. This is good evidence of intractability in practice.

Nevertheless there are special cases which can be solved efficiently. If the C_j are pairwise disjoint the problem is obviously trivial. More generally, EXACT COVER BY 3-SETS is solvable in polynomial time if each x_i appears in at most two of the C_j [5].

We can identify a second easy special case based on the concept of a *simple time selection*, which we define as a time selection with a time condition requiring only that the times be chosen from a given arbitrary subset of the set of all times. The problem of assigning times to any number of time-disjoint meetings, each containing any number of simple time selections, can be solved by bipartite matching in a graph whose edges connect nodes representing time slots to nodes representing times.

Based on these two special cases and the observation that heuristic methods usually succeed on this problem, it seems likely that a restricted version exists which encompasses most of the cases encountered in practice, and which is solvable in polynomial time for sets of time-disjoint meetings. Heuristics are certainly adequate if occasional violations of the conditions are acceptable.

Incidentally, we can reinterpret the assignment of times $\{c_{k,1}, c_{k,2}, c_{k,3}\}$ to meeting M_j as the assignment of student r to section k of meeting M_j. This shows that the assignment of sections of university courses to even a single student (as discussed in Section 3.1) is NP-complete.

3.5. Intractability of Assigning Two Forms Simultaneously

One useful line of attack is to discover large subproblems that can be solved efficiently. One such is the matching subproblem introduced by de Werra [10] and generalized to 'meta-matching' by Cooper and Kingston [1], which assigns times to all the meetings of one *form* (all meetings having a nominated student group in common) simultaneously, in such a way that the demand for the various types of teachers and rooms does not exceed their supply at any time.

The question naturally arises as to whether it is possible to assign suitable times to two forms simultaneously in polynomial time. In the following proof of NP-completeness, $MX_1, \ldots, MX_q$ stand for the meetings assigned previously, and $MY_1, \ldots, MY_q$ and $MZ_1, \ldots, MZ_q$ for the meetings of the two forms to which we wish to assign times.

Theorem 6. THREE DIMENSIONAL MATCHING $\propto$ TTC.

Proof: Recall that in the NP-complete THREE DIMENSIONAL MATCHING problem we are given three sets X, Y, and Z, each containing q elements, and a set $M \subseteq X \times Y \times Z$. The problem is to determine whether M contains a matching, that is, a subset $M' \subseteq M$ such that $|M'| = q$ and every element of X, Y, and Z occurs exactly once in M'. We transform this to a TTC instance whose groups are

timegroup T **is**
  $t_1; \ldots; t_q;$
end $T;$

group R **is**
  $r_X; r_Y; r_Z;$
end $R;$

and whose meetings are $MX_1, \ldots , MX_q, MY_1, \ldots , MY_q,$ and $MZ_1, \ldots , MZ_q.$ These meetings all have the same form, typified by

meeting MX_i **is**
  $1\ T;$
  $r_X;$
end $MX_i;$

where the MX_i select r_X, the MY_i select r_Y, and the MZ_i select r_Z.

But now, for each triple $m_j = (x_a, y_b, z_c)$ in $\overline{M}$, the complement of M in $X \times Y \times Z$, we create two new resources α_j and β_j and a resource subgroup R_j whose members are α_j and β_j, and we add the selection $1\ R_j$ to MX_a, MY_b, and MZ_c. This completes the transformation.

Suppose first that M contains a matching M'. For each triple $m_k' = (x_a, y_b, z_c)$ in M', where $1 \leq k \leq q$, assign time t_k to MX_a, MY_b, and MZ_c. Since M' contains each x_i exactly once, each MX_i is assigned exactly one time, and these times are distinct, as required by the presence of r_X in each one. Similar remarks apply to the MY_i and the MZ_i.

It remains to check that all the $1R_j$ selections are satisfied. Since R_j has two elements, the only possible violation would be if all three meetings MX_a, MY_b, and MZ_c scheduled for time t_k contained $1\ R_j$ for some particular j. But by construction this would imply ($x_a, y_b, z_c) \in \overline{M}$, contradicting $(x_a, y_b, z_c) \in M'$.

Conversely, if the TTC instance has a solution, the presence of r_X ensures that the MX_i are assigned different times, and similarly for the MY_i and the MZ_i. It follows that the solution can be expressed as a set of q triples (MX_a, MY_b, MZ_c) of meetings that occur simultaneously. By replacing each meeting by the corresponding element of X, Y, or Z, we arrive at a matching $S \subseteq X \times Y \times Z$. Since $MX_a, MY_b,$ and MZ_c occur simultaneously, they cannot all contain the selection $1\ R_j$ for any particular j, so by construction the corresponding (x_a, y_b, z_c) cannot be an element of $\overline{M}$. Hence $S \subseteq M$. $\square$

The complexity of the set $\overline{M}$ is easily achievable in real instances, owing to 'elective' meetings which select a number of teachers and rooms of arbitrary types. This would seem to rule out all hope of assigning two forms simultaneously.

4. Conclusion

This paper has demonstrated that the timetable construction problem is NP-complete in five quite independent ways. The instances constructed in our transformations are such as actually occur in practice. This is important, because it ensures that the intractability is real, not merely an artifact of the method of specification. Where known we have indicated special cases and compromises which may be used to work around the problems.

Against these negative results we can set the limited size of timetable construction instances. High schools with more than 100 teachers are rare; a week of more than 40 times is also rare. University problems are larger but seem to be easier. As ingenuity and computing power increase, timetable construction will become feasible in practice.

References

[1] Tim B. Cooper and Jeffrey H. Kingston. The solution of real instances of the timetabling problem. *The Computer Journal* **36**, 645–653 (1993).

[2] Tim B. Cooper and Jeffrey H. Kingston. A program for constructing high school timetables. In *First International Conference on the Practice and Theory of Automated Timetabling*. Napier University, Edinburgh, UK, 1995. Also URL ftp://ftp.cs.su.oz.au/pub/tr/TR95_496.ps.Z.

[3] J. Csima. *Investigations on a Time-Table Problem*. Ph.D. thesis, School of Graduate Studies, University of Toronto, 1965.

[4] S. Even, A. Itai, and A. Shamir. On the complexity of timetable and multicommodity flow problems. *SIAM Journal on Computing* **5**, 691–703 (1976).

[5] M. R. Garey and D. S. Johnson. *Computers and Intractability: A Guide to the Theory of NP-Completeness*. Freeman, 1979.

[6] C. C. Gotlieb. The construction of class-teacher timetables. In *Proc. IFIP Congress*, pages 73–77, 1962.

[7] R. M. Karp. Reducibility among combinatorial problems. In R. E. Miller and J. W. Thatcher (eds.), *Complexity of Computer Computations*, pages 85–103. Plenum Press, New York, 1972.

[8] G. Schmidt and T. Ströhlein. Timetable construction—an annotated bibliography. *The Computer Journal* **23**, 307–316 (1980).

[9] D. J. A. Welsh and M. B. Powell. An upper bound for the chromatic number of a graph and its application to timetabling problems. *The Computer Journal* **10**, 85–86 (1967).

[10] D. de Werra. Construction of school timetables by flow methods. *INFOR – Canadian Journal of Operations Research and Information Processing* **9**, 12–22 (1971).

Some Combinatorial Models for Course Scheduling

D. de Werra

Ecole Polytechnique Fédérale de Lausanne
Département de Mathématiques, CH-1015 Lausanne, Switzerland

tel: +41.21.693.2562, fax: +41.21.693.4250
e.mail: dewerra@dma.epfl.ch

Keywords: Graph coloring, timetabling, tabu search, preassignments, compactness, hypergraph, chromatic scheduling.

Abstract

Timetabling problems have often been formulated as coloring problems in graphs. We give formulations in terms of graph coloring (or hypergraph coloring) for a collection of simple class-teacher timetabling problems and review complexity issues for these formulations. This tutorial presentation concludes with some hints on some general procedures which handles many specific requirements.

1. Introduction

Course scheduling problems provide an excellent example of real problem for which O.R. methods were considered as the most natural techniques to use. Occurring by their nature in an academic world, these problems have expectedly been tackled by a huge variety of tools depending on the particular interests and fields of competence of the potential solvers. Our purpose is not to give a general survey of the various models which have been proposed but rather to focus our attention on combinatorial models and at the same time to show how extensions of classical models have been worked out to formalize and solve some type of timetabling problems. We will also present whenever it will be possible the limits between easy and difficult problems.

Timetabling problems are numerous: they differ from each other not only by the types of constraints which are to be taken into account, but also by the density (or the scarcity) of the constraints; two problems of the same "size", with the same types of constraints may be very different from each other if one has many tight constraints and the other has just a few. The solution methods may be quite different, so the problems should be considered as different.

Here we shall start from the simplest problems and introduce requirements consecutively while discussing the variations of the corresponding combinatorial models. Since they are more structured, we shall put the emphasis on class-teacher timetabling.

In fact, we shall essentially deal with timetabling problems as chromatic scheduling problems, i.e., we will concentrate on graph coloring models. After having presented node coloring in graphs or hypergraphs and edge coloring in graphs, we will very briefly mention some general approaches which may handle many types of requirements.

To keep the paper within a reasonable length, we shall not give standard definitions of graphs, they can be found in [1]. Similarly for concepts related to complexity, the reader is referred to [5].

2. The basic model: class-teacher timetabling problem

We shall start with the simplest situation which occurs in timetabling, the so called class-teacher timetabling problem. A class c_i will consist of a set of students who follow exactly the same programme. $\mathscr{C}=\{c_1,...,c_m\}$ will be the set of classes while $\mathscr{T}=\{t_1,...,t_n\}$ is the set of teachers. A requirement matrix $R=(r_{ij})$ gives the number r_{ij} of (one-hour) lectures involving c_i and t_j for all i,j.

The problem consists in constructing (when possible) a timetable in p periods. Each class (resp. teacher) is involved in at most one lecture at a time.

It is well known that a solution exists if and only if
$$\textstyle\sum_i r_{ij} \leq p \text{ for all } j \text{ and } \sum_j r_{ij} \leq p \text{ for all } i \text{ (see [14]).}$$

The problem may be viewed as constructing a generalized Latin square (GLS); a (pxp) Latin square (LS) is an array in which each cell (i,j) contains one of the p symbols $\alpha,\beta,...,\varphi$ and no symbol appears more than once in any line (row or column). If each symbol is associated with a period, we may consider that the LS corresponds to a requirement matrix R where $r_{ij}=1$ for each class c_i and each teacher t_j: cell (i,j) contains δ if c_i and t_j meet at period δ. Given an arbitrary R, a timetable corresponds to a GLS: cell (i,j) contains r_{ij} symbols in $\{\alpha,\beta,...,\varphi\}$; they are the periods where the meetings of c_i and t_j are scheduled; each symbol occurs at most once in each row and in each column. (Notice that a GLS need in fact not be square !) Figure 1 shows a requirement matrix R, an associated GLS and an extended GLS which is square and contains the initial one. It is always possible to transform a rectangle GLS into a larger square GLS which contains the first one, as can be seen easily.

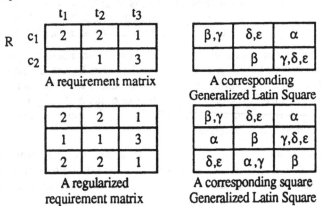

Fig. 1. Generalized Latin Squares

Another formulation would be to associate to R a hypergraph $H(R) = (X,\mathscr{E})$ constructed as follows: each unit in R is a node x in the node set X; for each line (row or column) of R we introduce an edge containing all nodes associated to units in this line. An example is given in Figure 2.

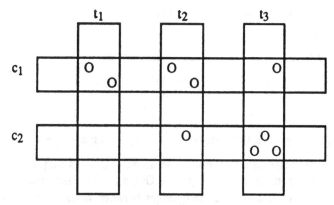

Fig. 2. The Hypergraph H(R) associated to the requirement matric R of Fig. 1

A timetable in p periods is a node p-coloring of H: each node gets one of the p colors in $\{\alpha,\beta,...,\varphi\}$ in such a way that no two nodes in the same edge get the same color.

We may at this stage consider with the same data R another problem which may be called the weekly problem (WP): instead of assigning the lectures at periods (of one day) as before, we may simply assign them to days: a_i (resp. b_j) will be the maximum number of meetings for c_i (resp. t_j) in each day; K_{ij} is the maximum number of meetings c_i-t_j in each day.

A weekly schedule in p days will be associated with a generalized node p-coloring of H(R): in each edge c_i (resp. t_j) there must be at most a_i (resp. b_j) nodes of the same color and in each intersection $c_i \cap t_j$ there will be at most K_{ij} nodes of the same color; this last requirement amounts to introduce new edges $c_i \cap t_j$ in H for each pair c_i,t_j with $c_i \cap t_j \neq \emptyset$.

An example of weekly schedule is given in Figure 3.

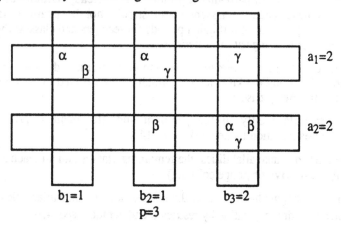

Fig. 3. A weekley schedule in p=3 days for the example of Fig. 1

It is well known that the following holds [13,14].

Proposition 2.1:

A weekly timetable in p days exists if and only if

a) $\sum_j r_{ij} \leq p \, a_i$ for each c_i

b) $\sum_i r_{ij} \leq p \, b_j$ for each t_j

c) $r_{ij} \leq p \, K_{ij}$ for each c_i and each t_j

Observe that we get back to the daily problem by setting $a_i = b_j = 1$; $K_{ij} = \infty$ for all i,j.

Finally it is also easy to observe that the above problems may be viewed as edge coloring problems in bipartite multigraphs $G=(\mathscr{C}, \mathfrak{T}, E)$ associated to R: each c_i is a node, each t_j is a node and there are r_{ij} edges between nodes c_i and t_j for all i,j. The daily problem is a classical edge p-coloring problem in G which can be solved in polynomial time [14]. The weekly problem is a generalized edge p-coloring problem and is also easy to solve. Related results with a combinatorial flavour are given in [11].

In the next sections we shall review some additional requirements which make the problem more realistic and more difficult.

3. Preassignments and unavailabilities

In almost all real timetabling problems we have to take into account so called unavailability constraints. These can be formulated as follows in a class-teacher timetable:

Teacher t_j is available only at a subset T_j of the p periods for each j and similarly class c_i is available for meetings only at a subset C_i of the p periods. Sometimes also meetings c_i-t_j may be scheduled only in a subset M_{ij} of the p periods.

Such requirements occur in particular if a timetable is already partially constructed: some meetings have been preassigned and should not be changed later. The consequence is the presence of forbidden periods for teachers and classes: they cannot be involved in other meetings at these periods.

As can be expected these requirements make the problem more difficult; it is indeed NP-complete [4]. Among the known cases which may be solved in polynomial time we mention the following cases:

a) there is one class only in the problem and all teachers have arbitrary unavailabilities (solution by network flow [14])

b) only one class has unavailabilities, the remaining classes and all teachers have no unavailabilities (trivial by edge coloring)

c) for each teacher t_j we have $|T_j| \leq 2$; the classes have no unavailabilities (solution of a boolean quadratic equation by restricted enumeration, see [4,14]).

We shall now mention another situation which gives rise to a problem which may be solved easily; observe first that when taking into account all the unavailabilities of teachers and classes we may simply consider that for each meeting e represented by an edge of the bipartite multigraph G=($\mathscr{C}$,$\mathfrak{T}$,E) there is a set φ(e) of feasible periods; let (G,φ) be the resulting problem. We can now state (see [17])

Proposition 3.1:

For the class-teacher timetabling problem (G,φ) with unavailabilities, we have the following:

if G is a tree, there exists either a timetable or a proof of nonexistence.

We sketch the solution procedure on the example given in Figure 4. We start by considering a star formed with pendent edges, for instance ab, ac, ad. Edge a$\bar{\text{e}}$ can have color 1 or color 2; we consider all these cases and try to color ab, ac, ad with feasible colors; in each case it is a maximum matching problem in a bipartite graph. We observe that the only possible color for a$\bar{\text{e}}$ is 1.

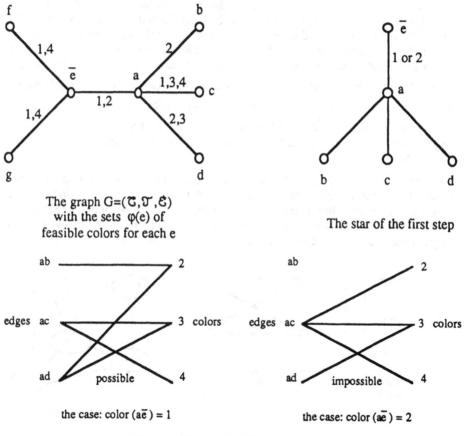

The graph G=($\mathfrak{T}$,$\mathfrak{T}$,$\mathscr{E}$)
with the sets φ(e) of
feasible colors for each e

The star of the first step

the case: color (a$\bar{\text{e}}$) = 1

the case: color (a$\bar{\text{e}}$) = 2

Fig. 4. Unavailability constraints

We go up the tree and consider the star formed with edges $\bar{\text{e}}$f,$\bar{\text{e}}$a,$\bar{\text{e}}$g (see Figure 5) (if $\bar{\text{e}}$f and $\bar{\text{e}}$g would not be pendent, we would have had to deal with the corresponding subtrees first).

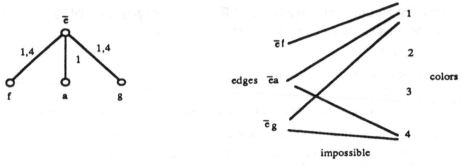

No timetable exists

Fig. 5. Unavailability constraints (continued)

Then we notice from the associated edge-color graph that no assignment can be found for this star. Since the whole of G has now been considered, there is no solution. The proof of non existence of a timetable follows from a simple argument: a set Γ of pairs (v,c) (where v is a node and c a color) can be found together with a collection $E(\Gamma)$ of edges $[v,w]$ such that for each $c \in \varphi$ $([v,w])$ at least one of (v,c), (w,c) is in Γ; furthermore $|\Gamma| < |E(\Gamma)|$ (see [17]). Here $\Gamma=\{(\bar{e},1), (\bar{e},4), (a,2)\}$ and $E(\Gamma) = \{\bar{e}f, \bar{e}a, \bar{e}g, ab\}$. Consider for example edge $\bar{e}f$. Coloring $\bar{e}f$ with a feasible color will set color 1 around node $\bar{e}$ (i.e. it will give $(\bar{e},1)$) or color 4 around $\bar{e}$ (it will give $(\bar{e},4)$). No two edges in $E(\Gamma)$ should give the same (v,c) in Γ. So we see that since $|\Gamma| = 3 < |E(\Gamma)| = 4$, no coloring exists.

Another way of dealing with unavailabilities is to consider a node coloring formulation for the problem: as in the hypergraph formulation, each meeting is a node of a graph G' and we link two nodes if the meetings cannot be simultaneous (i.e., if they involve the same class or the same teacher). In other words we link two nodes if they belong to a same edge of the hypergraph. An example is given in Figure 6.

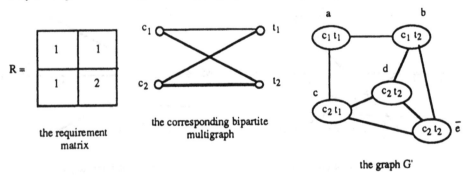

the requirement matrix

the corresponding bipartite multigraph

the graph G'

Fig. 6. Formulation in terms of node coloring in a graph G'

It is also known that there exists a node p-coloring of $G'=(X,E)$ if and only if there exists an independent set of $|X|$ nodes in a graph G^* obtained from G' by taking p copies $G^1,...,G^p$ of G' (each G^c has a node (v,c) for each v of G') and linking all nodes (v,c), (v,d) associated to the same v for each v and for all pairs c,d. An illustration is given in Figure 7 for the graph G' of Figure 5 with p=3.

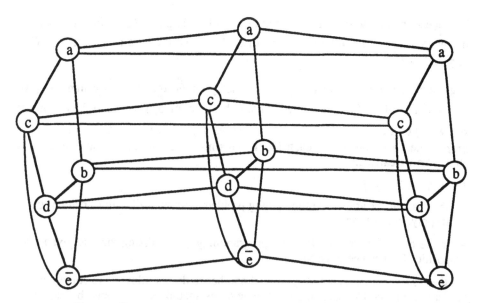

Fig. 7. The graph G* associated to G' in Fig. 6 with p=3

If (v,c) is in an independent set of G*, it may be interpreted by saying that node v gets color c. So if we have now for each node v a set $\varphi(v)$ of feasible colors, we remove from G* all nodes (v,c) such that $c \notin \varphi(v)$. Let $\tilde{G}$ be the remaining graph. So a node p-coloring exists for (G',φ) (the node coloring problem in G' with sets $\varphi(v)$ of feasible colors for each node v) if and only if an independent set of |X| nodes exists in $\tilde{G}$. An illustration of $\tilde{G}$ is given in Figure 8: thick nodes correspond to the independent set of |X|=5 nodes: a and d get color 1, b and c color 2 while $\bar{e}$ gets color 3.

$\varphi(a) = \{1,2,3\}$

$\varphi(b) = \{2,3\}$

$\varphi(c) = \{2,3\}$

$\varphi(d) = \{1,2\}$

$\varphi(\bar{e}) = \{1,3\}$

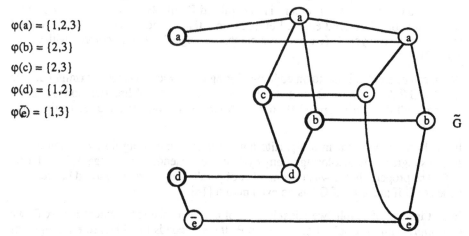

Fig. 8. The graph $\tilde{G}$ corresponding to the graph G' in Fig. 6
with sets γ of feasible colors for the nodes

The question is now to examine when one can find in polynomial time a maximum independent set in a graph of the form of $\tilde{G}$. It will be the case in particular if $\tilde{G}$ is *perfect* (see [1]).

A graph G is *perfect* if for every induced subgraph $\hat{G}$, the chromatic number $\chi(\hat{G})$ (minimum number of colors needed to color the nodes of $\hat{G}$) is equal to the maximum size $w(\hat{G})$ of a clique in $\hat{G}$. Here G* (and hence $\tilde{G}$) will be perfect if G' is a *block graph* , i.e., a graph where each block (maximal two-connected component) is a clique. So we can state:

Proposition 3.2: [8]

If G' is a block graph, the timetabling problem with unavailabilities can be solved in polynomial time.

A simple method based on dynamic programming (generalizing the one given after Proposition 3.1) can be devised.

All these solvable cases are very special and hence do not allow us to solve most of the real problems. However more solvable cases should be discovered by exploring other avenues.

One should at this stage mention some partial results about special unavailability requirements, i.e., the preassignment constraints.

It is known that the class-teacher timetabling problem with preassignments is NP-complete even if the number p of periods is 3 [4].

The problem may be formulated in terms of edge coloring (in a bipartite multigraph): given some precolored edges in G, can one extend the precoloring to an edge p-coloring of G ?

As mentioned above this problem is generally difficult. However we may consider special sets of precolored edges. Let us assume that the edges which are precolored form a bicolored cycle C (we may assume that its edges have been colored with colors 1 and 2).

When can one extend this to an edge p-coloring of G where p is the maximum degree $\Delta(G)$ of G ? A *mouth* in G consists of three chains which all link two nodes x and y and have all distinct intermediate nodes. A *mouth* is *even* if the three chains have even length.

It has been shown that in a bipartite multigraph G containing no even mouth as a partial subgraph the bicoloring of any cycle can be extended to an edge $\Delta(G)$-coloring of G. The property holds whatever number of parallel edges are introduced between the nodes of G if and only if G has no even mouth [16].

In fact instead of graphs we consider sets of entries in the requirement matrix R; we call *configuration* a subset of entries in R; it corresponds to all bipartite multigraphs obtained by inserting any number of parallel edges in the chosen cells. So we may ask what are the configurations in R such that any preassignment (in the form of a bicolored cycle) can be extended to a complete timetable in p periods (where p is the maximum degree $\Delta(G)$ of G i.e. the maximum line sum in R, where a line designates a row or a column of R).

Proposition 3.3: [16]

A configuration in R has the property that any cyclic preassignment can be extended to a complete timetable in p periods if and only if the corresponding graph contains no even mouth as a partial subgraph.

In the next section we shall briefly discuss another type of requirement where partial results are also formulated in terms of configurations.

4. Compactness

Quite often classes and teachers prefer to have so called *compact* timetables: they prefer to have their meetings grouped together as much as possible.

Consider the schedule of a teacher (or a class) in p periods; at each period the teacher is either active (i.e. involved in a meeting) or inactive (there is an idle period). A *block* is a maximal sequence of active (or of inactive) periods in the timetable of a teacher (or of a class).

An individual timetable (of a teacher or of a class) will be called *compact* if it consists of at most three blocks. A timetable with one block occurs when the class (or the teacher) is always active (A) or always inactive (I).

Observe that a timetable with AIA is by definition compact; in such a case we consider that the timetable is repeated day after day (or week after week), so the set $\{1,...,p\}$ of periods may be considered as a cyclically ordered set and the timetable now may really look compact in the sense that the active periods are cyclically consecutive. We may observe that timetables which are compact for all classes and all teachers may not always exist. Figure 9 shows a case where no compact timetable exists (edge coloring in G where at each node v the edges adjacent to v have colors which are cyclically consecutive): without loss of generality we may assume that c_2 meets t_i at period i (i=1,2,3). For compactness reasons color 7 can only be given to an edge $[c_1,t_1]$ and the same holds for color 6 to some edge $[c_1,t_3]$. This forces colors 8,9 for the remaining two edges $[c_1,t_1]$ and colors 4,5 for the remaining two edges $[c_1,t_3]$.

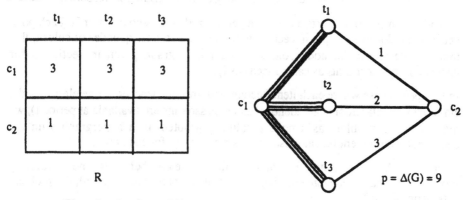

	t_1	t_2	t_3
c_1	3	3	3
c_2	1	1	1

R

$p = \Delta(G) = 9$

Fig. 9. A timetabling problem without compact solution

So we have colors 1,2,3 for the three edges $[c_1,t_2]$ and this is impossible.

This means that the configuration consisting of the six entries of R does not have the property that it has a compact timetable in p periods whatever positive values r_{ij} are given to the entries (where $p=\Delta(G)$ is the maximum line sum in R). Along this line we may state:

Proposition 4.1: [12]

For a configuration in R there exists a compact timetable in p periods whatever values r_{ij} are given to the entries chosen (where p is the maximum line sum in R) if and only if the associated bipartite graph has no mouth as a partial subgraph.

The graphs in the above proposition are precisely the bipartite outerplanar graphs; they can be recognized and their edges can be "compactly" colored in polynomial time (see [12]).

5. Chromatic scheduling

Timetabling problems may be regarded as special cases of chromatic scheduling problems; these are scheduling problems where graph coloring models may provide solutions.

In general we have a collection of items K_i (lectures) to be scheduled. A set $\mathcal{R}$ of (renewable) resources $R_1,R_2,...,R_u$ are given together with the amount r_{it} of resource R_i available during period t.

For each item K_i we are given the subset $\mathcal{K}_i \subseteq \mathcal{R}$ of resources which are needed (we assume that one unit of each one of the resources in $\mathcal{K}_i$ is needed to process K_i). All these items K_i have a unit processing time.

An item (lecture) K_i may be scheduled at period t if at least one unit of each resource in $\mathcal{K}_i$ is available (and not used by other items at the same time).

As an example each teacher v and each class w is a resource; we have $r_{vt} \le 1$, $r_{wt} \le 1$ for each t. Classrooms (or classroom types) may also be resources. A model of hypergraph H may be constructed as follows: each item (lecture) is a node; for each resource R_i we introduce an edge R_i containing all nodes using this resource.

A schedule in p periods corresponds to a generalized node p-coloring of H. Each node gets some color in $\{1,...,p\}$; in each edge R_i there are at most r_{it} nodes of color t; this model generalizes the node coloring model in a graph given in section 3 for unavailability constraints as can be seen easily.

In the special case where each item (lecture) requires one teacher t_j, one class c_i and a classroom (all classrooms are identical and r_t classrooms are available at period t), we may view the problem as a node p-coloring problem in a hypergraph with the additional requirement that at most r_t nodes have color t for each $t \le p$.

In spite of the special structure of H (which makes as before the node coloring problem identical to an edge coloring problem in a bipartite multigraph), the problem is NP-complete [2].

A polynomially solvable case is obtained when the values $r_1,...,r_p$ (ordered in such a way that $r_1 \geq r_2 \geq ... \geq r_p$) satisfy for some u $(2 \leq u \leq p)$

$$r_1 - r_u \leq 1, r_{u+1} - r_p \leq 1.$$

Other solvable cases are discussed in [2].

Another related situation is when in a class-teacher timetabling problem classrooms have to be rented. We are given a cost k_t for each classroom used in period t. The problem is to find a timetable (i.e. an edge p-coloring $(M_1,...,M_p)$ where each M_i is a matching in the bipartite multigraph G=($\mathscr{C}$,$\mathfrak{T}$,E)) such that its cost $\sum_{t=1}^{P} k_t |M_t|$ is minimum.

This problem is NP-complete in general even if p=3; however we can state

Proposition 5.1: [18]

If G=($\mathscr{C}$,$\mathfrak{T}$,E) is a tree, one can find in polynomial time a timetable (corresponding to an edge p-coloring $(M_1,...,M_p)$ with minimum cost $\sum_{t=1}^{P} k_t |M_t|$.

The method consists in solving a sequence of assignment problems in a dynamic programming framework.

Again in this case, many more nontrivial solvable cases should be discovered; at this stage, all solvable cases are still far from covering a huge subdomain of the main timetabling problems occurring in practice.

The search for more solvable cases is however encouraged first because this may give ideas of original methods for approaching - most likely in a heuristic way - the variety of problems which are present in real schools. Other reasons will be given later.

As a conclusion, we shall briefly mention general procedures which have been successful in tackling many types of combinatorial optimization problems.

6. Conclusions

In this paper we have concentrated on various basic combinatorial models occurring in timetabling. In some cases we have shown that they were easily solvable and we have noticed that many such problems are NP-complete.

Most practical problems are thus theoretically difficult; various approaches have been suggested in the literature, ranging from Tabu Search (see [3,6,7,10]) to Simulated Annealing [19], to Evolutionary Algorithms [21] and to Artificial Intelligence [22]. Other approaches start from integer programming formulations and by trying to use the structure of the problem in the solution technique they get close to some of the combinatorial problems discussed or to some others like the classical set covering. More references for the special case of examination scheduling can be found in [20].

So most of these general approaches are iterative procedures involving local search techniques or not. At each step of these algorithms we are facing some combinatorial problems which may be handled by some of the methods presented here.

Presently the most promising techniques seem to be interactive: using the experience of the specialist in timetabling and the power of general local search procedures with additional ingredients (like evolutionary methods) is likely to provide solutions which will be acceptable for the user.

We did not intend to present a general survey of the many approaches to be found in the vast literature of timetabling, but rather to stimulate non specialists to look at new combinatorial problems occurring in timetabling in order to discover new solvable cases.

7. References

[1]   C. Berge, Graphes, Gauthier-Villars, Paris (1983)

[2]   J. Blazewicz, D. de Werra, Some preemptive open shop scheduling problems with a renewable or a non renewable resource, Discrete Applied Mathematics 35 (1992) 205-219

[3]   D. Costa, A Tabu Search Algorithm for Computing an Operational Timetable, European Journal of Operational Research 76 (1994) 98-110

[4]   S. Even, A. Itai, A. Shamir, On the complexity of timetable and multicommodity flow problems, SIAM Journal on Computing 5 (1976) 691-703

[5]   M.R. Garey, D.S. Johnson, Computers and Intractability: a Guide to the Theory of NP-Completeness (Freeman, New York, 1979)

[6]   F. Glover, Tabu Search, Part I, ORSA Journal on Computing 1 (1989) 190-206

[7]   F. Glover, Tabu Search, Part II, ORSA Journal on Computing 2 (1990) 4-32

[8]   H. Gröflin, Feasible Graph Coloring and a Generalization of Perfect Graphs, IAOR Report 199 (1992) University of Fribourg

[9]   A. Hertz, V. Robert, Constructing a course schedule by solving a series of assignment type problems, ORWP 94/10, EPFL, November 1994

[10]   A. Hertz, Tabu Search for Large Scale Timetabling Problems, European Journal of Operational Research (1991) 39-47

[11]   A.J.W. Hilton, School Timetables, Annals of Discrete Mathematics 11 (1981) 177-188

[12]   N.V.R. Mahadev, Ph. Solot, D. de Werra, The cyclic compact open-shop scheduling problem, Discrete Mathematics 111 (1993) 361-366

[13]   D. de Werra, Graphs, Hypergraphs and Timetabling, Methods of Operations Research 49 (1985) 201-213

[14]   D. de Werra, An introduction to timetabling, European Journal of Operational Research 19 (1985) 151-162

[15]   D. de Werra, A. Hertz, Tabu Search Techniques: A tutorial and an application to neural networks, OR Spektrum 11 (1989) 131-141

[16] D. de Werra, N.V.R. Mahadev, U.N. Peled, Edge chromatic scheduling with simultaneity constraints, SIAM Journal on Discrete Mathematics 6 (1993) 631-641

[17] D. de Werra, A.J. Hoffman, N.V.R. Mahadev, U.N. Peled, Restrictions and Preassignments in preemptive open shop scheduling (to appear in Discrete Applied Mathematics)

[18] D. de Werra, N.V.R. Mahadev, Preassignment requirements in chromatic scheduling, ORWP 95/02, EPFL, February 1995 (submitted for publication)

8. Additional References

[19] D. Abramson, Constructing school timetables using simulated annealing: sequential and parallel algorithms, Management Science 37 (1991) 98-113

[20] M.W. Carter, G. Laporte, Recent Developments in Practical Examination Timetabling (in this volume)

[21] B. Paechter, A. Cumming, H. Luchian, M. Petriuc, Two Solutions to the General Timetable Problem Using Evolutionary Methods, Proceedings of the IEEE Conference of Evolutionay Computation, 1994

[22] M. Yoshikawa, K. Kaneko, Y. Nomura, M. Watanabe, A constraint-based approach to high-school timetabling problems: a case study, Proceedings of the 12th National Conference on Artificial Intelligence (AAAI-94) 1111-1116

The Phase-Transition Niche for Evolutionary Algorithms in Timetabling

Peter Ross[1], David Corne[2] and Hugo Terashima-Marín[3]

[1] Department of Artificial Intelligence, University of Edinburgh,
80 South Bridge, Edinburgh EH1 1HN, UK, Email: peter@aisb.ed.ac.uk
[2] Parallel Emergent & Distributed Architectures Laboratory,
Department of Computer Science, University of Reading, Reading RG6 6AY, UK
Email: D.W.Corne@reading.ac.uk
[3] Centre for Artificial Intelligence, ITESM, Monterrey, Mexico
Email: terashim@cia.mty.itesm.mx

Abstract. Constraint satisfaction problems tend to display phase transitions with respect to the effort required by specific problem solving strategies. So far, little is known concerning the causes of phase transitions, or the relative differences between performance of different algorithms around them, especially with respect to stochastic iterative methods such as evolutionary search. Also, work so far on phase transitions concentrates on homogeneous random problems, rather than problems displaying elements of structure typical of more realistic problems. We investigate some of these issues, and uncover some new phase transition regions on timetabling style problems, occurring in the context of varying degrees of problem homogenity as well as (the more standard) graph connectivity. Further, we find that a simple evolutionary algorithm outperforms a simple Stochastic Hillclimber in regions strongly associated with certain phase transitions, and not others. Finally, we discuss various clues to the underlying causes of these phase transitions.

1 Introduction

Constraint satisfaction problems tend to display phase transitions with respect to the effort required by specific problem solving strategies. For example, Prosser [8] and Smith [10] describe phase transition behaviour in binary constraint satisfaction problems (CSPs). Both Prosser and Smith tested the performance of a range of complete heuristic search algorithms on binary CSPs of varying tightness and density. Both found relatively small regions in the tightness/density parameter space where it grew sharply difficult for the algorithm used either to find a solution where one existed or to prove that no solution existed. Smith [10] coined the term 'mushy region' to describe the region of problem space where a given algorithm's performance deteriorates in this manner.

This kind of behaviour can also be shown to happen in the case of stochastic search algorithms applied to timetabling problems. For these kinds of technique, such as stochastic hillclimbing (SH) or evolutionary algorithms (EAs), the algorithm itself has no way of proving reliably that no solution exists; performance can only be discussed in terms of the empirically determined likelihood of finding a solution and this sort of measure is only useful if it is certain that at least one solution exists. Therefore in what follows only solvable problems are considered.

For example the performance of SH on solvable timetabling-style problems can be characterised in terms of the likelihood of SH finding a solution as the *allowed constraint density* of the problem is varied from 0% to 100%; allowed constraint density refers to the proportion of constraints used from a given maximally-constrained problem, so that 100 % density refers to the point beyond which the addition of more constraints would render the problem unsolvable. Experiments reported below demonstrate the general existence of a phase-transition region in which it becomes sharply more difficult for SH to find optima at certain intermediate levels of density, returning quickly to easier performance as constraint density increases beyond this point.

It might be argued that randomly-created problems are unrealistic in some way. An aspect of this concerns the typical homogeneity of a randomly generated problem. In contrast, real timetabling problems tend to be 'clumped' in the sense shown in figure 1. Following a standard convention in which vertices in a graph represent events, and edges joining two vertices indicate that those two events must not overlap in time, then the simple graph on the left of figure 1 represents a fairly homogeneous problem. There is no sense in which the events fall into distinct groups. The graph on the right, however, has the same number of edges, but falls into two distinct subgraphs, or clumps. There is no edge joining any two vertices in different clumps. Between these two extremes can be imagined varying degrees of homogenity, in which there are distinct clumps, but a relatively small number of edges exist between them. Real timetabling problems are typically rather more clumped than homogeneous. For example, exams within an arts faculty may typically form a distinct clump, largely separate from those within a science faculty. Later on, we begin to examine the effects of such varying homogeneity in relation to problem difficulty.

On many real and realistic timetabling problems, it is clear that SH generally performs better than previously reported evolutionary algorithm (EA) approaches. This is the case with regard to those addressed in papers by Abramson & Abela [1] and by Corne et al [5]. Other studies have also shown that simple hillclimbing strategies can outperform EAs on various instances of other sorts of problem [7, 6]. However, further study suggests that there are areas in timetabling problem space where this situation is reversed. By looking at a space of timetabling problems which vary in terms of constrainedness and homogeneity, our aim in this paper is to begin to discover where these regions are.

2 Generating solvable problems

In simple timetabling problems a number of events each have to be assigned to one of a given number of timeslots and there are various constraints each stipulating that two specific events may not occupy the same timeslot. In practice problems are much more complicated than this, involving further issues such as

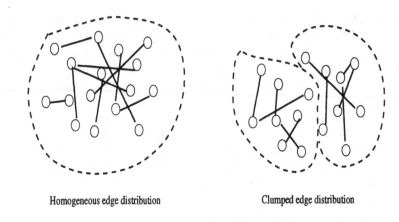

Homogeneous edge distribution   Clumped edge distribution

Fig. 1. Homogeneous and Clumped Problems

room capacities, inter-location travel times, varying sizes of timeslots, the need to space out some sets of events and so on. However these additional issues complicate the picture so that it becomes much harder to be able to explain phenomena in terms of the presence or absence of some features of the problem. For present purposes such extra issues are ignored, so that timetabling can be considered to be closely related to simple graph-colouring problems in which an edge corresponds to a constraint, timeslots correspond to colours, and the problem is to colour the vertices of the graph in such a way that no two vertices joined by an edge have the same colour. Graph theory provides some useful results about such problems.

The following procedure can be used to generate solvable problems in a suitably parameterised way. Suppose there are E events and S (time-)slots. The events are randomly placed into slots (making sure there is at least one event in each slot) and constraints are generated between each event and all others not in the same timeslot. Thus if events e_1 and e_2 had been assigned to the same slot, then no solution will exist in which they occupy different timeslots. After this constraint generation step, if any further constraint were then to be added it would have to be a constraint between two members of the same timeslot and that would cause there to be no solution at all to the problem. The problem is therefore a maximally constrained solvable problem. Note that the solution is not unique, of course; if a timetabling problem uses only transitive, non-slot-specific constraints then further solutions can always be created by permuting the slots.

Having generated a maximally-constrained solvable problem in this way, that has (say) A allowed constraints, the problem can be made easier by removing a proportion $1 - p$ of the constraints at random. The method used in this paper is to consider each constraint in turn, removing it with probability $1 - p$. The alternative would be to select a random subset of size $\lceil (1 - p)A \rceil$ and remove just those; this would produce problems which had precisely $\lfloor pA \rfloor$ constraints each, rather than problems which had this number on average.

It is now simple to introduce variable degrees of homogeneity into such a randomly generated problem. First, we need to define precisely what we mean by homogenity. A useful measure of homogenity, h, is as follows: suppose we have a problem with c clumps; $h = 0$ means that no edges at all exist between any distinct pair of these clumps, while $h = 1$ indicates complete homogeneity. That is, if $h = 1$ the clumps are no longer well defined, and the distribution of edges matches that of the simple random problem generator described above. An appropriate definition of h is N_o/N_w, where N_o is the average number of neighbours an event has which are outside its own clump, and N_w is the average number of neighbours within its own clump. To generate a random problem with a given homogeneity h and overall allowed connectivity k (the proportion of the A constraints we wish to retain), we first arbitrarily divide the events up into c clumps, generate a maximally solvable problem as above, and thus find the numbers A, A_w (the number of allowed constraints which are within clumps) and A_b (the number of allowed constraints that are between clumps). If we slightly alter the generation algorithm to remove constraints with either probability p_w, for within-clump constraints, or p_b, for between-clump constraints, it is simple to show that: $p_b = 1 - kA/(A_b + A_w/(h(c-1)))$, and then $p_w = (kA - p_b A_b)/A_w$.

Problems generated by the above means will be called (E, S, k, h, c, t) problems. A modest measure of realism can be added by not generating the maximum allowable set of constraints initially; instead, a constraint is included at the start only if it is between two events *more than* t slots apart or if the events are on different days (it is arbitrarily assumed that there are four lots per day; this is based on some difficult real-world exam timetabling problems that the authors have had to deal with). The quantity t is referred to as the *tightness* of the problem. Suppose, for example, that slots are numbered from 0 upward. Then if $t = 2$ and the algorithm is looking at events in slot 3, it would generate constraints between these and those in slot 4 (since slot 4 is on the second day rather than the first) and between these and those in slot 0. However, it would not generate constraints between the events in slot 3 and those in slots 1 and 2, since these slots are no more than t away from slot 3. Since there are four slots per day, it only makes sense to consider values of t in the range $0 \cdots 3$.

3 Experiments and Results

3.1 Algorithms

Being interested in the relative performance of EA and SH, especially within and around phase-transition regions, experiments concentrated on using a simple EA and a simple variant of SH as described below.

The Evolutionary Algorithm The EA used a population of 50 set out spatially on a 10×5 grid. Local mating selection [4] was employed with a random walk size of 2, and a steady-state reproduction strategy. The only operator used was 'event-freeing mutation' applied at a pressure of 0.2; event-freeing mutation is a fast local improvement operator described in [9]. It works by taking an event at random, and looking for a new timeslot for that event which 'frees' its from some of the conflicts (if any) it is involved in at its current timeslot. The pressure refers to the extent to which we look for the best possible new timeslot.

The Stochastic Hillclimber SH used event-freeing mutation at the same pressure, but was otherwise a straightforward hillclimber: a single current timetable was maintained, and mutations were attempted until a new timetable better or equal to the current was found. This would then replace the current timetable, and the process continued. In both EA and SH trials, computation was halted after 20,000 timetable evaluations, if an optimum (a timetable satisfying all constraints) was not found by then.

The Test Problems

Previous work has identified particularly sharp phase transitions on graph 3-colouring problems [3]. With tightness 3, a 12-slot (hence 3-day) problem of the kind described above is essentially isomorphic to a 3-colouring problem; a tightness value of 3 means that no two exams which are connected by an edge constraint can appear on the same day, making us able to identify days with slots[4]. We therefore decided to look first at such problems, confident of the appearance of a sharp phase transition, and interested to view the effect of varying homogeneity. We hence examined $(50, 12, k, h, 2, 3)$ problems with varying degrees of allowed connectivity k and homogeneity h, with homogeneity being with respect to two initially arbitrarily-defined clumps. Note that the interplay between allowed connectivity and homogeneity prevents us from being able to independently vary both between 0 and 1. Depending on other defining factors of the problem at hand, If connectivity is 1, for example, then every allowed edge constraint exists, which inevitably includes edges across clumps, hence it would be impossible to have connectivity 1 and homogeneity 0. This, and the fact that beyond certain values of connectivity the problems are all uninterestingly easy, explains the bounds on the axes in figures later on.

We also examined $(50, 12, k, h, 2, 2)$ problems; this lower degree of tightness remains realistic in many real (particularly examination) timetabling applications, and also renders the problem qualitatively distinct from simple graph colouring owing to the nature of the tightness constraints.

The experiments

For each tightness value (2 or 3), and each of a range of allowed-connectivity and homogenity values, ten different random problems were generated. A set of EA

---

[4] Note that the inclusion of any form of room capacity constraints destroys this isomorphism.

(SH) trials consisted of applying EA (SH) 5 times to each of the ten problems of given tightness, allowed-connectivity, and homogenity. The recorded results of a set of such trials were *Difficulty*, and Average Evaluations. Difficulty refers to the proportion of trials in the set in which an optimal solution was not found (recall: all problems are guaranteed to have an optimal solution which satisfies all constraints), and average evaluations records the mean number of evaluations over trials which *did* find an optimum.

Experiments on Problems with Tightness 3 Figure 2 shows the difficulty surface for the EA over allowed-connectivity/homogeneity space. Two phase transition ridges stand out. Ridge 'A' is already well-known, corresponding to the sharp increase in difficulty of 3-colouring problems at around 15% connectivity , falling back towards easy before and beyond that point. Interestingly, we find that this phase transition remains in place over a wide range of values of homogeneity.

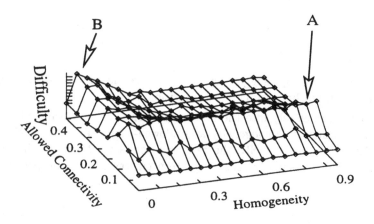

Fig. 2. EA difficulty on problems with tightness 3

Even more interestingly, we uncover a new phase transition ridge 'B', occurring over a wide range of allowed-connectivity values, corresponding to the point at which the problems are almost, but not completely, divided into distinct unconnected clumps. Beginning at 0 on the homogeneity axis, problems are divided entirely into two unconnected clumps. As we travel from left to right, increasing the homogeneity, we almost immediately hit phase transition 'B', suggesting that problems with distinct but very loosely connected clumps are particularly difficult. Travelling further to the right, as we further increase the connection between clumps (balanced by decreasing the connectivity within clumps), problems quickly become easy again.

Figure 3 shows very similar behaviour when using SH on the same problems.

A slight but notable difference is that phase transition ridge 'B' appears a little

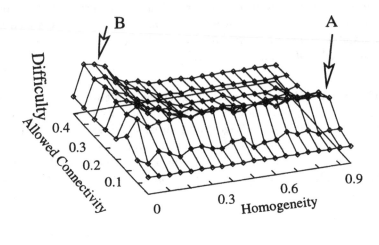

Fig. 3. SH difficulty on problems with tightness 3

smoother near the top, suggesting that SH takes longer to escape from this 'slight-connectivity-between-clumps' transition.

To look more closely into the relative performance of EA and SH here, we noted those values of homogeneity and allowed-connectivity at which the EA scored 5% or more above SH; the resulting points are those which stand out in figure 4. No particularly sensible pattern emerges, and a proper statistical

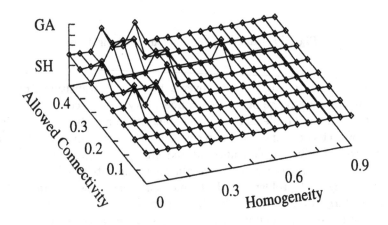

Fig. 4. Areas where EA beats SH on problems with tightness 3

examination of these studies is pending on further lengthy experimentation, but there is an unmistakable tendency for the EA to outperform SH within the 'B' phase transition ridge, with no such behaviour exhibited within the 'A' ridge.

Examining the 'Evaluations' (or 'time') surface for SH on these problems provides interesting clues as to this behaviour. Figure 5 gives this surface for SH (which is very similar to the equivalent surface for the EA); clearly, phase transition ridge 'A' on earlier figures is reflected in the extra search time and effort indicated here. However, phase transition ridge 'B' is now absent. This

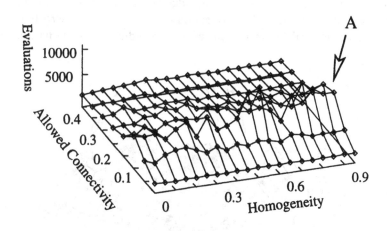

Fig. 5. SH average evaluations to find optimum on problems with tightness 3

suggests that the difficulty of problems along ridge 'B' is mainly due to persistent local optima, while on 'A' the difficulty is due more to the existence of awkward plateaus. On a plateau — a large collection of neighbouring timetables with the same fitness — EA or SH may spend considerable time visiting different points on the same plateau before finding an escape route to a fitter plateau. Around phase transition ridge 'A', it seems reasonable to conjecture that these plateaus become particularly difficult to escape from. Time spent on such plateaus is thus reflected in phase transition ridge 'A' being echoed by the similar ridge in figure 5. On the other hand, successfully solved problems on ridge 'B' don't take particularly long, suggesting that plateaus here are no more difficult to escape from than anywhere else outside ridge 'A'. Rather, we can tentatively infer that difficulty on ridge 'B' is due to occasionally getting trapped at plateaus or points which are *impossible* to escape from, or at least intractably difficult to find a way out in reasonable time, and hence form local optima.

These thoughts sit well with the observation that EA is often superior to SH around ridge 'B', but not around ridge 'A'. Enhanced ability to escape local optima is a solid and well understood expectation we would have of an EA as compared to SH. However, on ridge 'A' there is no 'getting trapped' issue –

rather, progress is slowed down by plateaus with infrequent escape routes: here we might expect SH to do at least as well, since increased attention to a single line of search reduces the time we would expect to wait before escaping from a plateau.

Experiments on Problems with Tightness 2 Figure 6 shows the difficulty surface for the EA over allowed-connectivity/tightness space on problems with tightness 2. On these problems, the situation is far less clear. Note that there is a wide phase transition ridge corresponding to a region of allowed connectivity between about 30% and 90%, echoing ridge 'A' on tightness 3 problems. There is no longer a clear ridge 'B' corresponding to low but nonzero homogeneity, however there is a fairly strong hint of one, as indicated in the figure. Figure 7

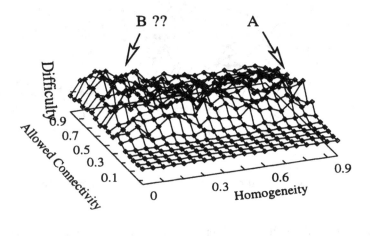

Fig. 6. EA difficulty on problems with tightness 2

is the SH version of this difficulty surface, which is again very similar to the EA difficulty surface.

Regions in which EA found optima on 5% or more trials than SH are recorded in figure 8. A rather different pattern is now revealed. Interestingly, the EA gives a generally better showing on these problems than on the earlier tightness 3 problems; again, those places where the EA seems superior to SH are almost entirely within a phase transition region. Notably, these points start a significant way into the transition (in terms of allowed connectivity).

Figure 9 shows the average evaluations surface for SH on this problem. Again, there is a hint of structure rather lost in considerable noise. It slightly seems (especially with the authors' benefit of being able to view this surface in a large number of orientations) that a peak in effort which is hit a short way into the ridge drops away slightly as allowed-connectivity increases further. Figure 10, showing the same graph in a revised orientation, lends some support to this

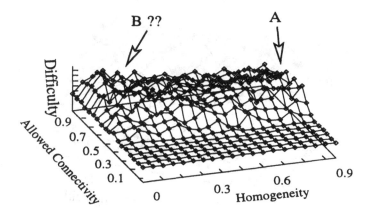

Fig. 7. SH difficulty on problems with tightness 2

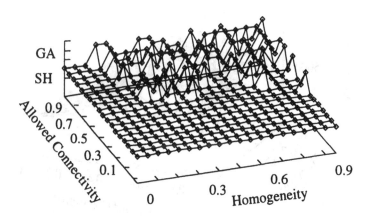

Fig. 8. Areas where EA beats SH on problems with tightness 2

observation. If these trends are real, then it seems the same general reasoning applies as in the tightness 3 case. That is, EA starts to do better on SH on those areas of the phase transition ridge in which search effort (when solutions *are* found) is not at a peak, in turn suggesting that these are areas in which local optima are strongly apparent, rather than awkward plateaus.

4 Discussion

A Note on Greedy Algorithms Other work reported in [11] has shown that for a very wide range of randomly-created timetabling problems, simple heuristic algorithms such as the *greedy* and the *Brelasz* graph-colouring algorithms can

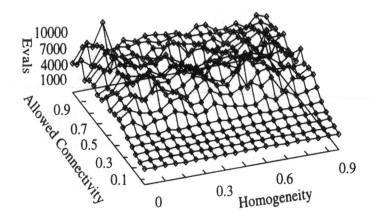

Fig. 9. SH average evaluations to find optimum on problems with tightness 2

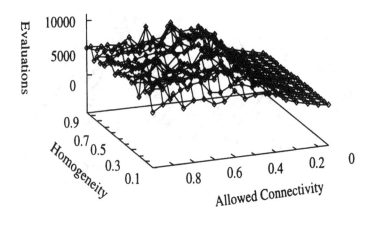

Fig. 10. SH average evaluations to find optimum on problems with tightness 2: a different perspective

often find a solution much faster than an EA that uses a simple penalty-function approach; indeed in many cases the EA may fail to find a solution. One version of the greedy algorithm merely chooses to colour vertices of highest degree first, backtracking as necessary; the Brelasz algorithm is a variant which sorts vertices according to the number of choices of colour remaining for a vertex, breaking ties by vertex degree and backtracking as necessary. The most basic greedy algorithm just colours vertices in turn, using as many colours as turn out to be necessary. It can be shown theoretically [2] that this does remarkably well; if a random graph is constructed by allowing each edge with fixed probability p then it will use $O(-n \log(1-p)/\log n)$ colours, where the constant of proportionality is no worse than 2 and is almost certainly 1. The one general reason to choose an EA or SH instead of the Brelasz method would seem to be that an EA can be set up to produce multiple solutions simultaneously, for example by penalising or even disallowing new candidate solutions that are too similar to ones already in the population. However, it remains to be seen to what extent algorithms such as the Brelasz method perform (with appropriate alteration) on real timetabling style problems, rather than simple graph colouring; also, of course, performance of such methods in phase transition regions such as those discussed here is an interesting and important topic for future work.

Explaining phase transitions via graph theory constructs It is natural to ask why phase transition regions exist. We have already made some partially founded conjectures based on the relative existence of local optima and awkward plateaus. In this section, we look briefly at available results in graph theory which might lead to an account of these matters, turning our attention more to cliques and other such graph-theoretical constructs.

First, the explanation of the phase transitions reported here is probably not the same one that would account for the kind of phase transitions reported in [10] and [8]. For example, Smith [10] studied phase transitions in constraint-satisfaction problems (CSPs) using a common form of forward-checking CSP algorithm; in her problems there are V variables each of which has a domain of size D. A precise proportion p_1 of the $V(V-1)/2$ possible edges are created, and for each edge a precise proportion p_2 of the D^2 possible combinations of values for the two variables linked by the edge are classed as acceptable in any solution. Thus Smith's problems may not be solvable, but the algorithm used may detect this and terminate, sometimes with little effort.

It seems clear (although not so far reported in print elsewhere) that Smith's phase transitions correspond precisely to those that can be proved to happen in the structure of random graphs [2]. Details of the following results can be found in that book. For example, suppose that a random graph has M edges, so that $0 \le M \le V(V-1)/2$. Various phase transitions happen as M increases. For small M up to about $V/2$ a random graph almost certainly consists of isolated trees and cycles; each such component will be easily solved by hillclimbers, EAs and so on. Then there is a phase transition; above $V/2$ the largest component will be of size ϵV and almost all vertices will lie on trees, so that again the problem will be easy to solve. As M grows even larger, the largest component continues to grow. It can be shown that almost certainly there will be no small components that have many edges; the graph will almost certainly be the union of its one giant component and a number of small isolated trees and unicycles. For still larger M the presence of cliques (sets of vertices each of which is connected to all other members of the set) becomes important, especially since these pose problems for most algorithms, including EAs. It can be shown that if $0 < p < 1$ and $0 < \epsilon < 1/2$ then almost every random graph in which each edge is chosen for inclusion with fixed probability p has a clique of order r for all r in the range

$$(1+\epsilon)\log_{1/p} n < r < (2-\epsilon)\log_{1/p} n$$

and for no values of r outside this range. All these results are probabilistic in nature and assume $V \to \infty$. They are not too surprising either; for example, very large cliques 'consume' a great many edges for their size, so it should not be at all suprising that very few among all the possible random graphs will have them. The typical scenario for M appreciably larger than V is therefore a graph that has a number of modest sized cliques and near-cliques more sparsely interconnected by other edges to form one giant component, and a number of very small isolated trees and unicycles. The giant component is what causes the trouble, and it is natural to believe that this is why there is a phase-transition in the performance of non-evolutionary constraint satisfaction algorithms when they try to solve such problems. Large cliques and highly-interconnected regions of the giant component would seem to make it easy for such algorithms to show that there is no solution. To summarise, graph theory literature holds various potential clues to phase transition regions in graph coluring and similar timetabling problems, by way of enabling us to predict the typical nature, number, and size, and connectedness of various graph components that may exist. Since we have some idea of how SH or EA may perform on these various types of components in isolation, phase transitions related to the nature, size, etc ... of the components are presumably closely related to phase transitions concerning difficulty of solution. However, the complexity of the interconnectedness of these components makes it hard to progress any further into a general explanation.

Explaining phase transitions via landscape features Earlier, we alluded to explanations of the phase transition ridge 'A' in terms of difficulty of escaping from plateaus, but of course this fails to address why this difficulty ceases to exist either side of the transition. An attempt to explain this might centre on the relative changes in size and nature of the plateaus as constraint density increases. Generally, as we increase the number of constraints, the sizes of the fitter plateaus reduces. There are several ways to see this; for example, a combinatoric analysis readily shows this to be true. It is similarly possible to see, with some thought, that the density of 'escape routes' within plateaus does not seem to significantly alter. Hence, after a point which we shall discuss next, increasing the number of constraints promises to reduce the time spent searching through and escaping from plateaus.

At very low levels of constrainedness, however, we are of course likely to find a solution without even trying, because so many exist. Increasing the number of constraints from tiny to small eventually takes us to a point at which the initial population of an EA (for example) is no longer likely to be only one or two steps from a solution, and so modest search is necessary. From this point onwards towards modest constraint density, the number of plateaus to travel through is increasing, and the number of available solutions is rapidly decreasing.

So, this rough analysis identifies three regions which would seem to correspond to before, at, and after the phase transition: before, solution density is so high, and the number of plateaus is so small, that very little search is necessary and the problem is easy. In the phase transition region itself, much fewer available solutions combines with an increasing number of plateaus to make the search rather more difficult. Beyond this point, the reduction in size (and hence extra ease in finding escape routes) of the fitter plateau starts to ease the search process again, despite number of available solutions still decreasing. One thing that counteracts the decrease in number of solutions after the phase transition is presumably the fact that it becomes increasingly harder to find new constraints to add which aren't already *implied* anyway; that is, many of the constraints left to add may not actually reduce the number of available solutions.

A related set of ideas concerning the existence of phase transitions, which is the subjectof work to be reported in due course, harps on two important descriptors of a plateau: its *escape density* – the typically small proportion of points on the plateau which have a neighbour on a fitter plateau, and its *escape ratio* – given a point on the plateau which has a fitter neighbour, this is the density of such fitter neighbours in this point's neighbourhood. Hence, with a high escape density and a low escape ratio, a hillclimber will not travel far along the plateau before finding a way out, but when it does, the low escape ratio will make it unlikely it will take the opportunity to escape. Alternatively, a low escape density and high escape ratio leaves a hillclimber meandering along plateau for ages at a time, but quick to take advantage of an escape route when it finds one. By inspection, it seems the actual escape densities and escape ratios in plateaus of the sort encountered in the problems we address here change only subtly and slightly as we increase constraint density. However, Markov modelling of the process, using escape ratio and density as central transition probabilities, reveals important and interesting interaction between these numbers. In particular, certain combinations lead to the expection of very lengthy 'plateau escape times', which drop quickly as we, for example, slightly decrease the escape ratio and increase the escape density. This suggests an explanation of certain phase transitions as an epiphenomon resulting from the interaction of subtle landscape features.

The reason for the existence of local optima (or perhaps very highly inescapable plateaus) around the 'B' phase transition region also needs addressing. An explanation seems ready in the tightness 3 case, in which this phase transition appeared when the problem consisted of two loosely connected subproblems. Marginal crosstalk between two subproblems means that the hillclimber spends most of its time ironing out the constraint violations in the two separate problems, with little effect on each other. Eventually, however, the slight connection between the subproblems rears its head. In the 3-colouring case, we can see how difficulty might arise: imagine the only connection between subproblems being the constraints (a, x), (b, y), and (c, z), where a, b and c are in one clump, and x, y and z in the other. Imagine further that a, b and c must all be in different days (slots), as also must x, y and z. Having perhaps effectively addressed the separate problems, the hillclimber may easily now be in the position of having, say, a and x on the same day, and this being the only violation left to remove. The difficulty, however, is that both a's and x's tighter interconnection within their own clumps means that either or both 'solved' subproblems must be very radically rearranged to remove this violation without affecting others. This suggests that very unfriendly plateaus, rather than true local optima, may be the cause of the 'B' phase transition. As further constraints are added to boost the connection between clumps, the hillclimber becomes much more likely to encounter and solve such problems earlier on, before they becomes too 'deep' to solve.

5 Conclusion

We have shown that interesting phase transition regions exist in the context of solvable timetabling style problems with varying connectivity and homogeneity. In addition, different phase transitions seem to exist for different reasons, a fact which manifests itself in the differential performance of EA and SH in these regions. In particular, certain phase transition regions seem to offer a platform on which an EA can outperform a hillclimber on timetabling problems.

We have speculated on the underlying causes of these phase transition regions, and pointed out several matters of potential importance and relevance in the study of such regions, particularly the plethora of available results in graph theory which seem to bear on these matters, at least as regards those problems which reduce to simple graph-colouring.

In conclusion, relative performance of different algorithms on timetabling problems is important to understand, because timetabling problems are ubiquitously important and can be notoriously difficult. We hope that studies such as this one, which concentrate on what seems to make timetabling problems particularly hard in some cases, and how this meshes with differential algorithm performance, will generally aid our understanding of these matters.

Acknowledgements

We are grateful to the EPSRC for support of the second author via an award with reference GR/J44513, and to ITESM, Mexico, for lending time and support for the third author to contribute to this work while on study leave in Edinburgh. Thanks also to two anonymous referees for many useful and insightful comments.

References

1. D. Abramson and J. Abela, 'A parallel genetic algorithm for solving the school timetabling problem', Technical report, Division of Information Technology, C.S.I.R.O., (April 1991).
2. B. Bollobas, *Random Graphs*, Academic Press, 1985.
3. P. Cheeseman, B. Kenefsky, and W.M. Taylor, 'Where the really hard problems are', in *Proceedings of IJCAI-91*, pp. 331–337, (1991).
4. Robert J. Collins and David R. Jefferson, 'Selection in massively parallel genetic algorithms', in *Proceedings of the Fourth International Conference on Genetic Algorithms*, eds., R.K. Belew and L.B. Booker, pp. 249–256. San Mateo: Morgan Kaufmann, (1991).

5. Dave Corne, Hsiao-Lan Fang, and Chris Mellish, 'Solving the module exam scheduling problem with genetic algorithms', in *Proceedings of the Sixth International Conference in Industrial and Engineering Applications of Artificial Intelligence and Expert Systems*, eds., Paul W.H. Chung, Gillian Lovegrove, and Moonis Ali, 370–373, Gordon and Breach Science Publishers, (1993).

6. A. Juels and M. Wattenberg, 'Stochastic hillclimbing as a baseline method for evaluating genetic algorithms', Technical Report UCB Technical Report CSD-94-834, Department of Computer Science, University of California at Berkeley, (1994).

7. U.-M. O'Reilly and F. Oppacher, 'Program search with a hierarchical variable length representation: genetic programming, simulated annealing and stochastic hill climbing', in *Parallel Problem Solving from Nature - PPSN III*, eds., Y. Davidor, H-P. Schwefel, and R. Manner, number 866 in Lecture Notes in Computer Science. Springer-Verlag, (1994).

8. Patrick Prosser, 'Binary constraint satisfaction problems: Some are harder than others', in *Proceedings of the 11th European Conference on Artificial Intelligence*, ed., A. Cohn, pp. 95–99. John Wiley & Sons, Ltd., (1994).

9. Peter Ross, Dave Corne, and Hsiao-Lan Fang, 'Improving evolutionary timetabling with delta evaluation and directed mutation', in *Parallel Problem Solving from Nature III*, ed., Y. Davidor, Springer-Verlag, (1994).

10. Barbara Smith, 'Phase transition and the mushy region in constraint satisfaction problems', in *Proceedings of the 11th European Conference on Artificial Intelligence*, ed., A. Cohn, pp. 100–104. John Wiley & Sons, Ltd., (1994).

11. H. Terashima-Marin, 'A comparison of ga-based methods and graph-colouring methods for solving the timetabling problem', Technical Report Technical Report AIGA-94-15, University of Edinburgh Department of Artificial Intelligence, (1994).

Tabu Search and Simulated Annealing

Three Methods Used to Solve an Examination Timetable Problem

Jean Paul Boufflet and Stéphane Nègre

URA CNRS 817 Heudiasyc

Université de Technologie de Compiègne (UTC)

Dpt Génie Informatique - BP 649

60 206 COMPIEGNE Cédex

FRANCE

Tel : (33) 44 23 46 91

Fax : (33) 44 20 48 13

Télex : Unitech 150110F

Electronic Mail : boufflet@hds.univ-compiegne.fr

snegre@hds.univ-compiegne.fr

Abstract

This paper describes the problem of examination timetables at the University of Technology of Compiègne and the solutions we devised. The problem we faced was drawing up a week-long the examination timetable, taking into account a number of different constraints. These constraints are administrative, physical and related to preferences. Three tools were developed to solve this practical problem. The first tool is an exact method based on a tree search, the second is based on the tabu technique, and the third is an interactive computer aided design system. The most effective is the tree search method, but the tabu search technique may be a convenient alternative for several reasons. The computer aided design system can be used if all the automatic techniques fail. In the first part of this paper we describe the problem. In the second part we present a model using a reduction of the problem and relaxed constraints. Next, the three methods are described, and we briefly present the related problem of the assignment of invigilators. The results we present in the fourth part show that there exists no solution which takes into account all the constraints. We have solved the related problem of invigilator assignment using the well known out-of-kilter method. Computational results are presented.

Keywords :   graph colouring techniques, tabu search, implementation, interactive vs. batch timetabling.

1. Introduction

Our aim is to solve the examination timetable problem of the University of Technology of Compiègne. Both automatic and interactive techniques should be used according to the nature of the problem. The basic problem in drawing up a timetable is to build a k-colouring of a graph [BRE 79][CAN 89][HER 87][HER 89]. This is an NP-hard problem. This kind of problem can be also modelled as a linear programming problem [TRI 84] or as a quadratic assignment problem [FER 83][FER 85]. In fact, each case is particular, and techniques used to solve it can be very different. We do not solve a general timetabling problem for a French university [BOU 92a][BOU 92b] as we would solve an examination timetabling problem [VDV 92][NEG 93]. A list of related papers can be found in [CAR 86][SCH 80]. But before tackling this kind of problem with specific methods, it is important to present the real case and the model we constructed using constraint relaxation and establishing a constraints hierarchy [VDV 92][NEG 93]. The importance of time instability should not be overlooked in this kind of problem. Consequently, building a unique sophisticated method exploiting the problem characteristics is not necessarily a good idea. So we develop three methods, implementing them in a simple way.

2. Formulation of the problem

In order to present the context of our work, we shall describe the curriculum of the University, the timetabling cycle, the constraints and the manual resolution method used up to now.

2.1. Curriculum and timetabling cycle

The curriculum of the University of Technology of Compiègne (UTC) is based on the principle of cumulative units of value (UV). A UV is a set of courses taught over a six months period. Twice a year examinations take place over a one week period (autumn and spring semesters). For each UV, one or several exams are set during the semester. At the end of the semester, a final exam has to be scheduled during the examination week. Even there are exceptions, the majority of UV's have a final exam. There are six types of students. The UTC has one preliminary diploma and five types of engineer diplomas. To graduate, each student has to obtain four different types of UV according to a curriculum. There are scientific (S), technical (T), general culture (C), and communication (L) units of value. Curricula are laid down by the administration which defines for each type of UV the set of UV's a student can choose during his or her studies according to the diploma wanted. Each semester, a student is enrolled for at most 7 UV and there are 1500 students. The curricula are heavily interconnected. Therefore the examination timetable problem is difficult to solve.

Between 90 (autumn semester) and 130 exams (spring semester) have to be scheduled. Several people are needed to draw up the timetable and the naming of supervisors. It takes one week to do this work.

Moreover, this work cannot be done far in advance. Indeed, as we shall describe it, information about UV's and exams are not known a long time before the creation of the exam timetable. At the beginning of the year, a list of students is set up. For each student, the list of chosen UV's is updated in a database. Students' choices are not always possible (scheduling or curriculum problems), thus some students have to change their UV's. Two weeks later, the modifications are taken into account. About 2 months before the exams, the Administrative Department distributes to teachers a document enabling them to specify whether they wish to set a final exam for their UV. If they wish it, they specify information about the exam (duration, location, wishes or impossibilities for planning periods, ...). The administration then waits for these documents to be returned and passes them to the Information Technology Department. A listing containing for each UV the list of compatible UV's and the number of students is created and returned to the schedulers who can begin to schedule the exams. They must take into account a number of constraints described below.

2.2. Constraints

The examination and supervision timetables have to be drawn up according to constraints :

- Exams have to be planned simultaneously in the same hall (except for few UV). This particular hall is available only one week each semester from Monday morning to Friday afternoon included. It can hold 390 students, so we have just one cumulative constraint;
- Some exams can however be planned in other locations. So, it is necessary to take into account the moves of the students between locations;
- Each UV has a principal teacher, who has to invigilate his or her exam. In this way, two UV's cannot be scheduled simultaneously if they have the same principal teacher;
- Two exams cannot be scheduled simultaneously if they have a common student;
- Exams have different durations : 1 hour, 2 hours or 3 hours;
- The number of students for each UV varies considerably (between 10 and more than 250). The number of invigilators must be proportional to the number of students;
- For a given exam, teachers who invigilate the exam are chosen according to this decreasing priority list : principal teacher of the UV; other teachers of the UV; other teachers;
- A teacher should not invigilate more than two exams except if he or she is the principal teacher of more than two UV's;
- We have to minimize the number of students having more than three exams a day;
- All the other constraints can be considered as prohibited planning periods in the week.

For example, wishes or impossibilities are given by teachers for their exams. General culture UV's have to be scheduled on Tuesday and Wednesday. Exams involving a large number of students have to be scheduled earlier in the week, Monday to Wednesday, so that marking can begin earlier. These last two constraints are preference constraints. A UV with more than 100 students is considered by the administration as an important one.

The problem was presented to us in this form (less concisely) by the people who drew up the timetable manually. But this list of constraints is insufficient to describe such a problem; we have to study both strategy and policy in order to understand the whole problem. Then, we complete the constraints description exposing briefly the manual resolution method and the tools used.

2.3. Manual resolution method

A number of documents were passed to the schedulers : a list of UV's having no common students (compatible UV's); a listing of the number of registered students for each UV; and a set of diverse information for each UV. This latter document containing exam duration, planning period constraints and exam location was provided by the principal teacher of the UV. Finally a timetable grid was drawn on a paper and was used to seek a solution.

The resolution method simply involved filling up each planning period. The idea was to fill the examination hall to capacity, adding other exams until, if possible, the hall was full of students. So they sought UV's which could be potentially added to this planning period using the listing of compatible UV's. This search of new UV was done using the following strategy.

They would attempt first to associate UV's from the beginning and from the end of the curriculum. Then, they would choose UV's from different courses from these two subsets. In this way, they would hope to minimize the risk of having common students. However, they had to verify systematically, using listings, that there were no common students each time a UV was added to planning period. This work meant handling a lot of listings, and consequently making a lot of mistakes. So many verifications were needed to validate the timetables. Moreover, a UV was added only if its constraints (particular planning period, special room, etc.) were met.

If a UV could not be scheduled in any planning period, the timetable had to be partially destroyed and remade. If it seemed impossible to solve the problem, the strategy was changed and some constraints relaxed. The problem might have had a solution without relaxing constraints, but it is impossible for a human to quickly explore all the solutions or a large part of the search space.

They attempted to build the timetable respecting the constraints as well as possible.

Once the timetable was built, they tried (still manually) to draw up the assignment of teachers to invigilate the exams according to administrative requirements.

Two persons were needed to perform these tasks.

3. Modelling

The problem is solved in two different steps, the timetable design and the assignment of teachers who invigilate the exams.

The first problem can be modelled as a graph colouring problem. The nodes of the graph represent the exams (the weights of the nodes are the exam durations) and the edges represent the impossibility of giving the same colour (same planning period) to two adjacent nodes (See Figure 1). An exact method has been developed by M. Cangalovic [CAN 89] to solve this problem. However, our problem is not a pure problem but a real one. Thus, our aim is to build software able to find a solution.

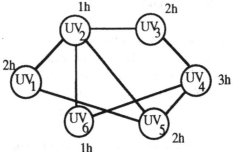

Fig. 1. Colouring problem with different exam durations

To tackle this problem, we first attempt to simplify it by studying the manual procedures. One can see that there are actually less than 5 exams of 3 hours duration. The schedulers use special rules for these exams, placing them at the end of the morning or at the end of the afternoon (See Figure 2).

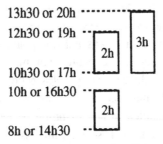

Fig. 2. Rules (2h, 3h)

We therefore obtain an easier problem and we can reduce the combinatorial problem. In the worst case, students either have one hour for lunch (and possibly to change locations) or they leave later in the evening. As regards automatic processing, this signifies that three-hour exams will have particular time period constraints.

This reduction will not cause problems in the future because the administration aims to phase out 3-hour exams.

There exists other rules to associate one-and two-hour exams. As we can see in Figure 3, there exist 3 rules to schedule simultaneously these exams.

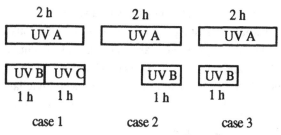

Fig. 3. Association rules (1h, 2h)

The only possible way is the third case (the one-and two-hour exams begin at the same time). The majority of exams have to be scheduled simultaneously in the same hall, so we have to avoid movements of students when others are still working. In the first case, there are students who go out of the hall and others who come in; in the second case, there are students who come into the hall during a two-hour exam; in the third case, there are students who go out of the hall during a two-hour exam. Only rule 3 is used by the administration. We must therefore place these students near the exit to minimize disturbance (this small problem was already solved automatically when the timetable was built manually). We can therefore treat one-hour exams like two-hour exams. The problem is simpler because the problem of exams with different durations is eliminated.

All the exams must be scheduled in one week. We saw that all exams can be considered as two-hour exams, which means we can use 20 planning periods (twenty colours).

Another constraint can be eliminated easily. We have to consider the students' moves from one location to another. These moves are very few because most of the exams take place in the unique examination hall. Moreover, distances between two examination rooms are short. So, if there is enough time between two exam periods, we can eliminate this constraint (See Figure 2).

If we consider that the colour 0 corresponds to Monday morning from 8 to 10 am, and so on, we take into account the basic time period constraints and the additional one related to exam durations.

In fact, before attempting a coloration, we are going to proscribe certain colours for exams which have these constraints. This will help us in a very important way to find a solution as we shall see later.

We have therefore to consider the 20-colouring problem of the graph $G(X,U)$ where the exams have the same duration. The set of exams to schedule is the set of the nodes. Furthermore, each node of X has a list of proscribed colours in order to deal with the marking constraint for large exams, the particular planning periods for general culture, teachers' wishes, and the rules concerning 3-hour exams. Two nodes i and j are linked by an edge if one of the following conditions applies :

- exams i and j have the same principal teacher;
- there is a common student between exams i and j;

- card (UVi) + card (UVj) > examination hall capacity;
- there is no possible planning period to schedule simultaneously exams i and j.

When seeking a 20-colouring we must take into account the cumulative constraint and proscribed colours, and minimize the number of students having 3 exams a day.

The second problem is the assignment of the teachers who invigilate the exams. We model this problem using a minimum cost flow problem (See Figure 4).

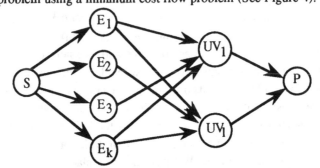

Fig. 4. Graph for the teachers assignment problem.

First, we create a source node (S) and nodes for each teacher (E_i) at the University (See Figure 4).

The source S is linked with all the nodes E_i (one node for one teacher). Between node S and a node E_i, we have a minimum flow equal to 0 (no invigilation for a teacher) and a maximum flow equal to 2, except if the teacher is the principal teacher of more than two UV's. The cost is up to now equal to 0, but we can use it to impose a penalty on a teacher. Thus we can take into account the past assignments of teachers as in the manual procedures. Indeed, we can prevent the same teachers invigilating a large number of exams (from one semester to another) even if they teach UV's each semester (there are about 350 permanent teachers).

Secondly, we create as many nodes as there are exams (See Figure 4) (from 90 to 130 UV). An edge is created between a teacher and an exam if the teacher can invigilate it. It should be noted that if a 20-colouring exists, two UV's having the same principal teacher cannot be scheduled at the same time. So an edge exists between each principal teacher and his or her corresponding UV, and its cost is equal to 0. However, all the edges are not created. Indeed, another teacher might have to invigilate two exams scheduled at the same period in the timetable. A filter is applied to avoid this situation, giving a preference to teachers of the UV. The minimum flow is equal to 0 (the teacher does not invigilate the UV) and the maximum is equal to 1 (the teacher invigilates the UV). The costs are set according to hierarchical criteria given by the administration.

Finally, exams (UV_i) are linked with sink P with edges. The minimum flow is equal to the number of students sitting the exam divided by 30, and the maximum flow is equal to this same number divided by 25. Indeed, the administration advises one teacher for 25 to 30 students, and we take the upper bound. The cost is equal to 0. We have to solve this problem to get an assignment of teachers to invigilate the exams. We use the out-of-kilter method with Edmons' and Karps' improvements [EDM 72]. In the following part of the paper, we are going to describe the methods used to solve the colouring problem.

4. Methods

Three methods have been used to solve the problem. The first one is a very simple tree search method, the second one is based on the tabu search method and the last one is a C.A.D.S (Computer Aided Design System).

4.1. Tree search method

As a first approach, we develop a tree search method in order to get a colouring of the graph $G(X,U)$. With this method, a complete exploration of the search space is unthinkable, since there are 20^N solutions (N is the number of exams to schedule). In order to limit computing time, we use separation rules based on problem specificities. We then seek separation criteria enabling us to generate a failure as early as possible in order to minimize computing time. Therefore, our tree search method has been designed to take into account some principles of the constraint programming. In order to prune the tree efficiently, the first fail and the forward checking principles have been used. We have to choose the node (exam), then the colour.

The rules we use to choose the node are (in order of precedence) :
- the nodes with the fewest colours;
- the nodes with the maximum degree;
- the node with maximum number of students.

If more than one UV remains using the first rule, the two other rules are successively applied. A large UV has many proscribed colours (Cf. § 3). Consequently, when the rules are applied, these UV's will be scheduled first. In the same way, general culture UV's will be considered early on. There are between 20 and 30 large exams and a similar number for general culture UV's. Consequently, our separation rules attempt to colour firstly these types of UV, and in so doing, we improve the tree search efficiency through reducing the width of the tree. Therefore we limit the backtracks which would be hard to avoid if we were to schedule a large UV at the end of the processing procedure. Indeed, it is easier to schedule a small UV with a lot of possible colours at the end of processing since a large UV would imply taking into account a cumulative constraint. Namely choosing the most constrained exam first allows us to apply the first fail principle.

We must now present the criteria when selecting a planning period (colour) to assign to the selected UV (node). We cannot consider a planning period if :
- the planning period is not authorized for the selected UV;

- the planning period has become impossible because a previous UV assignment does not allow the current assignment. This constraint propagation could be compared to the forward checking principle of the constraint programming;
- the planning period for this UV has been tried and has resulted in a failure.

If we have more than one possible choice, the rules we use to choose the colour are (in an hierarchical way) :

- the colour which best fills up the examination hall;
- the colour which minimizes the number of students having 3 exams a day.

We therefore have the best saturation of a planning period as with the manual procedures. If we have many possibilities (equal rate of fillings for many planning periods), we choose the colour which allows us to minimize the number of students having 4 exams a day. Let us notice that the constraint about the number of students having 4 exams a day is a minor constraint. Indeed this constraint was not taken into account in the manual method. Moreover, the event appears rarely.

After applying these filters, two situations can occur :

- we can find a colour for the selected UV. In this case, we remove this UV from the list of UV's to schedule and we chose the next UV in the list. Remark: once the list of UV's is empty, the problem is solved.
- we cannot find a colour for the selected UV. In this case, a backtrack occurs in the tree. We proscribe the colour given to the previous UV and we try to find for this UV another colour at this node of the tree. If there exists another colour for this UV, we continue to search. Otherwise, we continue to make backtracks in the tree.

Remark: if we make a backtrack to the root of the tree and if all the colours of the UV of the root have been tried, this implies that the problem has no solution.

This method has many drawbacks from a practical point of view. To seek a solution we systematically explore the whole tree. Therefore we cannot evaluate computing time. If no solution exists in the face of all the constraints, it is impossible to obtain an approximate solution. However, as we shall see below, with reference to actual case-studies, this method can give results with very good computing times. But, it should not be overlooked that the evolution of the problem is unpredictable. For this reason, it would appear desirable to use another automatic method to foresee the evolution of the problem.

We therefore decided to use a tabu search method.

4.2. Tabu search method

We briefly present the method. One can find more explanations and details in [GLO 88][GLO 90]. The aim is to find a good solution of a combinatorial optimization problem by improving step by step an objective function from an initial solution (not necessarily a feasible one), then generating and evaluating the neighbouring solutions. We can generate all the neighbours or a part of them. Some other techniques can be used to generate and explore the neighbourhood (intensification, diversification). We have to choose from the set of neighbours the one which best improves the solution. If there are no neighbours which improve the objective function, we consider the neighbour which decreases it the least. To avoid remaining in a local optima, a list of "taboo" neighbours is declared and updated. This list contains the T previous solutions explored, where T is the size of the tabu list. We cannot choose a neighbourhood solution belonging to this list. But the tabu status of a solution can be dropped if there exists no better solution in the neighbourhood and if one of the solutions of the tabu list can be selected by applying an aspiration function. The algorithm stops if a known optimum is reached or if a maximum number of iterations is made, or if no improvements occur between a fixed number of iterations. We can use one or more of these criteria to stop the algorithm.

A. Hertz and D. de Werra[HER 87] used this method to solve graph colouring problems. A k-colouring of a graph corresponds to a partition $s = (X_1, X_2, ..., X_k)$ of the nodes X in stable sets. Let S be a partition of the nodes X not necessarily corresponding to a feasible solution. $E(X_i)$ can be defined as the set of edges of X_i having the two ends in X_i. We can easily find the basic objective function by using :

$f(s) = \sum (|E(X_i)| / i \in \{1, ..., k\})$ which sums the number of edges having two ends in the same stable set (unfeasible colouring). This function has a known minimum ($f^* = 0$) if a feasible colouring exists. In order to solve our problem, we use the tabu method with the basic objective function of A. Hertz and D. de Werra. However, in our case, the resolution is not so simple. Indeed, we must build an initial solution, then we have to find an objective function able to evaluate the quality of a solution by taking into account all the constraints. Moreover, we must define how to generate the neighbourhood solutions and the aspiration function.

4.2.1. Neighbourhood and tabu list

We use the graph G(X,U) as presented above (See § 3) and 20 vectors to store the stable sets. Starting from a solution, we generate its neighbours, considering all the moves of exam from one stable set to another one. We generate all the feasible moves and we choose the one giving the best objective function. For each iteration, the number of neighbours is equal to (p-1) * n (where p is the number of planning periods and n is the number of exams to schedule). Of course, in order to decrease computation time, we compute the evaluation of each neighbour using the difference with the previous solution.

As commonly suggested in the literature, the size t of the tabu list is set to 7 and only the moves are stored.

4.2.2. Objective function and aspiration level

We must take into account five hierarchical criteria, therefore, the objective function is a multi-criteria one. We compute it by summing the different functions. Each function is weighted according to its priority. Formally, the function is :

$$f(s) = c_1 f_1(s) + c_2 f_2(s) + c_3 f_3(s) + c_4 f_4(s) + c_5 f_5(s)$$

where :

- $f_1(s) : \sum\limits_{i=1}^{k} |E(P_i)|$;

- $f_2(s) : \sum\limits_{i=1}^{k} \{ C(P_i) - Max \text{ / if } C(P_i) > Max \}$;

- $f_3(s) : \sum\limits_{i=1}^{k} \sum\limits_{j \in P_i} T_j$;

- $f_4(s)$: number of students having four exams a day ;

- $f_5(s) : \sum\limits_{i=1}^{k} | A(P_i) |$;

P_i is the set of exams at period i (colour i). $E(P_i)$ is the intersection (number of common students) of the set of exams P_i. Max is the capacity of the unique examination room. $C(P_i)$ is the number of students sitting an exam at period i (colour i). $T_j = 1$ if an exam j of set P_i at period i generates a violation of a period constraint , otherwise 0. $A(P_i) = Max - C(P_i)$ if $C(P_i) - Max/2 > 0$; $A(P_i) = C(P_i)$ otherwise.
We set $c_1 > c_2 > c_3 > c_4$ and $c_4 = c_5$ according to the constraints hierarchy.
We add an extra part to this objective function (f_5) in order to fill up the examination hall more completely. As we can see, f_5 is minimum (equal to 0) if, for each planning period, either the hall is full or empty. Otherwise, f_5 is maximum if, for each planning period, the hall is half full. In this way, we can create an empty planning period in which we can place exams which transgress a major constraint.
The aspiration level, $A(f(s))$, is set and updated at each step of the algorithm. If we get a better neighbour s than the best s^* found in the past iterations, then we set the aspiration level to $f(s)-1$. If we cannot find a neighbour s among the neighbourhood such that $f(s)$ is better than $f(s^*)$, and if there exists a neighbour s' belonging to the tabu list such that $f(s') \leq A(f(s))$, then we drop the tabu status of s' and consider the move as a valid one.

4.2.3. Initial solution

The initial solution is provided by a heuristic based on our tree search method. But no backtracks are allowed. So, if we cannot use one of the first 20 colours to schedule a UV, we create a new planning period. We obtain an initial solution which does not necessarily have 20 colours. In this case, we apply another procedure. Otherwise, the heuristic has directly found a solution and the tabu search need not be done. The exams which have a colour greater than 20 are distributed to the basic planning periods in order to minimize the number of violation of period constraints. Consequently, this constraint is fully respected at the beginning of the algorithm. Applying the tabu search, the changes we made to the solution will improve the two main constraints at the expense of the planning period constraint. Using this strategy, we hope to reach a solution which respects this preference constraint as well as possible.

4.2.4. Stopping criterion

The algorithm ends if the three main constraints are respected or if N iterations have been made (we set N = 200).

4.3. The C.A.D. system

The last method we propose is a very simple Computer Aided Design System. It can be used if the automatic methods failed. It is able to create a solution or to improve a partial one. For each UV, the C.A.D.S gives the list of compatible UV's and information useful for building a set of compatible UV's. We can build, manage and store lists of compatible UV with this tool.
One should note that it takes 1 day to build the timetable with this tool. The full manual method needed 3 or 4 days.

5. How to use the automatic systems

The idea is to build and submit to the automatic timetabling systems (tree search and tabu) a very difficult problem first. In this way, if a solution exists respecting all the constraints, then the tree search obtains it quickly because the search tree is small. If not, the computing time required to establish that there is no solution is also small. In this last case, after applying the tabu search, the tabu result can either be retained because only very few preference constraints are violated, or rejected but nevertheless used to build and submit another easier problem (less constrained) to the system. The decision is taken by the human designer according to his or her preferences and experiences. This scheme may be applied several times to arrive at a solution. We use this scheme to present our results.

6. Results

The different results we present correspond to real problems for autumn 1993, spring 1993 and autumn 1994. For each problem, we present three cases corresponding to different scheduling policies. These cases are :

- case 1 : general culture UV's prohibited on Monday and Friday afternoon, and large UV's prohibited on Thursday afternoon and Friday;
- case 2 : general culture UV's prohibited on Monday and Friday, and large UV's prohibited on Thursday and Friday;
- case 3 : general culture UV's prohibited on Monday, Thursday and Friday, and large UV's prohibited on Wednesday, Thursday and Friday.

The computational results obtained with our methods are presented below. The unit CPU time is expressed in seconds. For the tree search method, we indicate CPU time, whether a solution is reached or not, and the number of nodes developed. For the tabu, we present CPU time and whether a "good" solution is reached. We describe below what represents a "good" solution. For the heuristic, CPU time and the number of colours used are reported.

AUTUMN 93	94 EXAMS	Case 1	Case 2	Case 3
	CPU TIME	1.2 s	24.91 s	0.98 s
TREE SEARCH	correct solution (Y/N) ?	Y	Y	N
	NODES	91	8243	78
TABU SEARCH	CPU TIME	1.12 s	402.42 s	416.28 s
	correct solution (Y/N) ?	Y	Y(3)	N(*)
	CPU TIME	1.08 s	1.11 s	1.09 s
Heuristic	colour	20	21	25

SPRING 93	131 EXAMS	Case 1	Case 2	Case 3
	CPU TIME	22.54 s	1184.88 s	3.93 s
TREE SEARCH	correct solution (Y/N) ?	Y	N	N
	NODES	8850	294942	901
TABU SEARCH	CPU TIME	986.78 s	928.44 s	940.03 s
	correct solution (Y/N) ?	Y(6)	N(*)	N
	CPU TIME	2.63 s	2.65 s	2.67 s
Heuristic	colour	21	22	24

AUTUMN 94	109 EXAMS	Case 1	Case 2	Case 3
	CPU TIME	8.27 s	20.16 s	5.19 s
TREE SEARCH	correct solution (Y/N) ?	Y	N	N
	NODES	2292	5674	1442
TABU SEARCH	CPU TIME	651.58 s	651.58 s	759.51 s
	correct solution (Y/N) ?	Y(3)	Y(4)	N(*)
	CPU TIME	1.72 s	1.71 s	1.75 s
Heuristic	colour	21	22	26

The asterisk [*] in the results table indicates that we obtain a 20-colouring but the cumulative constraint is not respected. The number in brackets indicates the number of constraint period violations but, in these cases, we obtain the 20-colouring respecting the cumulative constraint. The tree search results are very good in terms of computational time. We get a solution, or conversely we prove there is no solution, in less than 20 minutes. However, the tabu search is a convenient alternative to obtain a good approximate solution (autumn 94, case 2). Moreover, for the autumn problems (case 3), the colouring constraint is respected. Only one or two exams with few students need to be scheduled in an extra room in order to obtain a feasible solution. At this stage, the human designer can decide to take or leave these approximate solutions.

The objective function curves (see Fig. 5 from 5.a to 5.f) for case 2 of the autumn 1994 problem are reported below. These curves correspond to an example where we attempt to minimize the number of students having four exams in a day. It takes more than 10 hours to compute. This constraint is a preference specified by the administration,

but not taken into account in the manual procedures because it takes too long to build intersection and union of students sets. Using the tabu method, we generate the full neighbourhood, then the computation time increases because we have to compute set operations. If this constraint became more significant, we would generate only a subset of the neighbours and increase the associated weight in the objective function. The second set of curves (see Fig. 6 from 6.a to 6.e) does not take into account this constraint. It presents case 3 for the three problems (autumn 1993, spring 1993 and autumn 1994).

341

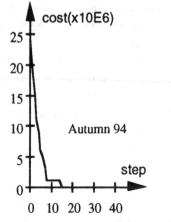

Fig. 5.a. Coloration constraint
f1(s).

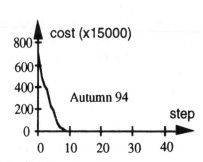

Fig. 5.b. Cumulative constraint
f2(s).

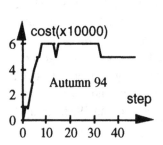

Fig. 5.c. Time period constraint
f3(s).

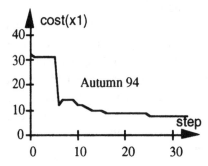

Fig. 5.d. 4 exams a day constraint
f4(s).

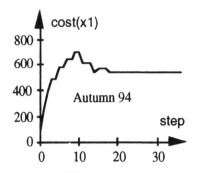

Fig. 5.e. Filling up of the hall
f5(s).

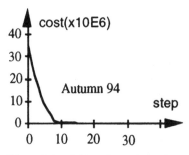

Fig. 5.f. Objective function.

Fig. 5. Tabu objective functions with minimization of students having
4 exams a day.

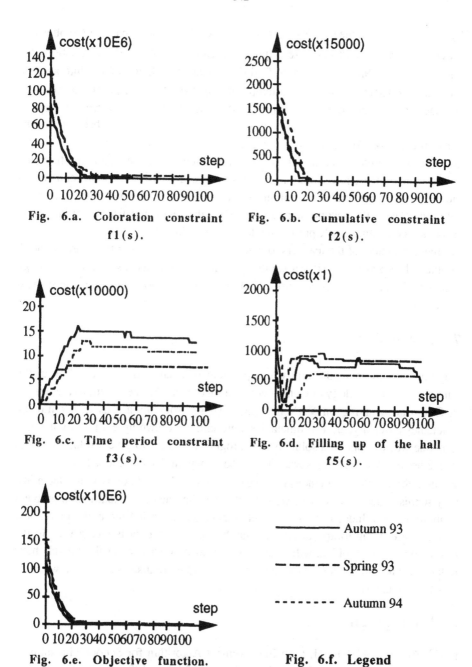

Fig. 6.a. Coloration constraint
f1(s).

Fig. 6.b. Cumulative constraint
f2(s).

Fig. 6.c. Time period constraint
f3(s).

Fig. 6.d. Filling up of the hall
f5(s).

Fig. 6.e. Objective function.

Fig. 6.f. Legend

Fig. 6. Tabu objective functions.

One can remark that the two first sets of curves for the f_1 and f_2 parts of the objective functions decrease and reach zero quickly because we set on these functions the highest weights. Namely, we try to find first a feasible solution taking into account the main constraints then, we attempt to improve the quality of the solution considering the secondary constraints. For this reason, one can observe two steps in the f_3 curves. The initial solution provided to the tabu algorithm has been built to be constraint period free but it did not consider the coloration and the cumulative constraints. Therefore, the initial solution is unpractical. This explains the first step where constraint period violations increase while the two other main constraints violations decrease until the minimum is reached (that is 0 if we reach a feasible solution). Then, the second step occurs. The tabu algorithm try to minimize the secondary constraints while preserving the feasible solution.

For the assignment of the teachers to invigilate exams, computing times are about 15 minutes. There always exists a solution to this problem because there are a large number of teachers. Consequently, finding a solution does not entail any great difficulty.

7. Conclusion

Our aim was to solve the real-world problem of examination timetabling at the University of Technology of Compiègne. We succeeded. All the programs are written in C and are running on VAX machines. These programs are used to build the timetables twice a year. The timetables were initially drawn up entirely by hand. It took one week to obtain a solution. Our programs are able to give a solution in less than 2 hours, by reapplying several times the policy until a solution is found.

We used three different methods to solve our problem. We did not try to use them in a very sophisticated way because we think that the lifetime of an examination problem is about 5 years. Indeed, the number of students is increasing more and more, new curricula are going to appear and the number of UV's taught is increasing. So the formulation of the problem will change in the near future and we shall probably have to take into account several examination rooms and more than one week in which to schedule the exams.

8. Bibliography

[AUS 76]   AUST, RJ. ; An Improvement Algorithm for School Timetabling. Computer J. Vol 19, N° 4 pages 339-343, 1976.

[BOU 92a]   BOUFFLET, J. P. ; Mémoire de doctorat "Emplois du temps dans un environnement fortement contraint : exemple de l'U.T.C". Thèse de Doctorat en Contrôle des Systèmes de l'Université de Technologie de Compiègne, Génie Informatique, 20 février 1992.

[BOU 92b]   BOUFFLET, J. P. et TRIGANO, P. ; "CELAME : Un Outil d'Aide à la Conception des Emplois du Temps de L'Université de

Technologie de Compiègne". ERGO IA'92, Ergonomie et Informatique Avancée, Biarritz France, 1992.

[BRE 79]   BRELAZ, D ; New Methods to Color the Vertices of a Graph. Communication of the ACM, Vol 22, N°4, pp 251-256, April 1979.

[CAN 89]   CANGALOVIC, M and SCHREUDER, A. M. ; Exact Colouring Algorithm for Weighted Graphs applied to Timetabling Problems with Lectures of different lengths. European Journal of Operational Research, Vol 51, pp 248- 258, 1991.

[CAR 86]   CARTER, M W ; A Survey of Practical Applications of Examination Timetabling Algorithms. Operations research vol 34, N°2, pages 193-202, 1986.

[EDM 72]   EDMONDS, J. and KARP, R. M. ; "Theoretical improvements in algorithmic efficiency for network flow problems"; Journal of the ACM Vol 19, N°2 pp 248-264.

[FER 83]   FERLAND,J et ROY, S et TRAN GIA LOC ; Quadratic Assignment Models for Examination Timetabling and Game Scheduling; Publication N° 485, Université de Montréal, 1983.

[FER 85]   FERLAND,J et ROY, S et TRAN GIA LOC ; The Timetabling Problem. Publication N° 531, Université de Montréal, 1985.

[GLO 88]   GLOVER, F. ; TABU Search. CAAI Report 88-3, University of Colorado, Boulder, 1988.

[GLO 90]   GLOVER, F ; TABU Search : a Tutorial. Interface, Vol 20, pp 74-94, 1990.

[HER 87]   HERTZ, A and DE WERRA, D ; Using Tabu Search Techniques For Graph Colouring. Computing Vol 39, pp 345-351, 1987.

[HER 89]   HERTZ, A. ; Coloration des Sommets d'un Graphe et son Application à la Confection d'Horaire. Thèse N° 785, Ecole Polytechnique Fédérale de Lausanne, 1989.

[NEG 93]   NEGRE, S. ; Algorithmes de Coloration de Graphe : Application à la Conception des Emplois du Temps de la Semaine d'Examen de l'Université de Technologie de Compiègne. Rapport de DEA de Contrôle des Systèmes, URA 817 Heudiasyc, Université de Technologie de Compiègne, 1993.

[SCH 80]   SCHMIDT,G and STRÖHLEIN,T ; Timetable Construction an annoted Bibliography. Comput J Vol 23, N° 4, pages 307-316, 1980.

[TRI 84]   TRIPATHY,A ; School Timetabling-A case in large binary integer linear programming. Management science Vol 30, pages 1473-1489, 1984.

[VDV 92]   VI CAO, N. and DU MERLE, O. and VIAL, J. P. ; Un Système de Confection Automatisée d'Horaires d'Examens; Revue des Sytème de Décision, Vol 1, N°4, pp 377-399, Editions Hermes, 1992.

General Cooling Schedules for a Simulated Annealing Based Timetabling System

Jonathan Thompson and Kathryn A Dowsland

European Business Management School,
University of Wales Swansea,
Singleton Park, Swansea,
U. K.,
SA2 8PP.
E-mail. j.m.thompson@swan.ac.uk
Keywords. Timetabling, simulated annealing, cooling schedule.

Abstract. The precise nature of the examination timetabling problem differs from institution to institution. Thus any general solution method must be suitably flexible and this paper is concerned with finding robust cooling schedules for a simulated annealing based approach. The motivation is TISSUE, a timetabling package developed and used successfully at Swansea University. Previous work has concentrated on the problem specific decisions, and with very slow cooling, TISSUE performs well on a variety of real life test data. Here, we concentrate on automating the cooling schedule with the objective of improving running times without sacrificing solution quality. The results of extensive tests on a variety of data sets demonstrated that adaptive schedules were flexible enough to produce high quality solutions with a reduction in solution time.

1 Introduction

Generic heuristic search methods such as simulated annealing (SA), tabu search (TS), and genetic algorithms (GA) are frequently hailed as being robust techniques, capable of maintaining a consistent standard of high quality solutions over a range of differing constraints and objectives. This makes them an attractive proposition for examination scheduling as the precise problem definition varies from institution to institution. However, all these methods depend on a suitable choice of parameters which control the way in which the solution space is searched. This suggests that some adjustments may be necessary in order to obtain maximum performance in different situations. This paper investigates the robustness of a simulated annealing approach to the examination scheduling problem and examines the extent to which this relies on the choice of a suitably adaptive cooling schedule.

The work is motivated by a very successful simulated annealing solution to the problem. The resulting system, TISSUE, has been used to schedule the examinations at University of Wales Swansea for the last three years. It has also performed well on a variety of test problems from other institutions, involving different data characteristics and objectives. However, this success has been achieved using a long slow cooling schedule over a wide temperature range. Here, we focus on the relationship between the cooling schedule and solution time and quality, and show how this is affected by the underlying structure of the problem data and the form of the objective function. Our ultimate aim is to identify an efficient adaptive cooling schedule which can be incorporated into TISSUE, to enable it to provide good results for a broad spectrum of problems with a minimal amount of computational effort.

We begin with a brief outline of SA and then go on to discuss the examination scheduling problem, using data from a variety of institutions to illustrate the differences and similarities in problem definition. This is followed by a full description of our SA implementation, together with some preliminary results which confirm the importance of the cooling schedule. A brief survey of the literature is then used to highlight a variety of generic or adaptive cooling schedules. A subset of these are selected for experimentation and compared empirically with some new developments, using a number of different data sets, neighbourhoods and cost functions.

2 Simulated Annealing

Simulated annealing as an optimisation technique was first suggested by Kirkpatrick et al. [1] in 1983. It is a variant of local search which allows uphill moves to be accepted in a controlled manner. In order to apply SA it is necessary to express the problem within the local search framework, by defining a solution space, neighbourhood structure, and cost function. This essentially defines a solution landscape which is searched by moving from the current solution to a neighbouring solution. Figure 1 outlines the basic procedure. Potential moves are sampled randomly and all improving moves are accepted automatically. Other moves are accepted with probability $\exp(-\delta/t)$, where δ is the change in cost function and t is a control parameter. The form of the acceptance probability function is derived from an analogy with the simulation of the physical cooling of material in a heat bath where the expectation of an increase in energy is given by Boltzmann's distribution. For this reason the parameter t is known as the temperature and the value of the cost function is sometimes referred to as the energy. It is well known that the quality of solutions is sensitive to the way in which the temperature parameter is adjusted - the cooling schedule. This is defined by the starting temperature, t_0, the stopping conditions, the reduction function, α, and the number of repetitions at each temperature, $nrep$. These values are problem specific as they must be chosen with respect to the shape of the solution landscape. Here we address the problem of finding appropriate cooling schedules for the simulated annealing approach to the examination scheduling problem described in the next section.

Select an inital solution s_0
Select an initial temperature $t_0 > 0$,
Select a temperature reduction function α;
Repeat
   Repeat
      Randomly select $s \epsilon N(s_0)$;
      $\delta = f(s) - f(s_0)$
      if $\delta < 0$ then
        $s_0 = s$
      else
        generate random $x \epsilon U(0,1)$
        if $x < exp(-\delta/t)$ then
          $s_0 = s$
        endif
      endif
   until $iteration\_count = nrep$
   $t = \alpha(t)$
Until stopping condition = true.
s_0 is the approximation to the optimal solution.

Fig. 1. Simulated Annealing for Minimisation

3 Examination Scheduling

The literature on examination scheduling indicates that there is no single definition of the problem, and a number of recent surveys confirm this view (Thompson
[2] and Loughlin [3]). The examination period is usually fixed and the primary objective is to schedule the exams so that any constraints on resources are obeyed
and student clashes are eliminated, or minimised. However, most institutions
also impose further, locally defined, constraints and secondary objectives. These
secondary objectives normally involve ensuring adequate gaps between pairs or
groups of exams taken by an individual student and are collectively referred to
as minimising second order conflict. The problem at Swansea is typical of many
and can be defined as that of finding a schedule which optimises the secondary
objectives subject to the binding constraints outlined below.

Binding constraints:
all exams to be scheduled within 24 time-slots
no student clashes to be allowed
certain pairs of exams to be scheduled at the same time
certain pairs of exams to be scheduled at different times
certain groups of exams to be scheduled in order
certain exams to be scheduled within time-windows
no more than 1200 students to be involved in any one session.

Secondary objectives:

minimise the number of exams with over 100 students scheduled after period 10

minimise the number of occurrences of students having exams in consecutive periods.

Our simulated annealing approach does not rely wholly on weights to deal with different aspects of the problem. Instead it solves the problem in phases. In the first phase a feasible solution which satisfies all the binding constraints is achieved. Phase two then searches the space of feasible solutions with the aim of optimising the secondary objectives. (In practice we have found that the objective of placing large exams early is relatively easy to achieve and we have included this as a time window constraint in phase one). A full discussion of the advantages of this phased approach can be found in Dowsland [4]. The implementation is derived from the SA solution to the graph-colouring problem suggested by Chams et al. [5] and by Morgenstern and Shapiro [6] and we therefore outline this model before detailing our simulated annealing framework.

The basis of the model is the standard graph-colouring representation of the problem. First, exams which must be scheduled together are merged and then each exam is mapped onto a vertex in the graph. Edges are defined between each pair of vertices representing exams which cannot take place in the same time period. A feasible colouring, in which vertices are allocated colours so that no two adjacent vertices have the same colour, then defines a clash-free timetable with the colours representing the different time-slots. Balakrishnan [7] extended this model to include time-windows by adding a set of dummy vertices representing the different time-slots. The problem of finding a feasible schedule for Swansea using the 24 available timeslots can then be regarded as that of finding a 24-colouring of the underlying graph, so that orderings and room capacity constraints are obeyed. Chams et al. report considerable success using SA to solve the problem of colouring a graph in k colours, and our phase one implementation is based on theirs, with additional restrictions on the solution space and extra terms in the cost function. They define the solution space as the set of partitions of vertices into k colour classes, and a neighbourhood move involves changing the colour of a single vertex. The cost is given by the number of edges between vertices in the same colour and the objective is to reduce this to zero. This model does not include capacity restrictions or pre-orderings and we have the choice of imposing these additional constraints on the solution space or penalising them in the cost function. We chose to impose orderings into our definition of feasible solutions, but to include desk capacities as a cost function term, as it is possible that the solution space may become disconnected if capacity constraints are tight.

This results in the following definitions.

Solution space: allocations of exams to 24 time-slots subject to ordering constraints

Neighbourhood move: change of time-slot for a single exam

Cost: $f_1 = w_1c_1 + w_2c_2 + w_3c_3 + w_4c_4$

where c_1 is the number of student clashes, c_2 is the number of exams clashing for other reasons, c_3 is the number of time-window violations and c_4 is the number of desk capacity violations. The objective is to reduce the cost to its optimal value of zero. Once a zero cost solution has been found phase two commences from the final solution of phase one and works on a reduced solution space from which all solutions with $f_1 > 0$ have been removed. The objective in this phase is to minimise the second order conflict given by cost function:

$$f_2 = c_5$$

In the case of Swansea, c_5 is the number of occurrences of a student having two exams in consecutive time periods. Initially we used the same neighbourhood structure as in phase one, but subsequent experiments showed that a wider neighbourhood suggested by Morgernstern and Shapiro and based on the idea of Kempe chains gave significantly better results. Essentially this neighbourhood involves swapping groups of vertices in two colour classes. When these vertices form a complete connected chain, the colouring remains feasible. Full details can be found in Thompson and Dowsland [8]. The resulting algorithm has been used live at Swansea for the last 3 years and has been tested on a variety of other data. In most cases phase one is relatively easy to solve, and is therefore less sensitive to the cooling schedule. The remainder of this paper will therefore concentrate on phase two.

We have already indicated that the problem details and data characteristics vary from institution to institution. Table 1 illustrates these differences with respect to eight institutions. Simple measures such as numbers of exams, students, and timeslots are obviously important but the ease or difficulty of a problem depends on the way in which these quantities interact to produce constraints. The graph-theoretic quantities of number of edges and density measure the number of constraints on the problem and the clique number is a lower bound on the minimum number of feasible time periods. Thus the difference between this and the number of periods available gives some idea of the difficulty of the problem. Also relevant is the mean spare desk capacity. These quantities give an indication as to how difficult it will be to find a feasible timetable, which in turn determines the size and connectivity of the solution space. The shape of the solution landscape will also be influenced by the distribution of exam sizes which has an effect on the difference in cost between neighbouring solutions.

The above differences will themselves give rise to a variety of landscapes, and these will become more diverse when the different cost functions are considered. Even if we restrict ourselves to the objective of spacing exams, the definition of cost depends on local conditions. For example, in Swansea all degree examinations are held in the mornings and so a straightforward objective of minimising the number of occurrences of students having exams on consecutive days is appropriate. Others (e.g. Nottingham) have three exams per day and wish to minimise the number of students with two exams on the same day

Table 1. Comparison of Examination Timetabling Details at Various Universities

Institution	No. Exams	No. Studs	No. Edges	No. Periods	Largest Clique	No. Cliques	Density	Mean No. Studs	Room Usage
EDIN	59	?	1907	28	13	3	42.70%	20.03	?
HEC	80	2823	1351	18	17	1	42.80%	132.78	?
LSE	381	2726	4531	18	17	2	6.30%	28.64	?
NOTT	800	7896	13208	32	14	5	3.68%	42.50	66%
QUEEN1	561	6502	2949	33	13	2	1.88%	33.15	40%
QUEEN2	632	6780	4043	33	14	6	2.03%	33.81	46%
SUNYAB	981	27600	18874	21	16	170	3.90%	24.69	?
SWAN	569	2657	8621	24	16	14	4.83%	21.15	40%

EDIN = Edinburgh University.

HEC = École des Hautes Études Commerciales, Montrèal.

LSE = London School of Economics.

NOTT = Nottingham University.

QUEEN 1 and 2 = Queens College, Belfast.

SUNYAB = State University of New York at Buffalo.

SWAN = University of Wales Swansea.

and to eliminate pairs of exams in adjacent time-slots on the same day. Belfast has different criteria depending on the 'level' of the student involved. They aim to eliminate situations where higher level students have exams on consecutive days and to minimise the number of lower level students with two exams on the same day. Any generic solution approach must be able to deal with this variety inherent in the problem.

Density is defined as the number of edges divided by the maximum number possible and includes where appropriate timeslot vertices. Mean No. Studs is the average number of students sitting each exam. ? indicates that the relevant figure is unknown.

Before we go on to discuss automatic and adaptive cooling schedules we will use the Swansea data and the objective of minimising second order conflict to illustrate the effect of the cooling schedule on solution quality. Table 2 shows the results of using four different cooling schedules, each with the same temperature range [20, 0.1], for both neighbourhood definitions. The lower value was chosen as the probability of accepting a minimum uphill move of just one unit is negligible at this temperature. The upper limit is chosen as it gives a reasonable probability (0.75) of accepting an 'average' sized uphill move. The first schedule is the slow geometric cooling schedule currently in use, which apparently gives good results for a wide spectrum of problems. However, for a problem the size of Swansea's this schedule requires around eight hours run time on a 486 pc under the standard neighbourhood. If we want to obtain faster solutions with a geometric schedule we have the choice of increasing the cooling rate, or reducing the cooling range. The results are given for a range of cooling ratios varying between 0.99 and 0.6. Solution quality clearly depends on the rate of cooling with very slow cooling giving the best results. Very slow cooling significantly increases the run times and the ratios for these four runs are 40:4:2:1. It is also worth noting that high quality solutions are not reached until near the end of a run, implying that time cannot be saved by cutting off a slow schedule early. This is confirmed by Figure 2 which shows the lower portion of the graph of cost function versus iteration number for a Kempe chain run. For a given number of iterations better results are obtained by adjusting the cooling ratio so that the full range is covered.

Table 2. Second order conflict resulting from SA runs with different cooling ratios on the Swansea data set. In each cell, the two figures refer to results obtained under a Kempe chain neighbourhood and standard neighbourhood respectively.

Cooling Rate	Seed 1	Seed 2	Seed 3	Seed 4	Seed 5
0.99	105/190	100/153	113/168	98/163	117/161
0.9	168/239	149/239	167/270	138/228	158/282
0.8	192/336	207/280	235/280	171/267	152/303
0.6	272/360	274/388	214/354	282/346	236/336

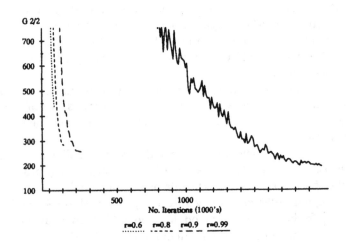

Fig. 2. Effect of Cooling Ratio on Cost

4 Determining Cooling Schedules

Many successful SA implementations use a geometric cooling schedule with parameters obtained by experimentation (see for example Jeffcoat and Bulfin [9], Kuik and Salomon [10]). However, there are many studies, both theoretical and empirical, which seek to improve upon this ad hoc approach. These range from approaches which simply determine upper and lower temperature limits using problem specific information and then use a fixed schedule between them, to those which are truly adaptive in that the temperature profile is adjusted dynamically according to information gathered during the search. Some of the latter category may even abandon the idea of monotonic cooling in favour of a system which also heats up when appropriate.

Theoretical approaches to fixing the starting temperature are frequently based on the concept of thermal equilibrium. For example, White [11] suggests that the starting temperature should be sufficiently high that the average energy (or cost) of visited solutions equals the average energy of the system as a whole. He gives a method for calculating this temperature and Abramson [12] has used this method successfully in his SA solution to the school timetabling problem. However, we have found that for the examination scheduling problem this method produces temperatures which are too high to be of any practical benefit.

Others take the view that the starting temperature should allow acceptance of a large proportion of moves. A suitable value can be found either by starting at a low temperature and heating until the required proportion is achieved or by sampling sets of random solutions and examining their neighbourhoods to obtain details of the expected move size. The stopping temperature may be determined in a similar way, or the run may be concluded when the system has obviously converged to a frozen state.

Having decided the cooling range it is necessary to determine the way in which the temperature will be reduced and the number of iterations executed at each temperature. The two most popular methods are simple geometric cooling in which the temperature is reduced by a constant factor after a fixed number of iterations and a Lundy and Mees schedule [13] in which temperature is reduced after each iteration according to $t \rightarrow 1/(1 + \beta t)$, for some small value of β. Many researchers, (e.g. Johnson et al. [14]) have carried out empirical testing to confirm the view that the shape of the temperature function over time is more important than the precise details of the cooling schedule. In spite of the popularity and simplicity of these schedules there are a number of other suggestions as to how the cooling rate should be controlled. For example Hajek [15] advocates using $t_k = c/log(1 + k)$, where k is the number of iterations and c is the depth of the deepest local, but not global, optimum. This leads to two practical problems in that c is not usually known and all but very small values of c will lead to extremely long run times. Nevertheless, Chams et al. use a schedule which is based on this idea for the graph colouring problem. They use $\exp(2/t)$ iterations at temperature t, (where 2 is their approximation to c in Hajek's formula), together with a reduction factor of 0.93 and a starting temperature of $\sqrt{n}$, where n is the number of vertices.

Anderson et al. [16] report than none of the standard schedules they tried worked well for a class of network design problems arising in telecommunications and suggest a quadratic cooling schedule given by $t_k = a.k^2 + b.k + c$. The upper limit on the temperature (C_0) is determined by considering a number of pre-determined neighbours and setting the initial temperature so that the largest such move has a small, but significant, probability of acceptance. The lower limit (C_F) is also set using problem specific knowledge. If the total number of iterations, max I, is fixed then these limits can be used to define a, b and c as follows.

$$a = (C_0.C_F)/(maxI)^2$$
$$b = 2.(C_F - C_0)/(maxI)$$
$$c = C_0$$

Truly adaptive schedules do not fix the cooling schedule before-hand but determine the number of iterations or the reduction factor dynamically as the search progresses. At the simplest level they use acceptance rates, for example reducing the temperature when a pre-specified number of moves have been accepted. More complex schedules use the concept of equilibrium. For example Huang et al. [17] suggest a schedule which aims to reach equilibrium at each temperature. This is monitored by counting the number of accepted moves lying within a given range of the average cost at that temperature and comparing this with the number outside the range. Equilibrium is reached if the former reaches a prespecified value before the latter. Once equilibrium has been detected the temperature is reduced by a factor which is adjusted automatically to ensure that the average energy of the system decreases uniformly.

A number of researchers have abandoned the idea of monotonic cooling. Connolly [18] shows that constant temperature annealing works well for the quadratic assignment problem and suggests a method for finding this temperature. Dowsland [19] extends this idea to allow more flexibility with a schedule which allows temperature to move up and down while keeping the acceptance ratio more or less constant. This is achieved by reducing temperature according to the Lundy and Mees function when a move is accepted and heating up according to $t \to 1/(1 - \alpha t)$ when a move is rejected. The ratio $\alpha : \beta$ determines the ratio of rejected to accepted moves. Other non-monotonic cooling schedules have been suggested. For example Walsh and Miller [20] define target energies at a series of temperature values and then adjust temperature up or down depending on whether these targets have been reached. This method relies on a good estimate of the optimal value of the cost function. Li and Jiang [21] partition the solution space into subspaces and adjust the temperature level according to the current subspace. Subspaces have temperatures which are higher or lower than the global temperature depending on the ease with which they can be entered. This allows a space which may contain good local optima, but which cannot be entered without significant hill climbing, to be approached more easily by taking advantage of a higher temperature at its boundaries. When moving from one subspace to another the temperature local to the old space is used. This allows more freedom of movement between subspaces and makes it easier for the search to escape from areas surrounding local optima.

5   Experiments

The objective of our experiments is threefold. First we want to compare geometric cooling with some of the adaptive methods to see whether the adaptive methods are able to produce better, or more consistent solutions. Second we want to examine the effect of data characteristics and cost function on the relative performances of different methods. Third, we want to identify the best option if solution time is limited. We have selected four of the eight data sets given in Table 1 to form the basis of these experiments. These are:

Swansea - average size, average difficulty
HEC - small, but tight problem with large exams
LSE - similar to HEC but with smaller exams and lower density
Nottingham - large, but relatively sparse problem.

Four different cost functions, based on real requirements at different institutions have been applied to each data set, three based on the objective of spacing exams out, and one on uniform space utilisation. In order to define the spacing objectives we introduce the following notation. Gx/y defines the number of occurrences of a student having x exams in y consecutive timeslots, and Dx/y defines the number of students having x exams in y consecutive periods in a single day. Our cost functions use $G2/2$ (the number of occurrences of pairs of consecutive exams), $G3/3$ (the number of triples), $D2/2$ (the number of occurrences of exams in consecutive slots on the same day), and $D2/3$ (the number of occurrences of 2 exams in 3 periods on the same day). This latter measure is used in situations like that at Nottingham where there are 3 slots per day, and therefore measures the number of occurrences of two exams on the same day. Our three spacing cost functions are $G2/2$, $G2/2 + 10G3/3$ and $10D2/2 + D2/3$, where the latter assumes 3 slots per day. The weighting factor of 10 has been chosen arbitrarily to produce significantly different cost functions for our experiments and we do not claim it produces the best trade-off between the different objectives. The fourth function will be denoted EU and is defined as the sum of the squares of the variation from the mean desk utilisation, summed over the set of timeslots.

Each data set / cost function pair has been run on a number of cooling schedules, spanning the spectrum of adaptive and non-adaptive methods. In addition to the basic geometric schedules using 4 cooling rates over a wide range, we opted for the following:

Geometric cooling with variable repetitions as suggested by Chams et al.
The quadratic cooling schedule of Anderson et al.
The adaptive schedule of Huang et al.
A modification of the non-monotonic method of Dowsland.

From now on, these will be referred to as CHA, AND, HUA, and DOW respectively and standard geometric cooling will be abbreviated to GC.

The starting temperature for the geometric cooling schedules differs from problem to problem and is chosen so that the probability of accepting an uphill move of average size is 75%. Of the other methods, only AND is truly automatic in that the only parameter required is the number of iterations. In our experiments, this was set equal to the number of iterations used under the standard geometric cooling schedule, thereby allowing a fair comparison. However we chose not to use the method of Anderson et al. in setting the initial temperature as this requires the generation of a thousand feasible solutions and their neighbours. In this case finding a feasible solution is itself a difficult task and we chose to generate one thousand neighbours of the same feasible solution instead.

The method of Chams et al. requires estimation of the parameter, c. Using the value of 2, which had proved suitable for a graph-colouring objective, on the Swansea data, resulted in very fast cooling and poor results. This was attributed to this value being too low and, as calculations using more realistic values indicated very long run times, this schedule was abandoned.

Both of our adaptive methods also require preset parameters. Huang et al. adjusts the temperature according to the equation

$$t \rightarrow t.exp(-\delta t/\sigma(t))$$

where $\sigma(t)$ is the standard deviation in energy at temperature t. Mirkin et al. [22] suggest that the results are insensitive to the parameter δ, although it has a significant effect on run time. Our initial choice of 0.7 as suggested by Huang et al. resulted in fewer iterations being conducted in comparison to the other cooling schedules. Further experiments with values of δ ranging between 0.7 and 0.1 showed improvements in solution quality between 0.7 and 0.3 but lower values increased solution time but not solution quality. With the value of 0.3, the number of iterations is about half that required under slow geometric cooling. This schedule also uses parameters in determining its equilibrium conditions. It is possible that changing these would result in extended run times but we have used the values recommended by Huang et al. throughout. We did not however use the method suggested by Huang et al. for choosing the starting temperature as this is based on White's method which produces unnecessarily high values. Instead we set t_0 to the same value as was used for the geometric cooling schedule. Further experiments confirmed that this did not have a detrimental effect on solution quality.

Dowsland's schedule requires a value for β and a ratio for rejected to accepted moves. The suggested value of $\beta = 0.02$ proved satisfactory but initial experiments suggested that keeping the ratio constant was not appropriate. We therefore combined the non-monotonic schedule with the principle of cooling by allowing the ratio to increase geometrically, multiplying by a factor of 1.005 after a fixed number of iterations. This left the decision as to what range of ratios should be used. In order to ensure convergence the lower limit should be equal to the proportion of zero cost neighbours expected at local optima, when uphill moves are effectively outlawed. After some experimentation based on the Kempe chain neighbourhoods the upper limit was then set at twice this value.

Before considering the quality of results produced by these different schedules, we compared the temperatures produced over time on a single run using Kempe chain neighbourhoods on the Swansea data to ensure they are significantly different. The results are shown in Figure 3 with values being plotted every 10,000 iterations. The three monotonic schedules are similar. However AND tends to be the hottest throughout. The adaptive cooling schedule HUA is of similar shape to that of the geometric cooling schedule, but converges far more quickly and shows evidence of kinks where equilibrium is reached more quickly. DOW reaches high temperatures during the search but has a general downward trend as the system is cooled. We conjectured that these differences would lead to different behaviour during the search and this is confirmed by Figure 4 which shows the corresponding cost function values.

Having established that all four cooling schedules were worth further investigation, we conducted a series of runs on the various datasets and cost functions described earlier. With the exception of HUA, the results in Table 3 are based on the number of iterations required by very slow geometric cooling. HUA was run with $\delta =0.3$. As predicted by previous studies (Thompson and Dowsland [8]) Kempe chain neighbourhoods achieve higher quality results across the spectrum of data sets and cost functions. Under Kempe chain neighbourhoods and the G2/2 cost function, all methods give solutions of similar quality although HUA tends to be slightly inferior. Under standard neighbourhoods DOW is not competitive with the current parameters which were chosen after experiments with the Kempe chain neighbourhood. However when we consider different cost functions, greater differences in solution quality are apparent. DOW is far superior on the weighted cost functions. Closer inspection showed that it was successful in removing more of the heavily weighted terms. This is probably a result of its flexibility in reaching high temperatures later in the run.

Throughout the experiments, the largest discrepancies occurred on the HEC data set indicating that the landscape produced by this tight problem with large exams may be more sensitive to the cooling schedule. This is particularly apparent with the EU cost function which can produce particularly spiky landscapes due to its quadratic term. It appears that this problem is very difficult to solve due to this landscape and the large average exam size and therefore, the results are poor.

Although three of the schedules were run over the same number of iterations, solution times vary. These discrepancies are due to the time taken to update solution details after accepted moves so that those schedules which spend more time at higher temperatures tend to be slower. The times taken for the runs shown in Figure 3 were 25, 30, 16, and 3 minutes for GC, AND, DOW, and HUA respectively. Even the fastest of these corresponds to more than an hour on a standard 486 pc. Thus we were interested in evaluating the effects of faster cooling.

In line with Table 2, the experiments were repeated with the number of iterations used for AND and DOW set to equal those required for cooling ratios of 0.9, 0.8 and 0.6. HUA was run with $\delta =0.7$, corresponding approximately to

Fig. 3. A Comparison of Temperature Levels

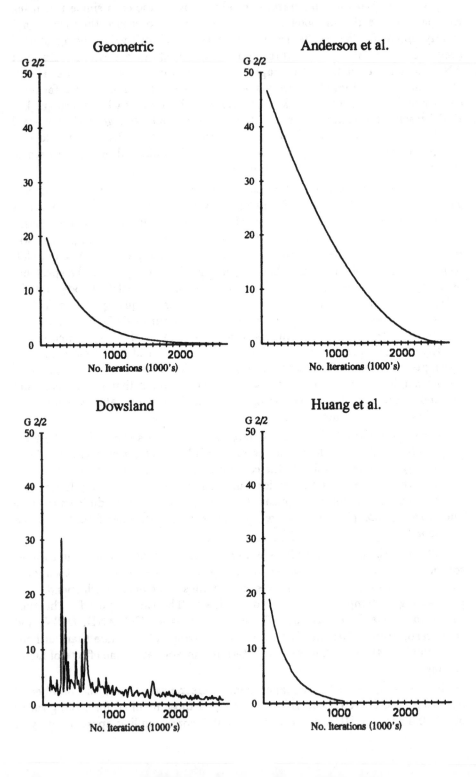

Fig. 4. A Comparison of Cost Function Levels

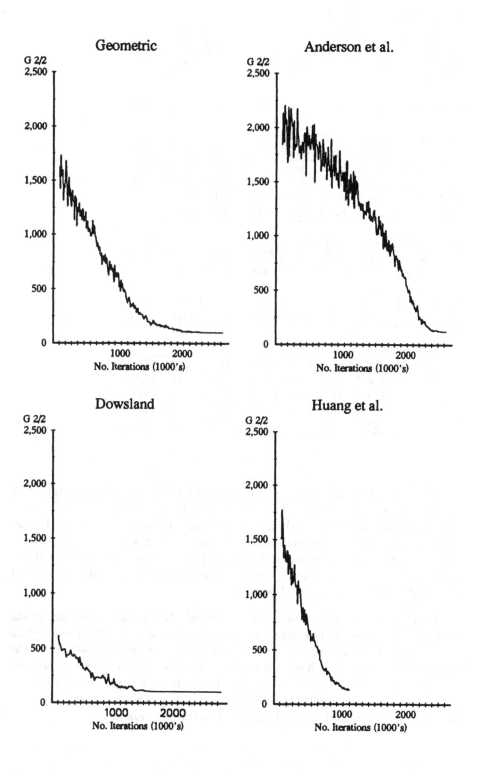

Geometric

Anderson et al.

Dowsland

Huang et al.

Table 3. Comparison of Cooling Schedules for Slow Cooling

(i) Cost Function = G2/2

	Kempe				Standard			
	SWAN	HEC	LSE	NOTT	SWAN	HEC	LSE	NOTT
GC	106.6	200.2	202.6	0.0	167.0	262.6	312.6	0.0
AND	113.2	200.8	210.4	0.0	178.6	280.2	298.6	0.0
DOW	100.6	202.8	208.4	0.0	249.0	292.6	329.8	0.0
HUA	127.0	225.8	235.8	0.2	218.0	368.2	400.0	0.0

(ii) Cost Function = G2/2+10G3/3

	SWAN	HEC	LSE	NOTT	SWAN	HEC	LSE	NOTT
GC	120.6	230.8	211.8	0.0	187.8	301.4	542.4	0.0
AND	121.6	258.4	258.2	0.0	197.0	454.0	435.6	0.2
DOW	118.2	239.6	266.2	0.0	246.2	441.6	944.6	0.0
HUA	147.4	274.4	240.8	0.0	224.0	564.0	896.0	0.0

(iii) Cost Function = 10D2/2+D2/3

	SWAN	HEC	LSE	NOTT	SWAN	HEC	LSE	NOTT
GC	662.2	892.4	1002.2	70.2	964.0	1676.4	1575.2	88.4
AND	698.0	894.2	935.0	109.8	965.8	1226.0	1550.0	176.0
DOW	641.2	1002.2	1205.2	112.8	891.4	2158.0	2031.8	100.8
HUA	655.4	927.8	1125.0	106.2	961.2	1532.0	1942.6	138.0

(iv) Cost Function = EU

	SWAN	HEC	LSE	NOTT	SWAN	HEC	LSE	NOTT
GC	0.0	59823	0.0	0.0	2122.4	105405	0.0	283.4
AND	0.0	63552	0.0	0.0	1.0	106387	0.0	60.0
DOW	0.0	74932	0.0	0.0	20.4	178946	34.0	1113.2
HUA	0.0	78874	0.0	0.0	258.2	139733	0.0	508.4

the number of iterations with a cooling ratio of 0.6. These results, together with random descent, are given in Table 4. The quality of results under GC, AND, and DOW fall away significantly when compared with the results obtained under HUA. Given limited computational time, this cooling schedule is preferable. However it needs the full run in order to converge to good solutions. Thus if it is likely that the user may want to break the run early, it may be better to adopt the schedule of Dowsland (see Figure 4).

Another important attribute of a cooling schedule is the consistency of the results obtained using different random number streams. All the results given are averages of five different runs and these sometimes mask wide variations. The standard deviations of each set of five solutions indicated little difference between methods, except for HUA which occasionally produced a very poor solution due to its stopping condition being satisfied prematurely. This is conjectured to be due to the presence of large plateaux in the solution landscapes.

Table 4. Comparison of cooling schedules when faster cooling is required.

(A) Cooling Ratio = 0.9

(i) Cost Function = G2/2

	Kempe				Standard			
	SWAN	HEC	LSE	NOTT	SWAN	HEC	LSE	NOTT
GC	156.0	235.0	231.2	0.0	251.6	398.2	518.4	1.6
AND	171.8	225.6	248.0	0.0	293.2	329.0	429.4	2.8
DOW	372.6	231.4	275.6	0.0	372.6	740.8	662.0	3.0

(ii) Cost Function = G2/2+10G3/3

	SWAN	HEC	LSE	NOTT	SWAN	HEC	LSE	NOTT
GC	170.4	271.2	277.2	0.0	248.2	458.8	948.2	0.0
AND	186.0	327.6	344.0	2.0	270.4	566.0	770.0	9.2
DOW	174.6	268.6	316.8	0.0	345.2	386.0	1036.6	0.0

(iii) Cost Function = 10D2/2+D2/3

	SWAN	HEC	LSE	NOTT	SWAN	HEC	LSE	NOTT
GC	662.2	892.4	1002.2	70.2	964.0	1676.4	1575.2	88.4
AND	698.0	894.2	935.0	109.8	965.8	1226.0	1550.0	176.0
DOW	641.2	1002.2	1205.2	112.8	891.4	2158.0	2031.8	100.8

(iv) Cost Function = EU

	SWAN	HEC	LSE	NOTT	SWAN	HEC	LSE	NOTT
GC	0.0	70667	0.0	0.0	2122.2	162535	0.0	347.4
AND	4.2	71982	0.0	9.6	5.0	141116	0.2	27.4
DOW	0.0	88084	0.0	0.0	18.4	209138	74.2	1127.2

(B) Cooling Ratio = 0.8

(i) Cost Function = G2/2

	Kempe				Standard			
	SWAN	HEC	LSE	NOTT	SWAN	HEC	LSE	NOTT
GC	191.4	233.0	253.2	0.0	293.2	471.4	577.0	2.8
AND	221.6	250.6	279.0	0.8	309.2	437.0	453.2	4.2
DOW	160.8	241.6	317.0	0.0	427.6	742.6	661.0	10.0

(ii) Cost Function = G2/2+10G3/3

	SWAN	HEC	LSE	NOTT	SWAN	HEC	LSE	NOTT
GC	211.6	291.2	317.4	0.0	297.0	459.8	1000.4	1.6
AND	325.0	354.6	396.4	17.0	273.6	560.8	952.6	40.4
DOW	267.0	285.6	356.4	0.0	411.8	619.4	1043.0	1.2

(iii) Cost Function = 10D2/2+D2/3

	SWAN	HEC	LSE	NOTT	SWAN	HEC	LSE	NOTT
GC	800.0	1008.8	1125.6	160.6	1175.0	2098.8	2122.0	174.8
AND	1066.8	1025.8	1268.2	691.8	1307.2	1320.4	1897.0	626.4
DOW	783.0	1043.8	129.8	179.0	1216.8	2540.2	2404.4	219.2

Table 4. Comparison of cooling schedules when faster cooling is required (continued).

(iv) Cost Function = EU

	SWAN	HEC	LSE	NOTT	SWAN	HEC	LSE	NOTT
GC	0.0	79103	0.0	0.2	2124.8	171334	0.2	337.8
AND	4.2	71078	0.2	9.6	6.2	146629	0.0	27.4
DOW	0.4	91991	0.0	0.0	773.2	231624	37.2	1124.8

(C) Cooling Ratio = 0.6

(i) Cost Function = G2/2

	Kempe				Standard			
	SWAN	HEC	LSE	NOTT	SWAN	HEC	LSE	NOTT
RD	182.2	310.4	304.6	0.0	509.0	403.8	759.2	0.0
GC	255.6	242.4	278.8	0.4	356.8	489.2	654.4	7.4
AND	310.0	261.0	334.8	20.4	377.4	386.6	502.4	13.6
DOW	201.4	247.4	317.4	0.0	472.2	796.4	688.0	29.6
HUA	156.4	226.6	247.8	0.0	197.0	381.2	492.6	0.0

(ii) Cost Function = G2/2+10G3/3

	SWAN	HEC	LSE	NOTT	SWAN	HEC	LSE	NOTT
RD	440.4	440.8	372.2	0.0	840.8	1214.	1188.0	0.0
GC	255.8	301.4	332.2	0.0	393.2	620.6	1037.6	10.4
AND	368.0	388.8	459.8	78.8	397.0	662.4	946.0	72.0
DOW	392.2	305.0	389.6	0.4	478.4	578.4	1103.4	5.2
HUA	171.4	300.8	282.0	0.0	246.0	616.8	953.2	2.2

(iii) Cost Function = 10D2/2+D2/3

	SWAN	HEC	LSE	NOTT	SWAN	HEC	LSE	NOTT
RD	746.8	1141.4	1156.0	118.0	1465.2	3766.4	3870.0	173.8
GC	918.2	1033.8	1236.8	219.6	1263.8	2337.8	2204.4	291.8
AND	1283.4	1060.6	1459.8	1045.8	1606.4	1465.2	1609.2	914.6
DOW	833.8	1035.4	1228.4	236.4	1230.8	2798.2	2648.0	284.2
HUA	655.4	925.8	907.2	106.2	978.2	1758.4	3804.4	151.4

(iv) Cost Function = EU

	SWAN	HEC	LSE	NOTT	SWAN	HEC	LSE	NOTT
RD	0.0	167433	256.2	0.0	2449.0	327353	2512.8	64.0
GC	0.0	90290	0.0	0.0	2229.6	200786	0.0	343.4
AND	42.2	79867	6.8	53.4	20.8	151245	23346	68.0
DOW	0.2	137540	0.0	0.0	763.0	239601	59.8	1147.6
HUA	0.0	87053	0.0	0.0	228.8	151222	0.0	506.8

These experiments have shown the importance of the cooling parameters and the difficulties associated with setting them at the right levels when dealing with different data sets and cost functions is apparent. It is interesting to note that similar difficulties would be encountered with tabu search. Limited experiments with a simple version of tabu search showed that solution quality is very sensitive to the length of the tabu list and that this varies from data set to data set. So far these experiments have been unable to match the simulated annealing solutions.

6 Conclusions

These experiments have confirmed that problem specific decisions have a greater effect on solution quality than the generic decisions. The results under the Kempe chain neighbourhood are far superior in every case and indeed, the results obtained using random descent are comparable with those obtained under very slow geometric cooling using the standard neighbourhood. Nevertheless the cooling schedule has been shown to be important. Our results show that wherever possible, very slow cooling should be used. Typical run times for very slow cooling equate to no more than an overnight run on a 486 pc. The examination timetabling problem will normally only be solved once or twice a year and as the need for the timetable is not instant an overnight run is acceptable.

If less solution time is available, the results indicate that the schedule of Huang et al. is the most likely to produce good results quickly, but the occasional bad results obtained with this schedule suggest that more than one run should be undertaken. If the quality of solution is vital, then the cooling schedule of Dowsland has been shown to be flexible and robust and capable of achieving results of high quality in reasonable time on a wide range of problems. It should be noted that the best results to date have been obtained by tinkering with the Dowsland cooling schedule and future research may lead to even further improvements.

With the right problem specific decisions, simulated annealing has been shown to be capable of producing high quality results for a wide range of problem instances. These results suggest that if the cost functions are similar, then any suitably slow cooling schedule between appropriate limits will form the basis of a robust heuristic. However the results with the EU cost function suggest that some modification may be necessary if the cost function takes on a significantly different form. If time is limited solution quality is more sensitive to the schedule but the results with the schedule of Huang et al. suggest that good quality results can still be obtained. As a result of this work, the most appropriate schedules for TISSUE appear to be those of Dowsland and Huang et al. with that of Dowsland being used for long runs and that of Huang et al. recommended when less run time is available. This will result in a considerable reduction in average solution times without any degradation in solution quality.

References

1. Kirkpatrick, S., Gelatt, C. and Vecchi, P.: Optimization by simulated annealing. Science 220 (1983), 671-679.

2. Thompson, J.: A survey of the examination timetabling problem at British universities. Internal Report, European Business Management School, University of Wales Swansea (1995).

3. Loughlin, B.: Private communication.

4. Dowsland, K. A.: Simulated annealing solutions for multi-objective scheduling and timetabling. Proc. ADT95, Modern Heuristic Search Methods, UNICOM Seminars, Brunel (1995), 205-220.

5. Chams, M., Hertz, A. and de Werra, D.: Some experiments with simulated annealing for coloring graphs. EJOR 32 (1987), 260-266.

6. Morgenstern, C. and Shapiro, H.: Chromatic number approximation using simulated annealing. Technical Report CS86-1, Department of Computer Science, University of New Mexico (1989).

7. Balakrishnan, N.: Examination scheduling: A computerized application. OMEGA 19, (1991), 37-41.

8. Thompson, J. and Dowsland, K. A.: Variants of Simulated Annealing for the Examination Timetabling Problem. To appear in Annals of OR.

9. Jeffcoat D. E. and Bulfin, R. L.: Simulated annealing for resource-constrained scheduling. EJOR 70 (1993), 43-51.

10. Kuik, R. and Salomon, M.: Multi-level lot-sizing problem: Evaluation of a simulated-annealing heuristic. EJOR 45 (1990), pp25-37.

11. White, S. R.: Concepts of scale in simulated annealing. Proc. of IEEE international conference on computer design (1984), 646-651.

12. Abramson, D.: Constructing school timetables using simulated annealing: sequential and parallel algorithms. Man. Sci. 37, (1991), 98-113.

13. Lundy, M. and Mees, A.: Convergence of an annealing algorithm. Mathematical programming 34 (1986), 111-124.

14. Johnson, D.S., Aragon, C. R., McGeoch, L. A. and Schevon, C.: Optimization by simulated annealing: An experimental evaluation; part II, graph coloring and number partitioning. Operations research 39, (1991), 378-406.

15. Hajek, B.: Cooling schedules for optimal annealing. Mathematics of OR 13 (1988), 311-329.

16. Anderson, K., Vidal, R.V.V. and Iverson, V. B.: Design of a teleprocessing communication network using simulated annealing. Lecture notes in Economics & Mathematical Systems 396 (Ed. R. V. V. Vidal). (1993) 201-216.

17. Huang, M. D., Romeo, F. and Sangiovanni-Vincentelli, A.: An efficient general cooling schedule for simulated annealing. Proceedings of the IEEE International conference on Computer Aided Design, Santa Clara (1986), 381-384.

18. Connolly, D. T.: An improved annealing scheme for the QAP. EJOR 46 (1990), 93-100.

19. Dowsland, K. A.: Some experiments with simulated annealing techniques for packing problems. EJOR 68, (1993b), 389-399.

20. Walsh, P. A. and Miller, D. M.: Goal-directed simulated annealing and simulated sintering. Microelectronics Journal 25, (1994), 363-382.

21. Li, Y. H. and Jiang, Y. J.: Localized simulated annealing in constraint satisfaction and optimization. Proc. ADT95, Modern Heuristic Search Methods, UNICOM Seminars, Brunel (1995), 221-230.

22. Mirkin, G., Vasudevan, K. and Cook, F. A.: A comparison of several cooling schedules for simulated annealing implemented on a residual statics problem. Geophysical research letters 20, (1993), 77-80.

How to Decompose
Constrained Course Scheduling Problems Into
Easier Assignment Type Subproblems

Vincent ROBERT and Alain HERTZ

Contact Person.
Alain HERTZ
Département de Mathématiques
E.P.F.-Lausanne, 1015 Lausanne, Switzerland
tel : +41-21-693 2568
fax: +41-21-693 4250
email : hertz@dma.epfl.ch

Keywords :   course scheduling, assignment type problems, tabu search.

Abstract

We propose in this paper a new approach for tackling constrained course scheduling problems. The main idea is to decompose the problem into a series of easier subproblems. Each subproblem is an assignment type problem in which items have to be assigned to resources subject to some constraints.

By solving a first series of assignment type subproblems, we build an initial solution which takes into account the constraints imposing a structure on the schedule. The total number of overlapping situations is reduced in a second phase by means of another series of assignment type problems.

The proposed approach was implemented in practice and has proven to be satisfactory.

1.   Introduction

When trying to solve real-life course scheduling problems with a set C of constraints, it often turns out that a subset C'⊆C of constraints cannot easily be taken into account. The constraints in C' are usually considered as secondary in comparison with avaibilites or non overlapping constraints.

However, important courses should preferably be given in the mornings. Also, most teachers ask for a compact schedule (i.e. they want to give their courses within as few days as possible, and preferably without any break). Such constraints impose a structure on the schedule. Relaxing them (i.e. putting them in C') may lead to timetables which are considered as non satisfying at all.

Many approaches have been proposed for solving the course scheduling problem [Car66,Tri80,Gan81,Mul82,Wer85]. In most approaches, the scheduling problem is solved in a first phase without taking care of the constraints in C'. Then, in a second phase, the constraints in C' are treated while trying not to deteriorate the schedule obtained in the first phase. This means that the structure of the schedule is built in an early phase, and it can hardly be modified in the subsequent steps.

We propose a different approach which first deals with the constraints imposing a structure on the schedule. It is based on the following observation. When solving real-life course scheduling problems, we often had in hands an initial solution provided by the timetable planner of the considered school. Such initial solutions were a kind of skeleton of the desired schedule. They violated many hard constraints while satisfying most constraints in C'. We have observed that by improving such initial solutions, we could obtain much better schedules than by starting from scratch. Therefore, it became evident that tools needed to be developed for generating initial schedules taking care of the constraints in C'.

Our proposed solution approach is based on a decomposition of the course scheduling problem into a series of easier subproblems. Each subproblem is an assignment type problem (ATP) in which items have to be assigned to resources subject to some constraints. In some special cases, network flow techniques can be used for solving an ATP. Also, small ATP instances can be solved by means of a branch-and-bound algorithm. For the other cases, we suggest the use of tabu search techniques whose flexibility allows to deal with many kinds of constraints.

2. Description of the Problem

Each student of the school has its own curriculum. A curriculum consists of a given set of courses. The courses are divided into lectures of given length, and each lecture must be taught during consecutive time periods.

The set of available periods of the week within which all curricula must be completed is given. Each day consists of at most two half days. When courses are given in the morning and in the afternoon of a same day, there is a fixed lunch time in-between. The periods in each half day are consecutive. Some periods (for example in the late afternoon) are called bad periods in that sense that important courses should not be scheduled at these periods.

The students are classified according to their level. The curricula of two students with the same level can be considerably different. In general, a course is followed by students with the same level. The level of a course (resp. level of a lecture) is defined as the level of the students following this course (resp. lecture). Some courses appear in the curriculum of each student having the same level. Such courses are called compulsory courses as opposed to option courses.

Large courses on which numerous students are registered have to be repeated several times during the week. Students registered in such courses must then be assigned to a specific course section. Note that a course which is not repeated has only one section. Given teachers are assigned to each course section. All sections of a same course need not be taught by the same teacher. Hence, two sections of a same course which do not involve the same teacher may have periods in common.

The availabilities of the teachers as well as the set of course sections in which they are involved are known in advance. Moreover, each teacher has a set of preferred periods during which he would like to teach.

The classrooms may have limited availabilities and some of them can be intended for particular courses (for example, a laboratory for courses on chemistry or physics). All lectures of a course section must be given in the same classroom.

We use the following terminology. An assignment of a starting period to each lecture is called a *timetable*, while an assignment of the students to the sections of the courses is called a *grouping*. Finally, an assignment of a classroom to each course section is called a *classroom assignment*.

A course schedule is completely characterized by a triplet (t,g,a) where t is a timetable, g is a grouping and a is a classroom assignment. Solving a course scheduling problem is then equivalent to finding a triplet (t,g,a). We consider the following constraints.

a) *No overlap*
. Two lectures having students in common, a same teacher or a same classroom should not have any period in common.

b) *Constraints on the teachers*
. The availabilities and preferences of the teachers must be taken into account.
. Because of syndical norms, a teacher should have a minimum number of half days off.
. The load of a teacher (i.e. his total number of teaching periods) at any working day should be large enough. For example, no teacher will accept to have a working day with only one teaching period.

c) *Constraints on the students*
. The load of a student (i.e. his total number of lecture periods) at any day is bounded by given minimal and maximal amounts. Typically, students should not have a free day in the week.

d) *Constraints on the timetable*
. The lectures of a course section must be scheduled in different days and distributed as uniformly as possible on the grid.
. A subset of specified courses should not be scheduled during bad periods.
. The lectures of length 2 should preferably start at an odd numbered period of a half day (i.e. the first one, or the third one, etc.).

e) *Constraints on the grouping*
. The sections of a course should have balanced numbers of students. Moreover, an upper bound on the number of students per section is given for each course.
. It can be imposed that given students should be assigned to a specific section of a course, or to any section except a specific one.

f) *Constraints on the classroom assignment*
. The availabilities of the classrooms must be satisfied.
. Some courses (for example, physics or chemistry) can only take place in a subset of classrooms.
. All lectures of a course section must be given in a same classroom.

3. Assignment Type Problems

An Assignment Type Problem (ATP) can be summarized as follows:

Given n items and m resources, the problem is to determine an assignment of the items to the resources optimizing an objective function F and satisfying K additional side constraints.

The associated mathematical model is the following:

(ATP)   Min $F(x)$

$$\text{Subject to} \quad \sum_{j \in J_i} x_{ij} = 1 \qquad 1 \le i \le n \qquad (1)$$

$$G_k(x) \le 0 \qquad 1 \le k \le K \qquad (2)$$

$$x_{ij} = 0 \text{ or } 1 \qquad 1 \le i \le n, \ j \in J_i \qquad (3)$$

where x_{ij} is a decision variable

$$x_{ij} = \begin{cases} 1 & \text{if item i is assigned to resource j} \\ 0 & \text{otherwise} \end{cases}.$$

and $J_i \subseteq \{1,2,...,m\}$ is the set of admissible resources for i, $1 \le i \le n$.

The assignment constraints (1) together with (3) indicate that each item i has to be assigned to exactly one resource j. The objective function F and the side constraint functions G_k are not restricted to having any specific property.

Several well known problems are ATP instances with a specific objective function F and specific side constraints (2). For example, the classic Assignment Problem, the Generalized Assignment Problem [Ros75] and the Timetabling Problem [Fer92] can be seen as special ATP instances.

Assignment type problems in general are NP-complete. However, some special ATPs can be solved in polynomial time. Assume for example that the objective function F is linear and that there is an upper bound b_j on the number of items which can be assigned to a resource j. If there is no additional side constraints, then the ATP can be solved in polynomial time by determining a maximum flow of minimum cost in a network [Edm72].

Also, the weighted stable set problem can be viewed as an ATP in which the items are the vertices which have to be assigned to exactly one among the two available resources, i.e. the stable set S and V\S. Each edge (v_i,v_j) of the graph is associated with a side constraint imposing that at most one item among i and j can be assigned to resource S. The objective is to maximize the total weight of the items assigned to resource S. The weighted stable set problem is known to be NP-complete [Gar79]. Efficient branch-and-bound algorithms have been designed for solving the weighted and unweighted versions of this problem to optimality [Fri90,Bal91,Man92].

When the considered ATP does not have one of the above special structures, we suggest the use of a heuristic solution method based on the tabu search technique (TS). Indeed, TS has proved to be a powerful tool for solving hard combinatorial optimization problems [Glo89,Glo90].

4. Proposed Approach

The proposed solution approach is based on a decomposition of the course scheduling problem into a series of easier subproblems. Each subproblem is an ATP. The main process is divided into two phases: an initialization phase and an improvement phase.

In the initialization phase, we build an initial solution which takes into account the constraints imposing a structure on the schedule. Indeed, we have noticed that the main objective of the planner is to give a certain structure to the initial solution so that overlapping situations will easily be handled in the improvement phase. To this purpose, the planner colors the periods of the grid so that he can visualize a desired structure on the schedule. Let y_{pl} be the color assigned to period p at level l. We have derived the following rules for assigning colors to the periods:

(1) each set of periods with a given color at a given level must be made of pairs of consecutive periods;

(2) at a given level, each pair of consecutive periods with a same color must start at an odd numbered period;

(3) for any period p and two different levels l_1 and l_2, we must have $y_{pl_1} <> y_{pl_2}$;

(4) the total number of colors must be as small as possible. This means that we must use only L colors, where L is the total number of different levels; moreover, each period must have different colors at different levels;

(5) at a given level, the distance between two pairs of periods with the same color must be as large as possible.

Such a coloring with L=4 colors for a grid with 45 periods is represented below.

Monday	Tuesday	Wednesday	Thursday	Friday
Bad period	Bad period	Bad period	Bad period	Bad period
lunch	lunch		lunch	lunch
Bad period	Bad period		Bad period	Bad period

It is not difficult to see that the problem of coloring the periods of the grid is an ATP in which the objective is to have a uniform distribution of the colors on the grid taking into account constraints (1)-(4).

The coloring of the periods is then used to assign colors to the lectures. Since all lectures of a given teacher must have the same color, overlapping situations for teachers can only occur for courses with a same level. The problem of coloring the lectures can then be expressed as an ATP. For a student s, the total number of periods having a given color y at a given level must be at least equal to the total duration of the courses given to s and having color y. However, in practice, it is often not possible to satisfy this constraint for all students. This is mainly due to the heterogeneous choices of the students for their option courses. Minimizing the total violation of these constraints is therefore considered as the objective of the ATP. In addition to the constraints imposing that all lectures given by a same teacher must have a same color, we take into account all teachers' availabilities.

It is then possible to generate a initial schedule by choosing at random feasible starting periods for each lecture taking into account the coloring of the grid and the availabilities of the teachers. We then improve the quality of this initial schedule by solving three different ATPs. The first one tries to decrease the total number of overlapping situations by modifying the starting times of the lectures. It is imposed that a lecture with color y can only be assigned to periods with color y. The second ATP improves the grouping of the students by moving them from one course section to another section of the same course. The objective is to minimize the total number of overlapping situations involving students. The third ATP improves the classroom assignment. All the ATPs described above can be solved by means of an adaptation of the tabu search method.

In the second phase of the process, we improve the quality of the initial schedule by solving another series of ATPs. These ATPs are very similar to those described in the first phase. The main difference is that the colors of the periods are ignored. All ATPs solved in the improvement phase as well as their solution methods are summarized in the following table.

Aim	Objective	Solution method
Improvement of the timetable	To avoid overlapping situations with teachers, students and classrooms	Tabu search in which only lectures involved in an overlapping situation are possibly moved
Global improvement of the grouping	To avoid overlapping situations with students	Tabu search in which only students involved in overlapping situations are possibly moved
Improvement of the grouping on a given course	To minimize the total number of overlapping situations for the students of a given course	Maximum flow of minimum cost in a network
Improvement of the classroom assignment	To avoid overlapping situations with classrooms	Tabu search in which classroom assignments are possibly modified only for overlapping situations
Improvement of the grouping for a given student	To optimize the assignment of a given student to the sections of the courses on which he is registered	Branch-and-bound procedure for a formulation of the problem as a weighted stable set problem

The general process for the construction of a feasible course schedule can now be summarized as follows.

Initialization Phase

Step 1	Color the periods.
Step 2	Color the lectures.
Step 3	Determine a first timetable, a first grouping and a first classroom assignment.
Step 4	Try to improve the timetable.
Step 5	Try to improve the grouping.
Step 6	Try to improve the classroom assignment.
Step 7	If an improvement has been obtained in Step 4, 5 or 6, then go to Step 4. Else go to Step 8.

Improvement Phase

Step 8	Try to improve the timetable.
Step 9	Try to improve the global grouping.
Step 10	If the grouping is not satisfying for a subset of courses, then try to improve it for each course in this subset.
Step 11	If the grouping is not satisfying for a subset of students, then try to improve it for each student in this subset.
Step 12	Try to improve the classroom assignment.
Step 13	If the course schedule is satisfying or if no improvement has been obtained in Steps 8, 9, 10, 11 and 12, then STOP. Else go to Step 8.

For more details and a more precise formulation of each ATP, the reader is refered to [Her94].

5. Application to a Real-Life Probem

The development of a new flexible approach for solving constrained course scheduling problems was initially motivated by a real-life problem in a Swiss school. The proposed approach was implemented in practice and has proven to be satisfactory.

The 518 students of the considered school had four different levels and were registered on 110 courses. There were 339 course sections, among which 26 were divided into 3 lectures, 145 into 2 lectures and 168 had only one lecture. The duration of most lectures was 2, but some of them were of length 1 or 3. The schedule of the lectures of length 3 was fixed in advance (preassignment requirements).

The courses were given on five different days, each day being divided into two half days of length 5, except one day which only contained 5 consecutive periods. This gives a grid with 45 periods which is equivalent to the grid represented in Section 4.

The load of the students (i.e. their number of lecture periods) varied from 23 to 40 with an average of 32.

The idea of coloring the periods and the courses was suggested to us by the timetable planner of the considered school. He was using such colorings for several years and was absolutely convinced that it was a helpful tool for visualizing a desired structure and for avoiding many overlapping situations.

The 85 teachers of the school had a working load (i.e. a number of teaching periods) which varied from 1 to 30. In average, the teachers were not available during 5 of the 45 periods, and about 80% of their available periods were preferred periods.

As already mentioned, it often happens in practice that the set of feasible schedules is empty. Hence, several constraints have to be modified in order to get a feasible schedule. Typically, changes on the availabilities of the teachers can help avoiding overlapping situations. Also, the timetable planner can decide to contact students registered on a large set of option courses. He can let them know that it will certainly not be possible to build a schedule in which all courses their have chosen are given during different periods. As a consequence, some of these students may indicate to the timetable planner which among their choices are considered as less important. In summary, phone calls, meetings and discussions are needed in order to negotiate for changes on the constraints.

For our real-life problem, the timetable planner needed about 10 hours on a PC486-66 MHz for generating a first schedule by means of the general process described in section 4. In this first schedule, 45 students were involved in overlapping situations. The timetable planner initiated negotiations with some teachers and students. He obtained changes on the constraints and modified part of the schedule manually. He then performed a second run of the improvement phase of our general process. For this second run, he used the first schedule as initial solution and part of it was considered as fixed (preassignment requirements). A second schedule has been obtained after a few minutes in which 25 students were involved in overlapping situations. Hence, this second schedule was better than the first one, but still not feasible. Therefore, additional phone calls, meetings, manual modifications of the schedule and runs of our procedures were needed. As a result, a third schedule has been generated which only contained 3 overlapping situations. The timetable planner considered this third schedule as satisfying since he was convinced that the 3 overlapping situations were unavoidable. All this process of building a satisfying schedule lasted about two weeks (150 men-hours). For comparison, before using our approach, the school needed seven different persons during about 700 men-hours for building a satisfying schedule.

6. Final Remarks and Conclusion

The development of a new flexible approach for solving constrained course scheduling problems was initially motivated by a real-life problem in a Swiss school. The proposed approach was implemented in practice and has proven to be satisfactory.

As a conclusion, we want to mention that there are at least three possible ways for extending or modifying our work. First of all, the proposed decomposition of the course scheduling problem into assignment type subproblems should only be considered as an example of decomposition. Other subproblems can be defined having an ATP structure.

The second possible extension of our work is based on the fact that the objective function F and the side constraint functions G_k are not restricted to having any specific property other than being computable. It follows that the set of constraints which has been considered in this paper can easily be enlarged.

Notice that the proposed solution methods described in section 3 are not necessarily the best ones for solving specific ATPs. Other solution methods may be preferred and this leads to a third possible extension.

7 . References

[Bal91]   Balas, E. and Xue, J., "Minimum weighted coloring of triangulated graphs, with application to maximum weight vertex packing and clique finding in arbitrary graphs", *SIAM J. Comput.* 20/2 (1991) 209-221.

[Car66]   Carlson, R.C. and Nemhauser, G.L., "Scheduling to minimize interaction cost", *Operations Research* 14 (1966) 52-58.

[Edm72]   Edmonds, J. and Karp, R.M., "Theoretical improvements in algorithmic efficiency for network flow problems", *Journal of the A.C.M.* 19/2 (1972) 248-264.

[Fer92]   Ferland, J.A. and Lavoie, A., "Exchanges procedures for timetabling problems", *Discrete Applied Mathematics* 35 (1992) 237-253.

[Fri90]   Friden, C., Hertz, A. and de Werra D., "TABARIS: an exact algorithm based on tabu search for finding a maximum independent set in a graph", *Computers and Operations Research* 17 (1990) 437-445.

[Gan81]   de Gans, O.B., "A computer timetabling system for secondary schools in the Netherlands", *European Journal of Operational Research* 7 (1981) 175-182.

[Gar79]   Garey, M.R. and Johnson, D.S., "Computers and Intractibility : a Guide to the Theory of NP-Completeness", Freeman, New York (1979).

[Glo89]   Glover, F., "Tabu Search, Part I", *ORSA Journal on Computing* 1 (1989) 190-206.

[Glo90]   Glover, F., "Tabu Search, Part II", *ORSA Journal on Computing* 2 (1990) 4-32.

[Her94]   Hertz, A. and Robert V., "Constructing a course schedule by solving a series of assignment type problems", ORWP 94/10, Dept of Maths, EPFL, Switzerland (1994).

[Man92] Mannino, C. and Sassano A., "An exact algorithm for the stable set problem", IASI-CNR Report No. 334, Rome, Italy (1992).

[Mul82] Mulvey, J.M., "A classroom/time assignment model", *European Journal of Operational Research* 9 (1982) 64-70.

[Ros75] Ross, C.T. and Soland, R.M., "A Branch and Bound Algorithm for the Generalized Assignment Problem", *Mathematical Programming* 8 (1975) 91-103.

[Tri80] Tripathy, A., "A Lagrangian relaxation approach to course scheduling", *Journal of the Operational Research Society* 31 (1980) 599-603.

[Wer85] de Werra, D., "An introduction to timetabling", *European Journal of Operational Research* 19 (1985) 151-162.

Other Timetabling Papers

Other Timetabling Papers

Other papers presented at the conference are listed below together with the addresses of the authors.

Title: Analysis and Implementation of Automated Timetabling System
Authors: I.Beender and L.Chernenko
Address: Odessa State University, Box 37, 270011 Odessa, Ukraine

Title: GET: An Interactive Timetabling System using CIM Concepts
Authors: C.Berard and J.Grislain
Address: Laboratoire d'Automatique et de Productique: GRAI, 351 Cours de la Libération, 33405 TALENCE, Cedex, France

Title: An Interactive Computer Aided Design System to Build the General Timetables of a University
Authors: J.P.Boufflet, R.Benouaghram and G.Boufflet
Address: URA CNRS 817 Heudiasyc, Université de Technologie de Compiègne (UTC), Dpt Génie Informatique - BP 649, 60 206 COMPIEGNE, Cédex, France

Title: A Simulated Annealing with Tabu List Algorithm for the School Timetable Problem
Authors: F.Carmusciano and D.De Luca Cardillo
Address: Dipartimento di Matematica, Ulisse Dini Universita' di Firenze, Viale Morgagni 67/a, 50139 Firenze, Italy

Title: Roster Scheduling at an Air Cargo Terminal: A Tabu Search Approach
Authors: H.W.Chan and J.Sheung
Address: Department of Computing, Hong Kong Polytechnic University, Hung Hom, Kowloon, Hong Kong

Title: Spatial Reasoning for Timetabling: The Timetabler System
Authors: F.P.Coenen, B.Beattie, T.J.M.Bench-Capon, M.J.R.Shave and B.M.Diaz
Address: Department of Computer Science, The University of Liverpool, Chadwick Building, PO Box 147, Liverpool L69 3BX, UK

Title: Conflict Reduction in Examination Schedules
Authors: A.W.Colijn and C.Layfield
Address: Department of Computer Science, University of Calgary, Canada

Title: Interactive Improvement of Examination Schedules
Authors: A.W.Colijn and C.Layfield
Address: Department of Computer Science, University of Calgary, Canada

Title: A Program for Constructing High School Timetables
Authors: T.B.Cooper and J.H.Kingston
Address: Basser Department of Computer Science, The University of Sydney, 2006 Australia

Title: A Constraint Programming Library Dedicated to Timetabling
Author: A.Dresse
Address: DECIS sa-nv, av. Louis Bertrand 100 A 12, B-1030 Brussels, Belgium

Title: Syllabus Plus: A State-of-the-Art Planning and Scheduling System for Universities and Colleges
Author: G.Forster
Address: Scientia Ltd, St John's Innovation Centre, Cowley Road, Cambridge CB4 4WS, UK

Title: Nationwide Scheduling of Examinations: Lessons from Experience
Authors: M.P.Hansen, V.Lauersen and R.V.V.Vidal
Addresses: M.P.Hansen, Institute of Mathematical Modeling, Building 321, Technical University of Denmark, DK-2800 Lyngby, Denmark
V.Lauersen, Ministry of Education, Department of Upper Secondary Education, Frederiksholms Kanal 25, DK-1220 Copenhagen, Denmark
R.V.V.Vidal, Center for Teleinformation, Building 371, Technical University of Denmark, DK-2800 Lyngby, Denmark

Title: School Timetabling System: SECTA
Authors: H.Ikeda, F.Kitagawa and Nakajima
Addresses: H.Ikeda, Ritsumeikan University, Japan
F.Kitagawa, Okayama Science University, Japan
Nakajima, Kusatsu High School, Siga, Japan

Title: Timetabling in an Integrated Abductive and Constraint Logic Programming Framework
Authors: A.C.Kakas and A.Michael
Address: University of Cyprus, 75 Kallipoleos St Nicosia, PO Box 537, Cyprus

Title: School Timetabling: A Knowledge-Based Approach
Authors: A.T.Khader and J.T.Buchanan
Addresses: A.T.Khader, School of Computer Science, Universiti Sains Malaysia, 11800 Penang Malaysia
J.T.Buchanan, Department of Computer Science, University of Strathclyde, Glasgow G1 1XH, UK

Title: Fine-Tuning a Genetic Algorithm for the General Timetable Problem
Authors: H.Luchian, C.Ungureanasu, B.Paechter and M.Petriuc
Addresses: H.Luchian, C.Ungureanasu, "AI. I Cuza" University of Iasi, Romania
B.Paechter, Department of Computer Studies, Napier University, 219 Colinton Road, Edinburgh EH14 1DJ, UK
M.Petriuc, "Gh Asachi" Technical University of Iasi, Romania

Title: University Timetabling at the Blackboard
Author: R.Macdonald
Address: Macdonald Research Institute, 10 Hollow Park, Ayr KA7 4SR, UK

Title: Timetabling at Southern African Tertiary Institutions
Authors: T.Nepal and S.Melville
Address: Department of Computer Studies, ML Sultan Technikon, PO Box 1334, Durban, South Africa

Title: Local Search Techniques for High School Timetabling
Authors: A.Schaerf and M.Schaerf
Address: Dipartimento di Informatica e Sistemistica, Università di Roma "La Sapienza", Via Salaria 113, 1-00198 Roma, Italy

Title: Timetabling in Dutch Secondary Schools: The Problem and the Strategy to Tackle It
Authors: J.A.M.Schreuder and A.J.Visscher
Addresses: J.A.M.Schreuder, Department of Applied Mathematics, University of Twente, PO Box 217, 7500 AE Enschede, The Netherlands
A.J.Visscher, Faculty of Educational Science and Technology, University of Twente, PO Box 217, 7500 AE Enschede, The Netherlands

Title: Interactive Bi-Level Course Faculty Assignment
Author: J-M Thizy
Address: Systems Science Programme, University of Ottawa, 136 Jean-Jacques Lussier, PO Box 450, Station A, Ottawa, Ontario K1N 6N5, Canada

Author Index

Bardadym, V.A., 22
Boizumault, P., 130
Boufflet, J.P., 327
Burke, E.K., 76, 241

Carter, M.W., 3
Cheng, C., 112
Cooper, T.B., 283
Corne, D., 227, 309
Cumming, A., 251

Dowsland, K.A., 345

Elliman, D.G., 76
Erben, W., 198
Ergül, A., 212

Ford, P.H., 76

Gudes, E., 93
Guéret, C., 130

Henz, M., 162
Hertz, A., 364

Jussien, N., 130

Kang, L., 112
Keppler, J., 198
Kingston, J.H., 283

Lajos, G., 146
Laporte, G., 3
Leung, N., 112
Luchian, H. 251

Meisels, A., 93

Nègre, S., 327
Newall, J.P., 241
Norman, M.G., 251

Paechter, B., 251
Prins, C., 130

Ram, V., 106
Rankin, R.C., 266
Rich, D.C., 181
Robert, V., 364
Ross, P., 227, 309

Scogings, C., 106
Solotorevsky, G., 93

Terashima-Marín, H., 309
Thompson, J., 345

Weare, R.F., 76, 241
de Werra, D., 296
White, G.M., 112
Wren, A., 46
Würtz, J., 162

Springer-Verlag and the Environment

We at Springer-Verlag firmly believe that an international science publisher has a special obligation to the environment, and our corporate policies consistently reflect this conviction.

We also expect our business partners – paper mills, printers, packaging manufacturers, etc. – to commit themselves to using environmentally friendly materials and production processes.

The paper in this book is made from low- or no-chlorine pulp and is acid free, in conformance with international standards for paper permanency.

Lecture Notes in Computer Science

For information about Vols. 1–1083

please contact your bookseller or Springer-Verlag

Vol. 1084: W.H. Cunningham, S.T. McCormick, M. Queyranne (Eds.), Integer Programming and Combinatorial Optimization. Proceedings, 1996. X, 505 pages. 1996.

Vol. 1085: D.M. Gabbay, H.J. Ohlbach (Eds.), Practical Reasoning. Proceedings, 1996. XV, 721 pages. 1996. (Subseries LNAI).

Vol. 1086: C. Frasson, G. Gauthier, A. Lesgold (Eds.), Intelligent Tutoring Systems. Proceedings, 1996. XVII, 688 pages. 1996.

Vol. 1087: C. Zhang, D. Lukose (Eds.), Distributed Artificial Intelliegence. Proceedings, 1995. VIII, 232 pages. 1996. (Subseries LNAI).

Vol. 1088: A. Strohmeier (Ed.), Reliable Software Technologies – Ada-Europe '96. Proceedings, 1996. XI, 513 pages. 1996.

Vol. 1089: G. Ramalingam, Bounded Incremental Computation. XI, 190 pages. 1996.

Vol. 1090: J.-Y. Cai, C.K. Wong (Eds.), Computing and Combinatorics. Proceedings, 1996. X, 421 pages. 1996.

Vol. 1091: J. Billington, W. Reisig (Eds.), Application and Theory of Petri Nets 1996. Proceedings, 1996. VIII, 549 pages. 1996.

Vol. 1092: H. Kleine Büning (Ed.), Computer Science Logic. Proceedings, 1995. VIII, 487 pages. 1996.

Vol. 1093: L. Dorst, M. van Lambalgen, F. Voorbraak (Eds.), Reasoning with Uncertainty in Robotics. Proceedings, 1995. VIII, 387 pages. 1996. (Subseries LNAI).

Vol. 1094: R. Morrison, J. Kennedy (Eds.), Advances in Databases. Proceedings, 1996. XI, 234 pages. 1996.

Vol. 1095: W. McCune, R. Padmanabhan, Automated Deduction in Equational Logic and Cubic Curves. X, 231 pages. 1996. (Subseries LNAI).

Vol. 1096: T. Schäl, Workflow Management Systems for Process Organisations. XII, 200 pages. 1996.

Vol. 1097: R. Karlsson, A. Lingas (Eds.), Algorithm Theory – SWAT '96. Proceedings, 1996. IX, 453 pages. 1996.

Vol. 1098: P. Cointe (Ed.), ECOOP '96 – Object-Oriented Programming. Proceedings, 1996. XI, 502 pages. 1996.

Vol. 1099: F. Meyer auf der Heide, B. Monien (Eds.), Automata, Languages and Programming. Proceedings, 1996. XII, 681 pages. 1996.

Vol. 1100: B. Pfitzmann, Digital Signature Schemes. XVI, 396 pages. 1996.

Vol. 1101: M. Wirsing, M. Nivat (Eds.), Algebraic Methodology and Software Technology. Proceedings, 1996. XII, 641 pages. 1996.

Vol. 1102: R. Alur, T.A. Henzinger (Eds.), Computer Aided Verification. Proceedings, 1996. XII, 472 pages. 1996.

Vol. 1103: H. Ganzinger (Ed.), Rewriting Techniques and Applications. Proceedings, 1996. XI, 437 pages. 1996.

Vol. 1104: M.A. McRobbie, J.K. Slaney (Eds.), Automated Deduction – CADE-13. Proceedings, 1996. XV, 764 pages. 1996. (Subseries LNAI).

Vol. 1105: T.I. Ören, G.J. Klir (Eds.), Computer Aided Systems Theory – CAST '94. Proceedings, 1994. IX, 439 pages. 1996.

Vol. 1106: M. Jampel, E. Freuder, M. Maher (Eds.), Over-Constrained Systems. X, 309 pages. 1996.

Vol. 1107: J.-P. Briot, J.-M. Geib, A. Yonezawa (Eds.), Object-Based Parallel and Distributed Computation. Proceedings, 1995. X, 349 pages. 1996.

Vol. 1108: A. Díaz de Ilarraza Sánchez, I. Fernández de Castro (Eds.), Computer Aided Learning and Instruction in Science and Engineering. Proceedings, 1996. XIV, 480 pages. 1996.

Vol. 1109: N. Koblitz (Ed.), Advances in Cryptology – Crypto '96. Proceedings, 1996. XII, 417 pages. 1996.

Vol. 1110: O. Danvy, R. Glück, P. Thiemann (Eds.), Partial Evaluation. Proceedings, 1996. XII, 514 pages. 1996.

Vol. 1111: J.J. Alferes, L. Moniz Pereira, Reasoning with Logic Programming. XXI, 326 pages. 1996. (Subseries LNAI).

Vol. 1112: C. von der Malsburg, W. von Seelen, J.C. Vorbrüggen, B. Sendhoff (Eds.), Artificial Neural Networks – ICANN 96. Proceedings, 1996. XXV, 922 pages. 1996.

Vol. 1113: W. Penczek, A. Szałas (Eds.), Mathematical Foundations of Computer Science 1996. Proceedings, 1996. X, 592 pages. 1996.

Vol. 1114: N. Foo, R. Goebel (Eds.), PRICAI'96: Topics in Artificial Intelligence. Proceedings, 1996. XXI, 658 pages. 1996. (Subseries LNAI).

Vol. 1115: P.W. Eklund, G. Ellis, G. Mann (Eds.), Conceptual Structures: Knowledge Representation as Interlingua. Proceedings, 1996. XIII, 321 pages. 1996. (Subseries LNAI).

Vol. 1116: J. Hall (Ed.), Management of Telecommunication Systems and Services. XXI, 229 pages. 1996.

Vol. 1117: A. Ferreira, J. Rolim, Y. Saad, T. Yang (Eds.), Parallel Algorithms for Irregularly Structured Problems. Proceedings, 1996. IX, 358 pages. 1996.

Vol. 1118: E.C. Freuder (Ed.), Principles and Practice of Constraint Programming — CP 96. Proceedings, 1996. XIX, 574 pages. 1996.

Vol. 1119: U. Montanari, V. Sassone (Eds.), CONCUR '96: Concurrency Theory. Proceedings, 1996. XII, 751 pages. 1996.

Vol. 1120: M. Deza. R. Euler, I. Manoussakis (Eds.), Combinatorics and Computer Science. Proceedings, 1995. IX, 415 pages. 1996.

Vol. 1121: P. Perner, P. Wang, A. Rosenfeld (Eds.), Advances in Structural and Syntactical Pattern Recognition. Proceedings, 1996. X, 393 pages. 1996.

Vol. 1122: H. Cohen (Ed.), Algorithmic Number Theory. Proceedings, 1996. IX, 405 pages. 1996.

Vol. 1123: L. Bougé, P. Fraigniaud, A. Mignotte, Y. Robert (Eds.), Euro-Par'96. Parallel Processing. Proceedings, 1996, Vol. I. XXXIII, 842 pages. 1996.

Vol. 1124: L. Bougé, P. Fraigniaud, A. Mignotte, Y. Robert (Eds.), Euro-Par'96. Parallel Processing. Proceedings, 1996, Vol. II. XXXIII, 926 pages. 1996.

Vol. 1125: J. von Wright, J. Grundy, J. Harrison (Eds.), Theorem Proving in Higher Order Logics. Proceedings, 1996. VIII, 447 pages. 1996.

Vol. 1126: J.J. Alferes, L. Moniz Pereira, E. Orlowska (Eds.), Logics in Artificial Intelligence. Proceedings, 1996. IX, 417 pages. 1996. (Subseries LNAI).

Vol. 1127: L. Böszörményi (Ed.), Parallel Computation. Proceedings, 1996. XI, 235 pages. 1996.

Vol. 1128: J. Calmet, C. Limongelli (Eds.), Design and Implementation of Symbolic Computation Systems. Proceedings, 1996. IX, 356 pages. 1996.

Vol. 1129: J. Launchbury, E. Meijer, T. Sheard (Eds.), Advanced Functional Programming. Proceedings, 1996. VII, 238 pages. 1996.

Vol. 1130: M. Haveraaen, O. Owe, O.-J. Dahl (Eds.), Recent Trends in Data Type Specification. Proceedings, 1995. VIII, 551 pages. 1996.

Vol. 1131: K.H. Höhne, R. Kikinis (Eds.), Visualization in Biomedical Computing. Proceedings, 1996. XII, 610 pages. 1996.

Vol. 1132: G.-R. Perrin, A. Darte (Eds.), The Data Parallel Programming Model. XV, 284 pages. 1996.

Vol. 1133: J.-Y. Chouinard, P. Fortier, T.A. Gulliver (Eds.), Information Theory and Applications II. Proceedings, 1995. XII, 309 pages. 1996.

Vol. 1134: R. Wagner, H. Thoma (Eds.), Database and Expert Systems Applications. Proceedings, 1996. XV, 921 pages. 1996.

Vol. 1135: B. Jonsson, J. Parrow (Eds.), Formal Techniques in Real-Time and Fault-Tolerant Systems. Proceedings, 1996. X, 479 pages. 1996.

Vol. 1136: J. Diaz, M. Serna (Eds.), Algorithms – ESA '96. Proceedings, 1996. XII, 566 pages. 1996.

Vol. 1137: G. Görz, S. Hölldobler (Eds.), KI-96: Advances in Artificial Intelligence. Proceedings, 1996. XI, 387 pages. 1996. (Subseries LNAI).

Vol. 1138: J. Calmet, J.A. Campbell, J. Pfalzgraf (Eds.), Artificial Intelligence and Symbolic Mathematical Computation. Proceedings, 1996. VIII, 381 pages. 1996.

Vol. 1139: M. Hanus, M. Rogriguez-Artalejo (Eds.), Algebraic and Logic Programming. Proceedings, 1996. VIII, 345 pages. 1996.

Vol. 1140: H. Kuchen, S. Doaitse Swierstra (Eds.), Programming Languages: Implementations, Logics, and Programs. Proceedings, 1996. XI, 479 pages. 1996.

Vol. 1141: H.-M. Voigt, W. Ebeling, I. Rechenberg, H.-P. Schwefel (Eds.), Parallel Problem Solving from Nature – PPSN IV. Proceedings, 1996. XVII, 1.050 pages. 1996.

Vol. 1142: R.W. Hartenstein, M. Glesner (Eds.), Field-Programmable Logic. Proceedings, 1996. X, 432 pages. 1996.

Vol. 1143: T.C. Fogarty (Ed.), Evolutionary Computing. Proceedings, 1996. VIII, 305 pages. 1996.

Vol. 1144: J. Ponce, A. Zisserman, M. Hebert (Eds.), Object Representation in Computer Vision. Proceedings, 1996. VIII, 403 pages. 1996.

Vol. 1145: R. Cousot, D.A. Schmidt (Eds.), Static Analysis. Proceedings, 1996. IX, 389 pages. 1996.

Vol. 1146: E. Bertino, H. Kurth, G. Martella, E. Montolivo (Eds.), Computer Security – ESORICS 96. Proceedings, 1996. X, 365 pages. 1996.

Vol. 1147: L. Miclet, C. de la Higuera (Eds.), Grammatical Inference: Learning Syntax from Sentences. Proceedings, 1996. VIII, 327 pages. 1996. (Subseries LNAI).

Vol. 1148: M.C. Lin, D. Manocha (Eds.), Applied Computational Geometry. Proceedings, 1996. VIII, 223 pages. 1996.

Vol. 1149: C. Montangero (Ed.), Software Process Technology. Proceedings, 1996. IX, 291 pages. 1996.

Vol. 1150: A. Hlawiczka, J.G. Silva, L. Simoncini (Eds.), Dependable Computing – EDCC-2. Proceedings, 1996. XVI, 440 pages. 1996.

Vol. 1151: Ö. Babaoğlu, K. Marzullo (Eds.), Distributed Algorithms. Proceedings, 1996. VIII, 381 pages. 1996.

Vol. 1153: E. Burke, P. Ross (Eds.), Practice and Theory of Automated Timetabling. Proceedings, 1995. XIII, 381 pages. 1996.

Vol. 1154: D. Pedreschi, C. Zaniolo (Eds.), Logic in Databases. Proceedings, 1996. X, 497 pages. 1996.

Vol. 1155: J. Roberts, U. Mocci, J. Virtamo (Eds.), Broadbank Network Teletraffic. XXII, 584 pages. 1996.

Vol. 1156: A. Bode, J. Dongarra, T. Ludwig, V. Sunderam (Eds.), Parallel Virtual Machine – EuroPVM '96. Proceedings, 1996. XIV, 362 pages. 1996.

Vol. 1157: B. Thalheim (Ed.), Conceptual Modeling – ER '96. Proceedings, 1996. XII, 489 pages. 1996.

Vol. 1158: S. Berardi, M. Coppo (Eds.), Types for Proofs and Programs. Proceedings, 1995. X, 296 pages. 1996.

Vol. 1159: D.L. Borges, C.A.A. Kaestner (Eds.), Advances in Artificial Intelligence. Proceedings, 1996. XI, 243 pages. (Subseries LNAI).

Vol. 1160: A.K. Sharma, S. Arikawa (Eds.), Algorithmic Learning Theory. Proceedings, 1996. XVII, 337 pages. 1996. (Subseries LNAI).

Vol. 1161: O. Spaniol, C. Linnhoff-Popien, B. Meyer (Eds.), Trends in Distributed Systems. Proceedings, 1996. VIII, 289 pages. 1996.

Vol. 1162: D.G. Feitelson, L. Rudolph (Eds.), Job Scheduling Strategies for Parallel Processing. Proceedings, 1996. VIII, 291 pages. 1996.